D1599228

Software Metrics

Software Metrics:
An Analysis
and Evaluation

Alan Perlis
Yale University

Frederick Sayward
Yale University

Mary Shaw
Carnegie-Mellon University

(Editors)

The MIT Press
Cambridge, Massachusetts, and London, England

Publisher's Note
This format is intended to reduce the cost of publishing certain works in book form and to shorten the gap between editorial preparation and final publication. Detailed editing and composition have been avoided by photographing the text of this book directly from the editors' camera-ready copy.

Printed and bound in the United States of America.

Library of Congress Cataloging in Publication Data
Main entry under title:

Software metrics: an analysis and evaluation.

    Bibliography: p.
    Includes index.
    1. Computer programs--Evaluation. I. Perlis, Alan J.
II. Sayward, Frederick G. III. Shaw, Mary, 1943-
QA76.6.S633   001.64'25   80-28971
ISBN 0-262-16083-8

Table of Contents

Preface

During the spring of 1979 Marvin Denicoff of the Office of Naval Research asked us to assess and evaluate the current state of the art and the status of research in the area of *software metrics*. After a quick review of the literature it became apparent that the central issues revolved around the following question:

> Is it possible to identify or define indices of merit that can support quantitative comparisons and evaluations of software and of the processes associated with its design, development, use, maintenance, and evolution?

Preliminary surveys indicated that there is great need for quantitative software measures, both for management and for technical reasons — but that adequate measurement techniques do not exist. We decided that an in-depth study was needed to identify promising areas for research and development in software metrics and software experimentation, to analyze the research currently being done in these areas, and to recommend directions that are promising in the near term. Our hope was to help the software field develop a scientific basis for analyzing and evaluating software.

It was clear from the outset that a large fraction of the computer science research community holds software metrics in low esteem. Consequently we decided to devote part of our effort to focussing the attention of the research community on the problems and methods in software metrics that show promise of substantial contributions to the field.

We organized a Study Panel whose members would be assigned specific areas to study and evaluate. In order to best assess the software metric needs of everyone involved in software, we decided that the panel should consist of members both from industry and from academia. The following scientists served on the panel:

Vic Basili, University of Maryland
Les Belady, IBM Corporation
Jim Browne, University of Texas
Bill Curtis, General Electric Company
Rich DeMillo, Georgia Institute of Technology
Ivor Francis, Cornell University
Richard Lipton, Princeton University
Bill Lynch, Xerox Corporation

Merv Muller, World Bank
Alan Perlis, Yale University
Jean Sammet, IBM Corporation
Fred Sayward, Yale University
Mary Shaw, Carnegie-Mellon University

Alan Perlis served as chairman of the Study Panel with Fred Sayward and Mary Shaw serving as assistants.

An organizational meeting was held at Yale University September 10-12, 1979. At that meeting an initial state-of-the-art presentation was given and the software metrics issues were discussed. Members were initially asked to study the current status of a variety of software metric areas. A second meeting was held on January 31-February 1, 1980 immediately following the Principles of Programming Languages Conference at Las Vegas. Panel members presented their initial reports and final topics were assigned.

This book contains state-of-the-art evaluations and recommendations for research initiatives in several areas of software metrics. The papers were presented to a cross section of approximately 125 members of the computer science research community at a meeting held in Washington, DC on June 30, 1980 at the National Academy of Science. An edited version of the discussion which took place at the meeting follows each paper, where applicable.

In addition to the panel's position papers this book contains the editors' overview of the need for software metrics, a discussion of research initiatives by Marvin Denicoff and Robert Grafton, and an extensive annotated bibliography. We hope that the discussions and recommendations will serve to stimulate the development of a science of software metrics.

Acknowledgements

Several people have been particularly helpful in supporting the panel study and in preparing the reports for final publication. Brian Wichmann and Chris Harman of the National Physical Laboratory allowed us to incorporate material from a draft survey of studies on the usage of high-level languages. Richard Snodgrass of Carnegie-Mellon University provided his extensive annotations on software monitoring. The material from *Computing Reviews* is reprinted by permission of the copyright owner, the Association for Computing Machinery.

The book was formatted using the Scribe text editing system created by Brian Reid. Trish Johnson and Mary-Claire Van Leunen helped in entering the papers to the Scribe system. Sharon Carmack managed the data base for the annotated bibliography and helped with final copy preparation. Mary-Claire Van Leunen copy-edited the manuscript and Michele Boucher prepared the illustrations.

Alan Perlis
Fred Sayward
Mary Shaw
October, 1980

List of Figures

List of Tables

The Role of Metrics in Software and Software Development

The Life Cycle Model

Software metrics is a new area of computer science aimed at assigning quantitative indices of merit to software. Here software means more than simply source code; we use *software* as a generic for all the stages of tailoring a computer system to solve a problem. All software passes through the following seven stages in its life cycle:

1. requirements analysis
2. specification
3. design
4. implementation
5. testing and integration
6. maintenance and enhancement
7. replacement or retirement

Since software specification is always imprecise and since the demands on software change with time, backtrack cycles to earlier stages often take place. It is not uncommon for several stages to co-exist and influence each other's progress.

The Role of Software Metrics in Life Cycle Decisions

The purpose of software metrics is to help answer the questions which arise as the life cycle progresses. Two questions common to all the stages are: Is it time to go on to the next stage? Is a backtrack to an earlier stage needed?

At each stage there is also a set of questions about the software and the project whose precise answers are needed to dictate an optimal life cycle control flow. Software metrics addresses such questions but it is not sufficiently developed yet to provide precise answers to most of them.

Requirements Analysis

While this area of system development has an enormous influence on system software, questions about requirements must lie outside the domain of software metrics — for it is not until the requirements are fixed that the structure of the software can begin to take shape. What is needed is a link from requirements analysis to software specification, but this link cannot be software-oriented, just as a link from an informal to a formal model cannot be formal.

Specification

At this stage an informal statement of the problem and its proposed solution has been prepared. Questions to be answered include:

- What is the cost of production?
- What are the memory requirements of the software?
- What are the speed requirements of the software?
- How long will it take to produce?
- When will it have to be replaced?
- What manpower loading should be used?
- Is the project feasible? That is, does the expected production time exceed the time when the software will be of use?

Design

At this stage a detailed formal statement of the problem and its proposed solution have been prepared. This includes a development plan for all future stages of the life cycle. Questions to be answered include:

- What machine configuration to use?
- What language to use?
- Is it possible to incorporate the work of others or must everything be built in house?
- How will the availability of tool X affect factor Y?
- How close to its limits is the system expected to run?
- What are the potential future enhancements?
- Should the system be all-encompassing, with subsystems carved out, or should the system be primitive, on which specific systems are built?

Implementation

Some questions need to be answered before implementation begins and others arise during implementation. They include:

- What developmental technology should be used? Should the system be built all at once or should it be constructed through a sequence of executable prototypes?
- What programming discipline should be used?   Chief programmer? Cottage industry?

- Is the project on schedule?
- Is the project on the budget?
- Is the implemented code correct? If not, how close is it to meeting the specification?
- What is the quality of the implemented code? Is it understandable? Is it maintainable? Is it enhanceable?

Testing and Integration

At this stage the chief question is: Does the implementation meet the specification? This usually reduces to questions concerning what the implementation actually does, what resources it uses, and how easy it is to use. Such questions can be asked about individual modules and about integrated modules working in concert. The decisions to be made include:

- Should testing be done top down or bottom up?
- Which of the available testing methodologies should be used?
- What levels of satisfactory testing are sufficient?
- How well does the testing environment approximate the execution environment?
- How will subsequent error reports be handled?

Maintenance and Enhancement

These two very different activities are often linked because both result in re-release of the system. Maintenance is similar to testing except that the software execution environment has changed from the controlled world of testing to the hurly-burly of actual use. Every repair and update must be tested, so the questions generated by maintenance are similar to the ones above in the testing stage. Enhancement, on the other hand, is a post-release augmentation of the system specifications to meet unforeseen demands. Enhancement may cause a backtrack all the way to the requirements analysis stage. The questions we ask about enhancement include:

- What is the cost of the enhancement? Is it worthwhile?
- Will the enhancement speed up or delay replacement?
- What is the re-release strategy?

Once it has been decided that an enhancement should take place, there is an automatic backtrack to the specification stage of the life cycle.

Replacement and Retirement

Among the questions asked when considering replacement or retirement of a system are:

- Has the problem outgrown the program?
- Has technology moved beyond the program?
- Has a critical support resource for the system become unavailable?
- Would it cost less to re-build the system than to maintain and enhance?
- How should the system be phased out?
- Should there be a change in the language in which the system is written? In the machine on which the system runs?

Summary of Panel Findings

Observations and Limitations

Because of the time constraints on our study, the size of the problems under investigation, and the extremely uneven level of quality attained by software projects, we have not attempted to present a complete survey. We have concentrated on those issues in software metrics that will benefit from research in the near future.

Except in a small way we have not addressed the issue of manpower, although undoubtedly the competence, availability, and training of manpower play an important role in defining the set of metric-oriented questions for a particular software project.

We have come to recognize the existence of certain critical issues in relating software metrics to other areas of computer science. For example, software should be seen as very different from algorithms — not so much in representation but in size, variability, and rate of change. In software, evolutionary complexity is probably more important than the classical time and space measures with which computer science has been concerned so far.

There is a tendency in studying software (or anything else, for that matter) to be satisfied with mere curve-fitting rather than with developing models whose inherent structure illustrates one or more important aspects of the topic being investigated. Indeed, throughout our work we have had a growing awareness that software management needs overwhelm current insights in computer science. Needs have overwhelmed insights to such an extent, and there has been so little order, discipline, and content in the resulting practice of software metrics, that a significant portion of the computer science research community is completely turned off and chooses not to perform research in software metrics. But it is important that computer science not focus on premature or incorrect developments to discredit the field. Software will grow more complex, not simpler, and the need for software metrics will grow apace.

No matter what aspect of software one studies, there is a noticeable lack of collected and categoried field data on which to build. RADC has recently initiated the categorization of the information which does exist, but since past software projects have rarely integrated data collecting into their production schedule there is really not much to go on. Serious large-scale data collection is imperative if order is to be brought into the software field.

Of course, collected field data is more meaningful when related to the data and conclusions of software experiments. We view the need for a variety of well thought out and well designed software experiments as crucial if software metrics is to develop as a science.

A natural dichotomy exists in the interests of those who study software metrics. There are those whose interests lie in studies of the creation and management of programs — in human performance. And there are those whose interests lie in studies of the objects produced — in program performance. Although it is generally agreed that there ought to be a natural relationship between these two types of studies, we see no unifying theory developing in the near future.

Software metrics suffers at the moment in that virtually everything it studies is incommensurate with everything else. Consider how extraordinarily difficult it is to make a definitive comparison on software design, management, or construction between a project using APL and one using COBOL. For the field to become more of a science there must be a dramatic increase in the number of precisely defined universally accepted software objects and parameters. But how do we arrive at such a desirable state? There is little doubt that the task would be significantly easier if there were one well-defined sufficiently powerful programming language used by all. But this has not come to pass.

Since there is little likelihood that anyone will accept constraints on language, machine, and methodology merely in order to advance software metrics, we must first study the relationships among the languages, machines, and methodologies we use and attempt to find the nature of the transformations between one and another. Otherwise the experiments, the data, the models, and the consequent theory of software metrics will have little value outside the realm of the laboratory.

Software seems almost infinitely malleable, and each individual change seems to require almost no effort. Yet to shape a piece of software to a precise end with no unforeseen consequences can paradoxically seem to require almost infinite effort. It is the task of software metrics to attach values and costs to every aspect of software between these two extreme views.

The Role of Software Metrics in Life Cycle Decisions

We now present an overview of the state-of-the-art assessments and the research recommendations made in the papers which appear in this volume. Three themes keep surfacing in the papers — a need for more and better data, a need for a way to translate ideas and results from one domain to another, and a need for taxonomies on metric terms and definitions.

In *Toward a Scientific Basis for Software Evaluation* Browne and Shaw explain how a great deal of energy is regularly invested in making measurements on software and its development. The techniques of description, measurement, and evaluation are, however, mostly ad hoc. Most of the analysis and data collection techniques haven't been generalized beyond the local system for which they were developed. There is no scientific foundation in this area on which to derive invariant principles from observations and experiments.

They recommend that future experimental work be based on the traditional principles of science, where the first considerations are principles which are invariant across all software and hierarchies of abstract models. Although there now are several popular predictive models, they see more long-term benefits coming from structural models of software. It is this area for which they recommend support, with concentration first on structural models for specific systems.

In *Design of Software Experiments* Sayward summarizes the principles used in conducting the many ongoing software experiments aimed at understanding and improving software development, testing, and maintenance. of these experiments have nearly all followed the orthodox many subject random-group design popularized by Sir Ronald Fisher. This area has led to the formulation of many interesting hypotheses. However, there are some basic problems with internal and external experiment validity.

Sayward recommends continued support for more small-scale many subject experiments since lead to interesting new hypotheses and they will produce a gradual refinement of design techniques for strengthening internal validity. He also suggests that a new approach, the single subject design, might be more natural for software experiments and recommends conducting intermediate-scale single subject experiments as a potential way of strengthening external validity.

In *Experimental Evaluation of Software Characteristics* Curtis finds that most experimental studies on software metrics do not demonstrate causal relationships between software characteristics and programmer performance. Many uncontrolled factors could have influenced the data. The biggest problem lies in replicating the conditions under which real-world software is built.

Curtis recommends long-term multiple-institute research programs that attempt to replicate software experiments. He also recommends that experimental work be initiated on two forgotten areas — differences among programming languages and the early life cycle stages such as requirements and specification.

In *Software Project Forecasting* DeMillo and Lipton assert that attempts at predicting the cost of large-scale software efforts are very likely to fail. They explain how measurement theory rejects most of the formulae that have been suggested. On a positive side, they feel that the other popular method, predicting cost from historical data, is more likely to produce useful results.

They recommend that predicting from historical data receive continued support and that more effort and thought go into a data base for these studies. They also note that an analogy with weather forecasting suggests a refinement: the development of micro theories of software costing (which don't necessarily scale up) and the use of large-scale computational techniques (such as clustering) to integrate the micro theories to make cost predictions for large systems.

In *Controlling Software Development Through The Life Cycle Model* Perlis states that almost no present systems are designed by taking a total view of the software life cycle into account. Systems are designed to minimize backtracks, to localize the effects of maintenance, and to delay enhancements. No one ever thinks about making replacement easy. This is what Perlis calls the *pre-structured approach.* It assumes that there is but one pass through the life cycle which, if all else is held constant, yields a perfect system. Little attention is paid to building prototype systems — they aren't necessary under this view.

Perlis recommends looking at the sequence of executable prototype systems approach to software design as an alternative to the pre-structured approach. When coupled with the proper language choice this approach might be more effective in dealing with the inevitable design changes, maintenance activities, and system enhancements.

In *Resource Models* Basili identifies two ways of predicting the resources (such as computer time, personnel, and dollars) needed for large-scale software projects: models based on historical data and equations based on assumptions such as assumptions about how people solve problems. He recommends experiments aimed at substantiating the equations and gaining insights on the software life cycle from them.

In *High Level Language Metrics* Sammet observes that language metrics and program metrics are quite different, although they are often confused in casual discussion. High level languages are intellectual entities worthy of study and measure in their own right. Language metrics have been used for comparison, selection, and design. Some of the issues and measurements are subjective, others can be objective.

Sammet wants measures of non-procedurality of languages; measures of programmer productivity derived from measures of language functionality; measures of the deviations from one language to another; measures of the relationship of the language to various program measures; and measures of the usefulness of a language in a specific application.

In *Data Collection, Analysis, and Validation*, Basili gives a variety of means for collecting data on software projects and suggests approaches to dealing with the validity of the data-forms and automated data-collecting programs. Validity considerations include incorrectly filled-out forms and redundant data.

He recommends that more effort be put into defining terms, reporting error bounds on collected data, and establishing and refining a very large data base on the software life cycle. It would be helpful to find ways of integrating metrics into the process of classifying the data base.

In *A Scientific Approach to Statistical Software* Francis summarizes what has been done in evaluating statistical packages. Two questions of concern are software accuracy and convenience for users. Some metrics have been defined for both questions and experiments have been conducted using these metrics on standard test problems. Francis recommends that a set of standard experiments be developed.

In *Performance Evaluation: A Software Metrics Success Story* Lynch and Browne find that performance evaluation of software systems has a set of generally accepted metrics for both external aspects (e.g., response time) and internal aspects (e.g., queue length). There is also a set of generally accepted abstract models which capture the salient concepts of performance and system tuning. They recommend that support be given to software engineering procedures for developing systems with desired values on given performance metrics.

In *Statistical Measures of Software Reliability* DeMillo and Sayward list two current scales of software reliability. The first is the Boolean scale of formal verification, formal testing, and special programming disciplines. These don't really address reliability. The other is the continuous scale gotten mainly by applying hardware reliability theory to software. These attempts have led to unnatural and often contradictory assumptions. Among other difficulties is the problem that software is not a fixed object and hence the stochastic requirements of hardware reliability theory cannot be satisfied.

They recommend that, rather than striving to assign a probability of correct operation to software, attempts be supported to assign a probability to the processes used to validate software be supported. Because these validation processes are fixed over time, their distributions can be studied empirically. Then a Baysian *level of confidence* in the correct operation of software validated by the process can be derived.

In *The Measurement of Software Quality and Complexity* Curtis explains that while there are many software metrics for measuring the product, programs, there are few metrics for measuring the process, programming. There have been several software experiments relating these two concepts so that product metrics could be used to predict the process time. Several interesting relationships have resulted, but it is far too early to accept them as laws. Curtis recommends support for efforts to refine metrics, weeding out the redundant ones, for validating metrics on larger data bases, and for the development and validation of predictive equations.

In *Complexity of Large Systems* Belady finds that there are many speculative ideas around on the complexity of small programs but that few of them have been adequately tested. There is much duplicated, uncoordinated effort. For the complexity of large systems, the two most important concepts are evolutionary complexity and the time required to do a programming task. Little is known about evolutionary complexity.

Belady sees the need for a DOD-coordinated effort to establish a large data base for validating a small standard set of complexity metrics. This data base could be searched for patterns and trends in the evolution of large systems. This would lead to models of software evolution from which would emanate testable hypotheses. Another potentially fruitful study would be on the use of locality of information in large systems.

In *Software Maintenance Tools and Statistics* Muller finds little actual use of metrics in the maintenance stage of the life cycle. Although considerable data is gathered, there is no conceptual model of maintenance, and hence no related set of software metrics has developed. The best things available are software tools such as the Programmer's Workbench, which are aimed at easing bookkeeping tasks. In order to improve this situation, Muller proposes precise definitions of maintenance terms, a refinement of the maintenance data-collection process, ways of detecting program deterioration, and ways of detecting errors introduced by maintenance activities.

In *When is 'Good' Enough? Evaluating and Selecting Software Metrics* Shaw examines the methods researchers use to evaluate their proposed metrics and to compute the efficiency of metrics. Software metrics are either direct (e.g., cost) or indirect (e.g., time for cost), the majority are indirect. Software metrics proliferate because there is little attempt to find a basis set of direct metrics with models relating them to indirect metrics. And metrics are applied without regard to precision or cost.

She recommends research on finding a small set of basis metrics which span most needs. This would avoid the syndrome of inventing new metrics for each study and would entail finding models which relate direct and indirect metrics. Also recommended is a more critical use of classical statistics in evaluating metrics.

Software Metrics: A Research Initiative

Marvin Denicoff

Office of Naval Research
800 North Quincy
Arlington, VA 22217

Robert Grafton

Office of Naval Research
800 North Quincy
Arlington, VA 22217

Introduction

Traditional engineering disciplines are marked by the availability of precise and well understood parameters of measurement. Numerous examples come readily to mind: pressure, temperature, volts, length, area, and volume. Much less well known are metrics for viscosity, illumination, and characteristics of fluid flow such as the Reynolds and Mach numbers. There are literally thousands of metrics available for workers in every scientific and engineering field. These all have elements in common: they are precise, well understood, standardized, and accepted by the scientific communities that use them. Moreover, they have evolved to their present useful state through a long-term process of scientific examination and investigation.

Of course, metrics for the traditional scientific and engineering fields are in a process of dynamic evolution with new metrics being proposed, examined and evaluated, and old one falling into disuse. The analogy here is clear. Computer science and software engineering need metrics and presumably they would evolve through a similar process of scientific evaluation and investigation. Unfortunately, the analogy is incomplete. Metrics for the established science and engineering disciplines are based in the physical sciences while those for computer science, like software itself, will be derived from human ingenuity. Computer science does not suffer from a lack of proposed metrics; however, many are being used out of necessity without the benefit of a deep understanding. Time is not on the side of software metrics. The demand is high thereby inhibiting a detailed examination, gradual acceptance, and eventual standardization.

Thus, while the analogy is interesting, it leaves researchers without particular avenues of approach. Perhaps software and computer science as disciplines have more in common with economics, psychology, and political science than with the physical sciences. These disciplines deal with human activities and they are also struggling with problems of measurement. Whether or not software and computer science can benefit from the experiences of these fields is at best debatable. However, one lesson stands out clearly; where there is no confirmed scientific theory, there is need for a high quality experimental paradigm, accepted by the scientific community, so that hypotheses can be tested, confirmed, and evaluated. This need is abundantly clear in software and computer science.

An Initiative in Software Metrics

While the availability of metrics in itself will not necessarily assure computer software the status of a science, it is safe to say that quantitative evaluation techniques are necessary for the evolution of software from an art form to an engineering discipline and eventual to qualifying as a science. If, indeed, the conventions of measurement and controlled experimentation are essential elements of any science, then one must conclude that computer software is not yet a science. The absence of these elements has been underscored, if not actually deplored, at numerous conferences in the past decade. The need was most recently articulated as an important conclusion of the jointly supported NSF/Industry *Software Engineering Workshop* of June 1979. To quote:

> Measurement techniques and parameters are desperately needed for assessing the quality and reliability of software as well as for the prediction and measurement of software production.

Acknowledging that the Office of Naval Research and other Defense Research agencies have been aware of this deficiency for some time, we cannot report that great progress has been made. Recognizing the continuing need for metrics, ONR has begun a new initiative focused on software measurement. Our first effort has resulted in this publication of contributions from the academic, industrial, and government communities. From a disciplinary viewpoint, this work includes computer science, statistics and psychology. The research initiative placed a high priority on developing indices of merit that can support quantitative comparisons and evaluations of software in terms of its design, use, maintenance, and evolution. The difficulties inherent in this initiative are illustrated by the fact that no one knows an objective measure for comparing competing software designs or for choosing between competing programming languages.

Beyond this quest for developing indices of merit, the objectives of the ONR initiative are: designing a philosophical framework for understanding and defining software measurement; and focusing the attention of the scientific community on computer software metrics.

Software Concerns

Recently, it was reported that software costs are growing at the rate of 15% per year while productivity is increasing at less than 3%. ONR is primarily concerned that this growth is proceeding without scientific foundations. The absence of experimentation and measurement has led to doubts about the fundamental design and introduction of software packages. It has raised questions on cost-effectiveness tradeoffs over the entire software life cycle. Computer software is accused of being undirected and unstructured because of its lack of metrics and experimentation.

Further evidence on this universal concern comes from a GAO report of June 1978 on managing weapons systems. It stated that *there exists no DOD performance criteria to measure software quality and to establish a basis for its acceptance or rejection.* The Secretary of Defense's response to this reported deficiency was brief and candid. *We concur. We regret and underscore the importance of the need. The Department of Defense will quickly embrace such measures when they are available.* Thus, an additional purpose of the ONR initiative is the long term satisfaction of the DOD interest in metrics.

Some Metric Concerns

The current DOD effort to develop and implement a standard programming language for tactical software exemplifies a problem often confronted in the software field — choosing among competing languages. The software field lacks formalism; thus such decisions must be resolved by exclusive reliance on *expert judgment.* We do not want to replace expert opinion in these situations; rather, our purpose is to permit the supplementing of opinion with empirical data.

Continuing the example of evaluating programming languages, a software measurement research program might develop hypotheses, metrics, and experiments for comparing language traits such as: portability, maintainability, extensibility, capability for interfacing with other language code, efficiency of object code, and ease of learning and training. More difficult would be to address issues such issues as: How one assigns weights to the importance of the individual features; varying the weights in consonance with the requirements of different programming environments; providing an answer to the question of whether one can or should develop a figure-of-merit-scoring approach over all features; and assessing the tradeoffs across language properties. Inherent to the language comparison problem are some non-trivial research issues: reaching agreement on an appropriate set of metrics, establishing the feasibility of collecting relevant data, exploring methodologies for comparing different measures of the same gross property, coping with a multitude of competing, if not conflicting, metrics, and defining a task-specific objective function that epitomizes the relation between properties and priorities.

Software metrics needs to determine to what extent the experimental constructs of psychology and statistics apply to software. A useful beginning would be the identification of software hypotheses. Further investigation might lead to a scientific approach accepting or rejecting the hypotheses based on experiments involving the collection and analysis of software data. Some examples of software hypotheses are: Programming language X is better than Y for a given set of programming tasks in a given programming environment; and software test method X is stronger than method Y for a given evaluation objective.

Before there can be progress, it is essential to distinguish those elements of software which can be measured from those which defy measurement. Few disciplines are able to make precise measurements of large, complex, heterogeneous systems; consequently we must avoid the trap of insisting on precise measurements for all aspects of software.

In addition to building mechanisms for objective evaluations and comparisons of software designs, software metrics should address an external concern — the comparison and evaluation of alternative software systems. Successful metrics-work in this area will have a very strong impact on the Navy and military decision process by which software is acquired. There must be convincing evidence that investment in new software technology truly constitutes a significant, measurable improvement. Military interest in this area are with command and control, logistics, and intelligence systems.

Experimentation is crucial if we are interested in substantiating or refuting hypotheses. Relevant experimental design factors were noted in the discussion on the choice of competing programming languages. Several other issues should be, but almost never are, taken into account in designing software experiments. To ensure validity in an experiment consisting of two or more programming teams coding the same application, it is necessary to certify that the teams are balanced in terms of the quality and qualifications. It is altogether too easy for a naive experimenter to let bias enter because of mismatched groups of programmers.

The matter of choosing *real world applications* on which to conduct software experiments is another research issue. Too often in the past, we have arbitrarily chosen a single application for our experiment without addressing the question of whether that choice accidentally, unconsciously, or worse, deliberately satisfied our exact a priori biases on the outcome. Again, the complex research issue here is building a methodology for choosing that application, or set of applications, which ideally and fairly exercises all features across all competitors.

Another factor is the degree to which experience and learning contribute to the result when one is conducting experiments on evaluating a new language. Particularly difficult is the case where a previously programmed application is being redone in the new language.

There are, of course, many other important concerns; for example, the number and duration of the tests, and the costs of the experiment in terms of money and people. This last factor may require a radically new approach to designing large scale software experiments.

Conclusion

The approach to software metrics must be made in a careful, scientific way marked by the traditional scientific paradigm of hypothesis, evaluation, criticism, and review. Progress will most likely be incremental. The search for exact truth may never end and we need to put value in approximations to the truth. Hopefully this book will inspire many solid follow-up research activities. A survey of extent measurement methodologies is needed as well as an evaluation of domains to which they apply and some insights into their utility.

Finally, we are deeply interested in this research initiative because we have made the first step of a long-term research effort that will define those metrics and experimental methodologies that might become the basis for a science of computer software. We continue to believe that progress in all the areas embraced by software metrics will inspire the evolution of computer software from an art or engineering form to a science.

Chapter 1:
Toward a Scientific Basis for Software Evaluation

J. C. Browne

Computer Science Department
University of Texas at Austin
Austin, TX 78712

Mary Shaw

Department of Computer Science
Carnegie-Mellon University
Pittsburgh, PA 15213

Abstract

An examination of the general practice of science, and in particular the interaction of experiment and analysis to generate structurally based system models, suggests a paradigm for the development of a science of software evaluation. We present a view of the development of structured models that is appropriate to software evaluation. We suggest research problems and research techniques which can lead to improvement in software measurement and evaluation methods.

The Problem of Software Evaluation

Most quantitative techniques for describing and evaluating software systems have been developed on a largely ad hoc basis. Large-scale software development has been forced on us by the unprecedented speed with which computer systems have been integrated into the economic life of this country. The need for control over the software development process has created a *software engineering* discipline whose purpose is to establish operational procedures for the development of *quality* software. Unfortunately, techniques for predicting and evaluating software *quality* and performance have not yet emerged in practice. The purpose of this paper is to examine the intellectual tools and research attitudes that will be required before reliable metric techniques can be developed.

A great deal of energy is regularly invested in making measurements of software and of its development process. The techniques of description, measurement and evaluation are, however, largely ad hoc. Most of the analysis techniques and even the data collection techniques have not been generalized beyond the local system or application for which they were developed. As a result, large-scale comparisons of systems and evaluations at a level abstract from particular implementations are rare, and new measurement efforts can be expected to require the development of tools from scratch.

In other words, present metric techniques are not readily extended to new kinds of systems, new kinds of questions, or new development environments. As a result, there is no direct quantitative basis for comparing programs or software engineering methodologies. The economic ramifications of this lack of extendibility are twofold. Each major software system requires a software engineering job starting almost from scratch. In many cases this engineering task is either slighted or totally ignored, leading to severe economic penalties in terms of effort, cost and delay. In addition, software engineering remains a high-technology discipline without adequate rules of standard practice; every system development requires expert skills and defies automation. This has serious economic significance, for the productivity of a group of technical personnel important to the economy is of paramount interest.

At present, software engineering is a technical activity for which we have developed a large set of ad hoc engineering techniques without a corresponding scientific foundation. We believe that this shortcoming is at the heart of many software engineering problems, including software metrics. There is substantial economic incentive for developing such a scientific basis for software evaluation. In Section 2 of this paper, we explore the proper relation between science and engineering and the role of modelling techniques in both. Section 3 discusses the role of scientific techniques and attitudes in software methodology. Section 4 examines current practice and points out discrepancies. Section 5 proposes steps to reduce the differences.

The Role of Models in Science and Engineering

Our description of the need for a scientific software metrics basis begins by examining the related techniques of abstraction and modelling and by discussing the proper science-engineering relationship.

Complexity and Abstraction

Programs are not the only complex systems that people deal with. The national economy is far more complex; even the motion of the molecules in a simple physical object is much more complex than the most complex program. However, no human *completely* understands the national economy or molecular structure in all their fine detail. In order to deal with complex situations we use a powerful technique — abstraction. We deal with complex systems by ignoring their details; we develop *models* which reflect only macroscopic behavioral properties that we believe to be important.

For example, Newton's laws of motion define one model of physical reality. This model abstracts from the precise details of the motion of an object's component particles, which are irrelevant for almost all purposes, and describes gross properties of their aggregate behavior. The only relevant information is expressed by summarizing the individual motions in some way. For example, we speak of the velocity of the object (which is actually the average velocity of all its molecules), its temperature (a measure of the kinetic energy of the molecular motion), and so on. When we summarize many details in a single property (velocity or temperature, for instance) we are *abstracting* from the details, or creating a *model* of the system.

For some purposes these gross abstractions may be inadequate. For example, the structure of a crystal depends on the properties of its constituent molecules. The abstraction used to describe crystalline properties must contain more detail about the crystal than is used to describe the temperature of an object that merely happens to be a crystal. If we wish to understand chemical reactions we must consider an even more detailed model: the atomic structure of the materials. But even then we can suppress information about the properties of subatomic particles. In each of these cases we merely use another *model*, another *abstraction* of reality. Each model contains just enough detail to explicate the phenomena under study. To analyze the motion or temperature of an object, we can totally ignore its molecular structure. To analyze its simple chemical properties, we can ignore, for example, the wave-like behavior of subatomic particles. Only if we were to study nuclear reactions would we need a still more detailed model, namely quantum mechanics.

It is clear, then, that a deep philosophical assumption underlying modern science is that the complexity of reality can be understood by understanding a *hierarchy* of models — some that describe macroscopic behavior by ignoring detail, others that successively explain increasingly lower-level behavior. In establishing a hierarchy of models, we make the assumption that natural causality corresponds to our hierarchy of simplifications. Whether this assumption is entirely valid can be debated, but our limited intellectual capacity *forces* us to make it; without such an assumption, we could not cope with the complexity surrounding us.

Science and Engineering

Engineering deals with the development and application of operational procedures for producing products or services. Science deals with models that explain relationships between the significant variables of systems. To do this, science must isolate and define the significant variables of the systems under study. These significant variables are usually identified by their appearance in statements of invariant relations or principles; system models established by science will incorporate these invariant relations. Engineering design of operational procedures is normally founded upon scientific models of systems.

Science usually starts with observations (measurements) and hypothesizes a set of principles or axioms to explain the observations. These axioms are used to derive or construct models of observable systems. The parameters or variables of these models may be derived from the axioms, or they may be estimated from observation. The model is then used to make new predictions about properties (metrics) of the observed system. The final step is to perform experiments (observations in controlled or understood environments) to determine the accuracy and robustness of models and of the statements of principles. The cycle of hypothesizing and validating models is then continued with the additional observations. Figure 1-1 illustrates this fundamental cycle of the scientific method; it is important to note that the scientific analysis process of figure 1-1 begins with measurements.

It is a crucial point that a single set of underlying principles generally serves as the basis for models of many systems in a broad variety of contexts. This modelling paradigm applies as well to the soft sciences as to the hard sciences. The difference is in essence that in the soft sciences such as psychology or social studies the problems are generally of a statistical or probabilistic nature.

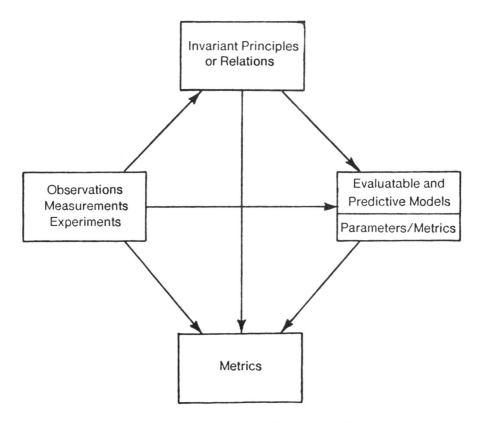

Figure 1-1: Model development cycle.

Two kinds of models can be supported by measurements and statistics. The first, and the one on which we concentrate here, is the *analytic* or *constructive* or *structural* model, in which a system is described in terms of the way it is presumed to work and predictions about its behavior are derived from measurements or predictions about the behavior of its components. The second kind is the *descriptive* or *empirical* or *phenomenological* model, in which no attempt is made to model the underlying structure and predictions about system behavior are made by extrapolating from previous observations about the relation of system behavior to the values of various inputs. Structural models are most likely to be feasible for systems that are small enough for the investigator to make reasonable hypotheses about how they work. Descriptive models are more appropriate for large systems in which the underlying structure is not well understood, but for which it is important to be able to make some sort of predictions. Although both kinds of models have legitimate roles in software engineering, good structural models are the mark of a mature engineering discipline. We therefore concentrate on the development process for structural models.

The determination of fundamental (metric) properties is an essential step in the formulation of a structured model. Fundamental properties are identified by their appearance in the invariant relations which unite observations across many environments; these invariants commonly express conservation relations. Identification of the fundamental properties is a major task of the model builder. However, instead of asking, "What are the fundamental properties of software systems?", we must seek to identify the invariant principles or relations which underlie experimental observations. The identification of fundamental properties or primitive metrics will emerge from the formulation of these invariants. We can then construct models for particular experiments, systems, or methodologies with the guidance that the models must be consistent with the invariant principles, and they will depend on values of measurable inputs. These models will incorporate the fundamental properties as integral parts of their structure; the models may be constructive (software development methodologies) or analytic (mathematical or logical relations).

The invariant principles are guideposts and constraints in the development of model systems. In science, operationally useful models of physical systems are typically based on invariant principles. Newton's laws are invariants for the mechanics of the material bodies of the normal environment; the fundamental laws of quantum mechanics — the Heisenberg uncertainty principle and the DeBrolie relation — are invariants for microscopic bodies. An active science has two threads of activity at each level of abstraction: one utilizes the invariant principles and their derived relations to study systems defined within the level of abstraction, and another attempts to resolve one level of abstraction with its upper and lower neighbors. Psychology is founded (loosely) on biology. Biology is based on chemistry. Chemistry is founded on physics, while physics seeks to resolve understanding to mathematical or symbolic relations.

The development of the gas laws in 19th century chemistry and physics illustrates both threads of development. In 19th century gas laws, Boyle's Law (the volume of a gas is inversely proportional to its pressure) and Charles' Law (the volume is proportional to temperature) were entirely phenomenological. The development of van der Waals' equation, which applies well to many real gases over a variety of conditions, was based on kinetic-molecular theory. Quantum mechanics allows direct computation of can der Waals' constants and indeed the precise virial equation of state. The conversion of mass to energy, for another example, occurs in many formats from solar fusion, to fusion reactors, to internal combustion engines. The models which can be used to compute the energy output for these classes of systems are very different, but we can always be assured that the invariant principle of $E = mc^2$ will not be violated. It must also be recognized that the models of science may vary enormously in resolution and detail. As an example, a model for the energy output of the sun may predict only total energy output or may be composed of flux into a wavelength spectrum and a kinetic energy spectrum for ejected particles on a local basis with respect to the sun's surface. These are further examples of the fundamental principle of hierarchical structuring. Similarly, models for software systems may legitimately be constructed to yield metrics at different levels of abstraction.

Both of the threads of understanding — relationships within the field and the relation of the field to adjacent fields — need to be pursued in the study of software. Software systems need to be understood in terms of appropriate metrics for the top level of concept abstraction, but it is also appropriate to try to map from programs to systems and from systems to programs.

The Practice of Science in the Context of Software Systems

We turn now to the application of this scientific paradigm to the analysis of software systems. This section discusses the lack of scientific foundations and sketches a suitable paradigm. The following section examines present practice in the field.

Lack of Scientific Basis

Software engineering has *leapfrogged* over the traditional engineering/science relationship. This leapfrogging has a number of consequences. The first and most obvious is that software engineering has been unable to produce broadly effective operational procedures for the development of large software systems with predictable characteristics. This assessment is not meant to decry or deride the enormous accomplishments of software engineering. On the contrary, there are few human endeavors since the pyramids where so much progress has been made in the face of so much difficulty and with so few tools in so short a time. It is simply not reasonable to expect that a given set of software engineering techniques can be extended beyond well-understood local environments without a basic scientific understanding of the structures and invariant principles underlying the systems involved. We do not yet have effective definitions of these underlying structures and principles for software systems, nor have we identified the significant variables by which software can be evaluated. Without a clear characterization of what is to be produced, we cannot hope to define an operational procedure for attaining the goal of producing software systems with desired characteristics. Another major impact of leapfrogging to engineering practice without a scientific basis is the confusion and intellectual disarray introduced into software engineering by the absence of basic scientific knowledge about the field. There has been a great deal of experimental and theoretical work on the creation and evaluation of methodologies for software development. This body of work, although carried out by careful and qualified practitioners, often contains inconsistencies, ambiguities, and contradictions. We attribute these problems to the lack of the unifying and integrating concept base which is developed through scientific principles of model building.

There is not now a well-established set of rules or concepts for analyzing or evaluating the properties of software systems. This is not to say that measurements of properties of programs and systems cannot be made; the problem lies in the fact that the variables which can be measured conveniently do not map readily upon properties or characteristics which are both quantifiable and comparable across a broad spectrum of contexts. Only properties or variables which satisfy both of the latter two requirements can be used reliably as metrics for evaluation of software systems. Since there is not a uniform basis for evaluating the software products we develop, it is difficult to make meaningful evaluations or comparisons of the methodologies used to produce these products. There is an excellent chance that the software measurements now being taken are not fundamental and that (even quantitative) descriptions of software do not refer to primitive and comparable concepts. There is an excellent chance that the relationships now observed and inferred in empirical models do not represent the actions of well-understood or fundamental mechanisms. In the absence of system-level metric properties or variables it is often the case that immediate metrics, which may be properties of languages or programming styles, are regarded as ends in themselves rather than pieces in the larger puzzle of a software system.

A given methodology may lead to software properties that are predictable by some metrics, but these metrics may not be relevant to products developed by other and competing methodologies. The next section discusses the traditional practice of the science in the context of software development and software evaluation problems. It is our contention that metrics for the evaluation of software can be developed only in the context of a scientific approach to the analysis of software.

Abstraction and Structure

Having argued that abstractions and models are essential, we now need to consider what constitutes a good abstraction or model. In the physical sciences the Occam's Razor principle has long been accepted as a criterion for choosing between competing models. In effect, Occam's Razor says "Pick the simplest model that adequately describes a phenomenon." The emphasis on simplicity is important, for the whole rationale for modeling is to accommodate our limitations in dealing with complexity. This is consistent with our use of simplicity as a criterion for good programming abstractions; in software design, too, we choose abstractions or models that are both simple (easy to understand) and yet adequate to describe the desired program behavior.

The classic Bohr atom is an excellent example of a simple model. There are only two kinds of parts: the nucleus and its orbiting electrons. Both parts can be characterized in terms of their weight and charge, and the relation between them is characterized in terms of the simple laws governing orbital motion.

The notions of models and abstraction play a central role in software design, but the situation is somewhat different from the situation in the classical sciences. For the chemist and physicist, reality is fixed, given by the physical systems they study; they propose models to describe and predict reality. For them, the degree to which a model is successful can be tested by performing experiments and comparing the results to predictions from the model. The software engineer, on the other hand, is building an artificial reality. He can also use abstractions to control complexity, but he has the ability, in principle, to make these models exact by changing the reality they model. That is, he can (in principle) *make* the program perform at some level of abstraction exactly as predicted by the model under all circumstances. Thus, in a sense, the notions of modeling and abstraction are even more powerful in programming than in the physical sciences. Still, in practice the abstract descriptions used in program specification are almost always somewhat incomplete, just as they are in the physical sciences; for example, we seldom specify the exact running times of our programs.

Further, as the physical systems of chemistry and physics illustrate a hierarchy of models, each more detailed than the last, so is a similar hierarchical structure applicable to programming. An entire program is usually too complex to comprehend, so we describe it in terms of an abstract model. That model is defined in terms that, in turn, must be implemented with fairly complex programs. Generally we need to explain each of these subprograms in terms of still more detailed models. Thus, in a large program you should expect to find many levels of abstraction. Only in this way we can hope to avoid an explosion in complexity.

The illusion of malleability implied by this ability, in principle, to precisely control system behavior leads to problems in the development and maintenance of software. It also affects our present concern with measurement: The very malleability of the medium allows different models to be used for the development or analysis of very similar systems, and it allows the structure of programs to be changed by human design — unlike physical systems, which are strongly constrained by natural laws. The implication of this lack of constraint on system organization is that any natural laws that operate must operate at a low level. Solid understanding of these primitive relations will be crucial to modelling large systems. In addition, the software metrician can re-emphasize the observation of many software builders that the illusion of malleability is misleading. More rigid rules governing system organization may well lead to more tractable systems.

Models for Software

A structural model explains a system in terms of component parts and presumed relations among those component parts. In the programming domain, the *parts* we deal with are data objects and portions of programs. The relations among them are such things as how control and data values flow from one part of a program to another, what kinds of assumptions each portion of a program makes about its execution environment, and the ways the humans working with the program are organized. As scientists, engineers, and programmers, we strive to make both the individual parts and the relationships between them as simple — as good — as possible.

For example, if our overall objective is to measure program quality, we might decide to characterize quality as a composite of a number of other, more specific, properties such as correctness, efficiency, maintainability, completeness, cost of development, quality of documentation, and so on. This reduces the problem of measuring quality to the subproblems of measuring the individual characteristics and of combining those results into an overall quality measure. We can address each of the subproblems in the same way — we might, for example, work from a conceptual model that suggests maintainability depends on program structure, readability, size, number of authors, age, and so on. This generates yet another set of subproblems that could be addressed in the same way. Interestingly, some of these individual characteristics may reasonably be expected to contribute to the measurement of some of the properties of the original set: readability may also be a factor in cost of development and quality of documentation, program structure may also affect correctness and efficiency, size may also affect correctness and cost of development, etc. We speculate that a good structural model for program quality may in addition lead to better understanding of the factors that affect quality in programs. Severe problems are associated with making measurements such as these in such a way that they are valid across computers, programming languages, and even human organizations. The invariant relations that can help to normalize measurements across such differences have not yet been identified.

Structure is often cited as a good property or an indicator of the quality of a program. Several measures for program structure have been proposed. These include syntactic measures [7,8,13], counts of modules and modular connections in a program [1,7], various properties of the graph of the program's control flow [11,12], and the amount of information shared among modules [5]. Each proposal for a metric is supported by one or more tests or algorithms for collecting data to evaluate the metric. It would be remarkable if all these tests were measuring the same characteristic of a program; we have not yet seen adequate work on validating these proposed metrics, either individually or collectively. Although these studies do not view measures of structure as components of a more global metric methodology, we can imagine using them in that way. In order to accept structure as a measurable property, we must ask both about the pertinence of the proposed metrics to the property we call structure and about the accuracy with which the tests embody those metrics. We must also consider whether it is economically feasible to gather the data in practice.

Indeed, a given property may be measurable in more than one way. Certain aspects of operating system performance are often measured by modelling the operating system as a simple single-server queueing system and estimating the parameters of the model on the basis of empirical measurements [10]. To accept the results of such an analysis, we must consider both the degree to which the model represents the actual system and the accuracy with which the parameters are estimated. Operating system performance is also measured with benchmark tests [6]. A user of these tests must consider whether the jobs in the benchmark set correctly model the intended usage of the system and whether enough (and accurate enough) data is collected. Further, to the extent that queueing models and benchmarks are used to measure the same properties, we must be able to discuss how well they actually do so.

The Current Status of Experimental Science in Software Evaluation

Two aspects of the general methodology of science are missing from software evaluation as currently practiced. These are the use of a hierarchy of models and the iterative cycle of hypothesis formation and validation.

The current cycle for experimental studies which should be establishing the foundation of a science of software evaluation is mostly conducted as shown in figure 1-2.

Some quantifiable abstract property — *metric* — is selected for study (understandability, complexity, etc.). Some set of directly measurable quantities — number of statements, reproducibility of code, etc. — is selected. A model which relates the measurements to the metrics is assumed. The model is normally frankly phenomenological. The measurables are used in the model to generate values for the metric properties. These values are then commonly analyzed in an external context or correlated with other experiments. Sometimes the variables of

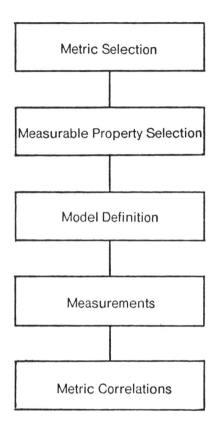

Figure 1-2: Current Practice for Experimental Software Science.

the model are adjusted from analysis and correlation and new values of metric properties generated.

The well-known studies of program structure of McCabe [11] are an example. McCabe's work aims at establishing a property of programs which he labels complexity. Complexity is not given an abstract meaning or scale nor related to other properties at a similar level of abstraction. Rather, complexity is postulated to be a function of the program's control flow structure.

If this process is compared to the traditional processes of science it is quickly seen that an important step has been left out; the development of invariant principles from observations and experiments. Programs unfortunately lack characteristics that can readily be quantified or expressed on a linear numerical scale. For example, control structures are not entirely comparable across programming languages even when extracted to graph structures. There is no intrinsic quantification of program complexity; it is regarded as a *derived* quantity.

A second shortcoming of current software evaluation practice is the lack of attention to hierarchical structure in metrics. The paradigm of science suggests a search for invariant relations involving complexity and attempts to *quantify* complexity in absolute terms or to relate it to other properties at similar levels of abstraction. Such relations could then be used to calibrate models with intermediate, perhaps not comparable, variables. The absence of a foundation of first principles renders the model entirely empirical. Such a model may have predictive value in a given situation, but it is not likely to contain enough structural information to be extendable to other situations. It will be very surprising for coherence and consistency to develop in experimental studies of software development until the field develops some basis of invariant principles. It is not necessary that the invariant principles be rigid mathematical structures; they may be expected to be statistically probabilistic for those aspects of software system evaluation which involve human judgment or human usage.

Models for productivity have often been developed purely empirically. For example, Walston and Felix [14] develop equations for several aspects of programmer productivity based on the assumption that equations of the form

$$\text{EFFORT} = a * \text{SIZE}^b$$

adequately model the situation. Based on empirical data, they obtain equations for a number of characteristics of productivity, including

$$E = 5.2\,L^{0.91}$$

$$D = 49\,L^{1.01}$$

where E = effort in man-months
        L = thousands of lines of delivered code
        D = pages of documentation

In discussing the first equation, they remark that it is nearly linear, but they do not hypothesize a structural explanation and they do not attempt to revise the model to express effort as a linear function of code size with second-order effects. In another paper in this report, Basili describes an attempt to apply the Walston-Felix model in a different environment. He finds that historical data for the second environment yields equations including

$$E = 1.41 \, L^{0.94}$$

$$D = 29.5 \, L^{0.92}$$

These are again close to linear, but again the linearity is noted but not incorporated in the model. Basili also notes that Lawrence and Jeffery [9] have successfully used a linear model. These models for productivity serve an immediate role in providing predictive information for cost planning of current development projects. However, they do not serve to illuminate the basic causal relations that underly the model.

The work of Walters and McCall [15] on the development of metrics for software reliability and maintainability is an example of careful and thorough analysis which proceeds by the entirely phenomenological model represented in figure 1-2. They, in fact, go beyond typical current practice by including a hierarchically structured model. They postulate that reliability and maintainability are functions of other more resolved concepts of programs, modules, and systems. Reliability is postulated as deriving from error tolerance, consistency, accuracy, and simplicity. Maintainability is said to derive from consistency, simplicity, conciseness, modularity, and self-descriptiveness. These assumed metric properties of modules and systems are in most cases evaluated for each module and for the entire system. Values for a top-level metric such as maintainability are derived from independent measurements. Linear regression fits between the metrics at the top level and the module system metrics are assumed and coefficients determined by regression analysis. This paper found significant correlation between values of top-level metrics and the values of module/system metrics such as effectiveness of comments and complexity. This work is thorough and professional. It is, however, deficient with respect to the traditional practice of science in two regards. The model structure is assumed. There is no effort to determine other than linear relationships between metrics or model parameters. There is no attempt to look beyond correlations for invariant principles or to determine further model structures. It is these latter two aspects which we feel must be added to observation and correlation in order to lay a scientific basis for software evaluation metrics.

Another attempt to devise a structural model addressed the more general concept of software *quality* [2]. In this study, Boehm and his colleagues proposed an extensive model for the relation between a number of quality measures and base properties. This model is, however, largely unvalidated.

The absence of a basis of invariant principles not only hinders the formation of coherent models or relations between the variables of a system, it also hinders the specification of measurement. The invariant principles are relations between fundamental quantities. It is often difficult to discern what properties are fundamental in the absence of the guidelines given by invariant principles. It is thus difficult for current experimental work to pose questions (hypotheses) in such a way that after the experiment it can be told whether or not the questions have been answered (tested). The situation is that persons doing experiments in software evaluation are faced with the circumstance of not having the basis for understanding what it is that they are supposed to be studying while trying to design and execute the experiments giving values for these quantities. They face the ultimate problem of experimentation — to demonstrate cause-and-effect relationships without having firmly based definitions of what is to be a cause and what effect is to be measured.

There are currently two main threads of experimental work. One is the direct analysis of software systems' measurable properties and properties presumed to be fundamental. Another is concerned with the evaluation of methodologies for software development in terms of the application of the methodology producing predictable values for assumed metric properties. These two streams of work now tend to use different metrics and to do generally incompatible experiments. A strong effort needs to be made to merge these two paths if true experimentation, which implies operational control, the ability to generate cause-and-effect relationships in experiments, is to be developed. The development methodologies need sound definitions of metrics and structural models for a sound base while experiments in software science must of necessity be constructive in nature.

The validation of models in this situation poses substantial difficulties. In the current structure, validation is showing that the given structure in a given set of variable values allows the model to map input to output in at least one case. This is a powerful validation procedure only if the model can be shown to conform to invariant principles which are known to be valid for a wide spectrum of system descriptions and if the model can be shown to generally conform to invariant structures.

The concept of successive refinement is not often invoked in current experiments in software evaluation. Rather, the intermediate metrics are often regarded as an end in themselves.

Response-time analysis of computer systems provides an example of a software evaluation experiment which conforms to a traditional paradigm for scientific analysis. Response can be measured as a function of transaction resource usage characteristics. A a queueing-network model representation of an interactive computer system might be as in figure 1-3, taken from Browne et al [3].

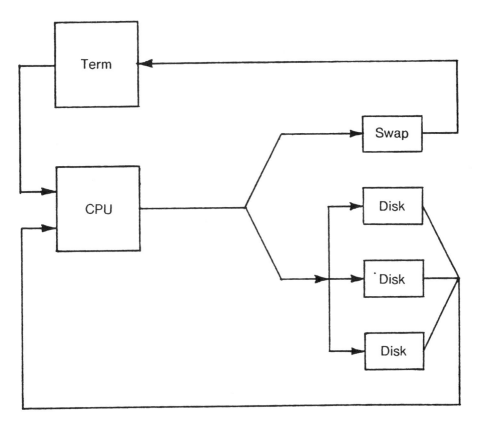

Figure 1-3: Queueing Network Model.

Response time is modeled on the time elapsed between a job's leaving the TERM queue and rejoining the TERM queue. The disk system is actually a two-phase process, involving both positioning and transfer.

Additionally, each disk sub-system probably consists of several drives on a single controller. Therefore each DISK queue is really a composite structure such as figure 1-4.

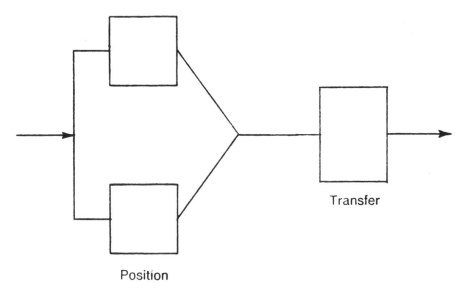

Transfer

Position

Figure 1-4: Disk System Model.

The service time for POSITION is normally a function of workload level. Measurements are made on each phase of the disk service and the model parameterized as a function of workload. The Chandy-Herzog-Woo (CHW) theorem [4] is then used to determine an equivalent single queue to represent DISK in figure 1-3. Figure 1-3 is then collapsed to figure 1-5 by the CHW theorem and response time becomes the service time of the queue labelled SYSTEM. The model relationships are determined by the structure of the several queueing network models and the parameters are taken directly from observations and invariant principles.

Steps Toward a Scientific Basis for Software Evaluation

The comparison of the successful development pattern for the sciences with the current ad hoc practice in software evaluation suggests directions for both long-term and short-term research and development. The current empirical and experimental work is vital. It should be

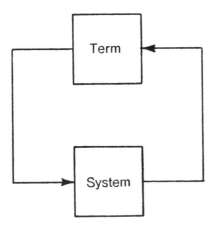

Figure 1-5: Collapsed System.

enhanced and extended by applying the general principles of traditional science.

1. *Invariant Principles:* The absence of invariance principles is the most serious deficiency in the field of software evaluation. Invariant principles are seldom created.   Rather they are synthesized from observation and from transfer of knowledge coupled with insight and a knowledge of the systems being studied. Thus analysis of observed properties of software is not wasted effort.   It is almost surely a prerequisite for eventual generation of invariant principles. Much more emphasis needs to be placed on attempts to identify abstract invariant principles from observations rather than the current attempts to create entirely empirical context-driven models.

2. *Successive Refinements:* The concept of hierarchical structuring of metrics and models needs to become a part of the experimental practice of software evaluation. The attempts to leap the vast conceptual distance from concepts such as maintainability directly to properties of programs written in the specific languages is unlikely to produce success. Experiments and models need to be constructed which attempt to define and evaluate programs or system concepts such as maintainability.

3. *Model Validation:* Model validation must be recognized as a principal problem.   Efforts need to be made to test models against even assumed invariant principles. The definition of the context of a validation and the precision of definition of the metrics and the variables in the model need to be an integral part

of every experimental study. Phenomenological and empirical models need to be analyzed for possible content of and effect on invariant principles. The principle of successive refinement is important with respect to the validation problem. The decomposition of the concept goals into intermediate metrics leads to the possible establishment of intermediate levels of validation which may be soundly based and perhaps well understood.

4. *Introspection:* We must iterate over our models to make them better descriptions of the systems they model. This is different from creating a hierarchy of successively more precise models — it is rather a requirement for better accuracy at each level of precision.

There is a strong need for experimental work based upon these traditional principles of science. A few such experiments, if successful, could lead to fundamental new directions for software system evaluation and software engineering. Although phenomenological predictive models will be useful, and they may yield higher cost returns in the short run, structural models provide a means for understanding the fundamental mechanisms at work in a system and for basing new models on existing sub-models. As a result, structural models offer substantial economic benefits in the long term. We recommend that investigations of techniques for developing, evaluating, and using structural models be supported as basic research. For the next few years, this must include support for the development of models for specific kinds of systems to serve as test beds and concrete examples of good practice.

References

[1]   L. A. Belady and C. J. Evangelisti.
        System partitioning and its measure.
        Technical Report RC 7560 (# 32643), IBM T. J. Watson
            Research Center, March, 1979.

[2]   B.W. Boehm, J.R. Brown, H. Kaspar, M. Lipow, G.J. McLeod,
        M.J. Merritt.
        Characteristics of software quality.
        North-Holland Publishing Co., 1978.

[3]   J.C. Browne, K.M. Chandy, R.M.Brown, T.W. Keller, D.F.
        Towsley, and C.W. Dissly.
        *Hierarchical techniques for the development of realistic models
            of complex computer systems.*
        Proceedings of the IEEE 63:966-977, 1975.

[4]   K. M. Chandy, U. Herzog and L. Woo.
         Parametric analysis of queuing networks.
         IBM Journal of Research and Development 19.36-42, 1975.

[5]   Robert N. Chanon.
         On a measure of program structure.
         Technical Report, Carnegie-Mellon University, 1973.

[6]   Dennis M. Conti.
         Findings of the standard benchmark library study group.
         Technical Report 500-38, National Bureau of Standards Special
             Publication, January, 1979.

[7]   Tom Gilb.
         Software Metrics.
         Winthrop, 1977.

[8]   Maurice H. Halstead.
         *Operating and Programming Systems: Elements of Software
             Science.*
         Elsevier Computer Science Library, 1977.

[9]   D. R. Jeffery and M. J. Lawrence.
         *An inter-organizational comparison of programming
             productivity.*
         Technical Report, University of New South Wales, Department
             of Information Systems.

[10]   L. Kleinrock.
         Queuing Systems, Volume II: Applications.
         John Wiley & Sons, 1975.

[11]   Thomas J. McCabe.
         A complexity measure.
         IEEE Transactions on Software Engineering SE-2(4), December,
             1976.

[12]   Barbara G. Ryder.
         Constructing a call graph of a program.
         IEEE Transactions on Software Engineering SE-5(3):216-226,
             May, 1979.

[13]   T. A. Thayer, et al.
         Software Reliability study.
         Technical Report RADC-TR-76-238, Rome Air Development
             Center, August, 1976.

[14]   C. E. Walston and C. P. Felix.
        A method of programming measurement and estimation.
        IBM Systems Journal 16(1), 1977.
[15]   Gene F. Walters and James A. McCall.
        The development of metrics for software reliability and
            maintainability.
        In *Proceedings of the 1978 Reliability and Maintainability
            Symposium*.

Questions Asked after the Conference

Fred Sayward

In trying to establish a science of software metrics, do you think that it would be more productive to initially view software metrics as a *hard* science or as a *soft* science? Why?

Jim Browne and Mary Shaw

The focus of this article is the development of a scientific basis for the evaluation of software. Establishment of a basis of metrics is only one aspect of software system evaluation. Evaluation of software is, as a science, still very much a *soft* science. It is likely to evolve slowly since some of the significant problems in evaluation of the development process (human factors, etc.) are intrinsically difficult problems of social and behavioral science. The important message is that evaluation of software should be systematically pressed toward evolution to a hard science just as is the case where possible in the soft sciences.

Fred Sayward

Your paper centers around a search for *invariant principles* of software which will form the basis of a software metrics science. You seem to assume that these principles exist and must be found. On what basis is your assumption made? I view software as a means of expressing a solution to a problem, there being an analogy to natural language being a means of expressing thought. Are there invariant principles in natural language? Must all science be based on invariant principles?

Jim Browne and Mary Shaw

Establishment of invariant principles is one of several distinguishing characteristics of a scientific approach to evaluation of software. Structurally-based models capable of successive refinement are also an integral part of the recommended approach.   Invariant principles or relations capture, at some level of abstraction, the common basis of a set of related objects and/or processes.   If software systems and their development and evaluation have any basis of commonality then invariant principles must exist. Yes, all science must have some basis of invariant principles. Yes, there are invariant principles for the evaluation of discourses expressed in a natural language.

Chapter 2:
Design of Software Experiments

Frederick G. Sayward

Department of Computer Science
Yale University
New Haven, CT 06520

Introduction

In this paper the current practices used in conducting experiments aimed at understanding and improving software development, testing, and maintenance will be summarized and critiqued. To date the designs used in *software experiments* have followed the traditional approach, in which subjects are randomly drawn from a population and then randomly assigned to two or more groups. The effect of the hypothesized improvement factor is then evaluated by comparing the mean intergroup change observed on some measured factor. In addition to the problems of internally validating current software experiments, external validation problems have led to little widespread acceptance of their conclusions. The chief research-directing recommendation given here is that a relatively new and controversial experimental design, called *single subject research* [16], should be explored as a possible cost-effective approach to the external validation problems of current software experiments.

In the next section the principles and terminology of experiments will be reviewed. A summary and analysis of the methods and conclusions of software experiments found in the literature is given in section 3. In section 4 the principles and problems of single subject experiments are given along with an indication of how this design type might be applied in software experiments. Suggested research directions are presented in the final section.

Experimental Principles and Terminology

Experiments of the type conducted for understanding and improving software usually start with an identification of three types of variables: *independent*, *dependent*, and *uncontrolled*. The independent variable is the hypothesised improvement factor (treatment). An example of an independent variable is using or not using structured programming techniques during program development. A dependent variable is some measurable factor (response) which is a function of the independent variable, for example, the cost of program development. Uncontrolled variables are any other factors (sources of variance) which influence the dependent variable, for example, years of programming experience, programming language, and program size. Hypotheses concerning the software life cycle are usually stated in terms of these variables; for example, "Structured programming reduces the cost of program development" and "The cost of developing 500 line FORTRAN programs is reduced by a factor of 3 when structured programming is used." Clearly, the more general the hypothesis the more effort required to design a valid experiment.

The next aspect is choosing a design type. The most popular choice in software experiments is the *many subject random group design*, which has evolved over the past hundred years from work initially done in agricultural experiments. After random selection, the subjects are randomly split into groups. Both uses of randomization are critical in accounting for the dependent variable measurement variance introduced by the uncontrolled variables. Also, groups are assigned instances of the independent variable for the duration of the experiment.

After subject selection and assignment, the material of the experiment must be determined. For software, this is usually the programming tasks to be done. Depending on the hypothesis, randomization may again be used to dampen variance.

The next decision is in the measurement technique used to monitor the dependent variable. For example, it may be too difficult under experimental conditions to measure cost in dollars. But if one makes the inference that time is money, then one is justified in measuring time. In the many subject random group experiment, measurements on the dependent variable are (effectively) taken only once, that being at the conclusion of the experiment. A single measurement is also in the agricultural tradition, where crop yield is the critical data. This point should not be taken lightly since a large body of statistical inference tests have evolved for analyzing this single (in time) data point. These tests form the analytic tools which have been used to analyze the data collected in software experiments in determining whether the hypothesis should be accepted or rejected.

The final and probably most important aspect concerns experiment validity. There are two forms of validity, *internal* and *external*. Internal validity is the degree of certainty that changes in the independent variable account for observed changes in the dependent variable. That is, all uncontrolled variables have been ruled out as contributors to the measurements taken on the dependent variable. External validity is the extent to which the results of the experiment can be generalized to different subjects, materials, statistical tests, and experiments. In general, do the experimental results scale up to the entire population? Internal validity is a minimum prerequisite for conducting an experiment since without it the results of an experiment are uninterpretable. For many subject random group experiments, there are several replication methods which have been used in the design of software experiments, such as factorization and Latin squares, aimed at ensuring internal validity.

State of the Art in Software Experiments

As stated above, the design of software experiments has followed the traditional many subject group orientation. The independent variables under investigation have fallen mainly into the following five categories: programming language constructs, programming methodologies, program complexity measures, types of debugging tasks, and programmer experience. The dependent variables have fallen mainly into the following four categories: time and accuracy of program development, understanding of existing programs, number of detected errors, and time and accuracy of modifications to existing programs. Depending on the study, one or more of the factors above are taken to be uncontrolled variables. It is noted that there is a surprising lack of using programming language as an independent variable. In software experiments programming language usually is a fixed parameter.

The number of papers on software experiments has grown rapidly in the past few years, indicating interest both in the computer science research and in the practitioner camps. What follows is a brief summary of the software experiments literature examined by the author, presented more or less in chronological order. Unless otherwise stated, each experiment used some form of many subject random group design.

Sackman, Erikson, and Grant [20] found that subjects doing on-line debugging required significantly less walk-clock time than did subjects doing off-line debugging for the same debugging tasks. Moreover, there was no significant difference in the CPU time needed by the two groups.

Sime, Green, and Guest [28] found that the IF THEN ELSE type of conditional statement was superior to the IF THEN GOTO in terms of programming time and number of errors made.

Gould and Drongowski [14] found up to a factor of five difference in the time required to detect different types of bugs and found up to a factor of four difference in the number of bugs detected by experienced programmers having equivalent backgrounds.

Weinberg and Schulman [30] found that programmers constructed quite different software to satisfy the same objectives of fast programming, efficient programs, minimal program size, and program readability.

Youngs [32] found that experienced programmers used different debugging strategies from those used by beginning programmers.

Weissman [31] found that commenting and paragraphing made programs easier to understand but more difficult to modify while good variable naming helped both program understanding and modification.

Gould [13] gave examples of debugging tasks and program modifications which required little to no understanding of the programs under consideration.

Shneiderman [21] found that using FORTRAN logical IFs rather than arithmetic IFs made small programs easier to understand for novice programmers.

Gannon [10] found that strong data typing in programming languages had positive effect over no data typing with respect to making fewer errors and taking fewer runs in arriving at the final program.

Green [15] found that professional programmers were better able to answer difficult questions about programs written in a language which used an IF THEN ELSE having redundant predicate information rather than the standard IF THEN ELSE.

Shneiderman [22] found that even a few months' difference in experience for intermediate level programmers can have a significant effect on performance, and he also advocated the use of memorization and recall as a basis of measuring program understanding.

Shneiderman, Mayer, McKay, and Heller [24] found that flowcharts were redundant and had a potentially negative affect on coding, comprehension, debugging, and modification.

Sime, Arblaster, and Guest [27] found that tools for helping format conditional statements reduced the initial program error content but didn't help in locating the errors initially present.

Sime, Green, and Guest [29] found that subjects, when programming in a language where the scope of conditional clauses is redundantly defined, tended to make more syntactic errors than semantic errors while when programming in traditional languages the reverse seemed to hold.

Brooks [3] found that dictionaries of program variables were superior to macro flowcharts as an aid to understand program control and data structures.

Chrysler [5], using no controlled groups, found that for COBOL programs the occurrence counts of output fields, input files, control breaks and totals, input edits, output records, input fields, and input records were the most significant predictors of development time and that programmer age and years of formal education were the most significant predictors of development time.

Myers [18], in comparing different debugging methods, found that surprisingly few errors (34%) were caught, that there were significant differences in the error types caught by group, and that code walkthrough was more costly than other methods but didn't give better performance.

Basili and Reiter [1] found that, in building a simple compiler, three-man teams which were required to use modern programming methods required less effort than uncontrolled teams or individuals.

Curtis, Sheppard, Milliman, Borst, and Love [7], in comparing Halstead's effort metric, McCabe's cyclomatic number metric, and the number of executable statements to programmer performance on two maintenance tasks, found there was little to choose among the three metrics with respect to time and accuracy of maintenance.

Curtis, Sheppard, and Milliman [6] in a replication of Curtis et. al. [7] using larger multimodular programs and a wider variety of subjects found that Halstead's effort metric was better than lines of code by a factor of two for predicting debugging effort.

Dunsmore and Gannon [8] found that low average variables referenced per statement and average low live variables per statement had a simplifying effect on program development and program maintenance.

Shneiderman and Mayer [23] found planned modularization rather than no or random modularization aided in the comprehension of programs.

Schneidewind and Hoffmann [25] found that the rates for making programming errors, detecting programming errors, and correcting programming errors are all dependent on structural program complexity.

Sheppard, Curtis, Milliman, and Love [26] found that one could use the number of languages known and the familiarity with FORTRAN concepts to predict comprehension, modification, and debugging performances for programmers having three years or less of FORTRAN experience, but not for programmers having more FORTRAN experience.

Dunsmore and Gannon [9], in investigating the effect program nesting, percentage of global variables, ratio of parameters to global variables, average variables referenced, and average live variables have on the effort required for program construction, comprehension, and modification, found that effort related to all five parameters and that modification was easier when the ratio of formal parameters to global variable was high and when the average live variables per statement was low.

Rarely in the software experiments above have hypotheses been formally stated at the outset. Rather, the paradigm is an informal introduction to the factors under consideration, the experiment design, the data collected, the application of statistical inference tools, and conclusions. The reported internal validity considerations are rarely satisfactory. Each paper usually ends with a note that the findings suggest further investigation should be done, indicating that even the authors have little faith, as yet, in the external validity of their software experiments.

Brooks [4] gives a detailed account of some internal validity flaws found in current software experiments. He cites several examples of subject and material selection, summarized below, which make many experiments suspect. With respect to measurement selection, he states that new measures of the effort required for program construction and program understanding based on cognitive models of program-programmer interaction are needed.

Brooks' criticism of subject selection is based on the methods used to circumvent the problems of cost, non-availability, and wide ability differences of using experienced professional programmers. Most software experiments have used beginning or intermediate-level student programmers as subjects. There is little proof of the necessary internal validation issue that experienced programmers use at a faster rate the same problem-solving procedures as do beginners. Also, guaranteeing that groups of begining programmers have equal ability is not trivial.

The problem with material selection is not so much internal as external. For internal validity, the programming tasks selected must be comparable across the uncontrolled variables. Program complexity measures have been somewhat helpful in this respect. Factorization designs can also be used.

For external validity, Brooks states that the programs used in software experiments are not representative of the programs being developed in the real world because of their small size. Since it is universally accepted that developing a large system is not just a matter of scaling up from developing a small system, small-scale material will be a potential source of external invalidity until an accepted model of the effects of program size is developed.

Brooks states that all of the experiments done to date need to be replicated on larger programs before any generality of their results can be accepted. Although it was not stated, presumably experienced professional programmers would also have to be used in attempting to generalize the current software experiments by replicating them on large-scale software.

It is the opinion of this author that Brooks' suggestion is not only economically infeasible but also premature. In the next section a more economical but equally risky alternative suggestion will be made, which is based on the following question:

> Given that the software life cycle is so dynamic over time, should we be content in our software experiments to draw conclusions based on a single ex post facto measurement?

Single Subject Research

The major difference between the orthodox many subject experiment and the single subject experiment is that in the latter approach the dependent variable is measured throughout the experiment to yield a *time-series* of observations. In their design, time is broken into phases during which different instances of the independent variable are applied (called interventions). Conclusions are then drawn from observed interphase changes in the dependent variable.

There are four basic types of single subject experiments: one individual, two or more individuals, one (small) group of subjects, two or more (small) groups of subjects. Hence, single subject is really a misnomer. Within each type of experiment there is further diversity in the number and order of interventions. However, in all designs the emphasis is on a time-series of measurements.

As usual, the design problems are in internal and external validity. It is more difficult to resolve the internal issue for single subject than for many subject experiments. Several recommendations on validity are given in [16] and some will be summarized below.

For now, some of the validity problems will be illustrated by considering a hypothetical single subject experiment on the hypothesis "Structured programming reduces the cost of program development." The single subject design will be of the *operant* or *ABAB* type which is used for one individual or one small group. For illustration purposes, let us assume we have a perfect definition of structured programming and a perfect measure of program development cost which can be applied in an unbiased fashion at any point in time.

In the ABAB design the time axis is broken into four phases whose sequence and terminology are illustrated in figure 2-1.

During baseline and withdrawal the single subject does not use structured programming techniques, while in the other two phases structured programming is employed. Suppose that the subject is writing a large system in some language and periodically the cost measure is applied to arrive at the raw data which is graphically presented in figure 2-2.

As will become evident, graphical presentation plays a central role in interpreting the data of single subject experiments. In [19] several methods of constructing line graphs, bar graphs, and cumulative graphs

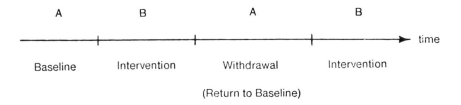

Figure 2-1: The ABAB single subject design

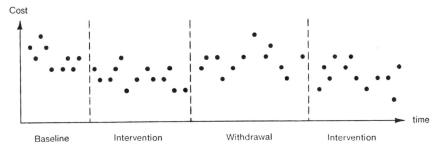

Figure 2-2: Hypothetical raw data

from the raw time-series data of a single subject experiment are given. Also, useful graph transformations are given. It is explained how the various graphical forms can be used as an aid in analyzing several experiment validity questions.

Two important graphs are illustrated in figures 2-3 and 2-4: a bar graph of the phase means and a within-phases least-squares fitted trend line.

Figure 2-3 indicates equal levels of better performance by the subject when structured programming is used, a necessity for internal validity. However, since the subject performed better under withdrawal than at baseline, there is a threat to internal validity due to *learning*. This is compounded in view of the decreasing baseline trend line illustrated in figure 2-4. Thus, there is a major threat to validity due to an unstable baseline. A prerequisite in single subject experiments is the establishment of stability in the baseline. Although not illustrated, variance in the phase data must also be considered.

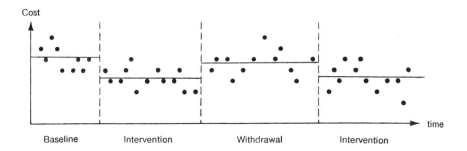

Figure 2-3: Bar graph of phase means

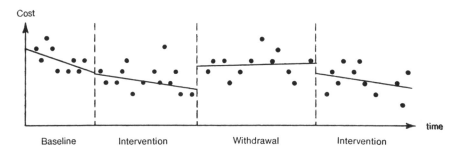

Figure 2-4: Least-squares fitted trend lines

Kratochwill [17] gives a summary of several validity issues which must be dealt with in single subject research. The threats to internal and external validity for single subject experiments are more or less the same threats present in many subject experiments. But the problems in dealing with the threats are more acute because of two facts: single subject experiments usually take more time to conduct and thus there is greater chance that a threat causing event will occur; and since there are fewer subjects, subject problems such as learning or dropout have greater negative impact on validity. In general, more attention must be paid to validity in single subject experiments since the design is less adequate for dealing with the influences of the uncontrolled variables.

On the positive side, the problem of representative material is somewhat easier. Also there are two emerging formal methods for data evaluation: graphical techniques [19] and statistical inference techniques [11,12]. In the latter area it has been shown how time-series analysis and Markov chains can be used as significance tests for baseline stationarity, interphase changes in level, and autocorrelation in the collected data.

Recommended Research Directions

The chief research-directing recommendation of this paper is that computer scientists engaged in software experiments should seriously consider using single subject designs in their subsequent experiments. Unlike the agricultural tradition of many subject designs, single subject designs have evolved from an educational psychology and therapeutic tradition. In these fields the difficulties of replication and the ethics of non-treatment led to a search for alternative designs. While the latter point doesn't appear to be a problem in computer science, the former certainly is.

A major potential advantage of single subject research to software experiments lies in retesting hypotheses which have been affirmed in past experiments. As stated above, these affirmations are often suspect because of the small scale material used and the selection of inexperienced subjects. Added strength can be gained through single subject experiments using larger scale material and more experienced subjects. Although these same goals could be accomplished by scaled-up replication of past experiments, as suggested by Brooks [4], it is not felt that there is adequate justification for the staggering costs this would entail at the present time. Also, some of the threats to internal validity would still be present in the replications since there are, as yet, many deficiencies in our knowledge of programmer-programming task interactions. In summary, single subject design offers a cost-effective opportunity to do larger-scale software experiments now.

From a philosophical view, the single subject approach is more appealing to this author because of its data collection over time mandate. Given that the software life cycle is very dynamic, it is difficult to accept hypotheses on the basis of data collected at a single point in time. Even if the validity issues of single subject software experiments prove too difficult to overcome, there is a good chance that conducting such experiments will lead to new insights on how to integrate the time variable into traditional software experiments.

Last, in addition to supporting the new single subject approach, it is recommended that small-scale many subject software experiments receive continued support. These experiments will continue to lead to interesting new hypotheses, a sharpening of subject, material, and measurement selection techniques, and a quick inexpensive rejection of false hypotheses. Integrating the recommendations, one can foresee the future possibility of hypotheses passing through a hierarchy of well planned software experiments: small-scale single subject, small-scale many subject, intermediate-scale single subject, intermediate-scale many subject, ...

Acknowledgement

I would like to thank Richard Lipton for making me aware of single subject research and for introducing me to an invaluable reference [16].

References

[1]   V. Basili and R. Reiter.
        An investigation of human factors in software development.
        Computer 12(12):21-38, December 1979.

[2]   S. Boies and J. Gould.
        Syntactic errors in computer programming.
        Human Factors 16:253-257, 1974.

[3]   R. Brooks.
        Using a behavioral theory of program comprehension in
            software engineering.
        *Proceedings of the 3rd International Conference on Software
            Engineering*, pages 196-201. IEEE, New York, 1978.

[4]   R. Brooks.
        Studying programmer behavior experimentally: The problems
            of proper methodology.
        Communications of the ACM 23(4):207-213, April 1980.

[5]   E. Chrysler.
        Some basis determinants of computer programming
            productivity.
        Communications of the ACM 21(6):472-483, June 1978.

[6]   B. Curtis, S. Sheppard, and P. Milliman.
        Third time charm: stronger prediction of programmer
            performance by software complexity metrics.
        *Proceedings of the 4th International Conference on Software
            Engineering*, IEEE, New York, 1979, pages 356-360.

[7]   B. Curtis, S. Sheppard, P. Milliman, M. Borst, and T. Love.
        Measuring the psychological complexity of software
            maintenance tasks with the Halstead and McCabe metrics.
        IEEE Transactions on Software Engineering SE-5, pages 96-
            104. March 1979.

[8]   H. Dunsmore and J. Gannon.
        Data referencing: An empirical investigation.
        Computer 12(12):50-59, December 1979.

[9]   H. Dunsmore and J. Gannon.
        Analysis of the effects of programming factors on programming
            effort.
        The Journal of Systems and Software 1:141-153, 1980.

[10]   J. Gannon.
        An experimental evaluation of data type conventions.
        Communications of the ACM 20(8):584-595, August 1977.

[11]   J. Gottman and G. Glass.
        Analysis of interrupted time-series experiments.
        In T. Kratochwill, editor [16], pages 197-235.

[12]   J. Gottman and C. Notarius.
        Sequential analysis of observational data using Markov chains.
        In T. Kratochwill, editor [16], pages 237-285.

[13]   J. Gould.
        Some psychological evidence on how people debug computer
            programs.
        International Journal of Man-Machine Studies 7, 1975, pages
            151-182.

[14]   J. Gould and P. Drongowski.
        An exploratory study of computer program debugging.
        Human Factors 16(3):258-277, 1974.

[15]   T. Green.
        Conditional program statements and their comprehensibility to
            professional programmers.
        Journal of Occupational Psychology 50, pages 93-109, 1977.

[16]   T. Kratochwill, editor.
        Single Subject Research: Strategies for Evaluating Change.
        Academic Press, New York, 1978.

[17]   T. Kratochwill.
        Foundations of time-series research.
        In Kratochwill, editor [16], pages 1-100.

[18]   G. Myers.
       A controlled experiment in program testing and code
           walkthroughs/inspection.
       Communications of the ACM 21(9):760-768, September 1978.

[19]   B. Parsonson and D. Baer.
       The analysis and presentation of graphic data.
       In T.Kratochwill, editor [16], pages 101-165.

[20]   H. Sackman, W. Erikson, and E. Grant.
       Exploratory experimental studies comparing online and offline
           programming performance.
       Communications of the ACM 11(1):3-11, January 1968.

[21]   B. Shneiderman.
       Exploratory experiments in programmer behavior.
       International Journal of Computer and Information Science
           5(2):123-143, June 1976.

[22]   B. Shneiderman.
       Measuring computer program quality and comprehension.
       International Journal of Man-Machine Studies 9:465-578, 1977.

[23]   B. Shneiderman and R. Mayer.
       Syntactic/semantic interactions in programmer behavior: A
           model and experimental results.
       International Journal of Computer and Information Science
           8(3):219-238, June 1979.

[24]   B. Shneiderman, R. Mayer, D. McKay, and P. Heller.
       Experimental investigation of the utility of detailed flowcharts in
           programming.
       Communications of the ACM 20(6):373-384, June 1977.

[25]   N. F. Schneidewind and H. M. Hoffmann.
       An experiment in software error data collection and analysis.
       IEEE Transactions on Software Engineering SE-5, May 1979,
           pages 276-286.

[26]   S. Sheppard, B. Curtis, M. Milliman, and T. Love.
       Modern coding practices and programmer performance.
       Computer 12(12):41-59, December 1979.

[27]   M. Sime, A. Arblaster, and D. Guest.
       Reducing programming errors in nested conditionals by
           prescribing a writing procedure.
       International Journal of Man-Machine Studies 9, pages 119-126,
           1977.

[28]   M. Sime, T. Green, and D. Guest.
         Psychological evaluation of two conditional constructions used
             in computer languages.
         International Journal of Man-Machine Studies 5(1):105-113,
             1973.

[29]   M. Sime, T. Green, and D. Guest.
         Scope marking in computer conditionals — a psychological
             evaluation.
         International Journal of Man-Machine Studies 9(1):107-118,
             1977.

[30]   G. Weinberg and E. Schulman.
         Goals and performance in computer programming.
         Human Factors 16(1):70-77, 1974.

[31]   L. Weissman.
         Psychological complexity of computer programs: An
             experimental methodology.
         SIGPLAN Notices 9(6):25-36, June 1974.

[32]   E. Youngs.
         Human errors in programming.
         International Journal of Man-Machine Studies 6:361-376, 1974.

Questions Asked at the Conference

Irwin Nathan, Xerox Corporation

I'm glad that you identified the fact that there is a time-series involved. Certainly nothing stops you from making an experiment where you are measuring the learning rate of any particular type of programming technique, structured or any other — or even the language. But the other aspect, which bothers me more, is the basic requirement that things be stochastic, that you are in an experiment, and it's closed, and it has all the properties of a probability distribution. You didn't mention anywhere that you know in fact that there is a probability distribution against which you can measure your hypothesis, or reject it. Do you know of any work that's been done there?

Fred Sayward

People have been formulating probability distributions that describe various aspects of the software process. I haven't seen too many results that aim at rejecting distributional assumptions, or even identifying them.

Most of the claims made from software experiments have been based on non-parametric analysis.

Irwin Nathan

But they still prescribe some kind of a distribution, and in a learning situation it may not be clear that you have one. There's been a lot of work done in human factors, which is essentially software in any real sense. Perhaps you might investigate work done there, particularly in the late 1960s. I think quite a bit of work was done, and maybe there might be some clues as to how to handle this kind of problem.

Sid Amster, Bell Labs

I wonder if the speaker has looked at all into the crossover designs, which have been extensively used in agricultural experiments for years. You feed some cows, say, one kind of diet, and then another diet, and then the first diet again. The idea is to allow for those effects that might be residual from the previous treatment. It sounds like there's a direct analogy here with your stuff.

Fred Sayward

Well, it wasn't illustrated in this example, but there are techniques aimed at seeing whether things are stochastic, or whether there is a prediction property of the data. It sounds like the crossover design you're talking about is one of these single subject designs. There is a problem of terminology in experiments because the educational psychologists tend to use one terminology, the agronomists another ...

Sid Amster

I would certainly agree with that comment. One of the problems in this whole area is that people are re-inventing things simply because they aren't aware of what's going on in another discipline.

H. E. Dunsmore, Purdue University

You propose conducting a large-scale single subject experiment, but I wonder how you would counter the objection that your results will be greatly confounded by the properties of that one single subject.

Fred Sayward

I'm not suggesting that you use a single particular subject. *single subject* is a misnomer — in some cases you do have to go to a group design. But the key thing is that you use small groups, to make it more cost-effective, and you measure over time, to try to account for the variance problems. You want to look into variance over time as well as the difference between treatment and non-treatment. Granted you can't resolve all of your problems if you have a single subject, but my major suggestion is to use fewer subjects, use larger material, and look at things over time.

Chapter 3:
Experimental Evaluation of Software Characteristics

Bill Curtis

Programming Technology Center
International Telephone and Telegraph
Stratford, CT 06497

Cause-Effect Relationships

Most studies on software metrics do not demonstrate cause-effect relationships between software characteristics and programmer performance. That is, there were uncontrolled factors in the data collection environment which could have influenced the observed data. These alternative explanations of the results dilute any statement of cause and effect. Although structural equation techniques [7,12] allow an investigation of whether the data are consistent with one or more theoretical models, a causal test of theory will require a rigorously controlled experiment. According to Cattell [4]:

> An experiment is a recording of observations...made by defined and recorded operations and in defined conditions followed by examination of the data...for the existence of significant relations.

Two important characteristics of an experiment are that its data collection procedures are repeatable and that each experimental event results in only one from among a defined set of possible outcomes [11]. An experiment does not prove an hypothesis. It does, however, allow for the rejection of competing alternative explanations of a phenomenon.

The confidence which can be placed in a cause-effect statement is determined by the control over extraneous variables exercised in the collection of data. For instance, Milliman and Curtis [15] reported a field study in which a software development project guided by modern programming practices produced higher quality code with less effort and experienced fewer test errors when compared to a sister project in the same environment which did not observe these practices. Although many of the environmental factors were controlled, an alternative explanation of the results was that the project guided by modern practices was performed by a more capable programming team.

An important characteristic of the classical experimental method in behavioral science is the random assignment of participants to conditions [8]. By removing any systematic variation in the ability, motivation, etc. of participants across experimental conditions, this method supposedly eliminates the hypothesis that experimental effects are due to individual differences among participants. Assigning a morning class to one condition and an afternoon class to another condition does not constitute random assignment, since students rarely choose class times on a random basis. However, if classes rather than students are the unit of study, the problem can be solved by randomly assigning a number of classes to each experimental condition. Random assignment is a problem in testing causal relationships in field studies on actual software development projects.

There is often a conflict between what Campbell and Stanley [3] describe as the internal and external validity of an experiment. *Internal validity* concerns the rigor with which experimental controls are able to eliminate alternative explanations of the data. *External validity* concerns the degree to which the experimental situation resembles typical conditions surrounding the phenomena under study. Thus, internal validity expresses the degree of faith in causal explanations, while external validity describes the generalizability of the results to actual situations.

In software engineering research, rigorous experimental controls are difficult to achieve on software projects, and laboratory studies often seem contrived. External validity is probably a greater problem in studying process factors such as the organization of programming teams than in studying product factors such as the complexity of control flow. That is, studying the environmental conditions surrounding software development, which are difficult to replicate in the laboratory and would probably have a greater effect on the functioning of programming teams than on a programmer's comprehension of code.

Reviews of the experimental research in software engineering have been compiled by Atwood, Ramsey, Hooper, and Kullas [1], Schneiderman [19], and Moher and Schneider [16]. Topics which have been submitted to experimental evaluation include batch versus interactive programming, programming style factors (e.g., indented listings, mnemonic variable names, and commenting), control structures, documentation formats, code review techniques, and programmer team organization. In the next section I will review one of the more extensive areas of experimental research in software engineering: the evaluation of conditional statements and control flow. This topic was not chosen because it was believed to be more important than other subjects. Rather, it was chosen because several programs of research have investigated this topic and because the conditional statement has been a focus of argument since it was originally assailed by Dijkstra in 1968. Control statements have been a concern of the structured programming movement, and the results reported here evaluate their most effective implementations.

Conditional Statements and Control Flow

Sime, Green, and their colleagues at Sheffield University have been studying the difficulty people experience in working with conditional statements. In their first experiment Sime, Green, and Guest [21] studied the ability of non-programmers to develop a simple algorithm with either nested or branch-to-label conditionals. Nesting implies the embedding of a conditional statement within one of the branches of another conditional. Nested structures are designed to make this embedding more visible and comprehensible to a programmer. Branch-to-label structures obscure the visibility of embedded conditions, since the *true* branch of a conditional statement sends the control elsewhere in the program to a statement with a specified label.

The conditional for the nested language was an **IF-THEN-ELSE** statement found in languages such as PASCAL, PL/I, and ALGOL. The conditional construct is written:

IF [condition] **THEN** [process 1] **ELSE** [process 2]

The branch-to-label conditional was the **IF-GOTO** construct of FORTRAN and BASIC which Dijkstra [5] considered harmful. This condition is written:

IF [condition] **GOTO** L1
[process 2]
L1 [process 1]

Participants used one of these micro-languages to build an algorithm which organized a set of cooking instructions depending on the attributes of the vegetable to be cooked. Sime et al. found that participants using the **GOTO** construct finished fewer problems, took longer to complete them, and made more semantic (e.g., logic) errors in building their algorithms than participants using the **IF-THEN-ELSE** construct.

In a second experiment, Sime, Green, and Guest [22] investigated different techniques for marking the scope of the processes subsumed under each branch of a conditional statement. In addition to the **IF-GOTO** conditional, they defined a nested **BEGIN-END** and a nested **IF-NOT-END** representing two different structures for marking the scope of each branch in nested conditionals. The **BEGIN** and **END** statements mark the scope of processes performed under one branch of an **IF-THEN-ELSE** construct, while the **IF-NOT-END** uses a more redundant scope marker by repeating the condition whose truth is being tested. The **IF-NOT-END** construct is written:

IF [condition] [process 1]
NOT [condition] [process 2]
END [condition]

Sime et al. [22] found that more semantic (algorithmic) errors occurred in the **IF-GOTO** language, while errors in the nested languages were primarily syntactic (grammatical). The **BEGIN-END** construct produced more syntactic errors and only half as many successful first runs as the other constructs. Errors were debugged ten times faster in the **IF-NOT-END** condition, which proved to be the most error free construct.

Based on the results of this second experiment, Sime, et al. [22] proposed that information is easier to extract from some languages than others. They distinguished two types of information: *sequence* and *taxon*. Sequence information involves establishing or tracing the flow of control and events forward through a program. Taxon information involves the hierarchical arrangement of conditions and processes within a program. Such information is important when tracing backward through a program to determine what conditions must be satisfied for a process to be executed. Sime et al. hypothesized that sequence information is more easily obtained from a nested language, while taxon information is more easily extracted from a nested language which also contains the redundant conditional expressions. In two subsequent studies Green [10] validated the hypothesis about differences between sequence and taxon information in research with professional programmers.

It is important to recognize that program comprehension is not a unidimensional cognitive process. Rather, different types of human information processing are required by different types of software tasks. Green demonstrated that certain constructs were more helpful for performing certain software tasks. Software engineering techniques may differ in the benefits they offer to different programming tasks, since they differ in the types of human information processing that they assist. Models of programmer performance need to take this interaction between task and process into account if valid hypotheses are to be derived from them.

Since the **IF-NOT-END** construct is not implemented in existing languages, Sime, Arblaster, and Green [20] investigated ways to improve the use of the **BEGIN-END** conditional markers for **IF-THEN-ELSE** constructs. They developed a tool which would automatically build the syntactic portions of a conditional statement once the user chose the expression to be tested. In a second experimental condition, they developed an explicit writing procedure for helping participants develop the syntactic elements of a conditional statement. This procedure involved writing the syntax of the outermost conditional first, then writing the syntax of conditionals nested within it. In the final condition participants were left to their own ways of creating the conditional constructs.

Sime et al. found that participants solved more problems correctly on their first attempt using the automated tool, but that a writing procedure was almost as effective. The writing procedure reduced the number of syntactic errors, which had been the major problem with the **BEGIN-END** construct in earlier studies. Syntactic errors were not possible with the automated tool. The writing procedure and automated tools helped participants dispense with syntactic considerations quickly, so that they could spend more time concentrating on the semantic portion of the program (i.e., the function which was to be performed). However, once an error was made, it was equally difficult to correct regardless of the condition. Thus, writing procedures and tools primarily increased the accuracy of the initial implementation.

The extensive program of research by Sime, Green, and their colleagues demonstrated:

- the superiority of nested over branch-to-label conditionals;
- the advantage of redundant expression of controlling conditions

at the entrance to each conditional branch;

- that the benefits of a software practice may vary with the nature of the task; and
- that a standard procedure for generating the syntax of a conditional statement can improve coding speed and accuracy.

Overall, these results indicate that the more visible and predictable the control flow of a program, the easier it is to work with.

In a separate attempt to evaluate the **GOTO** statement, Lucas and Kaplan [14] instructed 32 students to develop a file update program in PL/C, and half were further instructed to avoid the use of **GOTOs**. However, programmers in the **GOTO**-less condition were not trained in using alternative conditional constructs. Not surprisingly, the **GOTO**-less group required more runs to develop their programs. In a subsequent task, all participants were required to make a specified modification to a structured program. Contrary to results on the earlier task, the group which had earlier struggled to write **GOTO**-less code made quicker modifications which required less compile time and storage space.

Weissman [25] also investigated the comprehension of PL/I programs written in versions whose control flow was either 1) structured, 2) unstructured but simple, or 3) unstructured and complex. Participants were given comprehension quizzes and required to make modifications to the programs. Higher performance scores were typically obtained on the structured rather than the unstructured versions, and participants reported feeling more comfortable with structured code. Love [13] subsequently found that graduate students could comprehend programs with a simplified control flow more easily than programs with a more complex control flow.

Recently, a series of experiments evaluating the benefits of structured code for professional programmers was reported by Sheppard, Curtis, Milliman, and Love [18]. In the first two experiments three versions of control flow performing identical functions were defined for each of several FORTRAN programs. One version was structured to be consistent with the principles of structured coding [6]. Because structured constructs are sometimes awkward to implement in FORTRAN IV [24], a more naturally control flow was devised which allowed limited deviations from strict structuring: multiple returns, judicious backward **GOTOs**, and forward mid-loop exits from a **DO**. A deliberately convoluted version was developed which included constructs that had not been permitted in the structured and naturally structured versions.

The first experiment was on comprehension and required participants to reconstruct a previously studied program. As expected, the convoluted control flow was significantly more difficult to comprehend than naturally structured programs. Differences between naturally and strictly structured programs were insignificant.

In a second experiment Sheppard et al. [18] instructed programmers to make specified modifications to three programs, each of which was written in the three versions of control flow described previously. A significantly higher percentage of the steps required to complete each modification was correctly implemented in the strictly structured programs than in the convoluted ones. No statistically significant differences appeared between the two versions of structured control flow.

Results from the first two experiments suggested that the presence of a consistent structured discipline in the code was beneficial, and minor deviations from strict structuring did not adversely affect performance. This premise was tested in a third experiment, which compared the two versions of structured FORTRAN IV to FORTRAN 77. FORTRAN 77 contains the **IF-THEN-ELSE**, **DO-WHILE**, and **DO-UNTIL** constructs usually associated with structured coding. They measured how long a programmer took to find a simple error embedded in a program. No differences were attributed to the type of structured control flow, replicating similar results in the first two experiments. The advantage of structured coding appears to reside in the ability of the programmer to develop expectations about the flow of control — expectations which are not seriously violated by minor deviations from strict structuring.

The research reviewed here indicates that programs in which structured coding is enforced will be easier to comprehend and modify than programs in which such discipline is not enforced. It is not clear that structured coding will improve the productivity of programmers during implementation. However, some productivity improvements may be observed if less severe, more easily corrected errors are made using structured constructs (as suggested in the data of Sime and his colleagues). Structured coding should reduce the costs of maintenance since such programs are less psychologically complex to repair and modify. Experiments such as these can provide valuable guidance for decisions about an optimal mix of software standards and practices.

Problems in Experimental Research

It is important to recognize the benefits and limitations of controlled laboratory research. On the positive side, rigorous controls allow experimenters to isolate the effects of experimentally manipulated factors and identify possible cause-effect relationships in the data. However, laboratory research has an air of artificiality, regardless of how realistic researchers make the tasks.

Several problems attendant on most current empirical validation studies severely limit the generalizability of conclusions which can be drawn from them [2]. For instance, program sizes have frequently been restricted because of limitations in the research situation. This problem is characteristic of experimental research, where time limitations do not allow participants to perform experimental tasks involving the coding or design of large systems. Also, since new factors come into play in the development of large systems (e.g., team interactions), the magnitude of a technique's effect on project performance may differ markedly from its effect in the laboratory.

The nature of the applications studied is often limited by the environments from which the programs are drawn (e.g., military versus commercial systems, real-time versus non-real-time systems). Further, there is frequently little assessment of whether results will hold up across programming languages. It is extremely difficult to perform evaluative research over a broad range of applications. Results should be replicated over a series of studies on different types of programs and in languages other than FORTRAN.

Another problem arises with what Sackman, Erickson, and Grant [17] and Sheppard et al. [18] observed to be 25 or 30 to 1 differences in performance among programmers. This dramatic variation in performance scores can easily disguise relationships between software characteristics and associated criteria. That is, differences in the time or accuracy of performing some software task can often be attributed more easily to differences among programmers than to differences in software characteristics. Careful attention to experimental design is required to control this problem. One approach is to use the repeated measures designs employed by Sheppard et al. [18].

If generalizations are to be made about the performance of professional programmers, this is the population that should be studied rather than novices. As is true in most fields, there are qualitative differences in the problem-solving processes of experts and novices [23]. However, the advantage of some techniques is the ease with which they are learned, and novices are the appropriate population for studying such benefits. Attempts to generalize experimental results must also be tempered by an understanding of how real-world factors affect outcomes. Data should be collected in actual programming environments both to validate conclusions drawn from the laboratory and to determine the influence of real-world factors.

Measurement and experimentation are complementary processes. The results of an experiment can be no more valid than the measurement of the constructs investigated. The development of sound measurement techniques is a prerequisite of good experimentation. Many studies have elaborately defined the independent variables (e.g., the software practice to be varied) and hastily employed a handy but poorly developed dependent measure (criterion). For instance, program reconstruction is not a good measure of comprehension, since it is affected by memorization skills. Results from experiments with inadequate dependent variables are difficult to explain because they are confounded with other processes.

Results are far more impressive when they emerge from a program of research rather than from one-shot studies. Programs of research benefit from several advantages, one of the most important being the opportunity to replicate findings. When a basic finding (e.g., the benefit of structured coding) can be replicated over several different tasks (comprehension, modification, etc.) it becomes much more convincing. A series of studies also results in deeper explication of both the important factors governing a process and the limits of their effects. Performing a series of studies also affords an opportunity to improve measurement and experimental methods. Thus, the reliability and validity of results can be improved in succeeding studies.

Approaches to Experimental Research

There are three primary experimental approaches appropriate for research on problems in software engineering: the case study, the classical multi-participant experiment, and simulation. Each of these

Type of experiment	Focus of study	Source of criterion data	Extent of criterion data	Internal validity	External validity
Case study:					
single subject	individual programming processes	individual protocol	longitudinal	can be high or low	can be high or low
Field project	project outcomes & resources	project	longitudinal	low	high
Controlled study	cause-effect relations for manipulated variable	controlled-task performance	cross-sectional, occasionally longitudinal	high	low to moderate
Simulation	interactive causal chains among many factors	computer modeling analysis	depends on design	high	high to moderate

This table assumes that acceptable methodological standards are observed in each type of study.

Table 3-1: Summary of Experimental Approaches

approaches has advantages for studying certain types of problems. A summary of these approaches is provided in table 3-1. The paper by Fred Sayward in this collection reviews the case study approach, while I have concentrated on the classical multi-participant experiment. This latter technique is primarily a method of determining cause-effect relationships for a limited number of factors. Some of these designs can be intermixed to take advantage of their differing characteristics.

The *case study* approach can be used in either single-subject research or project field studies. In single-subject research the case study typically involves collecting continuous protocol data from a participant who is performing a software task, most frequently the design and implementation of an algorithm. A critical problem comes in defining a unit of behavior and in avoiding the many sources which contaminate protocol data. Such data are often difficult to interpret, but hold promise for modeling the human cognitive processes involved in software development. These models are more difficult to build from the results of classical multi-participant experiments. Thus, the single-subject approach may be more appropriate for initial data gathering, from which models can be built and experimentally tested using other approaches. In field studies of software development projects, longitudinal data can be collected which help describe actual software development processes and determine the effects of environmental factors not studied in the laboratory [15]. Such data are appropriate for developing the resource models described in the paper by Basili in this collection.

The experimental investigation of software design techniques for large systems would be difficult or impossible by any of the methods described previously. That is, funding is not available for implementing a quarter-million line software system in parallel by two or more project teams, each using a different design technique (e.g., data structured versus functionally structured). However, *simulation* tools are becoming available which will allow us to simulate the full implementation of a software design from the initial design specification. System size, performance, interface characteristics, and some quality metrics would be generated in such an experiment. If accurate distributions of productivity, costs, time, and resources could be established for various tasks included in a project work breakdown structure, simulations of project performance could be performed while experimentally manipulating various factors which affect these distributions. Simulation techniques hold great promise for many questions in software engineering which seem intractable to current experimental methodologies.

Conclusion

There is a steadily growing body of experimental research on software engineering techniques and their effects on programmer productivity. These experiments have been performed on problems which have been the easiest to define operationally and control in an experimental setting. Such problems involve the use of structured coding, flowcharts, indented listings, etc. Now that results are beginning to emerge on these topics, evaluative data are desperately needed on the most effective tools for assisting programmers in software development and maintenance.

The greatest opportunities for control over the outcomes of a software project are those gained during the development of requirements and the initial design specification. Almost no experimental research has evaluated various methods for creating and recording requirements and initial design specifications. Lance Miller and his colleagues at IBM's

Watson Research Center, however, have performed some research on problem-solving techniques which relate to software development during the early phases.

Another critical area of research involves language differences. Experiments such as those reported here on structured coding and those on strongly versus weakly typed languages performed by Gannon [9] have provided some initial results on language characteristics. However, larger experiments comparing the usefulness of various types of languages (e.g., APL vs. ADA vs. FORTRAN) for implementing different types of algorithms need to be performed. The advent of non-procedural languages invites such comparisons. New methodologies for performing such experiments need to be developed, and some may be an order of magnitude more difficult to implement than the methodologies currently in use. However, simulation techniques may provide a new source of data which avoids problems associated with individual differences among programmers. Such experiments will provide critical data on the most important factors affecting programmer productivity and software quality.

Acknowledgement

I would like to thank Laszlo Belady, Sylvia Sheppard, and Drs. Elizabeth Kruesi and John O'Hare for their thoughts and comments. Portions of this paper were drawn from work supported by the Office of Naval Research Engineering Psychology Programs (Contract # N00014-79- C-0595) and appeared in a paper published in the *Proceedings of the IEEE*, 1980, vol. 12, no. 9, pages 1144-1157. However, the opinions expressed in this paper are not necessarily those of the Department of the Navy. Most of the work leading to this paper was performed while Dr. Curtis managed the Software Management Research Unit at Information Systems Programs, General Electric Company in Arlington, VA.

References

[1]   M. E. Atwood, H. R. Ramsey, J. N. Hooper, and D. A. Kullas.
        *Annotated Bibliography on Human Factors in Software
        Development.*
        Technical Report TR-P-79-1 (NTIS # AD A071 113). Army
        Research Institute, Alexandria, Virginia, 1979.

[2]   R. Brooks.
        Studying programmer behavior experimentally: The problems
            of proper methodology.
        Communications of the ACM 23:207-213, 1980.

[3]   D. Campbell and J. C. Stanley.
        Experimental and Quasi-Experimental Designs for Research.
        Rand-McNally, 1966.

[4]   R. B. Cattell.
        The principles of experimental design and analysis in relation to
            theory building, page 20.
        In R. B. Cattell, editor, *Handbook of Multivariate Experimental
            Psychology*, pages 19-66. Rand-McNally, 1966.

[5]   E. W. Dijkstra.
        GOTO statement considered harmful.
        Communications of the ACM 11:147-148, 1968.

[6]   E. W. Dijkstra.
        Notes on structured programming.
        In O. J. Dahl, E. W. Dijkstra, and C. A. R. Hoare, editors,
            Structured Programming, pages 1-82. Academic Press,
            1972.

[7]   O. D. Duncan.
        Introduction to Structural Equation Models.
        Academic Press, 1975.

[8]   R. A. Fisher.
        The Design of Experiments.
        Oliver & Boyd, London, 1935.

[9]   J. G. Gannon.
        An experimental evaluation of data type conventions.
        Communications of the ACM 20:584-595, 1977.

[10]   T. R. G. Green.
        Conditional program statements and their comprehensibility to
            professional programmers.
        Journal of Occupational Psychology 50:93-109, 1977.

[11]   W. L. Hays.
        Statistics.
        Holt, Rinehart, & Winston 1973.

[12]   D. R. Heise.
        Causal Analysis.
        Wiley, 1975.

[13]   T. Love.
        An experimental investigation of the effect of program structure
          on program understanding.
        SIGPLAN Notices 12(3):105-113, 1977.

[14]   H. C. Lucas and R. B. Kaplan.
        A structured programming experiment.
        The Computer Journal 19:136-138, 1974.

[15]   P. Milliman and B. Curtis.
        *A Matched Project Evaluation of Modern Programming
          Practices.*
        RADC-TR-80-6, two volumes. Rome Air Development Center,
          Griffiss Air Force Base, New York, 1980.

[16]   T. Moher and G. M. Schneider.
        *Methods for Improving Controlled Experimentation in Software
          Engineering.*
        Technical Report 80-8, Computer Science Department,
          University of Minnesota, 1980.

[17]   H. Sackman, W. J. Erickson, and E. E. Grant.
        Exploratory and experimental studies comparing on-line and
          off-line programming performance.
        Communications of the ACM 11:3-11, 1968.

[18]   S. B. Sheppard, B. Curtis, P. Milliman, and T. Love.
        Modern coding practices and programmer performance.
        Computer 12:41-49, 1979.

[19]   B. Shneiderman.
        *Software Psychology: Human Factors in Computer and
          Information Systems.*
        Winthrop, Cambridge, Massachusetts, 1980.

[20]   M. E. Sime, A. T. Arblaster, and T. R. G. Green.
        Reducing programming errors in nested conditionals by
          prescribing a writing procedure.
        International Journal of Man-Machine Studies 9:119-126, 1977.

[21]   M. E. Sime, T. R. G. Green, and D. J. Guest.
        Psychological evaluation of two conditional constructions used
          in computer languages.
        International Journal of Man-Machine Studies 5:105-113, 1973.

[22]   M. E. Sime, T. R. G. Green, and D. J. Guest.
         Scope marking in computer conditionals - A psychological
            evaluation.
         International Journal of Man-Machine Studies 9:107-118, 1977.

[23]   H. A. Simon.
         Information processing models of cognition.
         In M. R. Rosenzweig and L. W. Porter, editors, *Annual Review of
            Psychology* 30:363-396, Annual Reviews, 1979.

[24]   T. Tenny.
         Structured programming in Fortran.
         Datamation 20(7):110-115, 1974.

[25]   L. M. Weissman.
         *A Method for Studying the Psychological Complexity of
            Computer Programs.*
         Technical Report TR-CSRG-37, Department of Computer
            Science, University of Toronto, Toronto, 1974.

Questions Asked at the Conference

Jim Browne, University of Texas

If you look at a great deal of the results that are published, one has the perspective that perhaps instead of asking the question "What is basic? What may be invariant from situation to situation?, that people have instead asked the question "What can I measure in this circumstance¿ I would hypothesize this as a principal problem, and I wonder if the speaker would agree with it?

Bill Curtis

Absolutely! That's why you have to start with a process model of how people work with software, of how they perform software tasks. Then you can get at how to measure the process based on what you wanted to understand or predict in the first place. It's a problem of not having models to begin with. You shouldn't start by just saying let's look at flowcharts versus this, that, or the other. Rather you should begin by questioning what type of information a programmer needs to perform a particular task, and what is the most effective way of presenting this information.

Jim Browne

But in order to get at the process, to ask questions and to answer questions, you may be prepared to go through many layers of perturbations. I think that's what we want to see.

Bill Curtis

As Fred Sayward implied in his earlier talk, that's not impossible in a controlled experiment. In fact it's advisable to build a data collection technique directed toward more than one final criterion, such as how long did it take this individual to find this bug. You can develop automated data collection procedures which watch people interact with a text editor in building a program and determine what approaches they use. This is something you can do in any experiment if you build a data collection technique which will get at the process. In building a process model of how people think about software, it's difficult to develop operational definitions of what's going on in a programmer's mind. That's a problem in cognitive psychology more than it is in software development. How can we measure those processes that various programming techniques are really going to affect? Our research group at GE has demonstrated that in structured programs we can develop expectancies about the control flow within a piece of software. Yet how do we measure the way someone develops expectancies? It's a very difficult problem.

Chapter 4:
Software Project Forecasting

Richard A. DeMillo

School of Information and Computer Science
Georgia Institute of Technology
Atlanta, GA 30332

Richard J. Lipton

Department of Electrical Engineering
and Computer Science
Princeton University
Princeton, NJ 08750

Introduction

A characteristic of the sciences is that they seek to explain, describe, and predict phenomena. While there are varying degrees of exactness in the sciences (the predictions of physics are of a quantitative character different from, say, the predictions of economics) the basis of scientific activity is rational and objective. This is what distinguishes economics from astrology — even though it might be argued that economic and astrological predictions are equally vague, economic predictions are the result of rational analysis of evidence. Thus we intend to divide sciences from non-sciences on the basis of the rational nature of the activities. (For a detailed discussion, see Helmer and Rescher [1].)

Let's now look at the problem of *measuring* software. It is evident from the remaining papers in this collection that aside from a well founded concern over methodological issues, the principal aim of studying software metrics is not the static determination of software properties but rather the scientific prediction of phenomena during the software life cycle. Indeed, Perlis, Sayward, and Shaw point out, "The purpose of software metrics is to provide aids for making the optimal choice...at several points in the life cycle" [2]. They go on to illustrate the nature of the decision points — how long it will take to produce the software, when it will have to be replaced, and so on. These are manifestly problems of prediction. As fascinating as explanation and description may be — and our ability to model software usefully is still primitive — the exigencies of governmental and commercial computing demand a reasonable facility in forecasting critical software project parameters. We will address this forecasting problem in the sequel; we can pretend to have no well-formed answers here. In fact, our goal is the rather modest one of pointing out that there is a scientific (although possibly inexact) component of the problem that is not adequately conveyed by the term *software metrics*: the use of past information to predict the future of a software system.

Analogies

Inevitably, primitive sciences are compared to physics, the standard of scientific rigor and success. Of course, inexact sciences fare very badly in the comparison, but often the reason they fare so badly is not understood. Physics stands almost alone among the sciences in the exactness and simplicity of its theories. The price paid is in the complexity of the situations that can be profitably handled by the theories. Predicting the behavior of complex systems — particularly those involving human interactions, is almost never carried out by deducing from first principles, that is, from physical theory. Tim Standish [3] points out that most scientific knowledge is organized so that phenomena at one level can be explained in terms of (or *reduced to*) phenomena at a more basic level; for example, physical chemistry explains chemical behavior in physical terms. Only rarely, however, is it possible to compose several such reductions in an intellectually manageable fashion. Thus while it is possible to imagine physical explanations of biological phenomena, biological explanations of psychological phenomena, and a psychological basis for social behavior, it is extremely unlikely that there will ever be a physical theory of social behavior.

Jim Browne [4] is correct: "There are analogies from other sciences." We even agree that the fundamental issues are predictive and phenomenological. We differ, however, in the choice of analogies, and we also differ on the role that measurement plays in constructing useful forecasts. It seems very unlikely that the theory of software forecasting is like physical theory at an early stage in its development. We have argued elsewhere [5] that software exhibits much complexity and ad-hocery, features that cannot easily be abstracted from real situations or simplified with approximations. The prediction problem for software is more akin to prediction in those disciplines that deal with complex systems. Rather than turn to physics for our methodology, we should turn to the less exact sciences — fields such as meteorology, economics, political science, and even the construction industry. These are fields in which the explanatory component is subjugated to the predictive component primarily because of the extreme public and social significance of the predictions.

Why distinguish at all between explanatory and predictive theories? After all, predictive and explanatory assertions are logically equivalent. They both use evidence to convince a listener of an hypothesis. They may both give *laws* concerning an effect X; the exactness of the laws may vary from that of the quasi-laws (X is asserted to be present except in certain cases) [1] to the more exact statistical laws (X is asserted to be present in a stated fraction of the observations) to the mathematically exact physical laws. Explanations and predictions are, however, distinguished in a fundamental way. In logical terms, an explanation must be more credible than its negation. A prediction need only be more credible than the alternatives.

Meteorology

The physical basis of meteorological theory fits comfortably on a large blackboard. It consists primarily of six equations of fluid dynamics that use the current local state of the atmosphere to predict the future state:

STATE(new) = F(STATE(old))

By observing pressure, temperature, and a few other meteorologically interesting variables (only six independent variables and a few thermodynamic constants are involved) and calculating their rate of change, the state equations allow extrapolation over short periods of time to new, or predicted, values [6,7].

It is amusing that the first attempts at meteorology were directed toward an explanatory theory, attempted by ancient Greek philosophers. But predicting the weather in the vicinity of the Mediterranean Sea is not a very pressing concern. To Europeans a thousand years hence, however, the state of the weather was a subject of intense interest — crops, harvests of fish, and trade routes depended on the vagaries of the less temperate climate. It is in the transition from Aristotle's speculation concerning the nature of the winds to the modern large-scale calculations that give rise to daily forecasts that there is a lesson for software forecasting.

The first stage in predicting weather most likely took the form of attempting to codify the portents of change: "They...were not so much concerned with explaining why weather happened as they were in predicting it, and...gradually built up a huge folklore and literature of portents — the unseasonable migration of birds, hibernation of wild beasts, unusual sexual behavior of farm animals, color of the sunset..." [6]. Such understanding is entirely qualitative, and although it is tempting to try, building a quantitative, predictive theory by improving on the portents is not productive. What was needed in meteorology was, first, a proper concept of *primary data*. Not until the middle of the seventeenth century were there means to observe atmospheric temperature and pressure. Measurements by themselves told little about climate beyond what was obviously revealed directly by observation (e.g., "It's cold out there!"). It was after Newton (and later Bernoulli, Euler, and Boyle) that a coherent fluid mechanics began to emerge.

It took nearly two hundred years to get from Bernoulli to the six equations of state for the atmosphere. These equations are, however, analytically intractable. The only hope of obtaining high quality quantitative predictions of the weather lay in massive computation. A proposal made by Richardson in 1922 involved the hand calculation of such nonlinear systems of equations by numerical techniques that are close to what is used today [7]. Without computers, however, Richardson could only speculate on the actual mechanism of carrying out the necessary calculations:

> [Richardson] describes a phantasmagorical vision of the *weather factory* — a huge organization of specialized human computers, housed in something like Albert Hall, directed by a mathematical conductor perched on a raised pulpit, and communicating by telegraph, flashing colored lights, and pneumatic conveyer tubes...In this fantasy, he estimated that, even using the newfangled desk calculators, it would take about 64,000 human automata just to predict the weather as fast as it actually happens in nature. Richardson's preface concludes with a rather wistful but prophetic statement: 'Perhaps someday in the dim future it will be possible to advance the computations faster than the weather advances and at a cost less than the saving to mankind due to the information gained. But that is a dream' ([6], p.138).

The nearly simultaneous advance of sophisticated numerical analytical techniques and high speed digital computation allowed the fulfillment of Richardson's dream in essentially its original form.

The characterizing features of modern meteorological forecasting are that, first, extensive primary data are gathered, second, accurate microscopic theories of atmospheric behavior are available, and, third the microscopic predictions — obtained from the local data — are pieced together using massive computation.

A Digression on Measurement

Since measurement of atmospheric pressure and temperature enter into our meteorological analogy, we should digress for a moment to consider the notion of measurement of software. The remaining papers in this collection refer to software *metrics*. The term metrics refers to "indices of merit that can support quantitative comparisons and evaluations..." [8]. In the context of predictive modeling (that is, of predicting the future from the past), it is more convenient to think in terms of observable software properties — particularly those that can be numerically characterized and objectively recorded — in other words, to think in terms of *measurements* instead of metrics. The distinction is not totally pedantic. There is a rich theory of measurement that guides the development of other models [9,10,11,12] and, most important, can be used to insure that there is a precise sense in which hypotheses that are formulated about the measured quantities are *meaningful*.

By a measurement is meant the assignment of numbers to represent properties of material systems; since by a system we mean a collection of objects or events, the properties of the system are given by relations between the objects/events. For reasons of intellectual economy a scientist usually isolates one *aspect* of the system to study; that is, he focuses on one relational system. So, a measurement — an assignment of numerals to objects or events according to certain rules [9] — can be defined to be a mapping f from a relational system (A,R), where A is a set and R is a binary relation defied on A, to a set of numbers. Since the numbers *represent* the relation, we should insist that

aRb iff $f(a) > f(b)$

whenever a and b are objects in A. More concisely, measurements are defined to be homomorphisms that preserve certain basic relations.

Thus, a basic measurement of, say, temperature is obtained by the assignment of a number by a well-defined rule (e.g., the height of fluid in a standard thermometer). This homomorphism is not uniquely defined, however. It is possible — and common — to define differing *scales* for measuring temperature. The scientifically meaningful statements that can be made about temperature do not depend on the scale; that is, they remain valid under rescaling. Just which rescalings are allowed depends on the properties of the relational system (A,R). Similarly, scale types can be characterized by the *admissible rescalings* as summarized in table 4-1 [10].

Admissible Transformations	Scale Type	Examples
$\Phi(x) = x$	absolute	census counting
$\Phi(x) = ax$ $a>0$	ratio	time interval length
$\Phi(x) = ax + b$ $a>0$	interval	time temperature
$x \geq y$ implies $\Phi(x) \geq \Phi(y)$	ordinal	preference
Φ is 1-1	nominal	labels

Table 4-1: Common Rescalings

Strictly speaking, an empirical statement is *meaningful* provided its truth is invariant under an admissible transformation. We can safely assert that 100 degrees Centigrad is the boiling point of water, since the statement is true under the rescaling $a = 9/5$ and $b = 32$. However, it makes little to no sense to assert that the temperature on March 15, 1980 was twice what the temperature was on November 4, 1979, since temperature is not defined on a ratio scale — the ratio of temperatures depends on the scale being used and therefore cannot be invariant under the rescaling.

As a warm-up, let's look at some empirical statements that one might make about software.

1. The length of Program A is at least 100.
2. Program A is 100 lines long.
3. Program B took 3 months to write.
4. Program C is twice as long as Program D.
5. Program C is 50 lines longer than Program D.

6. The cost of maintaining Program E is twice that of maintaining Program F.

7. Program F is twice as maintainable as Program E.

Statement 1 does not make reference to a particular scale, so it does not make sense, whereas statement 2 does make sense. Similarly, statement 3 is a perfectly reasonable factual statement. If the expected scales are provided for statements 4 and 6, they are meaningful, but as written they are technically meaningless. Statement 5, however, refers to a ratio scale, on which intervals make sense. Finally statement 7 forms a ratio on an ordinal scale, which is meaningless.

From the standpoint of measurement theory, many of the derived measurements of software that have been proposed [13] are meaningless.

Example 1. Programming Effort Equations

The total effort E in number of man months is

$$E = 2.7v + 121w + 12y + 22z - 497.$$

The interpretation of the variables and their scale types are given in table 4-2.

Variable	Interpretation	Scale
v	number of instructions	ratio
w	subjective complexity	ordinal
x	no. external documents	absolute
y	no. internal documents	absolute
z	size in words	ratio

Table 4-2: Typical Forecasting Variables

This example illustrates a common shortcoming of current attempts at fundamental and derived measurements. Not only is the equation dimensionally inconsistent (number of documents + number of instructions + words + complexity = man months), it does not rescale: The truth of the equation cannot be invariant under the required transformations.

and quality of interactions that must take place to produce a software system militate against a forecasting problem that can be easily solved on a hand calculator. The forecasting models that are the most realistic are also the most demanding in terms of computation and data gathering. For example, the controversial world dynamics model of Forrester [14] requires well over 500 pieces of primary data and massive computations.

By analogy to the meteorological prediction problem, we, therefore, reject the idea that there can be a single *correct* measurement of software. Instead, we look for *many* single measurements to aggregate - the large number of factors involved militate against the simplistic models cited above; in fact, they necessarily imply that the prediction problem **must** be associated with a computer-based solution! That is, we look for simple microscopic laws which interact in macro effects which are — either by necessity or by our lack of knowledge — beyond human understanding and by (possibly massive) computation combine them to obtain a prediction.

There are two relevant approaches to forecasting that deserve our attention here. The first approach is the classical econometric time-series approach to forecasting [15]. In this approach one looks for statistically meaningful patterns in past data and uses these patterns to predict future patterns. It seems to us that this approach is well-developed and has been applied with some success to certain kinds of software life cycle modeling [16].

From the standpoint of basic research, however, the traditional forecasting approach is not very satisfying, since it is an admission that the underlying mechanisms have not been understood. Returning to the meteorological analogy, it is an attempt to extend the portents. But that seems to be the stage of our current understanding of the software life cycle.

The exact approach to forecasting seems to require many more insights into the various facets of the software lifecycle than we currently have at our disposal. Rather than wait for the software equivalent of Newton (or Galileo, for those who believe that we cannot even measure temperature), we might try to use large-scale computation to build upon the primary data that we can collect. It should be possible to partition a wide variety of programming tasks into discrete, classifiable subtasks that are repeated anew for each project. We can imagine, for example, a and quality of interactions that must take place to produce a software system militate against a forecasting problem that can be easily solved on a hand calculator. The forecasting models that are the most realistic are also the most demanding in terms of computation and data gathering. For example, the controversial world dynamics model of Forrester [14] requires well over 500 pieces of primary data and massive computations.

By analogy to the meteorological prediction problem, we, therefore, reject the idea that there can be a single *correct* measurement of software. Instead, we look for *many* single measurements to aggregate - the large number of factors involved militate against the simplistic models cited above; in fact, they necessarily imply that the prediction problem **must** be associated with a computer-based solution! That is, we look for simple microscopic laws which interact in macro effects which are — either by necessity or by our lack of knowledge — beyond human understanding and by (possibly massive) computation combine them to obtain a prediction.

There are two relevant approaches to forecasting that deserve our attention here. The first approach is the classical econometric time-series approach to forecasting [15]. In this approach one looks for statistically meaningful patterns in past data and uses these patterns to predict future patterns. It seems to us that this approach is well-developed and has been applied with some success to certain kinds of software life cycle modeling [16].

From the standpoint of basic research, however, the traditional forecasting approach is not very satisfying, since it is an admission that the underlying mechanisms have not been understood. Returning to the meteorological analogy, it is an attempt to extend the portents. But that seems to be the stage of our current understanding of the software life cycle.

The exact approach to forecasting seems to require many more insights into the various facets of the software lifecycle than we currently have at our disposal. Rather than wait for the software equivalent of Newton (or Galileo, for those who believe that we cannot even measure temperature), we might try to use large-scale computation to build upon the primary data that we can collect. It should be possible to partition a wide variety of programming tasks into discrete, classifiable subtasks that are repeated anew for each project. We can imagine, for example, a catalog of subtasks (such as terminal handlers, hash table routines, and report writers) which are common in various applications software. Notice that we do not claim that these are *off-the-shelf* components — we merely claim that they must be recreated in approximately the same form for each new job. This catalog will be quite extensive, but it will be conceptually simple to structure and use.

The principal data gathering activity is to determine the cost estimates for each of these subtasks. These costs are influenced by many factors, including the potential application, the skill and experience of the programmers, and the restrictions imposed by the programming environment. There are many sources for such estimates. First, there is a great deal of historical data which can be carried forward; after all, we do have considerable experience with software projects and this experience can be codified. Second, we have expert advice concerning the cost of the projects. Third, experimentation can be carried out. Fourth, the cost estimation is from *managed* projects so feedback can be used to correct prior estimates.

If the data on the primitive tasks that make up the software system are reliable, then the task is to *piece together* a forecast of the total system cost by large-scale computation. By *reliable* we mean that the measurements have an accurate mean and small standard deviation, since in that case the Central Limit Theorem [17] guarantees that the overall estimate will have a small error term (in fact, one that grows as the square root of the total number of terms). It is important to distinguish in the approach between using standard cost and estimation data and advocating the use of *standardized software components*. Perhaps an analogy to a more familiar cost forecasting problem will make the point more clearly. To estimate the cost of a house, a contractor will consult extensive data sheets on the cost of installing doors (How big? How many?) and the hundreds of other basic components of a dwelling. These are not prefabricated items, they must be constructed completely from basic specifications and customized for the task at hand, but they are enough alike to permit an accurate assessment of the expected cost of construction. A cost estimate from a builder is pieced together from such estimates.

Now, it is entirely possible that this approach requires inordinate overhead; but there is still room for applying computational power to chip away at the forecasting problem from historical data. Often, the scale which one uses to assess the software project is even weaker than an ordinal scale: often all that is required is a measure of cohesion between software projects. A manager may need to know only whether the current project is enough like apparently similar projects which have succeeded (or failed) to justify his decision. In this situation the computation needed is a similarity analysis of the important project factors. A large clustering analysis of projected software tasks and historical data may provide such information [10]. The principal task in such an endeavor is to isolate the important factors through data gathering and experimentation.

Summary

We have argued that a major use of software metrics is in the forecasting problem for software projects. By analogy with weather forecasting, we may characterize the current state of knowledge in software forecasting as the gathering of *portents.* While these may be useful and sometimes decisive in project management, they are prescientific and qualitative. Further, it seems very unlikely that the portents can be developed into a useful theory of forecasting. To develop scientific forecasting tools, a rational way of predicting the future from historical primary data is required. It is also important that the primary data and the measurements used to obtain data satisfy some basic methodological requirements — for example, the hypotheses developed from the measurements should be meaningful in the sense implied by measurement theory.

Among the rigorous approaches to the prediction problem we distinguish the statistical and the exact approaches. We specifically reject the notion that such complex phenomena as software lifecycles can be dealt with in a global way using computationally simple *laws.* The statistical approach, seeking to predict future events on the basis of historical patterns, seems to be an attractive short range approach to the forecasting problem. There is certainly an extensive body of theory from econometrics and related areas which can be brought to bear on software forecasting. Unfortunately, the statistical approach is a recognition that the underlying mechanisms are not understood. We turn, therefore, to the exact approach. In the exact approach a great deal of effort is spent in attempting to understand — or at least quantitatively assess — the microscopic prediction problem. The goal of the exact method is to be able to apply large-scale computation to many micro predictions to synthesize a quantitative forecast. There may even be useful aggregations of statistical and exact techniques which give forecasting models. In both approaches, data gathering is an essential activity; it is, therefore, important to settle on the fundamental measurements to be performed on the software.

References

[1]   Olaf Helmer and Nicholas Rescher.
        On the epistemology of the inexact sciences.
        Rand Corporation Report # R-353, February 1960.

[2]   Alan Perlis, Fred Sayward, and Mary Shaw.
        Unpublished notes on software metrics.
        April 1980.

[3]   Tim Standish.
        Notes on Software Metrics and ADA.
        Las Vegas meeting of ONR Software Metrics group, January
           1980.

[4]   Jim Browne.
        A philosophy and justification for empirical software
           engineering and software science.
        Unpublished notes, 9/13/79.

[5]   R. DeMillo, R. Lipton, and A. Perlis.
        Social processes and proofs of theorems and programs.
        Communication of the ACM, May, 1979, pages 271-280.

[6]   P. Thompson.
        The mathematics of meteorology.
        In *Mathematics Today*, edited by L. Steen, Springer-Verlag,
           1979, pages 127-152.

[7]   M. Gleiser.
        The first man to compute the weather.
        Datamation, June 1980, pages 180-184.

[8]   Alan Perlis, Fred Sayward, and Mary Shaw.
        Unpublished notes on software metrics.
        April 1980.

[9]   F. Roberts.
        Measurement Theory.
        Addison-Wesley, 1979.

[10]   M. Anderberg.
         Cluster Analysis for Applications.
         Academic Press, 1973.

[11]   N. Weiner.
         A new theory of measurement: A study in the logic of
             mathematics.
         Proceedings of the London Mathematics Society, 1919, pages
             181-205.

[12]   D. Krantz et. al.
         Foundations of Measurement, Vol. 1.
         Academic Press, 1971.

[13]   Data and Analysis Center for Software.
         Quantitative Software Models.
         March 1979.

[14]   J. Forrester.
         World Dynamics, second edition.
         MIT Press.

[15]   R. Pindyck.
         Econometric Models and Economic Forecasts.
         McGraw-Hill, 1976.

[16]   L. Putnam and A. Fitzsimmons.
         Estimating software costs.
         Datamation, September, October and November, 1979.

[17]   W. Feller.
         An Introduction to Probability Theory and its Applications, Vol.
             I.
         Wiley, 1968.

Questions Asked at the Conference

This paper was presented in two parts at the conference; the first part by
Richard Lipton and the second part by Richard DeMillo.

Questions to Richard Lipton

Ben Shneiderman, University of Maryland

I too have been looking at analogies in other fields and have been
reading the Uniform Building Code used by architects. I think that kind of
direction will be a useful thing, of producing a uniform programming
code which looks at guidance and tests actually for different pieces of

code. But the analogy that I like to offer and look for comments from you is the idea of medical models, because each of these metrics that are being proposed, and there are hundreds of them being offered, is, I think, like a laboratory test about an individual person's health. Now, no one of them, nor small collection of them, will give us an adequate measure of a person's health. Ultimately, the decision about the diagnosis and what to do resides in a human, the physician who will use his or her judgment and decide what to do, and I like that analogy because it does emphasize the very much human component of the programming task. It's not the kind of task which will lend itself to measurement akin to physics measurements of specific gravity, or volume, or so on. But we must always remember that it is a human process and that there's enormous variability, as Bill Curtis pointed out, in humans. So the, the point is that the lab tests, each one of them can be seen as an additional indicator, and there is no normal range — there are normal ranges, but violations of them may still be acceptable. Have you thought about that model?

Richard Lipton

That seems like a reasonable point — One thing to go along with that is that we need, just as in any of these predictions processes, whether it be economic or medical or weather, a lot more primary data. I know Alan mentioned this earlier, and I think that's the major positive thing this committee will lead to. If we can get routine collection of basic data, we can start to make predictions. And I think that's an important thing that we have to do. And it's really not being done as universally as it should be.

Nicholas Zvegintzov, management consultant

I'm a management consultant here in Washington, and this comment grows out of that perspective. It's another comment about analogies, because I liked your statement about looking for wider analogies on what programming is. And here's one which seems to me to leap out of real life: the analogy to management. If you are put in charge of a new division of a company, or you take over a division of the company, you're going to ask yourself what are our inputs, what are our outputs, what are we trying to do, who do I have to work with, how will I assign them to tasks, and how will I assign decision processes to the sub-parts, and flows between them. Now this seems to me exactly what the program analyst is trying to do, so I recommend a slight study of *Datamation* every month, because there you have actual managers who say, we have this problem and we applied the computer to it in this way and that way, and you get some notion of the tradeoff between what the real resources are and what the computer help for it would be. I guess this isn't a question, just an idea.

Richard Lipton

I'm sympathetic with it, it seems clear, especially for very large Navy projects, one must have tremendous management overtones to any of the computer science issues.

Nicholas Zvegintzov

Not just the question of managing the project, but the analogy of what we're trying to do, to what the manager in real life is trying to do.

Dave Weintraub, Applied Physics Lab, Johns Hopkins

At the risk of adding another analogy, I think that the analogy to housing is nice, but I think there's one that's much more exact for software engineering, and that is the automobile construction industry, for the following reasons. When you build a house you're in one geographical area, the number of variables you have is actually fairly low, and the code matches up to that. The car it's a whole different story. The car has to deal with water in the gas, it has to deal with unleaded, it has to deal with premium. I'm not being funny here. The same thing is exactly true with software engineering. As you said, the ancient Greeks didn't worry about the weather because it didn't change too much. If you're building one program, the system isn't going to change too much. If you're building a system everything's going to change, continuously, since user requirements are going to change. It's why most things that data are collected on, that is, these high military single-purpose real-time systems, at least most of the data I've seen in my field, are really totally irrelevant to the area we are interested in for most other applications because the definitions for quality are totally different. I really don't care if a program takes thirty percent longer to run if it's five hundred times more difficult for the average user to be able to access the program. If I'm buying a car, it makes more difference to me whether the car gets fifty miles per gallon than it does to someone making a hundred thousand dollars a year, who only cares that the car will do a hundred and eighty miles per hour, because he doesn't care about traffic fines. I think the analogies are much more real there. "Metrics is crap" was your quote from Dijkstra, I think my quote would be "Quality is qualitative." What are you going to decide — I'm asking this of the panel, actually, not of the individual speaker. The implication of having metrics is that somebody somewhere wants to measure something, and my argument is, everybody involved in software thinks it's something different, and I think that everybody is right. My definition of what good software is is probably very different from your definition in a given application.

Mary Shaw

Since you addressed the question to the panel, one of the points I was trying to argue earlier was that if we can come to a genuine understanding of the models and the issues involved in measurement, which I think includes prediction, then we should be able to come to a paradigm for defining software quality that allows us to account very specifically for the situation objectives. If we are successful we should be able to generate in a reasonably straightforward way a quality objective function that will suit the multimillionaire who only wants a hundred and eighty miles an hour, and the same paradigm with different situation parameters will generate the car that drives fifty miles an hour, or fifty miles to a gallon...We certainly won't reach it if we don't start trying.

Questions to Richard DeMillo

Sid Amster, Bell Labs

I am a little confused by one point. Are you claiming that a regression analysis in which the independent variables have different units is not meaningful?

Rich DeMillo

I'm concerned about using regression analyses as explanatory laws. Certainly, you can get perfectly adequate information out of linear combinations of the independent variables. I guess my main concern is that it is an admission that you've decided not to understand the underlying mechanism. You're going to rely on making inferences from the data only.

Sid Amster

So what you're saying is that an underlying law by definition has to have commensurable, independent variables.

Rich DeMillo

No. As the paper describes, we're dealing now with explanatory laws and requiring them to be meaningful in the sense we've defined it here.

Sid Amster

May I offer my dissent to that opinion.

Laszlo Belady, IBM

I may add a little bit to the confusion by pointing out that there is some slight contradiction between the two recommendations given individually by Lipton and DeMillo. Lipton said, "Don't look for analogy in chemistry and physics, rather look for analogies with, say, social science." On the other hand, DeMillo said that the proper measures are those where the relationships are expressed in consistent dimensions and so forth. Now this is precisely what you find in physics and chemistry, where you have an insight and a detailed understanding of it. In social sciences you use those kinds of things that do not fit well into measurement theory. I buy, by the way, both arguments. I don't think there is anything wrong with them, but nevertheless I had an urge to point out this contradiction.

Rich DeMillo

That wasn't phrased as a question, but I'm going to extract one from it. The motivation for measurement theory comes in large part from the success of those fundamental methods in the physical sciences; the impetus for the theory has come out of the social sciences. Suppes and Carnap and others had grave concerns over making the fuzzy measurements Amster was referring to and combining them in ad hoc ways without being able to read out of that some logically significant information. That's really where this branch of logic has its home — in the social sciences, and in economics.

R. Skelton, Continental Telephone

I would like to ask whether we can really have a meaningful discussion on measurement without first of all deciding on what attributes we're trying to measure.

Rich DeMillo

That's what I meant when I suggested that we study the underlying relational systems. We have to isolate the relations that we want the measurements to preserve.

Chapter 5:
Controlling Software Development Through the Life Cycle Model

Alan J. Perlis

Department of Computer Science
Yale University
New Haven, CT 06520

Introduction

Software is more than *source code.* Software is used as a generic term for all of the stages gone through in tailoring a program (or programs) to solve some particular problem. The process is non-terminating and the product, software, is evolutionary and shaped both by the nature of its use and the intent of its design. Specification of software is generally incomplete and arrives at a satisfactory state through evolution and use.

Software is subject to a perpetual tension: Being purely symbolic, it can be perfected, guaranteed, arbitrarily extended, reproduced at almost no cost, completely understood, perfectly managed, and eternal. Being purely symbolic it can be easily changed, adapted, mishandled, corrupted, generalized, altered by use and discarded. Far from being reproducible at no cost, the replication of software induces significant extra cost in maintenance and replacement no matter who is responsible for these two activities.

If by software we mean programs, every piece of software is (a representation of) an algorithm. Hence the results of the study of algorithms in computer science should suggest methods for controlling and improving software. To a limited degree, computer science has already helped. But the behavior of software is different from the behavior of algorithms. We observe some of the differences between software and algorithms in the following list:

1. Software is rarely as precisely specified as algorithms. It is often pointless to speak of software as a map from domain to range and to study its computational complexity.

2. Unlike algorithms, software changes its intent, to say nothing of its mechanisms, while under specification, design, construction, use, and replacement.

3. Software is generally huge, algorithms are described as being precise. Huge objects get that way by processes of accretion and are rarely characterized as being thereby precise.
4. Software is managed (or mismanaged); algorithms are created, perfected, and proven correct.

Issues of performance over a wide range of data may force treatment of some algorithms as software: One speaks of a linear programming package, not merely the simplex algorithm.

Standardization may allow some software to be treated algorithmically (even as hardware), i.e., the recently announced chip for supporting connection of a processor to the Ethernet.

It seems reasonable to fix upon a model for software development in which the dynamics of software play a significant role. The model chosen is the life cycle model in which software is seen as passing through seven stages:

1. Requirements Analysis
2. Specification
3. Design
4. Implementation
5. Testing and Integration
6. Maintenance and Enhancement
7. Replacement or Retirement

In isolation, these stages occur at progressively later times but backtrack from a stage to an earlier one may occur at any time. Revision of specification and of demand, alteration of requirements arising from use, change in environment, and erroneous implementation may interrupt the flow of normal development or spawn sub-processes having their own life cycles.

What are the parameters of flow that will enable us to predict and control the behavior and performance of software as it passes through its life cycle? We must be careful that we not let the symbolic nature of software lead us to expect perfectible methods of prediction and control. Nevertheless, we seek methodologies within whose adherence questions can be asked whose answers will support quantitative comparisons and evaluation of software. Software metrics aid in making choices among options that arise in the life cycle.

The Software Life Cycle

The software life cycle captures one aspect of the evolution of software. The seven stages are attained by all software, but in a complex manner as a set of processes executing over time. To capture the diversity of process behavior, one is led to think of this passage through the life cycle as the set of execution states of a computation on a computer — another name for which is the software environment. What plays the role of the instruction code on this computer? We do not yet know this instruction code other than vaguely. However, if we attempt to epitomize software evolution, the set of actions we describe and thereby perform on a piece of software is an example of a program for that computer. The life cycle is the list of the gross procedures we must expect to perform.

The developing interest in software environments is understandable. The proper role of the software environment is much more than a catch-all of interpreters, source-language editors, debuggers, etc. It is precisely the computer milieu in which software exists as it negotiates its life cycle. One should not underestimate the importance of facile manipulation within a (real) computer of software by functioning software environments at every stage of the former's life cycle. It is in this manipulation that the symbolic nature of software becomes a matter of critical importance, first to control and then (ultimately) to automate the production of software.

Issues in Life Cycle Control

In the introduction, a set of typical questions was given associated with each life cycle stage. No questions were assigned to the requirements phase — the reader can undoubtedly supply a generous list. At each stage the questions "Is it time to go onto the next stage?" and "Is a backtrack to an earlier stage needed?" must be answered. Sometimes it is appropriate to answer both positively and thereby spawn another software development process. Let us consider the separate stages in more detail.

Specification

We know what function the software is to perform and have some suggestions of how the functions are to be performed. We are interested in determining (estimates of):

1. Feasibility. With the resources available (manpower and time) can the software be completed sufficiently before its predicted obsolescence to warrant its creation?
2. Generalizability. Can the problem be generalized so that the software becomes more feasible by postponing obsolescence or reducing resource requirements, or both?.
3. Competition. Is the software so critical or the proper design so unclear that competing efforts are worth supporting?

Design

At this stage a detailed formal statement of the problem to be solved and its solution have been prepared, including a development plan for every stage of the life cycle. We are interested in determining:

1. What machine configurations to use?
2. What language to use?
3. Is it possible to incorporate previous work or must everything be built from scratch?
4. How will the availability of tool X affect factor Y?
5. How close to its limits is the system expected to run?
6. What are the potential future enhancements?
7. Should the system be all encompassing from which subsystems are carved out as needed, or should the system be a base from which more limited and specific systems are built?

Implementation

At this stage there are some questions which need to be answered before implementation begins and others which arise during implementation. The questions before implementation include:

1. What developmental technology should be used? Should the system be built all at once or should it be constructed through a sequence of executable prototypes?
2. What programming discipline should be used? Chief programmer? Cottage industry?

The questions during and after implementation include:

1. Is the project on schedule?
2. Is the project on the budget?
3. Is the implemented code correct? If not, how close is it to meeting the specification?
4. What is the quality of the implemented code? Is it understandable? Will it be maintainable and enhanceable?

Testing

At this stage, the general question to be answered is: "Does the implementation meet the specification?" This usually reduces to questions concerning the implementation's functionality, performance, and usability. The decisions to be made include:

1. Should testing be done top down or bottom up?
2. Of the available methodologies for testing functionality, performance, and usability, which ones should be used?
3. What levels of satisfactory testing are sufficient?
4. How will subsequent error reports be handled?
5. How well does the testing environment approximate the execution environment?
6. How well does the software integrate into the larger system of which it is a part?

Maintenance and Enhancement

Maintenance, though similar to testing, is different because the software execution environment has changed from a controlled testing environment to the actual user environment. Enhancement, on the other hand, is a post-release augmentation of the system specifications to meet unsupplied and unforeseen demands. These two very different activities are often linked because both result in a re-release of the system. Note, however, that enhancement causes a backtrack cycle of greater distance than maintenance does. With this view, questions concerning maintenance can be thought of as questions concerning testing (see above). Questions concerning enhancement of a given piece of software include:

1. What is the cost of the enhancement? Is it worthwhile?
2. What is the re-release strategy?
3. Will the enhancement speed up or delay (ultimate) replacement?
4. Will the enhancement disturb or destroy the logical clarity of the system?

Once it has been decided that an enhancement should take place, there is an automatic backtrack to the specification life cycle stage.

Replacement and Retirement

Among the questions asked when considering replacement or retirement of a system are:

1. Has the problem outgrown the software?
2. Has technology moved beyond the software?
3. Has a critical support resource for the system become unavailable?
4. Would it cost less to redesign and rebuild the system than to maintain and enhance the system?
5. How should the system be phased out?
6. Do the benefits gained outweigh the costs incurred from changing the language in which the system is written? Changing the machine on which the system runs?
7. What are the requirements for the replacement?
8. What software is affected by its retirement?

What methodologies grease the passage of software through the life cycle? One might be tempted to argue that it is poor strategy to overdesign and build software with great care as though it would exist forever and be in eternal use. Experience shows that some software attains a perfection of design and construction, a complexity of function and a magnificence of size that assures its own future. The software shifts the burden of evolutionary costs to the milieu. Ultimately the milieu will reject the software — but the time of retirement can often be delayed considerably. Two methodologies seem attractive: careful use of prototype systems and use of high order languages).

Prototypes

There are two obvious choices for system development called the *pre-structured* method and the *prototypical* method. These two approaches are discussed and compared in this section.

The pre-structured method is the traditional approach in which the final system language, data structures, control structures, and modularization are fixed very early in the life cycle, usually in the design phase. The pre-structured choices influence enormously the direction of the later life cycle stages and tend to make significant design changes difficult and expensive and, hence, resisted. Nearly all current and past software has been developed using the pre-structured approach.

This method forces a view of software as being *hard,* since the costs of change tend to become enormous. Metaphors emphasizing the palpability, the material-like nature of software dominate; those which epitomize software — its *soft* character — are systematically avoided.

Management techniques and discipline enforcing methodologies play a key role in the life cycle passage.

In the prototypical approach, on the other hand, the software is seen as being developed through a sequence of executable prototypes possessing increased functionality, with more and more implementation detail and alternative designs being the rationale for the successive prototype systems. Here the design evolves with the implementation and the designer has the advantage of always having a model whose executions support design decisions. In a sense the prototypical approach, by *compressing* any single life cycle time span, allows many passes through the life cycle with more and more complex models of the software. Although the potential advantages of using the prototypical approach to software development have only recently begun to be recognized, the value of executable models has long been recognized in other disciplines, e.g., the value of rapid and flexible change has been recognized as crucial in evolutionary success of the MAXIMA system [1].

Successor prototypes have an important role to play in identification of enhancement possibilities and their costs. Their existence provides a source of executable software *history* that aids in maintenance activity and broadens the corps of specialists able to support software *in the field*.

These two development approaches differ radically in the language parameter. In the pre-structured method resource efficiency dictates that the final implementation language be chosen early and be the only language used. Most often this language is a compiler-oriented language. In the prototypical approach fast and flexible implementation permits, even dictates, that an interpretive language be used for the prototype systems. For it is interpretation, not compilation, which permits execution of incomplete programs and quick response to changes in both control and data structures. Later, for efficiency reasons, some prototype system may require (partial) translation to a language that husbands machine resources better.

The chief question that must be answered is, "In view of the total life cycle cost which approach is more cost effective?" Some advantages and disadvantages of the methods which must be analyzed in attempting to find an answer to this question are:

Pre-structured Advantages

1. Using one language throughout requires less training of personnel.
2. Since the design is more or less fixed early in the life cycle, one can concentrate on finding an efficient implementation, proving it correct, arranging personnel schedules, etc.

Prototypical Advantages

1. An executable prototype permits the design to evolve, often in ways not envisioned in the initial requirements.
2. It is natural to explore competing implementation strategies.
3. It is often easy to generalize the requirements and quickly reflect them in a new prototype system.
4. The average length of a life cycle backtrack cycle is lower.
5. Early prototype systems are potential starting points for evaluating, understanding, and performing future maintenance and enhancement.

Pre-structured Disadvantages

1. One is always working with a static, unproven and unobserved design.
2. Changes in the requirements often cause massive redesign of the system.

Prototypical Disadvantages

1. Separate languages for the prototypes and the production systems imply a need either for more or for higher qualified personnel.
2. The inherent inefficiencies of interpretation must be overcome in going from the final prototype to the production system.
3. There is an eighth (possibly costly) life cycle stage of translating from the final prototype to the production system.

Except in extreme cases, for today's software projects the benefits of the prototypical approach outweigh its disadvantages while the reverse is true of the pre-structured approach. This is supported by the following metaphorical thesis:

> The navigation of a software system through the life cycle is a realtime asynchronous process. The system must respond rapidly to the interrupts which will arise due to changing requirements, error corrections, etc. The ease of response materially diminishes the future cost of the software system.

Both development approaches start with flexible models during the initial *at the blackboard* requirements analysis and specification stages. But soon the schism occurs. In the pre-structured approach the informal design is massaged to fit the chosen language — in the prototypical approach, the informal design is directly reflected and studied in a prototype system. In the pre-structured approach commitment comes early and change is not only painful but often prohibited — the prototypical approach is based on rapid, easy design changes of almost any kind.

A bias toward the prototypical approach can be expressed in the following informal metaphorical hypotheses:

> The prototypical approach forces the inhibition of dramatically fewer life cycle interrupts than the pre-structured approach.

> The response time to life cycle interrupts is dramatically faster under the prototypical approach than under the pre-structured approach.

The prototypical approach leads to a more rapid development of software, and the developed software is more reliable, easier to maintain, and easier to enhance.

Programming Languages

What factors determine which language should be used for the software project? In general, how do we differentiate between programming languages and how do we connect programming languages to the tasks which are to be programmed in them?

Many important language and project dependent parameters have been identified. Numerous studies and controlled experiments have been and are being conducted in an effort to determine what, if any, distinguishable effects language choice has on life cycle costs. Nearly all of these studies have centered on comparing languages belonging to what can be called the ALGOL class of languages.

One can be skeptical concerning the conclusions of these studies — mainly because for every result which says, for example, "Maintenance is cheaper in language X than in language Y" one can find another result saying "Maintenance is cheaper in language Y than in language X." This is not surprising. Indeed, it supports a basic hypothesis:

> For any two languages in the *same* language class (see below) in the long run there is no *significant* financial gain in using one

language over another — the important parameters are not linguistic but depend on other issues, such as personnel training, software support, familiarity, and software environments.

There are four classes of language that are in heavy use in today's software:

1. Machine assembly language.

2. There are two classes at the second level:

    a. ALGOL-like such as ALGOL 60, FORTRAN, COBOL, and PASCAL.

    b. ALGOL-like with tasking such as JOVIAL, ALGOL 68, CMS-2, PL/I, and ADA.

3. Interpretive languages which operate in parallel on data structures such as APL and LISP.

The hypothesis does not mean that, for a given task, any language in class 2-a, for instance, is as good as any other language in 2-b and one chooses just to suit his fancy. On the contrary, there are intraclass language differences. However, the relevant social, educational, management, and emotional issues dominate the intra-class language differences when it comes to dramatically reducing life cycle costs. Experiments on hypotheses such as "Maintenance and enhancement is cheaper in ADA than in JOVIAL," and "Software written in PASCAL is more reliable than software written in FORTRAN" must lead to inconclusive interpretations.

This is not the case when comparing languages at the interclass level — e.g., there is hardly a software manager who would deny that using a class two language rather than assembly language dramatically reduces life cycle costs. This suggests a second hypothesis:

With proper integration into the life cycle, a dramatic decrease in costs can be realized by using a language from a higher level class.

How does one establish such claims? The general lack of theoretical models of the life cycle and programming language characteristics would seem to rule out formal studies.

A proposal has been made by Perlis and Sayward to investigate the use of program mutation as a means of relating programming languages to life cycle costs. A program's mutants are reasonable alternative programs and they have been used as a basis of the mutation analysis testing method [2]. It has been shown experimentally that the level of confidence in the mutation test for FORTRAN programs is proportional to the number of mutants considered in the test. That is, the larger the number of mutants considered, the larger the number of potential errors ruled out.

It is not unreasonable to relate the error proneness of a programming language to the influence on life cycle costs of using the language since error proneness materially affects all later life cycle stages. Consequently, Perlis and Sayward put forward two hypotheses:

> For a given task, to obtain a given level of testing confidence, there is no significant difference in the number of mutants which must be considered for programming languages in the same language class.

> For a given task, to obtain a given level of testing confidence, there is a significant difference in the number of mutants which must be considered for programming languages in different language classes. In particular, there is a dramatic reduction in going from class one to class two and in going from class two to class three.

Progress in programming languages is difficult to characterize, but one trend is clear: Languages show increased ability to produce contextual programs that execute but ignore arbitrary sets of details until such time as they become relevant to a subsequent program *refinement*. As our collective experience and insight have grown some of these sets have become *canonized* and their treatment hardened by syntactic and semantic language fixes. We have come to order languages from low to high strictly on the cardinality of their sainthoods. However it is not cardinality but ease of beatification that matters. This is Teitelman's principle.

If we append to that principle the observation that the invention of good notation or suggestive syntax is found rarely in humans, Occam tells us that, over the long run, that language is highest whose syntax and semantics is simplest subject to Teitelman's principle. Then our machine assembly languages should surely be highest, but aren't. Why? Backus says it's because our machines are inappropriate — and he's probably right. [3]

The appropriate machines are those which best fit the languages of class 3, not the languages of classes 2-a and 2-b. These machines will not be in large supply for some time, although some are begining to appear. Until they are widely available we must invent processes that can map a prototype with the aid of data accumulated on its performance into an efficient program in a lower class language.

Of course all this is hypothesis and experiments must be defined and metrics identified that will support or reject this view of software development.

Acknowledgement

The questions arising in the life cycle process were developed jointly with Fred Sayward and Mary Shaw. The hypotheses concerning comparison of languages within and across language classes and the prestructured versus prototype approach to the development of systems are the joint insight of the author and Fred Sayward.

References

[1]   Mathlab group.
         MACSYMA Reference Manual, Version 9.
         Laboratory for Computer Science, MIT, 1977.

[2]   R. DeMillo, R. Lipton and F. Sayward.
         Program mutation: A new approach to program testing.
         Infotech State of the Art Report: Software Testing, Volume 2
            (1979), pages 107-128.

[3]   J. Backus.
         Can programming be liberated from the von Neumann style? A
            functional style and its algebra of programs.
         Communications of the ACM 21:613-641, August 1978.

Questions Asked at the Conference

Capers Jones, ITT

Over the last five or six years I've dealt with a couple hundred companies and about fifteen hundred programming systems, mostly in large sizes, from fifty thousand up to, say, two million lines of code, and I want to make a few comments and raise a few questions about what goes on in the large commercial systems domain. First, the choice of a programming language rarely matters at all in that domain, because before you get around to selecting a programming language, you're probably going to have to do eighty to a hundred different kinds of text documents containing in some cases a hundred and twenty-five English words for every line of code in the final system, and the cost of that work is so much greater than the cost of code on big systems that the language hardly matters. Second, in the really large systems domain, as far as I can tell, there are no high-level languages that are used for a hundred percent of all large systems. In almost all cases you have to drop down to assembler for various performance reasons or for other reasons, and the domain of high-level languages is usually concentrated in the small to low-medium-size systems. Big systems almost always have to drop back into assembler, or at least the ones I've seen have. And second, the life cycle cost, the sixty percent figure that so many companies quote, is the cost of maintenance across the corporation, not the cost of maintaining any given program. Hardly ever does a single program's maintenance over its life cycle go to more than about twenty-five or thirty percent of the initial development cost. There are pieces, called error-prone modules, where the cost of maintenance will exceed a hundred percent of the development cost. The life cycle of a programming system varies enormously. The average or mode of system endurance is somewhat less than two years before the program disappears completely. What we see is an industry trend to a few very special and unique systems that last forever, e.g., things done on the 650 and then reprogrammed on the 1401, or later on the 360, but such systems are not common. The mode of industry is to develop programs that disappear in less than two years, and they aren't maintained in the traditional sense, they're reprogrammed. People reinvent the wheel because they throw away former programs and do them over. I guess the general thrust of my comments is that the academic orientation of this symposium seems to me to be dealing with one set of problems, where those of us in the business domain are dealing with another, and I've been surprised at how some of the academic speakers have talked of the future need to measure things, which the commercial side has been doing with reasonable success for the last couple of years. And while I'm glad to have a chance to talk to the academic group, I must say that the commercial side of the data processing industry is already, based on the morning's talks, somewhat ahead of the academic side in measuring the pragmatic aspect of real systems.

Alan Perlis

One of the reasons we're way behind is that we academics probably refuse to engage in handling software as you people do. We are searching for a better way. For example, have you ever asked yourself, what is a better way than *going down* to assembly code. Why do you accept that, since it's well known that working in assembly code is so less productive of programmers' time? Why do you accept it? Is it a fact of life that one must always do that? The commercial software world seems to assume it is. It isn't necessarily true. We may, for example, find that machines can be designed which will make that unnecessary by using better microcode, adapted to processing translations of a high oder language. In short, I regard this statement here somewhat as an implication that the academics are isolated from the real world. I would prefer to use not *real world*, but *old world.* The academics have a role to play and it is not of patching up the old world, but trying to create a better one.

Irwin Nathan, Xerox

One of the things that I think is interesting in that list is that it leaves out COBOL and NOMAD, which are higher-level data management languages, and probably more lines of code are written in those in the U.S. than any other language I can think of. Could you explain that?

Alan Perlis

Sure. I told you I left out some languages. I left out COBOL and NOMAD. (Laughter). I did not mean by leaving them out to imply that they are unimportant or irrelevant. COBOL belongs in there somewhere, probably in the same group as the multi-tasking languages, or somewhere between them and FORTRAN. But the phenomena associated with COBOL are no different — or with NOMAD for that matter, are no different from the phenomena associated with the others. That is, shifting from COBOL to FORTRAN or FORTRAN to COBOL isn't going to change things very much. And as long as one continues to program in COBOL, one is going to find that one is dealing with the same set of phenomena.

John Goodenough, Softech

I don't really disagree with the classifications that you have there for languages, but I do think the reasons for the classification are somewhat debatable. In particular putting PL/I and ADA in a different class from ALGOL because they deal with tasking seems to be saying that because the area of application in a language is somewhat wider that makes it a separate class. Whereas if you're using those languages in a non-tasking area, the classification would suggest that there's no difference between using PL/I or ADA and ALGOL, BASIC, and PASCAL. I would rather have said that the reason for the existence of the class three languages is perhaps they're more suitable for building large systems than for small systems, that is, for systems of fifty to a hundred thousand lines of code. Those languages have some facilities that would make it easier to deal with the problem arising from largeness than the ones in class two.

Alan Perlis

It is true that one can probably build larger systems with languages like ADA and Algol 68. One of the reasons that a language like ADA is supposed to be better for building large systems is its treatment of modularity. We have, with the modularity concept in languages such as ADA, gone the same path as the past, fixing these concepts in the language. Warren Teitelman of Xerox feels that in a programming language if somebody requests a feature, don't put the feature in, find a feature that will make it easier for the programmer to put the feature in. I call it Teitelman's principle. And I put it in a somewhat more picturesque way. The concept of modularity, which has gone into these new programming languages, is bound into the syntax and semantics of the language. One can, I think, look at things another way and observe that modularity, like optimization, is a process of gathering together and redistributing computations and definitions to ease something — optimization to ease execution, modularity to ease maintenance and enhancement. One can very well ask, since these are processes arising from use, why do they have to be bound into the language in the syntax and semantics? Often what we build into the language has come back to cost us, later on, in system handling. For example, the size of the support software that's needed for their support in a good environment.

John Gannon, University of Maryland

Do you think it likely that these languages affect the software development process equally?

Alan Perlis

I don't know whether some languages are better at the beginning and others later.

Jean Sammet

Let me express an opinion. It seems to me that those languages which are most suitable to provide good documentation are those which are likely to be useful in the long haul, and those which provide ease of programming are the ones more likely to be useful in the short haul, and the two languages which I think are the extreme ends of the spectrum, if you accept that spectrum, are COBOL for ease of reading and maintenance and APL for ease of writing, but hardly ease of maintenance.

Alan Perlis

I think I do have a response to what was said. What do we mean by a high-level language? I come to the conclusion that what we really mean by high-level language is not the number of details it contains, but the number of details that can be omitted from programs written in it at a stage of programming and still get running programs. I would say that a language is highest order when it is possible to write adequate running programs which omit all the details that are irrelevant at that stage in the life cycle.

Chapter 6:
Resource Models

Victor R. Basili

Department of Computer Science
University of Maryland
College Park, MD 20742

Introduction

It is important that we have a better understanding of the software development process and be able to control the distribution of resources such as computer time, personnel, and dollars. We are also interested in the effect of various methodologies on the software development process and how they change the distribution of resources. For this reason, we are interested in knowing the ideal resource allocation, how it may be modified to fit the local environment, the effect of various tradeoffs, and what changes should be made in the methodology or environment to minimize resources expenditure.

There has been a fair amount of work towards developing different kinds of resource models. These models vary in what they provide (e.g., total cost, manning schedule) and what factors they use to calculate their estimates. They also vary with regard to the type of formula, parameters, use of previous data, and staffing considerations. In an attempt to characterize the models, we will define the following set of attribute pairs. They can be characterized by the type of formula they use to calculate total effort. A *single variable model* uses one basic variable as a predictor of effort, while a *multi-variable model* uses several variables. A model may be *static* with regard to staffing, which means a constant formula is used to determine staffing levels for each activity, or it may be *dynamic*, implying staffing level is part of the effort formula itself. Within the multi-variable models, there are various subcategories: *adjusted baseline*, *adjusted table-driven*, and *multi-parameter equation*. The adjusted baseline uses a single variable baseline equation which is adjusted in some way by a set of other variables. An adjusted table-driven model uses a baseline estimate which is adjusted by a set of variables where the relationships are defined in tables built from historical data. A multi-parameter model contains a base formula which uses several variables. A model may be based upon *historical* data or derived *theoretically*. An historical model uses data from previous projects to evaluate the current project and derive the weights and basic formulas from analysis of that data. For a theoretical model, the formula is based upon assumptions about such things as how people solve problems. One last categorization is that some models are *macro* models, which means they are based upon a view of the big picture, while others are *micro* models, in that the effort is derived from knowledge of small pieces of information scaled up. We will try to discuss at least one model in each of these categories.

Static Single Variable Models

The most common approach to estimating effort is to make it a function of a single variable, project size (e.g., the number of source instructions or object instructions). The baseline effort equation is of the form

$$EFFORT = a * SIZE^b$$

where a and b are constants. The constants are determined by regression analysis applied to historical data. In an attempt to measure the rate of production of lines of code by project as influenced by a number of product conditions and requirements, Walston and Felix [1] at IBM Federal Systems Division started with this basic model on a data base of 60 projects of 4,000 to 467,000 source lines of code and of 12 to 11,758 man months. The basic relation they derived was

$$E = 5.2 L^{.91}$$

where E is the total effort in man months and L is the size in thousands of lines of delivered source code, including comments. Beside this basic relationship, other relations were defined. These include the relationships between documentation DOC (in pages) and delivered source lines

$$DOC = 49 L^{1.01}$$

project duration D (in calendar months) and lines of code

$$D = 4.1 L^{.36}$$

project duration and effort

$$D = 2.47 E^{.35}$$

and average staff size S (total staff months of effort/duration) and effort

$$S = .54 E^{.6}$$

The constants a and b are not general constants. They are derived from the historical data of the organization (in this case, IBM Federal Systems Division). They are not necessarily transportable to another organization with a different environment. For example, the Software Engineering Laboratory (SEL) on a data base consisting of 15 projects of 1.5 to 112 thousand source lines of code covering efforts of 1.8 to 116 staff months have calculated for their environment the following set of equations [2]:

$$E = 1.4\,L^{.93}, \; DOC = 30.4\,L^{.9}, \; D = 4.6\,L^{.26}$$

$$D = 4.4\,E^{.26}, \; S = .24\,E^{.74}$$

Some other variables, including other ways of counting code, were measured by the Software Engineering Laboratory and the equations derived are given here. Letting DL = number of developed, delivered lines of source code (new code + 20% of reused code), M = number of modules, DM = total number of developed modules (all new or more than 20% new) we have

$$E = 1.58\,DL^{.99} = .65\,M^{1.19} = .19\,DM^{1.0}$$

$$D = 4.6\,DL^{.26} = 2.0\,M^{.33} = 2.5\,DM^{.3}$$

$$DOC = 34.7\,DL^{.93} = 1.5\,M^{1.17} = 4.8\,M^{.99}$$

Most of the SEL equations lie within one standard error of the IBM equation and since the SEL environment involves the development of more standard software (software the organization has experience in building), the lower effort for more lines of code seems natural. It is also worth noting that the basic effort/lines of code equation is almost linear for the SEL — more linear than the Walston Felix equation. Remember that the project sizes are in the lower range of the IBM data. Lawrence and Jeffrey [3] have studied even smaller projects and discovered that their data fits a straight line quite well, i.e., their baseline effort equation is of the form

$$EFFORT = a * SIZE + b$$

where again a and b are constants derived from historical data. The implication here is that the equation becomes more linear as the project sizes decrease.

Static multi-variable models

Another approach to effort estimation is what we will call the static multi-variable model. A resource estimate here is multi-variable because it is based on several parameters, and static because a single effort value is calculated by the model formula. These models fall into several subcategories. Some start with the baseline equation just discussed based on historical data and adjust the initial estimate by a set of variables which attempt to incorporate the effects of important product and process attributes. In other models, the baseline equation itself involves more than one variable.

The models in the *adjusted baseline* class differ in the set of attributes that they consider important to their application area and development environment, the weights assigned to the attributes, and the constants of the baseline equations.

Walston and Felix [1] calculated a productivity index by choosing 29 variables that showed a significantly high correlation with productivity in their environment. It was suggested that these be used in estimating and were combined in a productivity index

$$I = \Sigma_i w_i x_i$$

where I is the productivity index, w_i is a factor weight based upon the productivity change for factor i and $x_i = +1$, 0, or -1, depending on whether the factor indicates increased, nominal or decreased productivity.

One model that fits into the single-parameter baseline equation with a set of adjusted multipliers is the model of Boehm [4], whose baseline effort estimate relies only upon project size. His attributes are grouped into four areas:

1. *product*: required fault freedom, data base size, product complexity, adaptation from existing software.
2. *computer*: execution time constraint, machine storage constraint, virtual machine volatility, computer response time.
3. *personnel*: analyst capability, applications experience, programmer capability, virtual machine experience, programming language experience.
4. *project*: modern programming practices, use of software tools, required development schedule.

For each attribute Boehm gives a set of ratings ranging from very low to very high and, for most of the attributes, a quantitative measure describing each rating. The ratings are meant to be as objective as possible (hence the quantitative definitions), so that the person who must assign the ratings will have some intuition as to why each attribute could have a significant effect on the total effort. In two of the cases where quantitative measures are not possible, required fault freedom and product complexity, Boehm provides a chart describing the effect on the development activities or the characteristics of the code corresponding to each rating. Associated with the ratings is a chart of multipliers ranging from about .1 to 1.8.

Another model which falls into this category is the model of Doty [5]. The Doty model, however, provides a different set of weights for different applications besides two ways to estimate size.

One model which falls into the category of adjusted table-driven is that of Wolverton [6]. Here the basic algorithm involves categorizing the software routines. The categories include control, I/O, pre- or post-algorithm processor, algorithm, data management, and time critical routines. Each of these routines has its own cost of development curve, depending upon the degree of difficulty (easy, medium, or hard) and the newness of the application (new or old). The cost is then the number of instructions by category and degree of difficulty times the corresponding cost taken from a table. Another model of this type, but more simplistic, is Aron [7].

The GRC model [8] involves a set of equations derived from historical data and theory for the various activities, several of which are *multi-parameter equations* of more than one variable. For example, the equation for code development is

$$MM_{CD} = .9773 * N_{OF}^{1.2583} * e^{-.08953 * Y_{EXP}}$$

where MM_{CD} is the baseline staff months for code development task group for a subsystem, N_{OF} is the number of output formats for a subsystem and Y_{EXP} is the average years of staff experience in code development. It is worth noting that size of the code is not a factor in this formula. Other formulas exist for the effort involved in analysis and design, system level testing, documentation installation, training, project control, elapsed time, and a reasonable check for the total staff months for the project (MM_{PROJ}).

$$MM_{PROJ} = .0218 * ((2 + N_{OF} * \ln(2 + N_{OF}))^{1.71}$$

where N_{OF} is as defined above.

Dynamic multi-variable models

Once an effort estimate is made, the next question of concern is how to assign people to the project so that the deadlines for the various development activities will be met. Here again there are basically two approaches, the one empirical, the other theoretical. Each of the methods discussed so far uses the empirical approach, which tries to identify the activities which are a part of the development process of a typical project for the software house. Then, historical data from past projects is used to determine what percentage of the effort was expended on each activity. These percentages serve as a baseline and are intuitively adjusted to meet the expected demands of a new project. For example, in the Wolverton model total cost is allocated into five major subareas: analysis cost (20% of total), design cost (18.7% of total), coding cost (21.7% of total), testing cost (28.3% of total) and documentation cost (11.3% of total). Each of these subarea costs are subdivided again, depending upon the activities in the subareas. In this way, each activity can be staffed according to its individual budget. Allocation of time is determined by history and good management intuition.

The theoretical approach attempts to justify its resource expenditure curve by deriving it from equations which model problem-solving behavior. In other words, the actual resource model lays out the staffing across time and within phases. We will refer to this approach as the dynamic multi-variable model. It is dynamic because the model produces a curve which describes the variation of staffing level across time. The model is multi-factor because it involves more than one parameter.

Two models in this category will be discussed which differ in the assumptions they make. The first model, which is the most widely known and used, is the Putnam model [9].

The model is based on a hardware development model [10] which noted that there are regular patterns of manpower buildup and phase out independent of the type of work done related to the way people solve problems. Thus, each activity could be plotted as a curve which grows and then shrinks with regard to staff effort across time. For example, the cycles in the life of a development engineering project are illustrated in figure 6-1. Similar curves were derived by Putnam for software cycles which are: planning, design and implementation, testing and validation, extension, modification and maintenance.

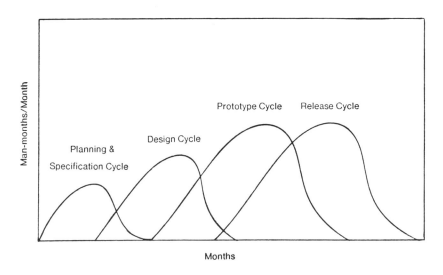

Figure 6-1: Typical Development Engineering Staffing

The theoretical basis of the Putnam model is that software development is a problem-solving effort and design decision making is the exhaustion process. The various development activities partition the problem space into subspaces corresponding to the various stages (cycles) in the life cycle. A set of assumptions is then made about the problem subset:

1. The number of problems to be solved is finite.
2. The problem-solving effort makes an impact on and defines an environment for the unsolved problem set.
3. A decision removes one unsolved problem from the set (assumes events are random and independent).
4. The staff size is proportional to the number of problems *ripe* for solution.

Because the model is theoretically based (rather than empirically based) some motivation for the equation is given. Consider a set of independent devices under test (unsolved problem set) subject to some environment (the problem-solving effort) which generates shocks (planning and design decisions). The shocks are destructive to the devices under test with some dependent conditional probability distribution p(t) which is random and independent with some rate parameter λ. Assume the distribution is Poisson and let T be a random variable associated with the time interval between shocks such that

$$\text{Pr}(T>t) = \text{Pr}[\text{no event occurs in interval } (0,t)] \tag{1}$$

where $t = 0$ is the time of the most recent shock. Letting $p(t)$ be the conditional probability of a failure given that a shock has occurred and λ be the Poisson rate parameter, then

$$\text{Pr}(T>t) = e^{-\lambda(\int_0^t p(x)dx)} \tag{2}$$

and

$$\text{Pr}(T\leq t) = 1 - e^{-\lambda(\int_0^t p(x)dx)} \tag{3}$$

and the p.d.f. associated with (3) is

$$f(t) = \lambda * p(t) * e^{-\lambda(\int_0^t p(x)dx)}, \, t>0$$

This leads to the class of Weibull distributions (known in reliability work) where the physical interpretation that the probability of devices succumbing to destructive shocks is changing with time. Based upon observed data on engineering design projects, a special case of (3) can be used

$$y = f(t) = 1 - e^{-at^2} \tag{4}$$

$$\text{where } p(t) = \alpha t \tag{5}$$

$$\text{and } a = (\lambda\alpha)/2 \tag{6}$$

Note that this implies engineers learn to solve problems with an increasing effectiveness (i.e., familiarity with the problems at hand leads to greater insight and sureness). Parameter a consists of an insight generation rate α and a solution finding factor α. Equation (5) is a special linear case of the family of learning curves: $y = a x^b$.

Equation (4) is then the normalized form of the life cycle equation. By introducing parameter K expressed in terms of effort, we get an effort curve, the integral form of the life cycle equation

$$y = K * (1 - e^{-at^2})$$

where

- y is the cumulative manpower used through time t.
- K is the total manpower required by the cycle stated in quantities related to the time period used as a base, e.g., man-months/month.
- a is a parameter determined by the time period in which y' reaches its maximum value (shape parameter).
- t is time in equal units counted from the start of the cycle.

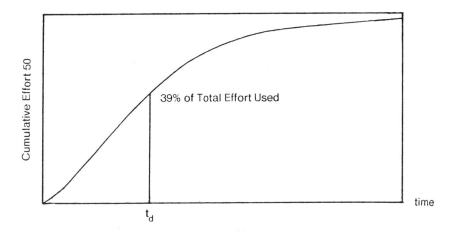

Figure 6-2: Optimum Cumulative Man Power Load

The life cycle equation (derivative form) is

$$y' = 2Kate^{-at^2}$$

where y' is the manpower required in time period t stated in quantities related to the time period used as a base and K is the total manpower required by the cycle stated in the same units as y'.

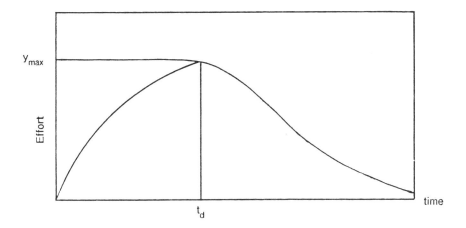

Figure 6-3: Optimum Man Power Load

The curve (called the Rayleigh Curve) represents the manpower build up. The sum of the individual cycle curves results in a pure Rayleigh shape. Software development is implemented as a functionally homogeneous effort (single purpose). The shape parameter a depends upon the point in time at which y' reaches its maximum, i.e.,

$$a = 1 / (2\, t_d^2)$$

where t_d is the time to reach peak effort. Putnam has empirically shown that t_d corresponds closely to the design time (time to reach initial operational capability).

From the life cycle equation it is a simple exercise in algebra to derive the following equations:

Development effort or time to t_d

$$y = .3935\, K$$

Life cycle cost

$$\$\, LC = K * MC$$

where MC is the mean cost in dollars per man year of effort and K is the total manpower (in man years) used by project. Note that the equation neglects computer time, inflation, overtime, etc.

Development cost

$$\$\, DEV = MC * (.3935\, K)$$

Putnam found that the ratio $K/(t_d^2)$ has an interesting property. It represents the difficulty of a system in terms of programming effort required to produce it. He defines

$$D = K/(t_d^2)$$

To illustrate how management decisions can influence the difficulty of a project, assume a system effort of 400 man years and a development time of three years. Then the difficulty is 44.4 man years per year squared.

Consider a management decision to cut the life cycle cost of the system by 10%. Now the system effort is 360 man years and the difficulty becomes 40. This results in a 10% decrease in assumed difficulty of the project. This decision assumes the difficulty is less than it really is, and the result is less product.

Now consider the more common case of attempted time compression. Assume management makes a decision to limit the expended effort to 400 man years but wants the system in 2.5 years instead of 3 years. Now the difficulty becomes 64, a 44% increase. The result of shortening the natural development time is a dramatic increase in the system difficulty.

The Putnam model generates some interesting notions. Productivity is related to the difficulty and the state of technology; management cannot arbitrarily increase productivity nor can it reduce development time without increasing difficulty. The tradeoff law shows the cost of trading time for people.

In deriving an alternative model, Parr [11] questions the assumptions of the Rayleigh equation since the initially rising work rate is due to the linear learning curve which governs the skill available for solving problems. He argues that the skill available on a project depends on the resources applied to it and that the assumption confuses the intrinsic constraints on the rate at which software can be developed with management's economically governed choices about how to respond to these constraints.

As an alternative to this assumption, his model suggests the initial rate of solving problems is governed by how the problems in the project are related, i.e., the dependencies between them. For example, the central phase of development is naturally suited to rapid rates of progress since that is when the largest number of problems are visible. Letting V(t) be the expected size of this set of visible (available for solving) problems at time t, Parr model yields the equation

$$V(t) = (Ae^{-\gamma\alpha t}) / (1 + Ae^{-\gamma\alpha t})^{\alpha + 1/\gamma}$$

where

1. α is the proportionality constant relating the rate of progress and the expected size of the visible set.
2. A is a measure of the amount of work done on the project before the project officially starts.
3. γ is a structuring index which measures how much the development process is formalized and uses modern techniques.

The curve represented by V(t) differs from the Rayleigh/Norden curve for Y'(t) in two important ways. The Rayleigh curve is constrained to go through the origin; the Parr curve is not. Making Y'(0) = 0 corresponds to setting an official start date for the project. Before that point, the effort expended on the project is assumed to be minimal. In reality, there is often a good deal of work done before that date, including such activities as requirements analysis and feasibility studies. In Putnam's environment, these were handled by a separate organization and could be ignored. Another factor that affects the problem space is past experience in the application area, or even more tangible is the influence of design or code taken from past projects. All of these have the effect of structuring the problem space at the begining, so that more progress can be made early. The Parr curve accounts for this, the Putnam curve does not.

A second distinction between the two curves is the flexibility in where the point of maximum effort can come. By using a structuring index greater than one, this point of maximum effort can be delayed almost to acceptance testing and still be able to reduce effort drastically before project completion. With the Rayleigh curve, a late point of maximum effort constrains the curve to have a slow buildup and almost no decay at the end.

Parr does not say how to estimate the parameters for V(t) in terms of data the project manager would have on hand. This is a problem in doing resource estimation currently, but the model could use the existing resource allocation schedule, based on early data points, to predict the latter part of the curve. The Parr model is only currently being tested on real software for the first time and the results are not yet in. The Rayleigh model, on the other hand, has been used in many environments and has been quite successful on the whole.

Theoretical Single Variable Models

The two previous theoretical models may be thought of as macro models in that the estimate of staffing levels relies on process oriented issues, such as total effort, schedule constraints, and the degree that structured methodology is used. Product oriented issues, such as source code, are not a factor. Most of the other models are less macro oriented in that they consider product characteristics, such as lines of code and input/output formats. In this section, we will discuss another type of theoretical model based upon lower level aspects of the product which we will call a micro model. The particular model discussed here deals with the idea that some basic relationships hold with regard to the number of unique operators and operands we use in solving a problem and the eventual effort and time required for development. This notion

Figure 6-4: Parr Model versus Putnam Model

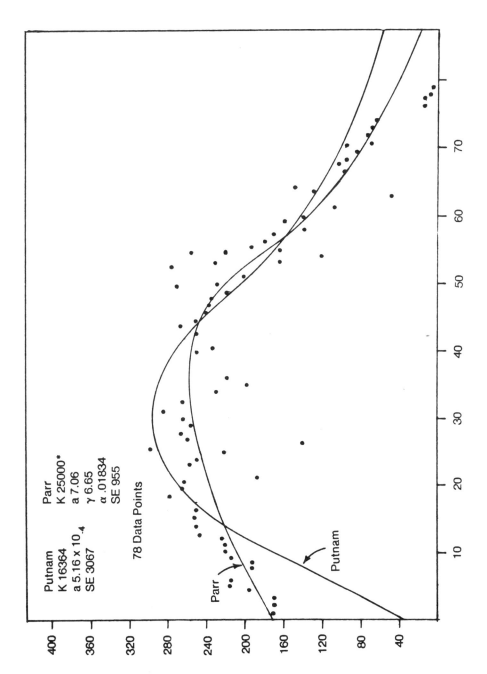

was proposed by Halstead as part of his software science [12]. Here there is only one basic parameter, size, measured in terms of operators and operands. The model transcends methodology and environmental factors. Most of the work in this area has dealt with programs or algorithms of module size rather than with entire systems, but that appears to be changing.

In the language of software science, measurable properties of algorithms are

- n_1 number of unique or distinct operators in an implementation.
- n_2 number of unique or distinct operands in an implementation.
- N_1 number of operator occurrences in an implementation.
- N_2 number of operand occurrences in an implementation.

From this comes the *vocabulary* n of an implementation:

$$n = n_1 + n_2$$

and the *length* N of an implementation:

$$N = N_1 + N_2$$

Based only on the unique operators and operands, the concept of *program length* N can be estimated as

$$\hat{N} = n_1 \log_2 n_1 + n_2 \log_2 n_2$$

Here $\hat{N}$ is actually the number of bits necessary to represent all things that exist in the program at least once, i.e., the number of bits necessary to represent a symbol table. Over a large set of programs in different environments, it has been shown that $\hat{N}$ approximates N very well.

To measure the size of an algorithm, software science transcends the variation in language and character set by defining algorithm size (volume) as the minimal number of bits necessary to represent the implementation of the algorithm. For any particular case, there is an absolute minimum length for representing the longest operator or operand name expressed in bits. It depends upon n, e.g., a vocabulary of 8 elements requires 8 different designators, or $3 = \log_2 8$ is the minimal length in bits necessary to represent all individual elements in a program. Thus, a suitable metric for size of any implementation of any algorithm is

$$V = N \log_2 n,$$

called *volume*.

The most succinct form in which an algorithm can be expressed requires a language in which the required operation is already defined and implemented. The potential volume V^* is defined as

$$V^* = (N_1^* + N_2^*) \log_2 (n_1^* + n_2^*)$$

where $V = N \log_2 n$. However, minimal form implies $N_1^* = n_1^*$ and $N_2^* = n_2^*$ because there should be no repetition. The number of operators should consist of one distinct operator for the function name and another to serve as an assignment or grouping symbol $n_1^* = 2$. Thus,

$$V^* = (2 + n_2^*) \log_2 (2 + n_2^*)$$

where n_2^* represents the number of different input/output parameters. Note that V^* is considered a useful measure of an algorithm's content. It is roughly related to the basic GRC model concept of input/output formats.

The level of the implementation of a program is defined as its relation to its most abstract form, V^*, i.e., $L = V^*/V$. Necessarily, $L \leq 1$ and the most succinct expression for an algorithm is a level of 1. The relation $V^* = L * V$ implies that when the volume goes up the level goes down. Since it is hard to calculate V^*, an approximation for L, $\hat{L}$, is calculated directly from an implementation

$$\hat{L} = (2n_2)/(n_1 N_2)$$

which is approximately equal to L. The reciprocal of level is defined as the difficulty, $D = 1/L$, which can be viewed as the amount of redundancy within an implementation.

Based on these primitives, formulas for programming effort (E) and time (T) are derived. Assuming algorithm implementation consists of N non-random selections from an n element vocabulary and that the selection is of the order of a binary search (implying $\log_2 n$ comparisons for the selection of each element), the effort required to generate a program is $N \log_2 n$ mental comparisons (equal to the program volume V). Each mental comparison requires a number of elementary discriminations which is a measure of the task difficulty (D). Thus, the number of elementary mental discriminations E needed to generate a program is

$$E = V * D = V/L = V^2/V^*.$$

This says the mental effort required to implement any algorithm with a given potential volume should vary with the square of its volume in any language. E has often been used to measure the effort required to comprehend an implementation rather than produce it, i.e., E may be a measure of program clarity.

To calculate the time of development, software science uses the concept of a moment defined by the psychologist Stroud as the time required by the human brain to perform the most elementary discrimination. These moments occurred at a rate of 5 to 20 per second. Denoting moments (or Stroud's number) by S, we have $5 \leq S \leq 20$ per second. Assuming a programmer does not *time share* while solving a problem, and converting the effort equation (which has dimensions of both binary digits and discriminations per unit time) we get

$$T = E/S = V/(SL) = V^2/(SV^*).$$

Halstead empirically estimated S = 18 for his environment, but this may vary from environment to environment.

Software science metrics have been validated in a variety of environments but predominantly for module size developments.

Other Resources

In what has been stated so far, resource expenditure and estimation have been predominantly computed in terms of effort. The formula for cost may be a simple multiplication of the staff months times the average cost of a staff member or it may be more complicated. It may include some difference for the cost of managers versus the cost of programmers versus the cost of support personnel whose role varies across the life cycle [13].

The schedule may be derived based upon historical data, with effort allocated to different activities based upon the known percentages or it may be dictated by the model itself, as with the Rayleigh curve. However, the dynamic models generate what they consider the ideal staffing conditions which may not be the actual ones available. Thus, in fitting actual effort to the estimated or proposed effort, some decisions and tradeoffs must be made.

Computer time is yet another resource. Unfortunately, none of the models treats this within the same formula. In general, they have a separate formula for computer time, again based upon computer use in similar projects. These models vary from a simple table type model [6] to some very sophisticated probability distribution based on reliability modeling for phases of the development, such as testing [14].

Effect of Resource Model Research

In general, modeling a process attempts to explain what is going on in that process by making assumptions about the underlying process and simplifying the environment by removing extraneous and less relevant factors. Modeling presents a viewpoint of the process, in our case the software development process or product by classifying various phenomena, abstracting from reality and isolating the aspects of interest.

Resource modeling can be useful in several ways. It can be used for initial prediction, i.e., given what we know or can guess about a project, it can be used to predict the effort required to produce the product, the cost, the staffing pattern, the computer time required, etc. The main point is to discover relationships between some set of characteristics that we can estimate or know and those resource elements we wish to find out about. It can be used in predicting the characteristics of the next phase of development from the current phase. We should be able to predict what should happen next and say, it doesn't happen, why not; is it a sign of trouble, etc.?

The most important research use of resource modeling is that it should give us insights into what is going on in the software development process. We can study how different environmental parameters, such as changes in specifications, the methodology or tools used, or the complexity of the requirements can change the pattern of software development. We can use the resource usage patterns to evaluate such things as methodology and tools and learn how better to engineer future developments.

We can use resource data to evaluate our various models of the software development process. For any model, does it explain our behavior and environment? Do the factors (parameters) agree with our environmental parameters and are they calibrated correctly? In this way, we can refine our models of the process and gain deeper insights into the qualitative and quantitative nature of software development.

From the empirical models, we can learn what basic relationships exist between various aspects of the software development process. We can learn what factors affect the development process and what their effects are. From the theoretical models, we can learn whether there are better ways to understand the underlying behavior of the process and test out some basic assumptions about group dynamics with regard to software development environments.

References

[1]   C. Walston and C. Felix.
        A method of programming measurement and estimation.
        IBM Systems Journal 16, Number 1, 1977.

[2]   Karl Freburger and Victor Basili.
        The software engineering laboratory: Relationship equations.
        University of Maryland Technical Report TR-764, May 1979.

[3]   M.J. Lawrence and D.R. Jeffery.
        Inter-organizational comparison of programming productivity.
        Department of Information Systems, University of New South
            Wales, March 1979.

[4]   Barry W. Boehm.
        Draft of book on software engineering economics, to be
            published.

[5]   Doty Associates, Inc.
        Software cost estimates study, Volume 1.
        RADC TR 77-220, June 1977.

[6]   R. Wolverton.
        The cost of developing large scale software.
        IEEE Transactions on Computers 23(6), 1974.

[7]   J. Aron.
        Estimating resources for large programming systems.
        NATO Conference on Software Engineering Techniques, Mason
            Charter, N.Y. 1969.

[8]   W. M. Carriere and R. Thibodeau.
        *Development of a logistics software cost estimating technique
            for foreign military sales.*
        General Research Corporation, Santa Barbara, California, June
            1979.

[9]   L. Putnam.
        A general empirical solution to the macro software sizing and
            estimating problem.
        IEEE Transactions on Software Engineering 1(2), 1975.

[10]   Peter V. Norden.
        Useful tools for project management.
        In M.K. Starr, editor, *Management of Production*, pages 77-101,
            Penguin, 1970.

[11]   Francis N. Parr.
         An alternative to the rayleigh curve model for software
            development effort.
         Transactions on Software Engineering, May 1980.

[12]   M. Halstead.
         Elements of Software Science.
         Elsevier North-Holland, New York, 1977.

[13]   Victor R. Basili and Marvin V. Zelkowitz.
         Analyzing medium scale software developments.
         *Proceedings of the Third International Conference on Software
            Engineering*, Atlanta, Georgia, May 1978.

[14]   John D. Musa.
         A theory of software reliability and its application.
         IEEE Transactions on Software Engineering, SE1(3):312-327.

Questions Asked after the Conference

Fred Sayward

In your paper you list several formulas relating macro software variables. The constants in these formulas, and sometimes the formulas themselves, are derived mainly from historical data with the goal of being able to predict the resource needs of future software projects. Which of these formulas, if any, do you feel are candidates for the needed *invariant principles* of a science of software metrics as discussed by Browne and Shaw? If the formulas are indeed principles or *laws of nature*, wouldn't the constants in them have to be universal constants, analogous, say, to the gravitational constant and Plank's constant in Physics? How would one go about establishing one of these formulaes as an invariant principle? How would one derived the universal constants?

Vic Basili

The best way to think of the formulas derived is as relationships that have been observed between various activities. We are not yet at a level of a law of nature! We are still at the early investigative stages where we do not know cause and effect, but only that two things appear to be related in a particular way. For example, the basic relation between lines of code and effort assumes that it may be possible to measure the amount of time it takes to write a line of code. Clearly, there are many other factors that influence that relationship, but if we agree that there is such a basic relationship, we can proceed to analyze the factors and their effect. In fact, physics may not even be a good analogy here. We are also dealing with the variations in human behavior and must rely on some of the investigative strategies of the psychologists.

Chapter 7:
High Level Language Metrics

Jean E. Sammet

IBM Federal Systems Division
10215 Fernwood Road
Bethesda, MD 20034

Introduction

There is a major difference between metrics for one or more *high level languages* (e.g., FORTRAN, COBOL) and metrics for one or more *programs*, although these concepts are often — and erroneously — used interchangeably. The high level language is clearly a major tool in producing a program, but the metrics are quite different. For example, programs can be measured with respect to their written length, time taken to prepare them, running time of the object program, length of object code, complexity, and error rate after completion. Of these measurable factors, two depend primarily on the *compiler* — namely running time and length of object code. Two are highly dependent on the ability of the *programmer* and the nature of the programming *problem* — namely time taken to prepare the program and error rate after completion. One is a less objective metric than the others — namely complexity. There have been numerous approaches to defining program complexity (e.g., Bell and Sullivan [2] and McCabe [9]), but there is no agreement on which of these or others should be used. This subject is discussed in Curtis [4] in this volume.

Program length seems as if it ought to be an objective measure, but it is not really. The obvious way to measure program length is by the ubiquitous "source lines of code," but that is not clearly defined even within a single language, since free form languages permit numerous statements on a single line. One might think that the number of characters in a program was a completely objective measure, but even here one runs into many questions, e.g., (1) should comments be counted within the program length, (2) should long data names really make a program seem longer than a program which is identical except for using short data names, and (3) in a language such as APL which permits overprinting of characters should such overprinted characters be counted as one or two characters? One approach to program metrics which is receiving increasing attention is that devised by Halstead [7].

There will be no further discussion of *program* metrics, because this paper is meant to deal with *language* metrics. The measures in this latter area tend to be somewhat more subjective, and harder to define. The main purposes for which language metrics have been used in the past are for language selection and/or comparison, and (separately) for language design. But there are numerous other issues involved in language metrics besides selection and design. However, they can all be classified under the heading of potential research. Such topics include levels of non-procedurality, deviations from one language to another, functionality of a language, and the relationship of the language to various program measurements. This paper discusses each of these very briefly and informally, and mentions the difficulties in carrying out experiments in language areas. Since languages are abstract intellectual entities worthy of being studied in their own right, the study of their measurements is an equally appropriate intellectual endeavor and in some cases could have useful concrete results.

The term "language" or "programming language" as used in this paper refers only to high level languages such as FORTRAN or COBOL. There is no discussion in this paper of assembly languages nor of such "midway" languages as PL/360.

Numerical Approaches to Language Selection/Comparison

Language selection involves technical and non-technical issues. Examples of the former are: the ability of the language to handle subscripts (e.g., how many, what type of subscript expressions); whether there is strong or weak data typing; whether elaborate data layouts can be specified. An example of a non-technical issue is the amount of training needed by the people who are going to use the language. There are some issues whose classification is unclear — the most notable one is the compiler. Most people ignore this important distinction between the technical and the non-technical issues, and get into intellectual and practical difficulty as a result. However, in all cases, the application area for which the language is to be used should be the major consideration for technical evaluation.

There are two basic numerical methods for doing language selection: numerical scoring against *requirements*, and *benchmarking*.

Numerical scoring of languages

Various attempts have been made to make the process of language selection more abstract, or at least more visible and objective and less dependent on handwaving and arbitrary human judgment. If the requirements of the problem for which the language is to be chosen are specified at the beginning, then a simple scoring technique can be used, although it is often difficult to apply. The technique simply assigns each requirement a weighting factor to indicate its relative importance among all the other requirements. Then each language is evaluated for its ability to deal with that particular requirement. The numbers in both cases are usually normalized, and then they are cross multiplied and a final score is obtained. For a more detailed explanation of this method, see Browne et al. [3] and Sammet [11]. The technique has been used in real situations (e.g., Browne et al. [3]).

Now nobody, least of all this author, would claim that such a method eliminates all arbitrariness; people can use unreasonable assignments of weights on both sides (i.e., both the importance of the requirements and the evaluation of the language against the requirements) to enable them to reach a predetermined conclusion. However, this method has the advantage of at least permitting all of these biases to be clearly visible to other people who will review the scoring process.

In some cases, a prior step must be taken before this technique can be used because the requirements themselves are not clearly determined at the outset. The requirements themselves could be determined by a similar type of weighted scoring method, or by some nonnumeric method of group decision. Again, there is no guarantee of objectivity, but at least the biases will become visible if a scoring technique is used here. The most extensive effort in comparing languages against requirements was the DOD sponsored work in evaluating about 20 languages against the TINMAN requirements described in Amoroso et al. [1].

Benchmarking

The basic principle of benchmarking is to choose problems and then write programs in the languages which are under consideration. The major difficulty of course is to select a fair set of problems which is representative of the application to be implemented. There are then three types of benchmarking that can be done. The first involves merely writing the programs on paper and then measuring both the length of the program and the time it takes a person to write it. Not much more can be done with regard to measuring paper programs of that kind.

A second possibility is to actually execute the programs and then measure those characteristics which are relevant to the eventual application. For example, one can measure the length of object code, the execution time for the running program, and any other environmental factors that are relevant. If a compiler which is to be used for the final project is actually available for these benchmarks, and if the problems are validly selected, then significant results can be obtained this way.

A third way of measuring for benchmarking is to measure the characteristics of the programs using measures such as those defined by Halstead [7] or McCabe [9]. The conclusions to be drawn from such measures will depend on how much one believes in either or both of those measurements. Such a discussion is beyond the scope of this paper.

The earliest of the benchmarking studies seems to have occurred in the early 1960s although the reference is currently unavailable. Certainly one of the early *thorough* attempts at comparing languages was Rubey et al. [10], which used benchmark problems to compare PL/I to COBOL, FORTRAN, and JOVIAL.

There are several difficulties with considering benchmarking as a very good metric. First, the capabilities of individual programmers tend to be more significant than the qualities of the languages themselves; there are generally ways around this by having the same programmers code problems in several languages, but then there is a difficulty in the person's having more familiarity with the problem when it is coded in the second language. A major — but often very subtle difficulty — arises in the actual choice of problems to be used for the benchmarks. It is entirely possible to choose problems that favor one language over another, and this is sometimes done unconsciously. Furthermore, this bias (whether deliberate or accidental) is often impossible to discover unless some objective person is expert in *all* the *problems* and *all* the *languages* under consideration.

Metrics for Language Design

In order to apply metrics to language design, there are two basic numerical approaches. The first involves feature comparison, and the second involves program metrics.

In order to do a feature comparison of the desirability of various language designs, one can carry out human experiments to compare features with respect to some desired criteria (e.g., readability, brevity). A number of people have conducted experiments in this area, e.g. Gannon and Horning [6] and Gannon [5]. These and many other experiments (including some of his own) are described in Schneiderman [12]. Among the most interesting of these is Gannon [5]; he designed two different simple languages and had two sets of programmers write programs. The language design issue being investigated was typed versus typeless languages. The measurements were made on the number and types of errors in the programs.

Another way of dealing with feature comparisons is by various linguistic approaches, e.g. examination of concrete and abstract syntax, types of grammar with various features. In particular, the size of the grammar can provide a metric for a language. One way to measure the size of a grammar is by counting the number of production rules it has. Another way is to count the numbers of individual grammar elements, e.g. key words, reserved words, data types, statement types, primitive elements, redundant features.

A third factor is the effect of various features on compilers. In this context, one determines which features or combinations thereof are easier (or more difficult) to implement with respect to a particular compiler design. An interesting study of the costs associated with such considerations was made in the Ph.D. thesis by M. Shaw [13].

As a fourth technique it is always possible to compare language features against already existing languages according to some specific criteria (e.g., number of subscripts allowed, presence of recursion) and reach some determination. This approach could provide relative metrics between two languages rather than an absolute measure for a language.

One can also use *program* metrics (e.g., Halstead) to measure one or more *language* designs. Thus if one is a believer in some of these program metrics, one could try writing programs in several alternate language designs and see what conclusions could be reached.

Potential Areas of Future Research

There are a number of fruitful areas for research in the area of language metrics. Each of the following sections provides a one sentence summary of a research task, followed by a paragraph explaining the intent of the task.

Technical vs non-technical issues

Strengthen the understanding and the measurement of the differences between technical and non-technical issues.

This would then enable the language selection to be done more abstractly. At best the results in this area will be subjective and relative, e.g., is the compiler a technical or a non-technical issue with respect to the language? In my opinion it is non-technical, but others will surely disagree, which simply reemphasizes the subjective nature of the issue.

Measurement of Language Deviation

Develop methods of measuring the deviation of one language from another.

This has implications which range all the way from the purely scientific to the practical area of contracting. Thus, if one knows the level or amount of deviation of one language from another, it may be possible to draw certain conclusions about programs to be written in one versus in the other. From a contractual point of view, it may become important to know whether or not a language is a major or minor "deviation" from some base language. Everybody uses the terms "dialect" and "language-L-like," but nobody has ever supplied a scientific meaning to these terms, and metrics should be developed to give meaning to the terms. A primitive attempt at starting this work is given in Sammet [11]. This seems to be a very fruitful area of research and a few good Ph.D. theses might solve this problem.

Measure of non-procedurality

Develop measures of *non-procedurality*.

It is agreed by virtually every knowledgeable person in the field that *non-proceduralness* is a relative term which changes as the state of the art changes. (See a discussion in Leavenworth and Sammet [8].) Since one objective of research in languages is to allow the user to specify as few of the details about his problem as possible, metrics of non-procedurality will enable us to measure our own progress towards this goal. In addition, people will have some choice about how many details about a particular problem they need to specify, by choosing a language at the right level of non-procedurality. Thus, the more non-procedural language will permit the user to specify fewer details. This is a very difficult — although very important — research topic. It is strongly related to the problem of measuring functionality discussed in the next section.

Measures of programmer productivity via functionality

Develop a good measure for programmer productivity using functionality.

Clearly this is one of the most crucial issues for which metrics are needed, but also seems to be the hardest. The only thing that is clear is that source lines of code is a poor measure, and yet it seems to be the most prevalent one. *What is desperately needed is a measure of functionality for a language and for a program written in the language.* From that we could derive programmer productivity. As an example, it is clear that a **CALL** to a subroutine provides more function than a simple **GOTO**. On the other hand, does a single loop statement provide more function than a single **CALL**? And in which case has the programmer accomplished more? Thus we need to derive measures of power or function or complexity of individual statement types.

Research is needed for both the language and the programs written in that language. With the technology of 1980, the use of a "statement count" is a more accurate measure of function accomplished in a program than a count of "physical lines of code" in the program. However, even the definition of a statement for these purposes needs research to have consistency from one language to another. For example, how many statements (for purposes of functionality and productivity) are there in **IF** A **THEN** B **ELSE** C? And does that answer change if A or B or C are themselves **IF**-statements or does the answer depend on the language?

Measuring languages vs measuring programs

Develop techniques to numerically bridge the gap between the measures of a language and measures of programs written in that language.

Right now, these measurements are frequently mixed up or interchanged or not even recognized as being separate concepts. A key issue is the "source lines of code" discussed in the previous section, which may have different measures depending on whether we are talking about the *language* or a *program* written in the language. This is as much an educational problem as a research problem.

Measuring definitional techniques

Develop measures of definitional techniques.

It is clear that the syntactical definitional technique which is used actually has a significant effect on the language if the syntactic method is chosen at the beginning. But we have no way of measuring this. This is a very difficult topic, but fortunately an area of relatively little importance.

Languages and the life cycle

Develop measures of a language, and its usefulness, over the whole life cycle of a program.

This probably involves consideration of some languages besides the classical high level languages, although measures of the latter in this context are also of interest. Some languages might be good for debugging and maintenance but poor for writing programs quickly. Thus we would like to be able to measure the appropriateness of a language with respect to each portion of the life cycle; clearly such a metric would be a major factor in language selection (as discussed in an earlier section).

Languages and applications

Develop techniques for measuring the applicability of a language to a particular application or class thereof.

As discussed in an earlier section, this is generally done by evaluating specific technical and non-technical features of a language in a subjective way. We know intuitively (and through experience) that COGO and GPSS are suitable for civil engineering and discrete simulation respectively and that trying to use each of those languages in the other's application area would be disastrous (and probably impossible). Other cases are less clearcut. For example FORTRAN and COBOL have traditionally been used for numeric calculations and business data processing respectively but interchanging them is not so disastrous as the COGO-GPSS case. There are currently no techniques for measuring these differences objectively and they are certainly needed.

Potential Experimentation

Unlike some other areas, it is difficult to suggest useful valid experiments in the area of language metrics. As with many other aspects of measuring software, the individual differences of programmers, or the individual differences in the applications involved may swamp the element(s) being measured.

Specifically with regard to languages, one of the obvious types of experiments involves language features (e.g. Gannon [5]). However, the issue here may be of the background language within which the feature is being tested rather than the feature itself. Thus, an issue of strong typing in a language, versus weak typing or typeless languages, cannot be separated entirely from the surrounding language.

Another fruitful area for experimentation is the cost occurring from the presence or absence of a particular feature in a language. Such costs occur in learning the language, the compiler, the maintenance of the programs in the language, and potential needs for portability. It is important to note that this experimentation applies equally well to presence *and* absence of a feature. As a simple example, the ability to allow any arithmetic expression as a subscript immediately leads to the need for rules about a floating point value as a subscript. Is the (apparent) generality of the rule just stated a help or a hindrance in learning the language and writing accurate maintainable programs? Perhaps some experiments about major features could be run, but this would probably be of intellectual interest only. Usually, time and economics don't permit this type of work to be done while the language is being designed!

References

[1]   S. Amoroso et al.
        *Language Evaluation Coordinating Committee Report to the
        High Order Language Working . group (HOLWG).*
        AD-A037634, January 1977, 2617 pages.

[2]   D. E. Bell and J. E. Sullivan.
        Further Investigations into the Complexity of Software.
        MITRE Technical Report MTR-2874, Volume II. MITRE
        Corporation, Bedford, Massachusetts, June 1974.

[3]   P. H. Browne et al.
        Data Processing Technologies, Volume I: High-Level Language Evaluation.
        Teledyne Brown Engineering, Huntsville, Alabama. Army Contract DAHC60-69-C-0037, May 1970.

[4]   B. Curtis.
        The measurement of software quality and complexity.
        This volume.

[5]   J. D. Gannon.
        An experimental evaluation of data type conventions.
        Communications of the ACM 20(8):584-595, August 1977.

[6]   J. D. Gannon and J. J. Horning.
        Language design for programming reliability.
        IEEE Transactions on Software Engineering 1(2):179-191, June 1975.

[7]   M. Halstead.
        Elements of Software Science.
        Elsevier, New York, New York, 1977.

[8]   B. Leavenworth and J. E. Sammet.
        An overview of non-procedural languages.
        Proceedings of the ACM SIGPLAN Symposium on Very High Level Languages. SIGPLAN Notices 9(4):1-12, April 1974.

[9]   T. J. McCabe.
        A complexity measure.
        IEEE Transactions on Software Engineering 2(6):308-320, December 1976.

[10]   R. J. Rubey et al.
        Comparative Evaluation of PL/I.
        Logicon Inc., San Pedro, California, AD-669096, April 1968.

[11]   J. E. Sammet.
        Problems in, and a pragmatic approach to programming language measurement.
        Proceeding of the AFIPS Fall Joint Computer Conference, pages 243-251. 1971.

[12]   B. Schneiderman.
        Software Psychology: Human Factors in Computer and Information Systems.
        Winthrop Publishers, Inc., Cambridge, Massachusetts, 1980.

[13]   M. Shaw.
        Language structures for contractible compilers.
        Carnegie-Mellon University, Computer Science Department
        Report, December 1971.

Questions Asked after the Conference

Capers Jones, ITT

I've measured the impact of high-level languages on development and maintenance productivity for seven or eight years, and, I would like to pass on a couple of observations.   First, John Gannon asked the question earlier about the impact of high-level languages on maintenance. I once interviewed twenty-six maintenance programmers, who were using various languages, to see if there was an impact. The gist of what they told me is that if a program is written in a high-level language and is well structured, they could make any given change in about one fourth the time of an equivalent assembler program, and the probability of introducing a fresh bug when they made a change (which is a very risky operation in maintenance) dropped by fifty percent. Usually, roughly one change out of every five will introduce a fresh bug if you write it in assembler. If you use a high-level language it's one bug per two and a half changes. There is an impact on maintenance from using high-level languages. Which brings up a point — if you want to measure cost reduction across an entire life cycle, high-level languages crudely, but generally, are effective. The difficulty is that if you add in all the costs of the cycle that have nothing to do with the language, like specifications, like paperwork, like integration, like configuration control, and you divide by the number of lines, high-level languages end up looking like they're diminishing productivity instead of improving it, even though in real life they're reducing the cost of the cycle. You have to be careful of the mathematical paradox when you try to measure programs in high-level languages contrasted to those in assembler.

Jean Sammet

With all due respect, and without wanting to contradict Capers about his comments, that's exactly the kind of comment that is orthogonal to the point that I'm trying to make. I'm trying to talk about languages as fairly abstract intellectual entities in and of themselves and not get into an issue on whether or not they are useful in writing programs. That is a very important area of discussion. It doesn't happen to be the one that

I'm trying to talk about, and it is not the message that I'm trying to get across to you. Again, let me emphasize, what I'm trying to convey is that languages need to be looked at as intellectual entities quite separate from the programs people write when using the language. That's not the only view of languages that needs to be looked at, but languages do need to be looked at from that point of view and not necessarily only from the point of view of what they do with regard to the programs. Now, obviously, if one looked at languages only as intellectual abstract entities, and if one had no concern about the eventual programs, this would be a fairly sterile exercise, but I submit that there is a proper kind of research that needs to be done on the languages quite independent of any programs that may or may not ever get written in them.

Dave Weintraub, Applied Physics, Johns Hopkins

It's not as much a question as a dilemma. I'm afraid I'm going to tread on toes as they were just treaded on, but what was bothering me during the very last part of your presentation is the growing number and high cost in the industry of preprocessors, which add one or two features to a given language. I think this is a bridge between what you're saying and Jones' comment, and I was hoping you'd say something about whether or not your study indicates that this is in fact a futile task, because thinking back to the comment made before, all the money spent on preprocessors is wasted.

Jean Sammet

I'm sorry. I don't mean to convey that I'm conducting an active research project in this area, because I am not. I think your phrasing of the question is a very reasonable one and is not treading on any toes. One of the areas of research that I mentioned was to bridge the gap between measuring languages and measuring programs, and I think it becomes quite legitimate to talk about the effect of language features on compilers, on preprocessors, and so on. I don't mean that the languages are completely to be looked at in a vacuum, but I want to separate these issues, and one of the characteristics of a language, for example, if one knew how to do this (I don't and I don't think anybody else does either), is what is the cost of adding a particular feature. Now I think that's a very legitimate area of concern and study for the language as an abstract entity.

Chapter 8:
Data Collection, Validation and Analysis

Victor R. Basili

Department of Computer Science
University of Maryland
College Park, MD 20742

Introduction

One of the major problems with doing measurement of the software development process and the product is the ability to collect reliable data that can be used to understand and evaluate the development process and product and the various models and metrics. The data collection process consists of several phases — establishing the environment in which the project is being developed, the actual data collection process itself, the validation of the collection process and the data, and, finally, the careful analysis and interpretation of that data with respect to specific models and metrics. We will discuss each of these phases.

Establishing the Environment

Before we begin collecting data, we must understand the various factors that affect software development. Data collection should begin with listing those factors one hopes to control, measure, and understand. In this way, we may characterize the environment, understand what we are studying, and be able to isolate the effects. One possible approach is to create categories of factors.

A partial list of factors is given below, categorized by their association with the problem, the people, the process, the product, the resources, and the tools. Some factors may fit in more than one category, but are listed only once.

People Factors

These include all the individuals involved in the software development process, including managers, analysts, designers, programmers, and librarians. People related factors that can affect the development process include: number of people involved, level of expertise of the individual members, organization of the group, previous experience with the problem, previous experience with the methodology, previous experience with working with other members of the group, ability to communicate, morale of the individuals, and capability of each individual.

Problem Factors

The problem is the application or task for which a software system is being developed. Problem related factors include: type of problem (mathematical, database manipulation, etc.), relative newness to state-of-the-art requirements, magnitude of the problem, susceptibility to change, new start or modification of an existing system, final product required (e.g., object code, source, documentation, etc.), state of the problem definition (e.g., rough requirements vs. formal specification), importance of the problem, and constraints placed on the solution.

Process Factors

The process consists of the particular methodologies, techniques, and standards used in each area of the software development. Process factors include: programming languages, process design language, specification language, use of librarian, walk-throughs, test plan, code reading, top down design, top down development (stubs), iterative enhancement, chief programmer team, Nassi-Shneiderman charts, HIPO charts, data flow diagrams, reporting mechanisms, structured programming, and milestones.

Product Factors

The product of a software development effort is the software system itself. Product factors include: deliverables, size in lines of code, words of memory, etc., efficiency tests, real-time requirements, correctness, portability, structure of control, in-line documentation, structure of data, number of modules, size of modules, connectivity of modules, target machine architecture, and overlay sizes.

Resource Factors

The resources are the nonhuman elements allocated and expanded to accomplish the software development. Resource factors include: target machine system, development machine system, development software, deadlines, budget, response times, and turnaround times. (Note there is a relationship between resource and product factors in that the resources define a set of limits within which the product must perform. Sometimes these external constraints can be a dominating force on the product and sometimes they are only a minor factor, e.g., it is easy to get the product to perform well within the set of constraints.)

Tool Factors

The tools, although also a resource factor, are listed separately because of the important impact they have on development. Tools are the various supportive automated aids used during the various phases of the development process. Tool factors include: requirements analyzers, system design analyzers, source code analyzers (e.g., FACES), database systems, PDL processors, automatic flowcharters, automated development libraries, implementation languages, analysis facilities, testing tools, and maintenance tools.

Collecting the Data

Once it is clear what the environmental factors are, it is important that what data is needed be carefully considered. The data needed should be driven by the basic models and metrics that will be used and studied. However, since this may not always be known beforehand, especially in a research environment, we must also include a second level set of data that involves what we may want to know, model, or measure. Data collected in this bottom-up manner can be used to refine and modify the existing models and metrics and be used to help characterize our environment.

The actual collection process can take four basic formats: reporting forms, interviews, automatic collection using the computer system, and automated data analysis routines. The reporting forms are usually filled out by the various members of the development team from senior management to clerical support. The benefit of participants' filling out the forms is that they can usually give detailed insights into what is really happening on the project and provide great detail in the data. Questions on a form can be much more specific than the kind of information one can collect automatically. On the other hand, automated data collection has the advantage of being more accurate since it is not as subject to

human errors. It can also be done without the participants' being aware
of what specific activities and factors are being studied.

Form development is an art all by itself. First one needs to know what
data is needed. This must be modified by what data the participants
would be willing and able to answer accurately. One large factor here is
sampling rate, that is, how often can the forms be filled out so that the
participant is willing to do it and still remembers what it is you want to
know. It is important that a certain amount of redundancy be built into
the data collection process so that reliability checks can be made across
the data forms.

Before forms are filled out, the participants should be given a training
course in filling out the forms. They should be supplied with a glossary of
terms, instructions on filling out the forms, and some sample filled out
forms. It would also be helpful if the training session covered some of
the models the data collectors had in mind so that the participants had a
better idea of the kind of information that was wanted. One
representative set of forms [1] may look as follows:

A General Project Summary

This form would be used to classify the project and will be used in
conjunction with the other reporting forms to measure the estimated
versus actual development progress. It should be filled out by the project
manager at the beginning of the project, at each major milestone, and at
the end. The final report should accurately describe the system
development life cycle.

A Programmer/Analyst Survey

This form would classify the background of the personnel on each
project. It should be filled out once at the start of the project by all
personnel.

A Component Summary

This form would be used to keep track of the components of a system.
A component is a piece of the system identified by name or common
function (e.g., an entry in a tree chart or baseline diagram for the system
at any point in time, or a shared section of data such as a common
clock). With the information on this form combined with the information

on the Component Status Report, the structure and status of the system and its development can be monitored. This form is filled out for each component at any point in time when a major modification is made. It should be filled out by the person responsible for that component.

A Component Status Report

This form would be used to keep track of the development of each component in the system. The form is turned in at the end of each week and lists the number of hours spent on each component. This form is filled out by persons working on the project.

A Resource Summary

This form keeps track of the project costs on a weekly basis. It is filled out by the project manager every week of the project duration. It should correlate closely with the component status report.

A Change Report Form

The change report form is filled out every time the system changes because of change or error in design, code, specifications, or requirements. The form identifies the error, its cause and other facets of the project that are affected.

Computer Program Run Analysis

This form is used to monitor the computer activities used in the project. An entry is made every time the computer is used by the person initiating the run.

Interviews are used to validate the accuracy of the forms and to supplement the information contained on them in areas where it is impossible to expect reasonably accurate information in a form format. In the first case, spot check interviews are conducted with individuals filling out the forms to check that they have given correct information as interpreted by an independent observer. This would include agreement about such things as the cause of an error or at what point in the development process the error was caused or detected.

In the second case, interviews can be held to gather information in depth on several management decisions, e.g., why a particular personnel organization was chosen, or why a particular set of people was picked.

These are the kinds of questions that often require discussion rather than a simple answer on a form.

The easiest and most accurate way to gather information is through an automated system. Throughout the history of the project, more and more emphasis should be placed on the automatic collection of data as we become more aware what data we want to collect, i.e., what data is the most valuable and what data we can or need to get, etc. More effort is required in the development or procurement of automatic collection tools.

The most basic information gathering device is the program development library. The librarian can automatically record data and alleviate the clerical burden for the manager and the programmers. Copies of the current state of affairs of the development library can be periodically archived to preserve the history of the developing product.

A second technique for gathering data automatically is to analyze the product itself, gathering information about its structure by using a program analyzer system. What data is gathered depends upon the particular product metrics.

The above data collected on the project should be stored in a computerized database. Data analysis routines can be written to collect derived data from raw data in the database.

The data collection process is clearly iterative. The more we learn, the better informed we are about what other data we need and how better to collect it.

Data Validation

After archiving, the next stage is to apply validation techniques to the encoded data. The first step in the validation process is a review of the forms as they were handed in by someone connected with the data collection process to make sure that all the forms have been handed in and that the appropriate fields have been filled out. The next step is to enter the data into the database through a program that checks the validity of the data format and rejects data which is outside of the appropriate ranges. For example, this program can assure that all dates are legal dates and that system component names and programmer names are valid for the project. The program does this by using a prestored list of component names and programmer names.

Ideally, all data in the database should be reviewed by individuals who know what the data should look like. Clearly, this is expensive and not always possible. However, several projects should be reviewed for errors in detail and counts of the number of errors and types of errors kept so that error bounds can be calculated for the unchecked data. This allows data to be interpreted with the appropriate care.

Another type of validity check is to examine the consistency of the database by examining redundant data. This can be done by comparing similar data from different sources to assure the data is reasonably accurate. For example, if effort data is collected at the budget level (resource summary data) and at the individual programmer level (component status data), there should be a reasonable correlation between the two total efforts. Another approach is to use cluster analysis to look for patterns of behavior that are indicative of errors in filling out the forms. For example, if all the change report forms filled out by a particular programmer fall into one cluster, it may imply that there is a bias in the data based upon the particular programmer.

It is clear that data collection is a serious problem, especially in the collection of data on large programming projects across many environments where one set of forms may not be enough to capture what is happening in each of the environments. Unfortunately, if we are to compare projects, we do need common data and we need to know how valid that data is in each case so as not to draw improper conclusions.

Data Analysis and Result Reporting

After the environment has been established, the appropriate data collected and validated, the process of data analysis can begin. The first step entails fitting the data to the specific models and metrics and the interpretation of the results. If the data supports the model, then it reinforces our understanding of the software development process and product. If the data does not support the model, then we must further analyze the model and its application to the data and the data collection environment. It is possible that the data collection environment did not satisfy some of the assumptions of the model, explicit or otherwise. We can use this data to refine or refute the model or to gain new insights into our software development environment. In any case, the application of the model to the data often generates more questions than it answers and sets the stage for new analysis and new data to be collected.

The data analysis process can be motivated by the different needs for understanding. When linked with various models and metrics, the data analysis can be used to evaluate the software development process and product, to help with software development, and to monitor the stability and quality of an existing product. The process of collecting and analyzing data varies with each area of interest.

Better understanding of the software development process and the software development product is a critical need. Metrics can help in that understanding by allowing us to compare different products and different development environments and providing us with insights regarding their characteristics. Too often we think of all software as the same. Metrics can be used to delineate the various software products and environments.

Many metrics have as a major goal the evaluation of the quality of the process or product in a quality assurance environment. Thus a low score on a metric like the number of errors, indicates something desirable about the quality of the process while a high score on the same metric indicates something quite undesirable about the product. Here data can be analyzed after the project is over.

A second use of metrics would be as a tool for development. In this case, the metric can act as feedback to the developer, letting him know how the development is progressing. It can be used to predict where the project is going by estimating future size or cost, or it may tell him his current design is too complicated and unstructured. Metrics should certainly be used across the entire life cycle and as early as possible to facilitate estimation as well as evaluation. Here data must be analyzed in real time and reports generated in a form easily understandable by the software developer.

A third use of metrics is to monitor the stability and quality of the product through maintenance and enhancement; that is, we can periodically recalculate a set of metrics to see if the product has changed character in some way. It can provide a much needed feedback during the maintenance period. If we find over a period of time that more and more control decisions have entered the system, then something may have to be done to counteract this change in character.

This last use of metrics is relativistic, requiring only a simple partial ordering to indicate what is changed. A relative measure is clearly easier to validate than an absolute measure. The first two uses of metrics — the evaluation of the process and product and the tool of development — are predominantly absolute metrics; that is, there is no basis of comparison within the same project. You may only compare their values with the values of the metrics on other projects. The drawback to an absolute metric is that we need some normalization and calibration factor to tell us what is good and what is bad. The data analysis environment here is somewhere between the two discussed above.

Data collected from any project must be interpreted with great care. One must know the nature of the project and its development environment. To use any model or metric, one must fully understand its assumptions as well as its strengths and weaknesses in order to interpret the results for the particular environment. One must generalize to other environments very cautiously and with great reserve. One unmeasured factor may account for a complete change in effect.

When reporting data, one should report the raw data, the various factors as they are understood, and, in the case of experiments, any statistical results independent of interpretation.   It is important in reporting results to define the terms used as precisely as possible. There is a large communication problem due to imprecise units of measurement. For example, if size is reported in lines of source code, the measure is dependent upon the language used, whether or not comments are counted and the commenting convention, and whether or not only executable statements are counted.   The difference in the figures could be of the order of two or three to one.   Whenever the results of an analysis are reported, it is important to publish error bounds, not just in the fit to the model, but in the actual data collection process itself.

There is a great deal of work to be done in the data collection process. More work must be done in defining terms. A variety of models must be developed which provide us with different viewpoints of the software development process, and we must not fall into the trap of assuming that there is a single overall model of software and the software development process. Most important, because of the nature of experimentational analysis and the many factors that contribute to software development, we must be ready to duplicate the studies and experiments of others and report our results in the open literature. It is only when a wealth of data is obtained to support a particular hypotheses that the software community will gain the confidence to believe in it.

References

[1]   Victor R. Basili, Marvin V. Zelkowitz, Frank E. McGarry, Robert W. Reiter, Walter F. Truszkowski, David L. Weiss. *The software engineering laboratory.* Technical Report TR-535, May 1977, University of Maryland, Computer Science Center, College Park, Maryland 20742.

Questions Asked at the Conference

Lorraine Duvall, IIT Research

We're under contract to the Rome Air Development Center to establish what is called a data and analysis center for software (DACS). One of our tasks is to establish a software experience data base with the kind of field data that Bill Curtis discussed. Now we do have in our data base the data from the NASA Software Engineering Laboratory, and the failure interval data from John Musa's reliability work at Bell Laboratories. In the last couple of months we have had a really aggressive data acquisition program, and from a preliminary look at what kind of data is really available out there, we could be swamped in six months. Now, the kinds of data we are dealing with now have been collected as part of a programming support environment. We have got some conversion data that has been collected through the Navy. Now my question is, not only to you but to any of the other members of the panel, if this kind of data base is available where you may have reports that discuss the collection of the data and the raw data itself, is this good enough to actually help you in your research efforts, or do you need more information to really make this data usable to you?

Vic Basili

What I would need to know if I were to use that data is whether I really understood what the numbers represented, how good the data was, and what the error bounds were. That is the only way I would feel secure in making use of the data. The data we have collected in the Software Engineering Laboratory I understand well since I was involved in its collection. I know what data is accurate, I know what data is missing, and I know what data is not very reliable. This way, when I test a model or metric or make a prediction, I understand how to interpret the data; that is, whether it is the model or the data which is in error.

I would be very hesitant to use someone else's data unless I had a real feeling for the collection and validation process as well as error bounds, and I would expect that someone else would be concerned about using data collected in the Software Engineering Laboratory at NASA, since they did not have enough feeling on the accuracy bounds. We are trying to validate the data, but as yet there is not enough information on error bounds available. In fact, I have a challenge for you. One thing that DACS could do is not just collect the data, but perform error analysis. For example, they could do redundancy analysis or cluster analysis to find error patterns in the data. This way, when you report the results you could also report about the consistency and error range of the data base.

Jean Sammet

Let me also respond to that. I believe that one of the standard problems in attempting to use heterogeneous data bases and data that has come from several sources is that the same information may be encoded in very different ways. The definition of terms, as Vic mentioned, is not consistent and the kind of data that is collected is irregular. Are you at DACS attempting to do anything to unify that? Are you, for example, trying to set up standards for consistency in data collection? I, personally, think that's a contribution that your project could make.

Lorraine Duvall

About two years ago we attempted to define a generic data base, trying to model the software development process, and realized that this was no easy task. The approach we're taking now is to work very closely with the IEEE group to define terms. We're looking to the IEEE task group for data collection terminology. However, we do have some data now and we can't wait for three years before we make it into one beautiful data base. So we're approaching it from two different directions. I think that definition of a generic data base for software experience data is really an interesting project and if anybody has the money, we'd really love to do it.

Merv Muller

As a statistician, one loves to see data, but I really feel it is a question of what society can afford versus what are the needs of society, and I really think that you ought to know why you want to have the data. In one sense, you want data for descriptive purposes, because this is how you get insight, and evolve, but I don't really believe that that's why we want metrics. I believe that we want it because we want to predict future events. In answer to the question of what kind of data you need, I think there's some kind of priority ranking based on what the important questions are that you're trying to find improved, prediction methods. I don't know what the priorities are, but I would think that some part of the money should be spent on trying to figure out where the real issues are.

Vic Basili

I agree one hundred percent with what you just said. I have to understand why I am collecting the data. Although another valid purpose of data collection is to understand how we do business, we must still start with a model, not with data. What is it I want, what is it I want to be able to understand, or predict, or whatever?

Wayne Bennett, National Bureau of Standards

Analogous to the efforts that I see here is the computer performance evaluation effort that's been going on for a long time. What they've learned, it seems to me, is that they've collected an inordinate amount of data: test data was providing them with data, accounting logs were providing them with data, and they've finally come to the conclusion that they don't know what they're collecting the data for. They've realized that without a purpose as a touchstone, that there is no reason to throw out this and keep that. The computer performance evaluation users' group is now in its sixteenth year and they've just now begun addressing these questions.

At the risk of sounding ignorant, I cannot understand, short of its impact on programming, what our interest in languages is. I can see, as usual, industry and academia passing like ships in the night. There's a question that still remains and I think it is something that could be explained to those of us that aren't as familiar with some of the reasons for data collecting. I would think that cost, either in computer performance evaluation or in software metrics, is the bottom line. If I have a measure of anything and I can't relate it ultimately to cost, pump it into some simple model that managers will understand, why am I getting that measure?

It could be that the most useful thing that the academic environment could do would be to help decide what those touchstones should be and formally define them. I guess the question that I'm asking is do you see that as your role? Do you see that as part of what you're trying to do as opposed to simply collecting data? Do you actually want to put forth the reasons for data collecting? I would ask this also of Ms. Sammet concerning her first slide on high level language metrics.

Jean Sammet

Well, I'm not about to repeat the whole talk which I'm sure you would consider a blessing. But let me give you one example of the cost element. One of the things we don't know how to do is measure the amount of deviation of one language from another. We use the term dialect and we use the term ALGOL-like language or PL/I-like language, PASCAL-like language, but we don't know what those things mean. Now, if I write a contract with somebody to produce me a language that has certain characteristics, it would be nice to be able to measure whether the terms of that contract had been fulfilled. In order to do that I may need certain measurements with regard to the languages. That's a cost element which doesn't relate to programming but relates to the contract, I asked to have some product created for me and I'd like to know whether or not it really has been.

Wayne Bennett

My question is whether or not it's not really important to ask what is the end result. If the gentleman in the back (Capers Jones) is correct and the cost of documentation requirements and specification are so large that they tend to swamp the choice of language question, then it could be that there is an initial limit on what kinds of questions we're even willing to ask about choice of languages. Those are the kinds of hypotheses, it seems to me, that should be tested first. And after one gets past those, if indeed you get past those, then you can ask the more interesting questions about classification of languages. If it turns out that the difference is a one percent difference in the end in the cost, once you count in this man's documentation cost, it could be that it doesn't make a lick of difference and it's not worth looking into. I don't believe that that's wholly true; however, it seems to me that because of that possibility one has to start to look at it from the top, at the driving forces first.

Vic Basili

Let me answer that question by coming back to data collection. Data collection has to be driven by the models or the metrics I'm interested in, and clearly cost is going to be one of them. It may be the prime one in the end. I can talk about cost by looking at cost models so that I will be able to predict future costs. But I'm also interested in studying other factors, such as complexity metrics. It may be important to understand whether it is going to be hard to develop software metrics. I believe or hypothesize that there's a direct correlation between complexity measures and the cost of maintenance. The more complex the program is going to be the more expensive it's going to be to maintain. So, my end goal is to minimize my costs. You're probably right, the goal of everything is cost.

Jean Sammet

The problem is the one of cost and we ought to solve it and delineate what the issues are before we tackle anything else. Fortunately or unfortunately, the world is very unhomogeneous and therefore you have to poke at bits and pieces of some of these problems and then hope that at some point one can synthesize. Let me give you an illustration of something I wouldn't want to happen again. One of the rationales for the development of ADA was that there were on the order of two thousand different languages being used in the Department of Defense. Now, I don't know where that number came from, but by my standards it's sheer nonsense. I think what was happening was that every different assembly language was being counted, every compiler was being counted, and every time anybody twiddled a bit anywhere was being counted as one of the numbers that went into this two thousand count. I submit that if we knew what a language was, if we knew how to measure how many of them we had, we would be a lot better off. I would also suspect that when large industrial organizations, regardless of whether their applications were business oriented or scientifically oriented, go to their management and say they are using three languages, or thirty-three, it would be better if they could all agree on what it meant when they counted to three or to thirty- three. That's again a cost factor.

Marvin Denicoff, Office of Naval Research

Certainly the last two questions were really the same question, and underscored the obvious, namely; we need an a priori specification of purpose, of objectives, of profound versus trivial issues, et cetera. It's not enough, obviously, to simply collect data. I made a note, because, unless we know what data to collect, what level of precision, from whom we're collecting the data, for whom we're collecting the data, for what purpose, for how long, for what decision models, unless all of those things are specified a priori, we tend to get into trouble — and if you've been involved in data collection programs for areas other than software, you know how much trouble you can get into. However, a word of caution, and that's really the purpose of my comment; namely, if we knew a hell of a lot about all of these elements I've talked about, if we could pre-specify all of these parameters, we'd be in great shape. However, my argument is that we know nothing, almost nothing, and that there is a hell of a lot of insights that come out of *overcollecting*. Looking at the data per se sometimes yields profound insights into how we do this a priori specification out there in the future. So I say at the beginning, in the inception period of this data collection program, I would argue that to gain the advantage of those surprises we ought to err in the direction of overcollection.

Alan Perlis

A question was asked before about why we are collecting this data about languages if documentation is such an important part of our work. I wonder why nobody has gotten up and said, "Isn't there something wrong with computing if saying what a line of code does is so much more extensive an effort than the writing of the code itself?" For whom are we writing the documentation? And why are we writing it? It's actually an insurance policy that we use to reduce the cost of catastrophe. The assumption is always made that a large number of the people involved in software are in management and not in code production. And one of the reasons for that too, possibly, is the language tools we use. That is, it's not obvious at all that the amount of documentation in a piece of code is independent of the way we program and the languages we use.

Capers Jones, ITT

I'm assistant director of programming measurements for ITT, and my job is to measure program quality, productivity, and other attributes for all programs put out by the corporation, some thousands of them. I've been in measurement for a long time. Let me give you a quick dump of how you ought to go about it.

First, overcollection of data is very common when people get set to measure software. The way you avoid that, or at least minimize it, is to start by trying to come up with the format of the output reports to be presented to the managers or the programmers, the people you want to convince that you've got valid information. Then you work backwards from the output format to the data base and the input requirements. If you do it the other way, if you set out trying to specify the input of the data base fist, you almost always overcollect, and you also have another problem. You occasionally leave out important variables that you should collect. IBM's federal systems division did that. They set up a data collection effort that was so massive that after the first wave of inputting data individual managers stopped doing it because it was too time-consuming and too bothersome. You've got to have some simplification. But the purpose of all this is to make things better, not just to record data and do academic research forever. Generally speaking, what you want to make better are costs, quality, and schedules. So you aim your data collection system to feed back the information on those three significant variables. And the only thing that seems constant across all sizes and kinds of programs in this very diverse industry is the fact that defect removal costs more than anything else. One of the reasons why language selection is important, even though the direct cost of coding is small, like three percent on a big system, is that the choice of language can minimize defect removal later and defect removal is a very large cost, from thirty to thirty-five to forty percent of development.

Second, the paperwork costs are extremely significant for medium to large systems. They're hardly significant at all for small programs. Another point about paperwork is that the range in the paperwork domain is astonishing, and seems to be due to individual human variances. For example, the smallest logic spec I ever saw was two pages per thousand lines of code and the biggest — and it was assembler that was the target language — the biggest was sixty-eight, which was a variance of thirty-four to one with no relationship to complexity or the language.   And paperwork is a controllable variable, and most companies do it too much. As Doctor Perlis suggested, it's to convince management that we really know what we're doing rather than because we really need it. So in the big system, while cutting down on paperwork actually is cost-effective and doesn't diminish the coding speed or the coding efficiency, it is a variable that gets out of control.

Measurement isn't a very tricky, difficult intellectual area, but if you try and think practically, then you only want to measure things that you can improve.

Chapter 9:
A Scientific Approach to Statistical Software

Ivor Francis

Department of Economic and Social Statistics
Cornell University
Ithaca, NY 14853

Abstract

This paper supports the scientific approach to the study of all phases of the development and use of software. It argues the case for including the user's viewpoint in describing and evaluating software. This requires that quantitative measures be defined to characterize a user's problem, to report the accuracy of computed solutions, and to assess the usefulness of the output. Examples of the use of quantitative measures are given from the evaluation of statistical software. A set of standard test problems is needed so that experiments can be conducted to compare the performance of software systems.

A Science of Software

In the early days of computer science the emphasis, as the name implies, was on the computer, the hardware and the algorithmic implications of the machine characteristics. The person who wrote a program would very likely be the person who used the program. Little attention was given to user convenience and protection, or to readability and documentation of software. But as programs began to be exported, attention was focused more on these software features. More recently, as programs have grown into very large software systems, interest has turned to the human, organizational, and managerial factors that influence the quality and cost of developing good software.

Thus computer science has grown from a study of hardware to include all these aspects of the emerging science of software. Marvin Denicoff, in his introduction to the first meeting of this Panel in New Haven, proposed that what is needed is the development of a science of software to provide a methodology or justification for choices among various competing software systems, either proposed or existing. Alan Perlis, in his statement of purpose to the Panel in June 1979, asked the fundamental question, "Can there be assigned to software and the processes associated with its design, development, use, maintenance, and evolution, indices of merit that can support quantitative comparisons and evaluation of software?" This paper argues for an affirmative answer.

The charge to this Panel, therefore, was to outline areas of study and a structure for a science of software. The list of areas suggested by this Panel is large and will undoubtedly be added to in the future. In 1977 Halstead [12] used the term *software science* in a restricted sense. Fitzsimmons and Love [6], in reviewing his work, said that "the basic concepts of software science [are] program length, program volume, program level, language level, effort, and programming time...based entirely upon measures which can be computed automatically from a computer program."

To this list we can add many other concepts, as other papers from this Panel show, including program complexity, language characteristics, problem specification and performance evaluation, maintenance, accuracy and user convenience, micro modeling of program development resources, and organizational and managerial aspects of program development. The Panel has chosen to adopt the concept of the *life cycle* of software to organize these concepts, to be a model or paradigm for this science of software. This model, borrowed from biology, will no doubt be supplanted in time by an indigenous one, but it will serve the immediate object of organizing the subject to aid our comprehension and communication. For science is "a mental construct, by means of which a collection of objective data is arranged in a model and expressed linguistically for certain ends" (Dingle [5]). The ends proposed by Denicoff and Perlis above are the quantitative comparisons and evaluation of existing or proposed software. The ultimate end is the improvement of the state of the software art.

On a final philosophical note we might observe the quotation carved over the door to this National Academy of Sciences. It reminds us that in proposing to assign numbers to represent aspects of perceived reality we are hardly proposing something startling or new: This is the basis of science itself. If we replace the word *mankind* by *software managers* we describe the quest for a science of software:

"Harken to the miseries that beset mankind. They were witless and I made them to have sense and be endowed with reason. Though they had eyes to see, they saw in vain, they had ears but heard not, but, like to shapes in dreams throughout their length of days without purpose they wrought things in confusion...They had no sign either of winter or flowery spring or fruitful summer, where on they could depend, but in everything they wrought without judgment, until such time as I taught them to discern the rising of the stars and their settings, aye, and numbers, too, chiefest of sciences, I invented for them, and the combining of letters, creative mother of the muses' arts, where with to hold all things in memory." [Prometheus Bound, Aeschylus, c. 470 B.C.]

Some might argue that a science of software is philosophically different from the science of, say, physics, that there is nothing as measurable as, for example, temperature. This sharp distinction will not stand up under philosophical examination, but will be seen to be a question of precision. Bartlett [1], commenting on a warning against endowing certain statistical measures with reality, continued, "While tending to agree with this warning I would at the same time point out that there is no *a priori* objection to any coefficient which appeared permanently and satisfactorily measurable in practice being regarded as possessing a certain degree of reality. (The temperature of a body is thought of as something real, but theoretically it appears as a mathematical coefficient in an equation of statistical equilibrium.)" We may find models or equations to usefully summarize aspects of software, and perhaps some coefficient will capture a sense of software complexity, for example.

Characterizing Software

Having adopted the life cycle model to organize this science of software, we can begin to characterize and describe the components of software which are, broadly speaking, 1) specification, 2) development, 3) testing, and 4) maintenance. Lists of the characteristics of each of these components can be drawn up. We can also group the people who will interact with this software into 1) managers, 2) computer scientists, 3) programmers, and 4) users.

We may attempt to compile a list of desirable properties for these lists of characteristics. The desirability of some properties may depend, however, on which group of people one is addressing and what the intended application is. Furthermore, some tradeoffs will have to be made, for example between low cost and ease of use.

From these characterizations and desirable properties, possibly with the help of some mathematical models, we can propose quantitative indices of merit.

One activity which is central to the comparison of software systems is the evaluation of performance, which consists of specification plus testing. The term *performance evaluation* has been used to measure completion time of workloads in certain machines, which is of paramount importance to computer scientists. But to users, *performance* means more: The user is also interested in the nature of the output from a software system in response to the practical problem facing him. He is interested in the content and the form of the output, that is, its accuracy and usability.

In the next section we discuss these two aspects of the software cycle from a user's point of view, and illustrate them with examples of quantitative measures, or metrics, which have been used to make comparisons and evaluations of statistical software.

Performance Measures for Statistical Software

Two questions that a potential user of some software will ask are "Will it accurately compute solutions to my problems?" and "Is it sufficiently convenient to use, presenting results in a sufficiently useful form, to be worth my investment of money and time in using it?" This user is asking for an evaluation of performance, which will require testing the software in the light of the specification of his problems.

For many types of software applications the *accuracy* of a program's output is well defined; for sorting, information retrieval, and maintaining payrolls there is one correct solution. For some applications, however, there may not be a single correct answer, and the notion of *accuracy* has to be defined. This is the case for many applications in statistics.

An example of the need and usefulness of quantitative measures is provided by the study of multiple regression programs. Longley [13] compared the performance of several widely used multiple regression programs by submitting a single test problem to each program, and *qualitatively* comparing their computed solutions with an extremely precise solution which he obtained using special subroutines on an extended precision machine. Chambers [4], in comparing the accuracy of various algorithms for regression calculations, used the *minimum number of significant figures* in regression coefficients that were in agreement with those of a *best* program as a *quantitative* measure of accuracy of an algorithm.

Beaton, Rubin, and Barone [2], however, showed that Longley's precise solution was not the best solution for that test problem, and they defined a *perturbation index* as a quantitative measure of the difficulty of the problem to be solved, which incorporated the variance of the data and the word length of the machine. Velleman and Francis [15] argued that Chambers' measure was inadequate and proposed other quantitative measures of accuracy.

Velleman, Seaman, and Allen [16] used these measures of difficulty for problems and these measures of accuracy for solutions in an experiment which measured the accuracy of several programs as a function of the difficulty of a sequence of problems. Thus it was possible to plot the *response curve* for a program, the accuracy of its computations for problems of increasing difficulty. One would expect that accuracy would decline monotonically with increasing difficulty, but this was not always the case.

We have seen, therefore, that this experiment did not just happen. It evolved over ten years, during which time different quantitative measures were tried and found wanting.

From such response curves it is possible to propose an index of merit incorporating both accuracy and difficulty to evaluate performance of competing programs, although a user would probably want to include measures of cost and convenience into an index of merit. Note that a physicist with very precise raw data may place greater weight on accuracy in his index than an economist who might prefer to use a cheaper program, provided it gave sufficient accuracy for well conditioned problems and advised the user when it encountered problems that were too difficult for it.

Quantitative measures of convenience and usefulness have also been used in comparing statistical systems. For example, Bryce and Hilton [3] conducted an experiment to compare the difficulty of installation of a number of statistical packages. They measured the effort of three systems programmers in installing each of three packages, using a Latin square experimental design. Francis and Valliant [11] describe an experiment to compare the ease of use of two packages for novices, using a simple crossover design. Thisted [14] performed a further experiment to assess the adequacy of user documentation and control languages of three packages for an audience with some computer experience and statistical training. Again, he used a crossover design. Finally, Francis and Sedransk [10] describe experiments, on the performance of software for analyzing survey data. Indices of merit were computed to measure tabulating power and the simplicity of the user language. These two concepts, which are apparently qualitative, required detailed, although admittedly debatable, definitions in order for them to be represented quantitatively.

Quantitative representation of qualitative properties also made possible a comparative review of over one hundred statistical systems, which used a model based on the *life cycle* of a statistical analysis to organize users' ratings of fifty-five program features and compared them with the corresponding developer's ratings (Francis [8]).

All of these experiments, and others listed in the bibliography of Francis [7], illustrate the need for the careful use of the techniques of experimental design. Statisticians have a particular role to play here in the choice of test problems and in removing the effect of the many controllable and uncontrollable factors from the comparative measures of performance.

Effect on Statistical Software Quality

In 1973 the Section on Statistical Computing of the American Statistical Association (ASA) declared its concern for the accuracy of statistical software. It established a committee which prepared a report summarizing the opinions of over one hundred contributors, in which desirable characteristics of statistical software were listed and discussed (Francis, Heiberger, and Velleman [9]). Since then there has been considerable improvement in the quality of at least the major statistical program systems. During this time sessions on the evaluation of statistical software have been held at virtually every annual conference of the ASA and of the Symposium on the Interface of Computer Science and Statistics. A growing interest has been seen in similar sessions of COMPSTAT, the European Symposium on Computational Statistics.

The publication of the results of comparisons and evaluations of statistical software has an effect both on developers and on users. No standards have been established for either the development or the use of statistical software. Some developers have given insufficient attention to the accuracy of their product and to methods of protecting the user against misusing the program. Users, on the other hand, in publishing the results of analyses in which computers have been used, typically fail to identify precisely the software and hardware used. Publication of software comparisons and evaluations encourages the developers to improve their products, and prompts users, and more particularly editors and referees of journals, to take a closer look at which packages are being used in statistical analyses.

The goal of these comparisons and evaluations is to promote both the best use of existing statistical software and the development of better software. Through the comparisons of the performances of packages in performing standard test problems, de facto standards for statistical software, both existing and proposed, are established, standards which will evolve over time as the state of the software art improves.

Further Work

This paper has argued the need to evaluate software performance with a user's perspective, that is, (1) to specify and characterize quantitatively the difficulty of the problem, (2) to measure the accuracy of computed solutions, and (3) to assess the usability of the output. Particular reference was made to statistical software. All three of these components of evaluation support the case for the need for quantitative measures of software. Implied also is the need for a set of standard test problems and solutions which can be used to evaluate existing software and write specifications for new software.

There is a need for well-designed experiments to evaluate certain features of software, particularly experiments which compare at least two software systems. There is a need for these experiments to be replicated under different environments.

To capture the many dimensions of problem difficulty, accuracy of solutions, and usefulness of output by a few quantitative measures presents challenges both applied and theoretical. To carry out the many and continuing experiments necessary to monitor the quality of software will require the contributions of many researchers.

References

[1]   M. S. Bartlett.
        The statistical conception of mental factors.
        British Journal of Psychology 28:97-104, 1937.

[2]   A. E. Beaton, D. B. Rubin, and J. L. Barone.
        The acceptability of regression solutions: Another look at
            computational accuracy.
        Journal of American Statistical Association 71(353):158-168,
            1976.

[3]   G. R. Bryce and H. G. Hilton.
        Local installation of packages.
        Proceedings of the Statistical Computing Section, American
            Statistical Association, pages 13-15, 1975.

[4]   J. M. Chambers.
        Linear regression computations: Some numerical statistical
            aspects.
        Bulletin of the International Statistical Institute, 45(4):245-254,
            1973.

[5]   H. Dingle.
        The rational and empirical elements in physics.
        Philosophy 13:148-65, 1938.

[6]   A. Fitzsimmons and T. Love.
        A review and evaluation of software science.
        Computing Surveys 10:3-18, 1978.

[7]   I. Francis, editor.
        A comparative review of statistical software I.
        *The International Association for Statistical Computing
            Exhibition of Statistical Software*, IASC, Voorburg,
            Netherlands, 658 pages, 1979.

[8]   I. Francis.
        A taxonomy of statistical software.
        To appear in COMPSTAT 1980: Proceedings in Computational
            Statistics, Physica-Verlag, Vienna, 1980.

[9]   I. Francis, R. M. Heiberger, and P. F. Velleman.
        Criteria and considerations for the evaluation of statistical
            program packages.
        American Statistician 29(1):52-56, 1975.

[10] I. Francis and J. Sedransk.
A comparison of software for processing and analyzing surveys.
Bulletin of the International Statistical Institute 48, 1979.

[11] I. Francis and R. Valliant.
The novice with a statistical package: Performance without competence.
Proceedings of Computer Science and Statistics: 8th Annual Symposium on the Interface, pages 110-114, 1975.

[12] M. H. Halstead.
Elements of Software Science.
New York: Elsevier North-Holland, 1977.

[13] J. Longley.
An appraisal of least squares programs.
Journal of the American Statistical Association 62:819-841, 1967.

[14] R. A. Thisted.
User documentation and control language: Evaluation and comparison of statistical computer packages.
Proceedings of the Statistical Computing Section, American Statistical Association, 1977.

[15] P. F. Velleman and I. Francis.
Measuring statistical accuracy of statistical regression problems.
Proceedings of Computer Science and Statistics: 8th Annual Symposium on the Interface, pages 122-127, 1975.

[16] P. F. Velleman, J. R. Seaman, and I. E. Allen.
Evaluating package regression routines.
Proceedings of the Statistical Computing Section, American Statistical Association, pages 82-83, 1977.

Questions Asked after the Conference

Fred Sayward

In your paper you argue that a standard set of test problems should be assembled so that experiments can be conducted to compare the performance of software systems. While this method has worked well for evaluating statistical packages, it must be remembered that although the specifications of the software were well known it still took several iterations by several researches to arrive at some agreeable test problems. Wouldn't the imprecise nature and the time constraints of the typical software project seem to rule out for most software the approach to performance analysis you are suggesting? Why not?

Ivor Francis

Our panel is making the case that specifications for the performance of software, both existing and proposed, be made more quantitative. The principal argument of my paper is that these specifications should include characteristics which are important to the ultimate users, namely accuracy and usability.

The proposal that test problems be designed to determine whether or not a product, existing or proposed, meets specifications is appropriate to any undertaking, whether it be the development of a new aircraft or the development of a new software system. It is not suggested that the designing of test problems, plus the choosing of quantitative measures (metrics) to characterize both these problems an a system's degree of success or failure, is either easy or static. Indeed it is the quantitative characterization of these problems and their solutions, not the solution of the problems, that presents the greatest challenges to the applied and theoretical researchers.

Chapter 10:
Performance Evaluation: A Software Metrics Success Story

W. C. Lynch

XEROX Systems Development Division
3333 Coyote Road
Palo Alto, CA 94304

J. C. Browne

Department of Computer Science
University of Texas at Austin
Austin, Texas 78712

Abstract

Performance evaluation has generally accepted metrics both for externally observable aspects of performance (response times, rates of completion for externally defined units of work, etc.) and for the performance of intermediate abstract machines (resource consumption for execution of a given externally defined unit of work, etc.). Values for these metrics are, however, often strongly context dependent. Performance evaluation has generated a scientific approach to the development of the field. There is an effort to extract and define invariant principles and there is a systematic hierarchic structuring of performance models to relate concepts and metrics at different levels of abstraction. The fundamental problem: the absence of operational (software engineering) procedures which will yield software systems with desired values for given metrics. The principal research directions recommended are (1) the development of invariant principles which establish direct relations between elementary units of work (abstract machine work) and externally defined units of work and (2) the development of technology for increasing the effectiveness and efficiency of the performance evaluation process. There is a strong need for the development of abstract machine models appropriate for different types of workload elements. An associated unmet requirement is a capability for describing and specifying performance characteristics for these abstract machines.

Definition and Overview

Performance evaluation is determining and evaluating in context the completion time and resource consumption of processes executing specified tasks on abstract machines. The early emphasis of performance evaluation (when hardware was the expensive element of a computer system) was on the definition and measurement of (incomplete) sets of internal (efficiency oriented) metrics for resource utilization. The goal was to maximize the efficiency of the computer system itself. Current emphasis is on the definition, measurement, and prediction of external metrics (such as response time and work throughputs). The goal is to maximize effectiveness and productivity of the total system.

An abstract machine may be a hardware realized machine or an abstract machine defined in terms of abstract operations such as the comparisons of a sort algorithm or the multiplies of matrix algorithms. A process may be a complex software system such as a data base transaction system operating under an operating system on a large mainframe or it may be a simple sort algorithm on a dedicated microcomputer. The task may be large, e.g., determine the flux of neutrons 1,000 kilometers from the epicenter of a given thermonuclear detonation, 30 degrees from the direction of a 10 mph prevailing wind, or small, such as sorting a short and almost sequential list of names. We confine ourselves here to considering performance evaluation of substantial software systems on non-trivial (although perhaps abstract) computer systems. The performance evaluation of systems executing elementary units of work appears here only as components of a hierarchic model, used systematically to lead to the evaluation of the performance of a substantial software system. The study of processing of elementary units of work, algorithm analysis, is a substantial sub-branch of computer science in its own right. It is logically a part of performance evaluation but is in practice largely executed by complexity theorists. The interested reader is referred to the classical books of Knuth [18,19,20], Horowitz and Sahni [16] and Aho, Hopcroft, and Ullman [1] for substantive works on algorithm analysis.

The very rapid rise in the role of person-machine interactions in work environments makes the external metric of responsiveness one of the most important criteria by which a software system can be evaluated. Lack of human scale responsiveness can have significant impact on the productivity of persons using a computer system and may lead to the propagation of increased cost throughout an organization. Factors such as long delivery times and costs of housing, operations and communications as well as hardware costs make the prediction of performance of software systems in advance of implementation a significant problem. The dramatic rise in the integration of computer systems into communication systems, monitoring systems and control systems (the generic class of imbedded computer systems) is also increasing the significance of performance metrics, both internal and external. The space and power limitations of process control environments often limit hardware capacity enhancement and force considerations of efficiency in the use of resources for imbedded systems. There have in the past few years appeared several texts and monographs on performance evaluation [10,11,15]. These books offer introductions to techniques and to representative applications.

Performance Metrics

The metrics for the evaluation of performance of large software systems are disjoint in concept from the metrics for the evaluation of other properties such as maintainability and understandability. The *-ability* properties are difficult to define. Their definition cannot now be based on independent concepts. The rates at which a computer system delivers completed externally defined units of work are definable and measurable. External performance metrics (e.g., transaction or interactive response time, work throughput) are thus simple and well defined and understood. Complexity arises from the fact that a performance metric value is not an intrinsic property of the software subsystem alone. Many metrics are meaningful only in the context of a specific hardware configuration and a specific workload to be executed by the software system. Thus interpretation of given metric values is subjective and context dependent. Note that performance evaluation has developed a hierarchically structured model where external metrics from one level become parameters for higher levels (see Section 3, following). The internal metrics of resource consumption by a given external unit of work or device utilizations under a given load of external work are also in principle directly measurable and have readily interpretable value sets. There is still here subjectivity and context dependence due to lack of comparability between different physical realizations of the same abstract machines.

There are two other aspects of performance evaluation which need comment. One is the concept of cost effectiveness to obtain a given level for an important metric such as responsiveness. It is here that an additional connection is made between internal and external metrics. It is often possible to quantify costs in terms of resource power or resource availability. Another is the concept of total system effectiveness where system definition includes the users who interface directly with the system. This area of the quality of human interfaces is an extremely significant problem in its own right. This article will confine itself only to the time responsiveness aspects of the human interface.

The Status of Performance Evaluation

The paper by Browne and Shaw [3] in this volume develops a paradigm for science in the context of software systems. This paradigm points to the need for invariant principles as a basis for a science and to the almost universal presence of a hierarchic concept structure relating more complex objects to less complex objects.

Performance evaluation has two serious streams of research aimed at development of basic invariant principles. The *software physics* work of Kolence [21], Hellerman [14], etc., is based upon information theory concepts. The theme of this work is to establish operational concepts for information transformations similar to the entropy concept in physics or information theory. Unit operations on unit objects would in these models create precisely known changes in state variables. The operational analysis work of Buzen and Denning [5,6] is a second and fundamental approach. Operational analysis is a sort of cosmology for software whereby the relationships between the macro metrics of a system are developed without resorting to the process through integration through micro metrics and models.

Performance evaluation also has a set of structural concepts and relationships which enable the hierarchic integration of individual unit models into a parametric system model. There are two sub-streams — the process-event model [12,22] which was developed for simulation languages and the network of queues model [17, 13] which was picked up by computer science as an analytical tool in the 1960's and has been extensively developed in the computer system problem area.

There is a third stream of work focusing on the development of a whole catalog of unit models which act as atoms in the hierarchic models developed by simulation or queuing network analysis. Included in this stream is the development of a large collection of single queue models whose integration into a system is addressed by the network queuing models refered to above. Some of the non-queuing models are quite simple but some (e.g., models of locality of reference effects) [30] are not. Algorithm analysis is currently the dominant source of unit models.

The interdependence of software system performance evaluation with hardware and workload concepts is easily seen in the queueing models. The queue-server pairs generally represent hardware devices (and their software schedulers) while the resource consuming units are labelled jobs. The actual service patterns (including the value of the response time metric) are controlled both by the system's internal service facilities (hardware and software) and by the external requests for service presented by the workload. Figure 10-1 is a simple queueing network model of a computer system including a processing unit (CPU), I/O devices (DISK), and user terminals (TTY). The units of work can be modelled as originating in the TTY server. There may be several types of requests, each with a distinct requirement for CPU and DISK service. The arcs in the figure represent the flow of job requests from device to device. The $P_{i,j}$ labeling the arcs are the probability that a job of type i takes branch j.

The dependence of software system performance evaluation on abstract machine execution and workload pervades through all hierarchic levels for system models. Algorithm analysis is performance evaluation of a simple system on an abstract machine under a given workload. A sort algorithm is, for example, said to require $O(n \log n)$ comparisons if the elements being collated are initially in a random sequence. The abstract execution machine is a comparison machine while the significant property of the workload, the initial state of the element sequence, is specified. This structure carries to the much higher levels of abstraction of queueing network models. A queue may represent a disk or a CPU while the service patterns of the servers are determined jointly by the specification of the workload, the application algorithms and the scheduling disciplines for the software system.

Courtois [8] discusses decomposability and hierarchic structuring in general and mathematical terms. Browne et al. [2] give a case study of the application of hierarchic modeling based upon queueing networks. Chandy, Herzog, and Woo [7] develop the formal basis for analytic

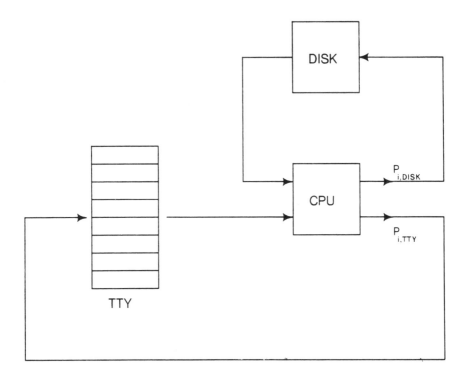

Figure 10-1: A Simple Queueing Network Model

determination of the single queue equivalent to a network of queues.

In a multi-level hierarchic system, the metrics of the lower level abstract machine are available as and become the parameters of the higher layers of the system. This systematic layer-by-layer construction methodology focuses attention on those metrics of the lower level abstract machine which are the required parameters for the performance evaluation of the upper levels.

This provides another explanation for the focus on response times as important metrics for computer systems. The response times of the lower layers become service times for the upper layers. In a person-machine system, the response times of the machine subsystem determine a subset of the service times in the upper, human interfacing system.

Performance evaluation can thus, in several senses, be regarded as conforming to the paradigm for a software science. There are, albeit not widely accepted, invariant principles which can be related to observables and used to define fundamental properties of scale for performance. There is a theoretical structure (models of systems) which establishes useful input/output relationships which can be used both for an ex-post-facto explanation of the observed behavior of an existing system and for the prediction of future behavior of systems perturbed from base line models.

While there is now emerging a methodology for the prediction of performance of a software system in a given hardware and workload context we do not yet have good synthesis or design capabilities. We are not at present able to achieve the software engineering of performance properties. There do not at present exist well established methodologies for the development of software systems which, put in the context of a hardware configuration and a workload, will deliver specific performance metric values. However, work in this area of design and synthesis is now in progress. Attention is called to [11] and to the papers of Smith and Browne [27,28,29], of Sanguinetti [25], and of Shaw [26] for several different aspects of this problem.

It is not difficult to identify the impediments to the achievement of a design methodology. A design methodology must have as its first step an understanding of the design space (or a useful subset of the design space) as a function of the system specifications. The second step of a methodology must be a set of procedures which selects a specific design from the space. Each potential design selected can then be evaluated by the analysis procedures described above. Additional procedures can then be used to select better designs sequentially until an acceptable one is achieved.

At present, we have only a modest amount of research attempting to describe the design space for synthesis of large software systems with most of the existing work concentrated in the data base area. The procedures which systems programmers use to select initial and improved designs is not well understood and not nearly ripe for automation.

The relationship of performance evaluation analysis to computer system design seems quite analogous to the relationship of finite element analysis to the design of structures in civil engineering. In the latter case, an adequate understanding of the design space and of procedures for selecting improved designs has permitted the substantial automation of all kinds of structures from bridges to airframes. It has also improved our knowledge of the relationships between requirements and the value of metrics in those areas.

Research and Development in the Performance Evaluation Area

A fundamental problem in performance evaluation is the requirement for a methodology which can predict both internal and external performance metrics from specifications rather than from base line cases. In imbedded systems, in particular, it is important to know performance metrics before a commitment is made to physically engineer a particular set of resources into a constrained environment. This general problem leads to a number of problems which must be solved to support this constructive capability.

First, our analytic capability still has some shortcomings in both unit models and the analysis of hierarchic systems integration. More realistic unit models need to be constructed, particularly addressing the question of service costs due to information accessing and due to algorithm setup times. Better unit models describing memory space requirements are also needed and most of the models could be improved by including parametric dependencies on workload characteristics. With respect to hierarchic systems integration, the representational capabilities of rapidly soluble system models, such as queueing network models, need to be greatly extended. Additional capabilities which are required include capabilities for rapid solution of finite queues and extended sets of scheduling disciplines. Attention also needs to be paid to the development of model structures appropriate to asynchronous (data flow control) concurrent executions. See the Petri net based models of Noe and co-workers [4,9,23,24].

Second, we need to develop design (or design sketch) methodologies which are capable of integrating the existing analysis capabilities if we wish to establish causal relationships between specific system requirements and specific values of system metrics. As noted before, this will require a substantial increase in our fundamental knowledge of the topology of the design space as a function of the system specification. Improvement in this area depends upon development of better unit model structures. It will also require a substantial increase in our fundamental knowledge of procedures for selecting good (or improved) designs from the design space. This is a very general problem pervading all of software development.

Third, as we develop fundamental invariant principles at various levels of the system, we will be able to validate model system representations against the invariant principles since they establish direct relationships between requirements and performance metrics. The current state of affairs is, however, that both the information theory and operational analysis approaches are currently in a state of flux and are not accepted widely as fundamental at their respective levels of abstraction. Continuing basic research in this area is sorely needed as the payoffs for any progress in this area are quite large.

References

[1]   Aho, A. V., Hopcroft, J. E. and Ullman, J. D.
        The Design and Analysis of Computer Algorithms.
        Addison-Wesley, Reading, 1974.

[2]   Browne, J. C., Chandy, K. M., Brown, R. M., Keller, T. W.,
        Towsley, D. F. and Dissly, C. W.
        Hierarchical techniques for the development of realistic models
            of complex computer systems.
        Proceedings of the IEEE 63 (1975), pages 966-977.

[3]   Browne, J. C. and Shaw, M.
        Toward a scientific basis for software evaluation.
        This volume.

[4]   Bryant, R. F. and Dennis, J. B.
        Concurrent Programming.
        In P. Wegner (editor), *Research Directions in Software
            Technology*, MIT Press, Cambridge, 1979.

[5]   Buzen, J. P.
        Fundamental laws of computer systems performance.
        *Proceedings of the International Symposium on Computer
            Performance Modeling, Measurement, and Evaluation*,
            Cambridge, Mass., March 1976, pages 200-210.

[6]   Buzen, J. P. and Denning, P. J.
        The operational analysis of queueing network models.
        Computing Surveys 10, 225-262 (1978).

[7]   Chandy, K. M., Herzog, U. and Woo, L.
        Parametric analysis of queueing networks.
        IBM Journal of Research and Development 19, 36-42 (1975).

[8]   Courtois, D. J.
        *Decomposability: Queueing and Computer System
           Applications.*
        Academic Press, New York, 1977.

[9]   Crowley, C. P. and Noe. J. D.
        Interactive graphics simulation using modified Petri nets.
        Proc. on Simulation of Computer Systems, Boulder, Colorado,
           August 1975, 177-185.

[10]   Drummond, M. E.
        *Evaluation and Measurement Techniques for Digital
           Computers.*
        Prentice-Hall, Englewood Cliffs, 1973.

[11]   Ferrari, D.
        Computer System Performance Evaluation.
        Prentice-Hall, Englewood Cliffs, 1978.

[12]   Franta, W. R.
        Process/Event Driven Simulation.
        American-Elsevier, 1975.

[13]   Graham, G.
        Guest Editors Overview: Queueing Network Models of
           Computer Systems Performance.
        Computing Surveys 10, 219-224 (1978).

[14]   Hellerman, L.
        A Measure of Computational Work.
        IEEE Trans. Comp. 21, 439-446 (1972).

[15]   Hellerman, H. and Conroy, T. F.
        Computer System Performance.
        McGraw-Hill, New York, 1975.

[16]   Horowitz, E. and Sahni, S.
        Fundamentals of Computer Algorithms.
        Computer Science Press, Inc., Potomac, MD, 1978.

[17]   Kleinrock, L.
        *Queueing Systems: Vol. 1, Theory and Vol. 2, Computer
           Applications.*
        John Wiley and Sons, 1975.

[18]   Knuth, D. E.
         *The Art of Computer Programming, Vol. 1: Fundamental
            Algorithms.*
         Addison-Wesley, Reading, 1968.

[19]   Knuth, D. E.
         *The Art of Computer Programming, Vol. 2: Semi-Numerical
            Algorithms.*
         Addison-Wesley, Reading, 1969.

[20]   Knuth, D. E.
         *The Art of Computer Programming, Vol. 3: Sorting and
            Searching.*
         Addison-Wesley, Reading, 1973.

[21]   Kolence, K.
         Software Physics and Computer Performance Measurements.
         Proc. ACM Natl. Conf. 25, 1024-1040 (1972).

[22]   MacDougall, M. H.
         Process and Event Control in ASPOL.
         Proc. Symp. on the Simulation of Computer Systems, Boulder,
            Colorado, August 1975, 35-51.

[23]   Noe, J. D. and Nutt, G. J.
         Macro E-nets for Representation of Parallel Systems.
         IEEE Trans. Comp. C-22, 718-727 (1973).

[24]   Peterson, J. L.
         Petri Nets.
         Computing Surveys, 9, 223-252 (1977).

[25]   Sanguinetti, J.
         A Technique for Integrating Simulation and System Design.
         *Proc. of Conf. on Simulation, Measurement and Modeling of
            Computer Systems*, Boulder, Colorado, August 1979, 163-
            172.

[26]   Shaw, M.
         *A Formal System for Specifying and.Verifying Program
            Performance.*
         Dept. of Computer Science Report, Carnegie-Mellon University,
            June 1979.

[27]   Smith, C. and Browne, J. C.
         Performance Specifications and Analysis of Software Designs.
         *Proc. of Conf. on Simulation, Measurement and Modeling of
            Computer Systems*, Boulder, Colorado, August 1979, 173-
            182.

[28]   Smith, C. and Browne, J. C.
         Modeling Software Systems for Performance Predictions.
         Proc. CMG, Group X, Dallas, Texas, December 1979.

[29]   Smith, C. and Browne, J. C.
         Aspects of Software Design Analysis: Concurrency and
            Blocking.
         To be presented at *Performance '80*, Toronto, May 1980.

[30]   Spirn, J. R.
         Program Behavior: Models and Measurements.
         Elsevier North-Holland, Ltd., New York, 1977.

Questions Asked after the Conference

Fred Sayward

In describing the state of the art and in recommending research
directions, most of the results on performance evaluation you listed are
of an asymptotic nature (e.g., sorting requires n log n time and job
response time under round robin scheduling is proportional to the
service time) where one is not concerned with the constants. However,
in tuning a system the constants play a critical role.

My experience has been that system tuning is black art understood by
few, if by anyone. Would you include system tuning under the heading of
performance evaluation? What is its state of the art? What steps should
be taken to make system tuning more of scientific discipline?

Bill Lynch and Jim Browne

Tuning a system is actually modifying a large complex system, the
operating system or a major basic software subsystem. The effects of
modification can often be predicted from appropriate performance
models. Logically, *tuning a system* usually consists of alterations in
scheduling algorithms. It is often possible to predict approximately the
effects of changes in complex real scheduling algorithms from a
knowledge of simple limiting cases. There are also a few simple
principles which guide design of scheduling systems. (See Browne in

the September 1980 issue of *IEEE Transactions on Computers*.) Thus there does exist a scientific basis for the engineering of performance of existing systems. The *black art* concept arises from the fact that in-depth knowledge of very complex systems is needed to apply this knowledge base. *Computing Surveys* is a good source for a state-of-the-art analysis of solution techniques and applications of queueing network models.

Chapter 11:
Statistical Measures of Software Reliability

Richard A. DeMillo

School of Information and Computer Science
Georgia Institute of Technology
Atlanta, GA 30332

Frederick G. Sayward

Department of Computer Science
Yale University
New Haven, CT 06520

Introduction

Estimating program reliability presents many of the same problems as measuring software performance and cost. The central technical issue concerns the existence of an independent objective scale upon which to base a qualitative judgment of the ability of a given program to function as intended in a specified environment over a specified time interval. Several scales have already been proposed. For example, a program may be judged reliable if it has been formally proved correct [1], if it has been run against a valid and reliable test data set [2], or if it has been developed according to a special discipline [3]. While these concepts may have independent interest, they fail to capture the most significant aspect of reliability estimation as it applies to software. Most software is unreliable by these standards, but the degree of unreliability is not quantified. A useful program which has not been proved correct is unreliable, but so is, say, the null program (unless by some perversity of specification the null program satisfies the designer); an operationally meaningful scale of reliability should distinguish these extremes.

What is needed is a measure R(t) which, for a given piece of software (i.e. a system, subsystem, program, or program module) gives an index of operational reliability in the time interval [0,t]. The most commonly proposed such index is the reliability function of traditional reliability theory [4,5,6]:

R(t) = *probability* of survival at time t

In the sequel, we will sketch the outlines of the traditional theory that is most relevant to software reliability estimation, give a brief critical analysis of the use of the traditional theory in measuring reliability, and describe another use of the R(t) measure, which we believe more closely fits the intuitive requirements of the scale we asked for above.

The Statistical Theory

R(t) is to be interpreted as the probability of satisfactory performance of the system in the time interval [0,t]. It is an underlying assumption that satisfactory performance at time t implies satisfactory performance in the interval [0,t]. A second assumption is that the form of the theory does not change from system to system; in particular, it should not matter whether one estimates R(t) for a total system, a subsystem, or a single component.

The second assumption suggests the following analysis of complex systems. Let R_i be the reliability function for the ith component of the system and define a random variable x_i for each component as follows.

$$x_i = \begin{cases} 1 \text{ if } R_i(t) \geq a_i \\ 0 \text{ otherwise} \end{cases}$$

The performance of the system is then determined by a 0-1 valued function.

$$\varphi(x_1,...,x_n)$$

Simple examples of such performance functions are the functions for series systems,

$$\varphi(x_1,...,x_n) = x_1 x_2...x_n = \min\{x_i \mid i \leq n\},$$

and for *parallel* systems,

$$\varphi(x_1,...,x_n) = 1-(1-x_1)...(1-x_n) = \max\{x_i \mid i \leq n\},$$

For more complex situations, one may place additional requirements on the performance function; for instance, the function may have to be coherent:

for all i, $x_i \leq y_i$ implies $\varphi(x_1,...,x_n) \leq \varphi(y_1,...,y_n)$

The reliability function for the entire system is then

$$R = Prob\{\varphi(x_1,...,x_n) = 1\}.$$

For extremely simple models of subsystem failure (e.g. fixed independent probabilities of satisfactory performance) such an analysis gives the combinatorial probabilities of success and failure in a very handy form.

For realistically complex systems, however, R(t) is determined by probability distributions that draw their properties from observable parameters of the system. For computer programs, as well as many other systems, it is inconvenient to estimate satisfactory performance directly. Instead one uses the observed *failures* of the system. Let F(t) be the failure distribution of the system and let f be the corresponding probability density function. Then

$$R(t) = 1 - F(t) = \int f(y)dy.$$

Often, the reliability distribution is more conveniently expressed in terms of the *failure* rate (or hazard rate). Let B(t,h) represent the conditional probability of failure by time t + h given survival at time t:

$$r(t) = \lim_{h \to 0} \{B(t,h)/h\} = f(t)/R(t)$$

The failure rate determines the reliability since

$$1-F(t) = R(t) = \exp\left(-\int r(y)dy\right).$$

One obtains a reliability function for a given system by a variety of paths: nontechnical considerations like mathematical tractability, empirical observations, and theoretical analysis of more fundamental properties of the system that is subject to failure.

The exponential distribution

The exponential distribution is exactly characterized by those systems that have constant failure rates.

$$R(t) = \exp(-\theta t)$$

$$r(t) = \theta\exp(-\theta t)/\exp(-\theta t) = \theta$$

The exponential distribution is the most widely used of the reliability models, even when there is slight evidence to justify its use. It is, of course, among the most tractable of the statistical models, but it can lead to serious errors when the underlying distribution corresponds to failures that do not occur randomly or that depend on the history of the system. The popularity of the exponential distribution (and the tendency to observe it in complex systems) is no doubt due in part to the following fact. Let R_i be the reliability of the ith component and let

$$R = \prod R_i.$$

If there are N components in the system, then define

$$r^*(N) = r_1(0) + \dots + r_N(0).$$

Then R tends to be an exponential distribution:

$$R(t) \rightarrow \exp(-r^*(N)t) \text{ as } N \rightarrow \infty.$$

whenever three technical conditions are met:

1. Each failure rate grows as $r_i(t) = r_i(0) + a_i t^\theta$ as $t \rightarrow 0$.
2. $r^*(N) \rightarrow \infty$ as $N \rightarrow \infty$.
3. $r^*(N)(a_1 + ... + a_N)$ is bounded by a fixed constant.

These conditions are, however, not easy to satisfy, and several of the most common distributions of reliability theory fail one or more of the restrictions.

The Weibull distribution

In an attempt to circumvent the more serious deficiencies of the exponential distribution, one is led to a family of distributions in which the failure rate is a function of time.

$$R(t) = \exp(-t^a/\theta),$$

$$r(t) = a\,t^{a-1}/\theta.$$

Obviously, the failure rate is increasing or decreasing depending on the value of a. The properties of the R(t) distribution for certain choices of a and θ make it a good descriptor of mechanical *breakdown* phenomena, such as failures due to metal fatigue or other kinds of stress. The Weibull distribution varies wildly from the exponential distribution in its statistical properties (compare, for example, the nth moments of the two) and thus cannot be used interchangeably with predictable results. A special case of the Weibull distribution, called the Rayleigh distribution is common in software reliability studies. This class of distributions fails to satisfy restrictions (1) and (3) above, so that it is difficult to argue that interconnections of Rayleigh-distributed components may behave with simpler failure rates.

Truncated normal distribution

The failure rate that is most commonly cited as applicable to software life cycles is the so-called bathtub curve illustrated in figure 11-1. As opposed to the Weibull-type distributions, the normal distributions model systems that wear out, such as light bulbs. Rather than dealing directly with the reliability functions, which may be applicable to only a portion of the system's life cycle, it is often convenient to combine several failure rates to model modes of failure that apply to specific stages of

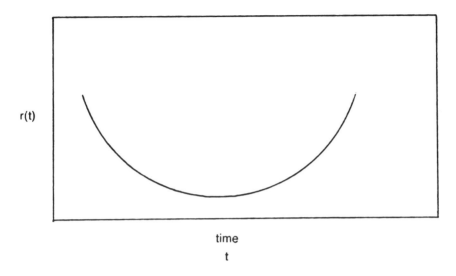

r(t)

time

t

Figure 11-1: The Truncated Normal Hazard Function

development. The wear-out models are particularly attractive in this regard. During the initial stages of operation of a large number of copies of identical systems, there is a high incidence of immediate failure (*infant mortality*). This initiation process is followed by a relatively stable region until, near the end of the useful lifetime of the systems, the incidence of failure rises.

If $\Phi(x)$ is the probability density function for a normal distribution and $\varphi(x)$ is the corresponding distribution function, then even though the expression for R(t) involves an integral that cannot be expressed in closed form, the failure rate is easily expressed:

$r(t) = a\varphi(at-t_0)/\Phi(at_0).$

Renewal theory

A common application for the reliability theory sketched above is in the prediction of the cost of operation as the system functions within some prescribed maintenance policy. By knowing statistical properties of operational periods (e.g. such statistics as mean time between failures) and repair periods (e.g. replacing a failed component reduces the number of failed components by one) a variety of useful system parameters can be calculated. In concert with system design and maintenance policies (for example, survival can be insured by redundancy and repair effort reduced by keeping a stock of spare parts) standard optimization models can be used to minimize total operating costs due to failure. The mathematics of the optimization techniques dictates very simple statistical models for these applications. Among the simplifications that seem to be essential one frequently finds:

1. Failures are immediately detectable and attributable to a single component.
2. During periods of reduced operation the remaining load is shared by the rest of the system.
3. The renewed system and its predecessor have identically distributed failures.

Software Models

The descriptions of extant software models presented here are obtained from the DACS summaries [7]. Although a wide variety of models is covered in the DACS extracts, we will highlight those that fall within the time-dependent reliability models of the traditional theory. Figure 11-2 illustrates the use of these models.

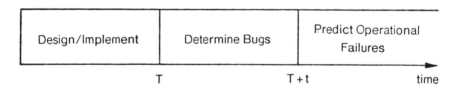

Figure 11-2: Applying Reliability Theory to Software

At time T in the system's software life cycle, the statistical model is determined, usually by controlled observations of system errors (the traditional *failures*). In the interval [T,T + t] enough data is gathered to determine a failure rate r(t). This coupled with a variety of subjective evidence concerning the behavior of the system in operation determines an estimate of the underlying failure distribution. The predictive model is then applied in the interval [T + t,T + t + k], where k is a *regenerative* time less than the operational lifetime of the system.

Table 11-1 summarizes the utilization of the traditional models summarized in the DACS report on quantitative software models [7].

Distribution	Number of Models
Exponential (including geometric and Poisson)	7
Rayleigh or Weibull	3
Normal	1

Table 11-1: Reported Software Reliability Models

As described above, the Exponential-Weibull distributions describe system failures when the system components are stressed materials. While there may be a body of experimental data that fits the appropriate failure rate functions, the assumption of one of these distributions as the underlying reliability distribution forces one or more of a number of questionable assumptions concerning errors in software. For example:

1. The number of initial program errors can be reliably estimated.
2. Error detection rate (failure rate) is proportional to the number of remaining errors.
3. Errors are discovered one at a time.
4. Once an error is detected, it can be found and removed immediately.
5. The rate at which errors occur is constant.
6. Removing an error reduces the total number of errors by one.
7. Errors are statistically independent.
8. The distribution of program inputs is known.
9. The rate at which errors are detected is proportional to the amount of time spent debugging.
10. The size of a program is constant over its lifetime.

The experimental evidence to support these assumptions is contradictory [8]. Common sense would suggest that statistical models intended to describe physical systems would be ill-adapted to software, but it is still possible that nature allows an aggregate description of the error occurrence rate in typical software that is useful in practice. One test of this is careful experimentation on the assumptions 1-10. Allen Acree of the Georgia Tech Testing Laboratory has, for instance, gathered extensive data on failure rates as related to the number of remaining errors in small programs (50-1000 lines) and found that it does support the exponential rate. In other studies, however, by Acree and Timothy Budd of the Yale Testing Laboratory, there is rather clear evidence that the strategic assumptions of independence of errors, single error occurrence, and immediate removal fail drastically in even moderately large systems. There is also considerable evidence that, for large systems, most remaining errors lie in unexecuted portions of code, which means that for these systems failure rates cannot depend on either the number of remaining errors or the debugging effort.

Certain of the remaining assumptions also appear hard to confirm. For example, there is no methodologically acceptable way of estimating initial error percentages. The most commonly proposed technique is the error seeding procedure described in Gilb [11], which is based on the population statistics calculations described in Feller's classic text [12]. While this procedure gives the best unbiased estimator for certain random populations, it can badly overestimate or underestimate the number of errors when there is nonrandom mixing of seeded and natural errors. There is experimental evidence that such nonrandom mixing must take place [9,10].

Finally, the use of the Rayleigh or Weibull distribution to model program modules presents severe mathematical difficulties for macro-modelling since these distributions are nonreproductive; that is, overall system description is not a simple aggregate of module descriptions.

The usual validation of these models is the posterior observation of failure rates and costs [14]. The experimental technique is deficient and lacks some essential size constraints to allow statistical sampling techniques to be used with acceptable confidence. Studies aimed at validating these model have led to even more confusion:

> Basically, the results of the goodness-of-fit tests and other aspects of the data analysis indicate that none of the models fit very well...The various data sets showed obvious tendencies to increasing (in time) error rates: more or less contrary to the model assumption that mean error rates should be nonincreasing. It also seems clear to us that the observed increasing error rate situation cannot simply be written of as due to the *introduction* of errors during the debugging process or due to chance...The data sets themselves have some problems of a nature unknown to us...With better data more fits might have been obtained [14].

Another set of difficulties has been clearly enunciated by Littlewood [15]. "We should be extremely careful of replacing the wealth of information in a probability distribution with simple summaries — whether these be parameters or moments of the distributions." In a sense,

Littlewood's criticisms are even more fundamental than those attained above since they go to the heart of the matter — the correct interpretation of the statistical theory.

If, indeed, the classical theory can be imported to software reliability there must be considerable attention paid to deriving relevant distributions from first principles and to developing the appropriate experimental and data gathering [12] techniques. It should be noted, however, that software errors must be viewed as design errors [8] (since there is no material wearing or stressing) and classical reliability theory does not deal satisfactorily with design errors.

Whatever the final resolution of these difficulties, it seems to us that there is no way around them. Estimations of reliability based on incorrect models, statistics improperly applied, or fuzzy notions of *error* can have unboundedly pernicious behavior. If the model doesn't fit there is simply no way to tell.

Confidence Estimation

In a sense, the goals of traditional reliability theory and software reliability measurement are fundamentally at odds with each other. We have little opportunity to create large populations of identical systems and observe failure rates to obtain statistically meaningful measurements of failure distributions as indications of relative frequencies.

The more common situation is that a *fixed* programming and/or testing validation method is used during development and/or testing in the hope to obtain some level of confidence that the software will behave as intended. The actual reliability of the system is then intertwined with this estimate of the system's reliability (since we stop testing when our estimate is satisfied).

We should then ask for experiments to confirm the level of confidence in the chosen methodology. In traditional statistical approaches to reliability, such objectively obtained parameters as number of errors observed per unit time are used to infer the appropriate distributions. We suggest that the observable parameters represent instead a *varying* quantity that represents a prior estimate of reliability. That is, we use a function r(R) to represent our level of confidence in the reliability level R of the software. For example, a program that has been subjected to mutation analysis [13] might be described by a function r with the shape shown in figure 11-3.

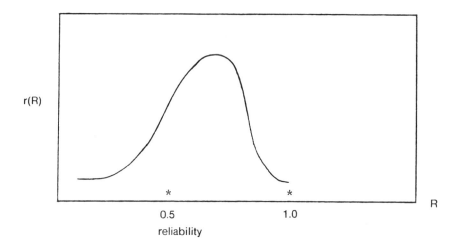

Figure 11-3: Mutation Analysis Reliability Function

It is important to note that r(R) is merely a quantitatively assessed judgment; it is not necessarily an objective probability obtained by classical techniques. The r function may, however, be based on solid evidence an may form the basis for a scientific hypothesis concerning the long-run behavior of a system. By applying Bayes' theorem [11], it is possible to gather hard evidence to support or deny the estimate of confidence r(R). From now on, we treat R as a random variable with probability density function r(R).

Suppose that in an experiment designed to refute a given reliability level R we make a large number of observations and gather a statistic, say x, that is distributed as E(x|R) for a given level R. Think of E as a distribution of errors for a given reliability; this is a quantity that can be observed and inferred in a given programming environment. The joint distribution for x and R is F(x,R). Let the associated pdf's be e and f, so that

$$f(x,R) = r(R)e(x|R).$$

The marginal density for x is:

$$g(x) = \int_R r(R)e(x|R)dR.$$

Then the conditional distribution for R is given by the density

$$h(R|x) = (r(R)e(x|R))/g(x),$$

which represents our level of confidence in R given the results of the experiment yielding x.

Even though these results merely restate Bayes' theorem, the interpretation implied by the results of the experiment yielding x is not necessarily subjective. The key is rather in the degree of objectivity with which r(R) is obtained. (See Feller's criticism of Bayesian analysis in reliability [12], page 124.)

At the heart of this treatment of software reliability is another view of the role of statistical statements. This point of view rejects the idea that a meaningful probability of correct operation can be assigned to a piece of software. Rather, any such assessment must be interpreted as a *level of confidence* in the process used to validate the program. This effectively shifts the statistical burden from the program to the methodology used to produce and validate it. One problem with the traditional approach, which we noted briefly above, is that there is no acceptable sense in which the frequency interpretation of the reliability function R(t) can apply to software; there is, for example, no reasonable application of the law of large numbers to obtain failure rates. This view of probability — the limit of a physically observable relative frequency — is not the only view. It is possible to construct alternative subjective probabilities. In fact, James Bernoulli in 1713 described probabilities as *degrees of confidence.*

Even though we use the term *subjective* in describing the non-frequency version of R(t), it does not follow that the measure represents an ad hoc assessment of reliability. For example, the prior distribution may not really represent a subjective estimate of reliability. It may be the result of experimental research an summarization. This suggests an iterative procedure for *updating* the state of knowledge regarding the reliability of the validation methodology.

Littlewood [15] also adopts the Bayesian approach — with an important extension to the software design phase. For essentially the reasons outlined above, Littlewood also rejects the frequency interpretation of R(t). He goes further, however, in exploiting the ability of Bayes' theorem to update previous reliability measurements in the light of new data: "Periods of failure-free working cause the reliability [i.e. the confidence] to improve...It is interesting to compare this with the [traditional methods in which] reliability improvements can only take place at a failure, since it is only at such a time that an error can be removed" [15]. This Littlewood cites as a contradiction to the common-sense approach to estimating software confidence — namely, that there is no a priori reason that confidence should *increase* as failures occur.

In other words, an assessment of reliability represents a judgment relative to a prior reference *standard,* which the user presumably understands and believes, and against which he is being required to wager.

A useful reliability theory, then, should incorporate notions that are so far untouched.   For example, an economic theory that develops a concept of utility for software would be extremely helpful. Hence, for the reliability measurement to be useful, it must only order uncertain events so that the user can consistently win when he adopts a rational betting strategy [16].

References

[1]   Z. Manna.
        Mathematical Theory of Computation.
        McGraw-Hill, 1974.

[2]   S. Gerhart and J. Goodenough.
        Toward a theory of test data selection.
        In R. Yeh, editor, *Current Trends in Programming Methodology
            Volume 2: Program Validation,* pages 44-79. Prentice Hall,
            1977.

[3]   E. Dijkstra.
        A Discipline of Programming.
        Prentice Hall, 1977.

[4]   K. C. Kapur and L. R. Lambertson.
        Reliability in Engineering Design.
        Wiley, 1977.

[5]   M. Zelen, editor.
        Statistical Theory of Reliability.
        University of Wisconsin Press, 1964.

[6]   R. E. Barlow and F. Proschan.
        Mathematical Theory of Reliability.
        Wiley, 1965.

[7]   DACS Software Engineering Research Review
        Quantitative Software Models.
        Data and Analysis Center for Software, Order Number SRR-1,
            IIT Research Institute, Rome, NY, March 1979.

[8]   R. Longbottom.
        Computer System Reliability.
        Wiley, 1980.

[9]   A. Acree.
        On Mutation.
        PhD thesis, Georgia Institute of Technology, 1980.

[10]   T. A. Budd.
        Mutation Analysis of Program Test Data.
        PhD thesis, Yale University, 1980.

[11]   T. Gilb.
        Software Metrics.
        Prentice Hall, 1978.

[12]   W. Feller.
        *An Introduction to Probability Theory and Its Applications
            Volume 1.*
        Wiley, 1968.

[13]   A. Acree, T. A. Budd, R. A. DeMillo, R. J. Lipton, and F. G.
            Sayward.
        Mutation Analysis.
        Report GIT-ICS-79/08, School of Information and Computer
            Science, Georgia Institute of Technology, 1979.

[14]   R. Schafer J. E. Angus, J. F. Alter, and S. E. Emoto.
        Validation of Software Reliability Models.
        RADC-TR-79-147, Rome Air Development Center, 1979.

[15]   B. Littlewood.
        Software reliability measurement, some criticisms and
            suggestions.
        Proceedings of the Software Life Cycle Management Workshop,
            pages 473-488, 1977.

[16]   M. DeGroot.
        Optimal Statistical Decisions.
        McGraw-Hill, 1970.

Questions Asked at the Conference

Martin Shooman, Polytechnic Institute of New York

You mentioned that some of the people working in the reliability modeling area compiled data showing that some modeling assumptions were false and had tried to explain this away by finding fault with the data. Can you cite some of the data? I'm not aware of any such studies.

Rich DeMillo

I don't remember the title of the report, but it was a June 1979 RADC report on validating reliability models. I'll be happy to send you the citation.

Martin Shooman

Do you know the author?

Rich DeMillo

No, no, I really don't know the author. [The report is RADC Report TR-79-147, *Validation of Software Reliability Models,* by R. E. Schafer, J. E. Angus, J. F. Alter, and S. E. Emoto, of Hughes Aircraft.]

Martin Shooman

I've worked in this area for over ten years and I don't know of any such studies so I'm a little puzzled.

Fred Sayward

One thing I might mention is that in all of the material I've seen in this area, there has been very little work done on using standard statistical tests to validate distributional assumptions. That seems to be a missing ingredient, and there are standard tests, like the chi square test and others of that nature.

Rich DeMillo

The Rome study analyzed a large mass of reliability data, some of it from internal Hughes Aircraft projects. The deficiencies of the data are discussed in the paper.

Martin Shooman

Yes, I think you're talking about a study that was done at Rome by Allan Sukert. A lot of the data did not have basic parameters on the time when certain failures occurred and other necessary data. These are necessary for some of the models that John Musa calls execution-time models. These models have been validated by other sets of data. Also, rather than make statistical tests, some people have made estimates. Then they have made measurements later when the software was placed into use. The estimates agreed to within twenty, thirty percent of the actual usage measurements. That's a rather strong proof that there is some validity to the model. One of the big problems in this area as in other areas is that it's very difficult and costly to gather data. So rather than say that the models are invalid because they haven't been validated, I think you should look at some of the studies where they have been validated.

Merv Muller

It's a comment. I think I've made it before to the panel. I get very uncomfortable when I hear people who are testing models using chi square tests. The problem of chi square is you don't know what the alternative is. It's every other possible point in the parameter space of all possible models that you could ever have thought of. It's obvious if you don't take very much data you will most likely accept the fact that you don't have enough data, or you might accept a model and you could take too much data. I don't care what the model is, you'll reject it.

Anonymous

All you need to do is go back and look at the Rand studies in the late 1940's on trying to test randomization. They put out a big thick book, and they ran many, many tests. What they really came down to on the bottom line was they couldn't come to any conclusion because the theory was lacking. And others have tried to adjust the chi square test for the fact that you have an interval of possibilities. If you insist that there's a single point (I don't care what distribution it is) you're ultimately going to reject it because you don't know what the power of the test is. You don't know what you're comparing it to. I think it would be a pity if we got hung up over a statistical test that we've developed for a certain class of statistical analysis. I like what Shooman said. I think the purpose of using data is not to test, but to try to estimate something...whatever that may be, because you're interested in the future. I may have worn out my welcome on this, but there is an inappropriate use of statistical techniques, and I don't know whether they answer the question of the validity of the model or not, but I would urge that people pay more attention to statistical theory.

Rich DeMillo

Let me ask a question of Martin Shooman, as long as he's here. It seems to me that the general consensus among people who work in engineering reliability theory is that the theory is just not well adapted to design errors. Is it your contention that the errors that you find in programs are not design errors, that they're somehow equivalent to wear-out errors? Failure errors?

Martin Shooman

Let me address the first statement. Each year at the annual Reliability and Maintainability Symposium you see between seven hundred and a thousand of these people. I regularly attend these symposia and I don't find that to be true.

Rich DeMillo

I'm talking now about the time-dependent theory.

Martin Shooman

The general consensus among these people is that this is not true. When you deal in failure of any type you find various modes of failure. It is true that in any failure of hardware the predominant mode of failure is wear-out, an actual physical failure of the device. Although you still find perhaps ten percent of the modes of failure are design errors. When you deal with software, the predominant modes of failure are design errors. This in no way invalidates the basic approach. All it means is that you end up making different models. True, your distributions may look different. But in general you're dealing with a very simplistic model. It's somewhat invariant to the distribution. People in a first-order model trying to fit data can fit an exponential model, can fit a gamma model, and so on. Sure, you may get errors of ten or twenty or thirty percent, but the techniques for estimating the parameters of the models are no more accurate than twenty or thirty percent, so the distribution is really not as important as how you're going to measure the parameters of the model. The measurement techniques are crude enough so that even using a one-parameter rather than a two-parameter model won't make very much difference in the results. The fact that software doesn't wear out is well known to all modelers and they take this into account and don't use models based on software wearing out.

Irwin Nathan, Xerox Corporation

The problem is that you have a very complex system, all kinds of subsystems routines, and human interfacing, and you really can't find out what's going on. All you know is that at certain intervals, which are randomly distributed, or distributed according to some probability distribution, you're going to get failures. You can forecast that, and as you keep improving, and finding these design anomalies, and correcting them the failure rate gets lower and lower. You eventually get to the point where you can tolerate it, OK? That's essentially what you do in hardware systems. Tolerate it. There are a number of design errors, and there are a number of components that are probably exceeding some design limit, in some way, and there are a few components that are wearing out. And you add all these things up, and you take a macro look at it, and you say, it's a constant failure rate (or whatever you have). And the same thing is probably true with software, based on what we have done up to date. I think that's where the situation is, as far as software reliability goes — to try an estimate those parameters. At least you know where you are, and you can have some statement of probability of success for a system that is going to operate and evolve. It's only when you get to the complex programs that it counts.

Rich DeMillo

The researchers that are involved in reliability estimation and in program testing should have a lot to say to each other. The assumptions that I chose for this slide [the assumptions made about the occurences of software errors] have been addressed by a number of studies in program testing. I gather from your comments and Shooman's comments that in reliability estimation you take a very summary view of the failure process. In program testing we take a microscopic view of the process. The observations that we get through program testing are fundamentally at odds with the assumptions that are built into these reliability models. For instance, take the assumption of statistically independent errors. Or constant program size.

Fred Sayward

I was going to add that one common thing you find in program testing is that most of the remaining errors are in code that hasn't been executed — or even, in some cases, can't be executed except under very bizarre conditions. That's certainly not consistent with continuous hazard functions.

Rich DeMillo

I guess what I'm doing is suggesting a number of experiments. The models, these time-dependent models, rise or fall on a given set of assumptions, and I'm saying that those assumptions can be dealt with empirically. Now, if we don't have adequate data to determine the validity of an assumption, I think that we should put it together.

Chapter 12:
The Measurement of Software Quality and Complexity

Bill Curtis

Programming Technology Center
International Telephone and Telegraph
Stratford, CT 06497

Uses for Software Metric

The measurement of software complexity is one facet of a larger effort to measure important software characteristics. Measurements of software characteristics can provide valuable information throughout the software life cycle. During development, measurements can be used to predict the resources which will be required in future phases of a project. For instance, metrics developed from the detailed design can be used to predict the amount of effort that will be required to implement and test the code. Metrics developed from the code can be used to predict the number of errors that may be found in subsequent testing or the difficulty involved in modifying a section of code. Because of their potential predictive value, software metrics can be used in at least three ways:

Management information tools

As a management tool, metrics provide several types of information. First, they can be used to predict future outcomes as discussed above. Measurements can be developed for costing and sizing at the project level, such as in the models proposed by Freiman and Park [21], Putnam [45], and Wolverton [54]. Other models have been developed for estimating productivity by Freburger and Basili [20] and Walston and Felix [52]. Such metrics allow managers to assess progress, future problems, and resource requirements. If these metrics can be proven reliable and valid indicators of development processes, they provide an excellent source of management vision into a software project.

Measures of software quality

Interest grows in creating quantifiable criteria against which a software product can be judged [38]. An example criterion would be the minimally acceptable mean time between failures. These criteria could be used as either acceptance standards by a software acquisition manager or as guidance to potential problems in the code during software validation and verification [53].

Feedback to software personnel

Elshoff [16] has used a software complexity metric to provide feedback to programmers about their code. When a section grows too complex they are instructed to redesign the code until metric values are brought within acceptable limits.

The three uses described above suggest a difference between measures of process and measures of product. Measures of process would include the resource estimation metrics described as potential management tools. Measures of cost and productivity quantify attributes of the development process. However, they convey little information about the actual state of the software product. Measures of the product represent software characteristics as they exist as a given time, but do not indicate how the software has evolved into this state. Measures used for feedback to programmers or as quality criteria fall within this second category.

Belady [3] argues that it will be difficult to develop a metric which can represent both process and product. Development of such a metric or set of metrics will require a model of how software evolves from a set of requirements into an operational program. Charting the sequential phases of the software life cycle will not provide a sufficient model. Some progress is being made on system evolution by Lehman and his colleagues at Imperial College in London [5,7,30]. In the remainder of this section, I will deal with measures of product rather than process.

Omnibus Approaches to Quantifying Software

There have been several attempts to quantify the elusive concept of software quality by developing an arsenal of metrics which quantify numerous factors underlying the concept. The most well known of these metric systems are those developed by Boehm, Brown, Kaspar, Lipow, MacLeod, and Merrit [8], Gilb [23], and McCall, Richards, and Walters

[33]. The Boehm et al. and McCall et al. approaches are similar, although differing in some of the constructs and metrics they propose. Both of these systems have been developed from an intuitive clustering of software characteristics which are illustrated in figure 12-1.

The higher level constructs in each system represent 1) the current behavior of the software, 2) the ease of changing the software, and 3) the ease of converting or interfacing the system. From these primary concerns Boehm et al. develop seven intermediate constructs, while McCall et al. identify eleven quality factors. Beneath this second level Boehm et al. create twelve primitive constructs and McCall et al. define 23 criteria. For instance, at the level of a primitive construct or criterion both Boehm et al. and McCall et al. define a construct labeled *self-descriptiveness*. For Boehm et al. this construct underlies the intermediate constructs of testability and understandability, both of which serve the primary use of measuring maintainability. For McCall et al. self-descriptiveness underlies a number of factors included under the domains of product revision and transition.

Primitive constructs and criteria are operationally defined by sets of metrics which provide the guidelines for collecting empirical data. The McCall et al. system defines 41 software metrics consisting of 175 specific elements. Thus, the metrics themselves represent composites of more elementary measures. This proliferation of measures should ultimately be reduced to a manageable set which can be computed automatically. Reducing their number will require an empirical evaluation of which metrics carry the most information and how they cluster. There are a number of multivariate statistical techniques available for performing such analyses on empirical data [39].

No software project can stay within a reasonable budget and maximize all of the quality factors. The nature of the system under development will determine the proper weighting of quality factors to be achieved in the delivered software. For instance, reliability was a critical concern for Apollo space flight software where human life was constantly at risk. For business systems, however, maintainability is typically of primary importance. In many real-time systems where space or time constraints are critical, efficiency takes precedence. However, optimizing code often lowers its quality as indexed by other factors such as maintainability and portability. Figure 12-2 presents a tradeoff analysis among quality factors performed by McCall et al. [33].

Figure 12-1: Software Quality Models

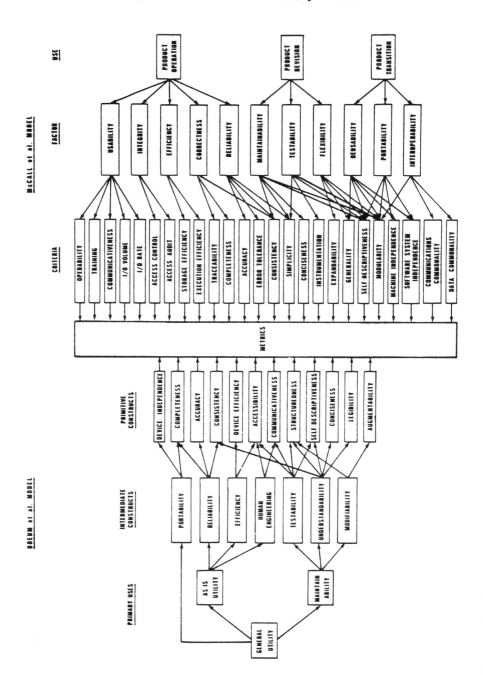

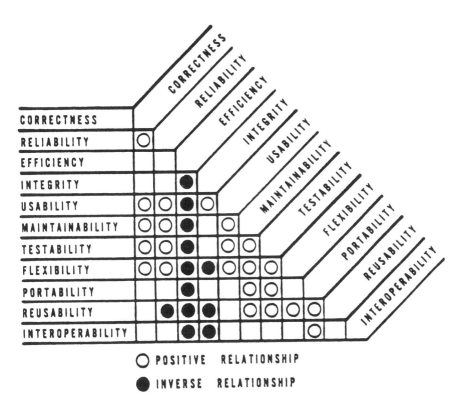

Figure 12-2: Software Quality Factors Tradeoffs

The omnibus approach to metric development had its birth in the need for measures of software quality, particularly during system acquisition. However, the development of these metrics has not spawned explanatory theories concerning the processes affected by software characteristics. The value of these metric systems in focusing attention on quality issues is substantial. However, there is still a greater need for quantitative measures which emerge from the modeling of software phenomena. Much of the modeling of software characteristics has been performed in an attempt to understand software complexity.

Software Complexity

The measurement of software complexity is receiving increased attention, since software accounts for a growing proportion of total computer system costs. Complexity has been a loosely defined term, and neither Boehm et al. nor McCall et al. included it among their constructs of software quality. Complexity is often considered synonymous with understandability or maintainability.

Two separate focuses have emerged in studying software complexity: computational and psychological complexity. *Computational complexity* relies on the formal mathematical analysis of such problems as algorithm efficiency and use of machine resources. Rabin [46] defines this branch of complexity as "the quantitative aspects of the solutions to computational problems" (p. 625). This topic is discussed in a later paper in this collection by James Browne and William Lynch. In contrast to this formal analysis, the empirical study of *psychological complexity* has emerged from the understanding that software development and maintenance are largely human activities. Psychological complexity is concerned with the characteristics of software which affect *programmer performance*.

The investigation of computational and psychological complexity has been carried on without a unifying definition for the construct of software complexity. There do, however, seem to be common threads running through the complexity literature which suggest the following definition:

> Complexity is a characteristic of the software interface which influences the resources another system will expend or commit while interacting with the software [12].

Several important points are implied by this definition. First, the focus of complexity is not merely on the software, but on the software's interactions with other systems. Complexity has little meaning in a vacuum; it requires a point of reference. This reference takes meaning only when developed from other systems such as machines, people, and other software packages. It is these systems that are affected by the *complexity* of a piece of software. Worrying about software characteristics in the absence of other systems has merit only in an artistic sense, and measures of *artistic* software are quite arbitrary. However, when there is an external reference (criterion) against which to compare software characteristics, it becomes possible to define complexity operationally.

Second, explicit criteria are not specified. This definition allows mathematicians and psychologists to become strange bedfellows since it does not specify the particular phenomena to be studied. Rather, this definition steps back a level of abstraction and describes the goal of complexity research and the reference against which complexity takes meaning. Complexity is an abstract construct, and operational definitions capture only specific aspects of it.

The second point suggests the third: Complexity will have different operational definitions depending on the criteria under study. Operational definitions of complexity must be expressed in terms which are relevant to processes performed in other systems. Complexity is defined as a property of the software interface which affects the interaction between the software and another system. To assess this interaction, we must quantify software characteristics which are relevant to it. A model of software complexity implies not only a quantification of software characteristics, but also a theory of processes in other systems. Thus, the starting point for developing a metric is not an ingenious parsing of software characteristics, but an understanding of how other systems function when they interact with software.

The following steps should be followed in modeling an aspect of software complexity:

1. Define (and quantify) the criterion the metric will be developed to predict.
2. Develop a model of processes in the interacting system which will affect this criterion.
3. Identify the properties of software which affect the operation of these processes.
4. Quantify these software characteristics.
5. Validate this model with empirical research.

The importance of this last point cannot be overemphasized. Nice theories become even nicer when they work. Preparing for the rigors of empirical evaluation will probably result in fewer metrics and tighter theories. Results from validation studies make excellent report cards on the current state of the art.

Belady [4] has categorized much of the existing software complexity literature. First, he distinguishes different software characteristics which are measured as an index of complexity: algorithms, control structures, data, or composites of structures and data. In a second dimension he describes the type of measurement employed: informal concept, construct counts, probabilistic/statistical treatments, or relationships extracted from empirical data. Most research has concerned counts of software characteristics, particularly control structures and composites of control structures and data. I will review some of the complexity research in these two areas and compare them to a system level metric.

Control structures

A number of metrics having a theoretical base in graph theory have been proposed to measure software complexity by assessing the control flow [6,10,24,32,47,55]. Such metrics typically index the number of branches or paths created by the conditional expressions within a program. McCabe's metric will be described as an example of this approach since it has received the most empirical attention.

McCabe [32] defined complexity in relation to the decision structure of a program. He attempted to assess complexity as it affects the testability and reliability of a module. McCabe's complexity metric, v(G), is the classical graph-theory cyclomatic number indicating the number of regions in a graph or, in the current usage, the number of linearly independent control paths comprising a program. When combined these paths generate the complete control structure of the program. McCabe's v(G) can be computed as the number of predicate nodes plus one, where a predicate node represents a decision point in the program. It can also be computed as the number of regions in a planar graph (a graph in regional form) of the control flow. This latter method is demonstrated in figure 12-3.

McCabe argues that his metric assesses the difficulty of testing a program, since it is a representation of the control paths that must be exercised during testing. From experience he believes that testing and reliability will become greater problems in a section of code whose v(G) exceeds 10.

Basili and Reiter [2] and Myers [41] have developed different counting methods for computing cyclomatic complexity. These differences involved counting rules for CASE statements and compound predicates. Definitive data on the most effective counting rules have yet to be presented. Nevertheless, considering alternative counting schemes to those originally posed by the author of a metric is important in refining measurement techniques.

Evidence continues to mount that metrics developed from graphs of the control flow are related to important criteria such as the number of errors existing in a segment of code and the time to find and repair such errors [13,17,48]. Chen [10] developed a variation of the cyclomatic

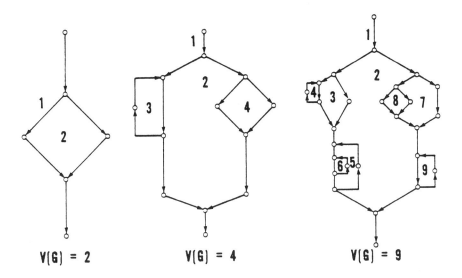

Figure 12-3: Computation of McCabe's v[G]

number that indexed the nesting of **IF** statements and related this to the information-theoretic notion of entropy within the control flow. He reported data from eight programmers indicating that productivity decreased as the value of his metric computed on their programs increased. Thus, the number of control paths appears directly or indirectly related to psychological complexity.

Software Science

The best known and most thoroughly studied of what Belady [4] classifies as composite measures of complexity has emerged from Halstead's theory of software science [26,28]). In 1972, Maurice Halstead argued that algorithms have measureable characteristics analogous to physical laws. Halstead proposed that a number of useful measures could be derived from simple counts of distinct operators and operands and the total frequencies of operators and operands. From these four quantities Halstead developed measures for the overall program length, potential smallest volume of an algorithm, actual volume of an algorithm in a particular language, program level (the difficulty of understanding a program), language level (a constant for a given language), programming effort (number of mental discriminations required to generate a program), program development time, and number of delivered bugs in a system. Two of the most frequently studied measures are calculated as follows:

$$V = (\eta_1 + \eta_2) \log_2 (\eta_1 + \eta_2)$$

$$E = [\eta_1 \, \eta_2 \, (\eta_1 + \eta_2) \log_2 (\eta_1 + \eta_2)] \, / \, [2 \, \eta_2]$$

where V is volume, E is effort, and

1. η_1 = number of unique operators
2. η_2 = number of unique operands
3. N_1 = number of operator occurrences
4. N_2 = number of operand occurrences

Halstead's theory has been the subject of considerable evaluative research [19]. Correlations often greater than .90 have been reported between Halstead's metrics and such measures as the number of bugs in a program [6,11,22,43], programming time [25,50], debugging time [13,31], and algorithm purity [15,27].

My colleagues and I have evaluated the Halstead and McCabe metrics in a series of four experiments with professional programmers. In the first two experiments [14] problems in the experimental procedures, a limit on the size of programs studied, an substantial differences in performance among the 36 programmers involved in each, suppressed relationships between the metrics and task performance. In fact it did not appear that the metrics were any better than the number of lines of code for predicting performance. However, in the third experiment [13] we used longer programs, increased the number of participants to 54, and eliminated earlier procedural problems. We found both the Halstead and McCabe metrics superior to lines of code for predicting the time to find and fix an error in the program.

In the final experiment [50], we asked nine programmers each to create three simple programs (e.g., find the maximum and minimum of a list of numbers) from a common specification of each program. The best predictor of the time required to develop and run the program successfully was Halstead's metric for program volume (see figure 12-4). This relationship was slightly stronger than that for McCabe's v(G), while lines of code exhibited no relationship.

The datapoints circled in figure 12-4 represent the data from a program whose specifications were less complete than those of the other two programs studied. The prediction of development time for this program was poor. We have observed in other studies that outcomes are

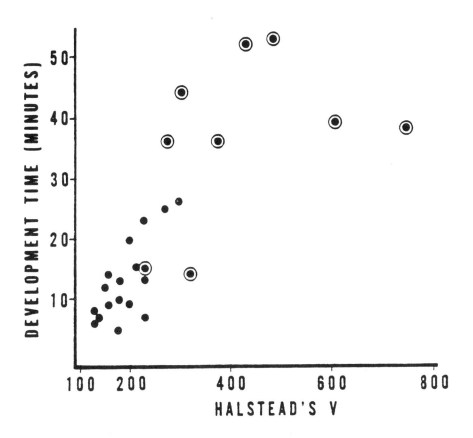

Figure 12-4: Plot of V against development time

more predictable on projects where a greater discipline regarding software standards and practices was observed [36,37]. This experiment suggests that better prediction of outcomes may occur when more disciplined software development practices (e.g., more detailed program specifications) reduce the often dramatic performance differences among programmers.

In these experiments we found Halstead's and McCabe's metrics to be valid measures of psychological complexity, regardless of whether the program they were computed on was developed by the programmer under study or by someone else. We concluded that there is considerable promise in using complexity metrics to predict the difficulty programmers will experience in working with software. Similar conclusions have been reached by Baker and Zweben [1] on an analytical rather than empirical evaluation of the Halstead and the McCabe metrics.

Halstead's metrics have proven useful in actual practice. For instance, Elshoff [16] has used these metrics as feedback to programmers during development to indicate the complexity of their code. When metric values for their modules exceed a certain limit, programmers are instructed to consider ways of reducing module complexity. Bell and Sullivan [6] suggest that a reasonable limit on the Halstead value for length is 260, since they found that published algorithms with values above this figure typically contained errors.

Regardless of the empirical support for many of Halstead's predictions, the theoretical basis for his metrics needs considerable attention. Halstead, more than other researchers, tried to integrate theory from both computer science and psychology. Unfortunately, some of the psychological assumptions underlying his work are difficult to justify for the phenomena to which he applied them. In general, computer scientists would do well to purge from their memories the magic number 7 ± 2 and the Stroud number of 18 mental discriminations per second. These numbers describe cognitive processes related to the perception or retention of simple stimuli, rather than the complex information processing tasks involved in programming. Broadbent [9] argues that for complicated tasks (such as understanding a program) the magic number is substantially less than seven. These numbers have been incorrectly applied in too many explanations and are too frequently cited by people who have never read the original articles [35,51]. Regardless of the validity of his assumptions, Halstead was a pioneer in attempting to develop interdisciplinary theory, and his efforts have provided considerable grist for further investigation.

Interconnectivity

Since the modularization of software has become an increasingly important concept in software engineering [44], several metrics have been developed to assess the complexity of the interconnectivity among the parts of a software system [3,34,40,56]. For instance, Myers models system complexity by developing a dependency matrix among pairs of modules based on whether there is an interface between them. Although his measure does not appear to have received much empirical attention, it does present two important considerations for modeling complexity at the system level [42]. The first consideration is the *strength* of a module

— the nature of the relationships among the elements within a module. The stronger, more tightly bound a module, the more singular the purpose served by the processes performed within it. The second consideration is the *coupling* between modules — the relationship created between modules by the nature of the data and control passed between them.

A primary principle of modular design is to achieve as much independence among modules as possible. This independence helps to localize the impact of errors or modifications to within one or a few modules. Thus, the complexity of the interface between modules may prove to be an excellent predictor of the difficulty experienced in developing and maintaining large systems. Myers' measure identifies data flow as a critical factor in maintainability. Nevertheless, his measure has not been completely operationally defined, and its current value is primarily heuristic. Yau and his associates [56] are currently working on validating a model of this generic type. Unfortunately, more empirical evidence is needed to assess the predictive validity of such metrics.

The focus of metrics measuring the interconnectivity among parts of a system is quite different from those that measure elementary program constructs or control flow. Metrics measuring the latter phenomena take a micro view of the program, while interconnectivity metrics view a macro level. An improved understanding of aggregating from the micro to the macro level needs to be achieved. For instance, summing the Halstead measures across modules leads to very different results from computing them once over the entire program [37].

Interconnectivity metrics may prove more appropriate parameters for macro-level models such as those which predict maintenance costs and resources. Macro-level metrics may prove better because factors to which micro-level metrics are more sensitive, such as individual differences among programmers, are balanced out at the macro or project level. Macro-level metrics are less perturbed by these factors, increasing their benefit to an overall understanding of system complexity and its impact on system costs and performance.

Conclusions

A major theme behind the effort to develop valid measures of software quality and complexity is the desire to provide predictors of the life cycle costs and resources which must be invested in a software system. A traditional measure of life cycle effort has been lines of code developed or modified per person-month. However, this is a terribly flawed measure of productivity [29], which does not provide insight into the processes that affect costs and resources. Software characteristics are believed to be much more directly related to processes which determine cost and resource outcomes. That is, the research reviewed here demonstrated that several software complexity metrics are related to the number of errors left in a section of code and the ease of debugging and modifying the code. Software errors and the effort required to find and eliminate them are a major driver of software costs and resources. For instance, an error caught during system specification may be 50 times cheaper to repair than one detected in system testing [29]. To the extent that software metrics can provide feedback on error-proneness throughout the life cycle, they become a means of estimating and controlling costs and resources.

Research needs to be conducted at two levels of analysis. At the macro level, appropriate metrics need to be developed that relate to system costs and effort. Most existing measures are computed directly from the code. If measures can be developed that use information available during the initial requirements allocation or software system specification, they could be used in costing and sizing models. Metrics computed on tested code could be used as input to software reliability models that require an estimate of delivered errors. Metrics computed at the macro level will be valuable for management information and prediction.

Software metrics computed at the micro level, such as those of Halstead and McCabe, will be of primary value in developing models of software development and maintenance processes. Continued research needs to determine the most important characteristics affecting software development and maintenance tasks. It is also possible that the importance of these characteristics will vary by the nature of the task and the capability of the programmer. For instance, should different software characteristics prove to be better predictors of performance based on the capability of the programmer, they may provide insight into how a programmer's method of understanding software matures. Such an understanding could lead to designing better training techniques.

The current state of the art is that interesting relationships have been demonstrated. Future research needs to refine the metrics, develop predictive equations, validate them on large data sets, and refine the metrics as software technology changes.

Four topics which deserve immediate attention because of their relevance to the current problems in software development are:

1. Define metrics relevant to the interface among program modules.
2. Define metrics relevant to the dataflow within a module.
3. Identify the types of information available in a functional specification which may be used to predict future project outcomes and product quality.
4. Develop measurement techniques which compare the relative attributes of a program written in different languages.

Acknowledgements

I would like to thank Laszlo Belady, Sylvia Sheppard and Drs. Elizabeth Kruesi and John O'Hare for their thoughts and comments. Some of this paper was drawn from work supported by the Office of Naval Research, Engineering Psychology Programs (Contract # N00014-79-C-0595) and has appeared in a paper published in the *Proceedings of the IEEE*, Vol. 12, no. 9, pages 1144-1157, 1980. However, the opinions expressed in this paper are not necessarily those of the Department of the Navy. Most of the work leading to this paper was performed while Dr. Curtis managed the Software Management Research Unit at Information Systems Programs, General Electric Company in Arlington, VA.

References

[1]   A. L. Baker and S. H. Zweben.
A comparison of measures of control flow complexity.
Proceedings of COMPSAC '79, pages 695-701. IEEE, New
    York, 1979.

[2]   V. R. Basili and R. W. Reiter.
Evaluating automatable measures of software development.
*Proceedings of the Workshop on Quantitative Software Models
    for Reliability, Complexity, and Cost*, pages 107-116. IEEE,
    New York, 1980.

[3]   L. A. Belady.
Software complexity.
Software Phenomenology, pages 371-383. AIRMICS, Atlanta,
    1977.

[4]   L. A. Belady.
         Complexity of programming: A brief summary.
         *Proceedings of the Workshop on Quantitative Software Models
            for Reliability, Complexity, and Cost*, pages 90-94. IEEE, New
            York, 1980.

[5]   L. A. Belady and M. M. Lehman.
         A model of large program development.
         IBM Systems Journal 15(3):225-252, 1976.

[6]   D. E. Bell and J. E. Sullivan.
         Further investigations into the complexity of software.
         MITRE Technical Report MTR-2874. MITRE, Bedford,
            Massachusetts, 1974.

[7]   G. Benyon-Tinker.
         Complexity measures in an evolving large system.
         *Proceedings of the Workshop on Quantitative Software Models
            for Reliability, Complexity, and Cost,* pages 117-127. IEEE,
            New York, 1980.

[8]   B. W. Boehm, J. R. Brown, H. Kaspar, M. Lipow, G. J. MacLeod,
            and M. J. Merrit.
         Characteristics of Software Quality.
         North Holland, Amsterdam, 1978.

[9]   D. E. Broadbent.
         The magic number seven after fifteen years.
         In A. Kennedy and A. Wilkes, editors, *Studies in Long-Term
            Memory*, pages 3-18. Wiley, New York, 1975.

[10]   E. T. Chen.
         Program complexity and programmer productivity.
         IEEE Transactions on Software Engineering 3:187-194, 1978.

[11]   L. M. Cornell and M. H. Halstead.
         Predicting the number of bugs expected in a program module.
         Computer Science Department Technical Report CSD-TR-205.
            Purdue University, West Lafayette, Indiana, 1976.

[12]   B. Curtis.
         In search of software complexity.
         *Proceedings of the Workshop on Quantitative Models for
            Reliability, Complexity, and Cost,* pages 95-106. IEEE, New
            York, 1980.

[13]   B. Curtis, S. B. Sheppard, and P. Milliman.
         Third time charm: Stronger prediction of programmer
              performance by software complexity metrics.
         *Proceedings of the Fourth International Conference on
              Software Engineering,* pages 356-360. IEEE, New York,
              1979.

[14]   B. Curtis, S. B. Sheppard, P. Milliman, M. A. Borst, and T. Love.
         Measuring the psychological complexity of software
              maintenance tasks with the Halstead and McCabe metrics.
         IEEE Transactions on Software Engineering 5:96-104, 1979.

[15]   J. L. Elshoff.
         Measuring commercial PL/1 programs using Halstead's
              criteria.
         SIGPLAN Notices 11:38-46, 1976.

[16]   J. L. Elshoff.
         A review of software measurement studies at General Motors
              Research Laboratories.
         *Proceedings of the Second Software Life Cycle Management
              Workshop,* pages 166-171. IEEE, New York, 1978.

[17]   A. R. Feuer and E. G. Fowlkes.
         Some results from an empirical study of computer software.
         *Proceedings of the Fourth International Conference on
              Software Engineering,* pages 351-355. IEEE, New York,
              1979.

[18]   A. B. Fitzsimmons.
         Relating the presence of software errors to the theory of
              software science.
         In A. E. Wasserman and R. H. Sprague, editors, *Proceedings of
              the Eleventh Hawaii International Conference on Systems
              Sciences,* pages 40-46. Western Periodicals, 1978.

[19]   A. B. Fitzsimmons and L. T. Love.
         A review and evaluation of software science.
         ACM Computing Surveys 10:3-18, 1978.

[20]   K. Freburger and V. R. Basili.
         The Software Engineering Laboratory: Relationship Equations.
         Computer Science Department Technical Report TR-764.
              University of Maryland, College Park, Maryland, 1979.

SOFTWARE METRICS: AN ANALYSIS AND EVALUATION

[21] F. R. Freiman and R. E. Park.
      PRICE software model version 3: An overview.
      Proceedings of the Workshop on Quantitative Software Models for Reliability, Complexity and Cost, pages 32-41. IEEE, New York, 1980.

[22] Y. Funami and M. H. Halstead.
      A software physics analysis of Akiyama's debugging data.
      Proceedings of the MRI 24th International Symposium: Software Engineering, pages 133-138. Polytechnic Press, New York, 1976.

[23] T. Gilb.
      Software Metrics.
      Winthrop, Cambridge, Massachusetts, 1977.

[24] T. F. Green, N. F. Schneidewind, G. T. Howard, and R. Pariseau.
      Program structures, complexity and error characteristics.
      Proceedings of the Symposium on Computer Software Engineering, pages 139-154. Polytechnic Press, New York, 1976.

[25] R. D. Gordon and M. H. Halstead.
      An experiment comparing FORTRAN programming times with the software physics hypothesis.
      AFIPS Conference Proceedings 45:935-937, 1976.

[26] M. H. Halstead
      Natural laws controlling algorithm structure.
      SIGPLAN Notices 7(2):19-26, 1972.

[27] M. H. Halstead
      An experimental determination of the *purity* of a trivial algorithm.
      ACM SIGME Performance Evaluation Review 2(1):10-15, 1973.

[28] M. H. Halstead
      Elements of Software Science.
      Elsevier North-Holland, New York, 1977.

[29] T. C. Jones.
      Measuring programming quality and productivity.
      IBM Systems Journal 17(1):39-63, 1978.

[30] M. M. Lehman.
      Programs, programming and the software life cycle.
      Proceedings of the IEEE 68(9):1060-1076, 1980.

[31]   L. T. Love and A. Bowman.
         An independent test of the theory of software physics.
         SIGPLAN Notices 11:42-49, 1976.

[32]   T. J. McCabe.
         A complexity measure.
         IEEE Transactions on Software Engineering 2:308-320, 1976.

[33]   J. A. McCall, P. K. Richards, and G. F. Walters.
         Factors in Software Quality.
         General Electric, Command and Information Systems,
            Technical Report 77CIS02, Sunnyvale, California, 1977.

[34]   C. L. McClure.
         *Reducing COBOL Complexity through Structured
            Programming.*
         Van Nostrand Reinhold, New York, 1978.

[35]   G. A. Miller.
         The magic number seven, plus or minus two.
         Psychological Review 63:81-97, 1956.

[36]   P. Milliman and B. Curtis.
         An evaluation of modern programming practices in an
            aerospace environment.
         Proceedings of the Third Digital Avionics Systems Conference.
            IEEE, New York, 1979.

[37]   P. Milliman and B. Curtis.
         *A Matched Project Evaluation of Modern Programming
            Practices.*
         RADC-TR-80-6 (two volumes), Rome Air Development Center,
            Griffiss Air Force Base, New York, 1980.

[38]   S. N. Mohanty.
         Models and measurements for quality assessment of software.
         ACM Computing Surveys 11:251-275, 1979.

[39]   D. F. Morrison.
         Multivariate Statistical Methods.
         McGraw-Hill, New York, 1967.

[40]   G. J. Myers.
         Software Reliability.
         Wiley, New York, 1976.

[41]   G. J. Myers.
         An extension to the cyclomatic measure of program complexity.
         SIGPLAN Notices 12(10):61-64, 1977.

[42]   G. J. Myers.
        Composite/Structured Design.
        Van Nostrand Reinhold, New York, 1978.

[43]   L. M. Ottenstein.
        Quantitative estimates of debugging requirements.
        IEEE Transactions on Software Engineering 5:504-514, 1979.

[44]   D. L. Parnas.
        On the criteria to be used in decomposing systems into
            modules.
        Communications of the ACM 15:1053-1058, 1972.

[45]   L. H. Putnam.
        A general empirical solution to the macro software sizing and
            estimating problem.
        IEEE Transactions on Software Engineering 4:345-361, 1978.

[46]   M. O. Rabin.
        Complexity of computations.
        Communications of the ACM 20:625-633, 1977.

[47]   P. Richards and P. Chang.
        Localization of variables: A measure of complexity.
        General Electric, Command and Information Systems,
            Technical Report 75CIS01, Sunnyvale, California, 1975.

[48]   N. Schneidewind and H. M. Hoffman.
        An experiment in software error data collection and analysis.
        IEEE Transactions on Software Engineering 5:276-286, 1979.

[49]   S. B. Sheppard, B. Curtis, P. Milliman, and T. Love.
        Modern coding practices and programmer performance.
        Computer 12:41-49, 1979.

[50]   S. B. Sheppard, P. Milliman, and B. Curtis.
        Experimental evaluation of on-line program construction.
        Proceedings of COMPSAC '80, pages 505-510. IEEE, New
            York, 1980.

[51]   J. M. Stroud.
        The fine structure of psychological time.
        New York Academy of Sciences Annals 138(2):623-631, 1967.

[52]   C. E. Walston and C.P. Felix.
        A method of programming measurement and estimation.
        IBM Systems Journal 16:54-73, 1977.

[53]   G. F. Walters.
        Applications of metrics to a software quality management (QM)
            program.
        In J. D. Cooper and M. J. Fischer, editors, *Software Quality
            Management*, pages 143-157. Petrocelli, New York, 1979.

[54]   W. R. Wolverton.
        The cost of developing large scale software.
        IEEE Transactions on Computers 23:615-634, 1974.

[55]   M. R. Woodward, M. A. Hennell, and D. Hedley.
        A measure of control flow complexity in program text.
        IEEE Transactions on Software Engineering 5:45-50, 1979.

[56]   S. S. Yau and J. S. Collofellow.
        Some stability measures for software maintenance.
        Proceedings of COMPSAC '79, pages 674-679. IEEE, New
            York, 1979.

Questions Asked after the Conference

Fred Sayward

Most of the current complexity measures are based on the product (e.g.,
source code) and their relationship to cost and effort have been
extensively analyzed. The number of metrics that one could define on
source code seems unlimited in number. Are there any accepted meta-
rules for proposing a new complexity measure? For example, all things
being equal, if P_1 cost more to build than P_2 then I would expect P_1 to be
more complex than P_2. That is, complexity measures should in some
sense be monotonic with respect to cost. What, if any, are the meta-rules
for validating complexity measures? What types of suggestions do you
have for filtering out anomalous and redundant metrics? Are controlled
experiments a possible way for establishing that a complexity measure
obeys meta-rules?

Bill Curtis

This is one of those questions you always get in your pre-dissertation
oral exams. The answer requires the regurgitation of several text books.
It is interesting to note, however, that most students in computer science
would be unprepared to handle this question. Research programs which
would like to emphasize this type of research must incorporate a heavy
dose of experimental design, measurement theory, and statistics. For a

more considered answer to your question, I would refer you to my article in the September 1980 issue of the *Proceedings of the IEEE*.

Chapter 13:
Complexity of Large Systems

L. A. Belady

IBM Watson Research Center
P.O.Box 218
Yorktown Heights, NY 10598

Domain of Study

At first approximation a program, including a large software system, is a piece of text, suitable for machine processing. This processing is usually compilation resulting in a bit-string of zeros and ones — the object code — which, when loaded into the machine, is capable of guiding further processing of information. Obviously, the compiler itself is a program whose bit-string, derived from its text, guides the machine to process other programs' text into object code.

A program first of all must be correct. But we also require that, during execution, machine resources be economically used. Programs may be equivalent in the sense that the same input data is always processed into the same output data. Yet programs may significantly differ in their execution time and memory demand on the same machine. Researchers active in the discipline of computational complexity study algorithms from this resource demand point of view. On the more empirical side, operating system designers and modelers study the interaction of programs sharing a single computer. The purpose is to find better coordination of program execution, i.e. to reduce idleness of resources and to increase system throughput.

These studies thus consider the complex execution *dynamics* of programs and seek answers to questions like: Which algorithm, expressed in the program text, is best for a given machine configuration; or which resource allocation strategy, or parameter setting, is to be applied in an operating system? Notice, however, that the structure, format, and appearance of the program text, and indeed the entire history of its development, the way it was created, are considered irrelevant in this context of machine performance. All but the execution dynamics have been abstracted away.

At this point we would like to distinguish between small programs and large scale software systems. This we base on whether the quality of the program text and of other documents is a significant factor in the total cost of data processing. A small program is usually the intellectual product of a single person or of an informally cooperating and communicating team, and the program text rarely serves as a working document for others than its creators. In contrast, we will call *software* those systems whose dynamics of evolution demands the planned and coordinated activity of a human organization, spans many project phases, and lasts several years. Here, program text and other documents play a significant role of communication within the organization.

In fact, program evolution can be pictured as a sequence of forms, or documents, the last one being the text ready for compilation. Forms in earlier phases are, for example, the requirements documentation, the specification sheets, the many design documents of increasing detail, and all of the above in different versions, as later on modifications are performed on the software system. The process of creating one form out of another is today a predominantly manual activity. This is why large scale programming is so costly and error prone. Since man-to-man communication is a significant component of the process, the structure, arrangement, availability, style, and clarity of representation of each of these forms strongly influence cost and quality. Again, the program, its text, is not only the input to the computer, but even more importantly the major means of human communication in development and maintenance.

The current question is: How can we capture, possibly numerically, properties of text and other software documents, to help predict development cost, schedule, and the reliability of the final product or to help evaluate the impact of new tools and techniques? We tend to use the word complexity to describe informally the difficulty we encounter in developing software, or the software's resistance to modifications. Note, however, that we want measures of complexity related to a human process, and not to a machine procedure as is the case with computational complexity, or with machine resource allocation. The latter is being studied quite well in other disciplines. We rather discuss here several quantification efforts being proposed for the programming process.

State of the Art

There seems to be a consensus that complexity of programming has to do with program properties other than the sheer size of program text or document. Intuitively, complexity has many other factors: preparedness of the crew (training and experience), connectedness of components, easy reach of relevant information (availability of files, libraries, consulting experts). Complexity also appears as variety vs. repetition, or surprise vs. predictability — just to give a few ideas. But all of these factors ultimately manifest themselves in the amount of time spent on the task. Thus time itself could be the global measure of at least the symptoms of complexity.

It is the decomposition of aggregate time, and the association of the resulting time components with particular software attributes, which are the main issues here. For example, one could treat separately the complexity of the distinct activities of specification, design, maintenance, etc. This makes even more sense if we consider that the early (design) phases of developing modularly structured large software are characterized by allocating functions into modules and then firming up the interfaces. In contrast, later (implementation) phases are involved with the intramodule aspects of programming in the syntax of some language. In fact, many of the metrics proposed so far and mentioned below can be classified into the two categories of intermodule and intramodule complexity.

In general, it is more difficult to capture the complexity of creating software than of modifying it. In fact, one of the earliest published complexity metrics was deduced from observations made on the evolution — maintenance and enhancement — of modularly structured operating systems. This metric was defined to be the extent to which changes get diffused into the software, measured as the fraction of modules changed while transforming the old into a new system version. The underlying idea is that the smaller the number of components involved, the less complex, i.e. less time consuming, the modification. Probably the effect is not linear: Twice as many components to work with may take more than twice as much time.

With such a variety of activities along the life-cycle phases, it is not surprising that so many, more or less relevant, papers on complexity can be found in the literature. A recent article [1] published in the *Proceedings of the Workshop on Quantitative Software Models* late last year presents a two-dimensional classification of papers related to complexity (see [1] and table 13-1). Some of the papers specifically study software,

	Informal	Counts	Probabilistic	Empirical
Software				
Algorithms	Chaitin	Aho Traub	Rabin Chaitin Pippinger	
Control Structure	Chapin	McCabe Farr Myers Cobb Woodward	Chen	Savage
Data		Valiant Yin	McKeeman	Basili Lehman
Composite Constructs	Hoare	McClure Rugaber Halstead Knuth Mills Gileadi/Ledgard		Walston/Felix Feuer Elshoff Kolence Uhrig Weissman Stucki
Non-Software				
Systems	Parnas Simon Myers Jones	Belady/Lehman Basili Gilb	Belady/Beilner Haney Williams Belady/Evangelisti	Ferdinand VanEmden
Hardware	Allan	Edwards Considine	Cook/Flynn	
Tools		Halstead Lawson	Laemmell/Shooman	Symes
Understanding	Weaver	Schorer	Klare McKee	VanGigch Curtis/Love Weissman

Table 13-1: Categories of Complexity Papers

and they are grouped in the upper half of the matrix. Papers in the lower half also contain ideas applicable to software, but are more general.

The approaches of the papers vary significantly. Some of them are descriptive and informal, others are of a quantitative nature. The latter can be further classified by approaches: Informal, counting objects, expressing events in probabilistic terms, or making use of organized observations. The four vertical subdivisions of the table correspond to these classes.

Another survey of the literature on complexity is an RADC report [2]. Although its classification scheme is somewhat different, the message from both is clear: We are not short of ideas but we have very few tested ideas, or validated metrics which we could safely recommend to measure and compare complexity of software. The current state of the art is that of early exploration of potentially useful approaches. Before presenting our recommendations for short term research in complexity metrics we would like to illuminate further the state of the art through a few representative examples. To do this we quote a passage from the mentioned survey [1]. Other examples, or some examples amplified, can also be found in the paper on "Programming Complexity" by Curtis in the same volume [3].

Some Examples[1]

"In the category of deterministic control flow complexity the best known work is McCabe's. With the control flow graph of the program given, he proposes as a complexity measure the number of distinct execution sequences which are possible along the directed graph. The application of this metric has become quite widespread, because the number of paths is easy to extract automatically from existing (and machine stored) programs. This approach also appeals to intuition: a person reading a program must mentally follow all control paths in order to fully understand the program. Unfortunately the even more complex activity of following data reference paths is completely neglected in this model.

"Another control flow based measure was proposed by Woodward, et al. The basis of their approach is program text, amended by lines which interconnect statements where control may be passed between them. These lines occasionally cross each other and thus create *knots*. The complexity then is assumed to be proportional to the knot-count. Indeed, well-structured, easy-to-read programs have less knots, but again data references are not included here (although the knot method could include data graphs as well).

---

[1]The examples are all referenced in the bibliography of [1], from which this entire section is quoted.

"Also related to the above approaches are Cobb's *reachability* measure, Myers' extension to McCabe's model, and an early paper by Farr and Zagorsky proposing the density of **IF** statement as a measure of complexity.

"Significantly different is the approach taken by Yin and Winchester. Here data flow complexity is considered basic, and the associated graph's departure from its spanning tree is defined to be the measure of complexity. The rationale is that in a tree a unique path leads to each node — a sort of minimum complexity.

"The most comprehensive of the deterministic approaches based on program object counts is unquestionably Halstead's software science. It is based on the four counts of: distinct operators, operands, and total occurrences of operators and operands in the program. From these numbers bounds and estimates of program size, programming effort, etc., are derived. The approach has received considerable attention. Often, experimentalists summarize their own results in terms of Halstead measures, or test and verify the claims of software science. Such work has been reported for example by Curtis.

"There are too many other deterministic proposals to mention them all. Due to its originality, however, we cite here Mills' proposal to measure complexity of a program by the length of text necessary to prove its correctness. (Will this motivate for simplicity?)

"However interesting and promising, information theory based approaches are rather rare in the literature and appear concentrated either around the study of probabilistic algorithms or of interconnected systems in general. More specifically for program systems, Belady and Beilner attempted to capture the complexity of program evolution by introducing distributions over the set of modules of the probability that (a) a change hits a given module and (b) another module becomes impacted by the change. The scheme is formally quite close to the entropy approach of van Emden's. Another, earlier, effort by Haney models the change propagation along the probability graph spanned by modules as nodes. Unfortunately, very little experience exists with these approaches and at present they are subjects of research.

"There are numerous papers...on readability, complexity of comprehension, frequency distributions of words and symbols in natural languages as compared to program symbols...But again, experience with respect to their usability is practically nil.

"Much more promising are the empirical approaches. In one of the earliest studies, L. Weissman at the University of Toronto identified a number of program constructs and attributes and ranked them according to the associated relative difficulty which a group of students encountered while programming. By implication, a construct is more complex the more difficult it is to apply and understand it in a program. Encouraged by earlier results, recently more professional psychologists turned their attention to the empirical evaluation of programming complexity. They usually conduct joint efforts with computer scientists, with the objective to understand human factors of programming tools and techniques and to test in practice the measures arrived at by speculation, which would otherwise be doomed to oblivion."

Potential Impact

Although reasons for using complexity metrics are manifold, ideally one would like to extract from measurements and observations a small set of numbers which could be used to predict quality, which in turn may help estimate maintenance load and the cost of further development and enhancement. In addition, it would be important to compare, and learn from, projects on different products and under different circumstances. To do so one would need *model rules*, as they exist and are applied in experimental physics.

Complexity metrics could also be instrumental in deciding whether a piece of software is ready for replacement because it is so complex that modifying it would cost more than redesigning it from scratch. Note that this implies the capability to predict costs of both modification and new design. New design is often done with advanced tools and techniques, which were not available while developing the old version. Absence of experience in this case makes prediction even more difficult.

There are some other, perhaps less important, potential applications of these metrics. Programming styles could for example be classified, and programmers easily identified on the basis of programs they wrote. Similarly, language classification could become more meaningful, at least as applied to the ranking of programmer — language pairs or program — programmer — language triplets. But detailed discussion of these issues is certainly beyond the scope of this writing.

Recommended Short-term Research

As already indicated, most of the early work on software complexity involved ad hoc, isolated, and uncoordinated efforts. As a result, the definition of objects (for example, lines of code, language constructs) in the domain of individual studies seems quite arbitrary, thus preventing systematic comparison either of different metrics or of measured values of the same metric applied to different systems and environments. Nevertheless, we should not ignore some promising results already reported, or the many efforts in progress. It is therefore necessary to

- Standardize terms and dimensions of observable and measurable attributes, that of programs and of the development — maintenance process, such that ongoing exploratory work in metrics be not disrupted and, instead, exchange of experience encouraged. This research effort, based on already existing reports and data, should be sponsored by DOD rather than a smaller organization, in order to enlarge the data base and to enforce commonality.

We already mentioned that quantification of from-scratch design and development of large software could be too hard a nut to crack. It is therefore recommended that

- Study of patterns in trends and measurements of evolving large systems be conducted, using standard definitions as suggested above. The resulting data should then be used to build models of software evolution, which in turn can be used to explore alternative approaches more rapidly and less expensively than with full scale experimentation. A byproduct of this effort could be metrics for complexity of maintenance and enhancement.

We feel that probabilistic, or information-theoretical, models of structural complexity, some of them studied already, should be refined. We recommend that

- Interdisciplinary research be started in the area of structural complexity, employing computer scientists, statisticians, and information theorists. For example, concepts such as locality (in this case, that of information required by participants of the life cycle) which was so successfully applied in program execution dynamics, should be examined and whether similar concepts are applicable to the quantitative evaluation of the impact of tools and techniques on development and maintenance.

A final note: Complexity studies related to the execution time behavior of programs, such as complexity of computation, are in good hands and these efforts do not need further reinforcement. It is the evolution dynamics of large software which needs attention.

References

[1]   L. A. Belady.
        Survey of software complexity measures.
        *Proceedings of the IEEE/NY Poly Workshop on Quantitative
            Software Models*, Kiamesha Lake, New York, October 1979.

[2]   Quantitative Software Models.
        DACS (Data & Analysis Center for Software), Griffiss AFB,
            March 1979.

[3]   Bill Curtis.
        In search of software complexity.
        *Proceedings of the IEEE/NY Poly Workshop on Quantitative
            Software Models*, Kiamesha Lake, New York, October 1979.

Questions Asked at the Conference

Klaus Gradischnig, University of Rochester

In my own experience, it looks like the programming and design of a distributed system is much harder than of a conventional one. Do you know about any (complexity) studies in this area?

Les Belady

Personally, I think, the answer could come from a reasonable extension, or fall-out, of a somewhat related but simpler case, but I wish we had at least that already, pretty firmly. And you are right that it is wrong to jump into a world which is even more complex than the current one, and not wait until we understand and can formalize the current.

Chapter 14:
Software Maintenance Tools and Statistics

Mervin E. Muller

Director of Computing Activities
World Bank[2]
1818 H Street N.W.
Washington, DC 20433

Abstract

Many of the activities involved with the maintenance of computing applications suggest areas of research into needed software metrics. Software metrics are needed to help evaluate what is taking place and to predict future demands for maintenance. Improvements in software metrics, in turn, can lead to more effective maintenance. Maintenance of a computing application tends to include more activities than are appropriate, and maintenance is typically more complex and costly than desired. In most respects we lack the tools and statistical techniques to gain an adequate picture of what is going on. We need a conceptual framework for maintenance and a related set of software metrics. These objectives raise a series of research questions, some of which are addressed in this paper.

The life cycle model is used as a reminder that earlier events in the design and development phases influence all future maintenance activities. The life cycle model is reviewed here as an aid in understanding what software maintenance tools and statistics can offer. Appropriate perspective is sought through better understanding of the possible relationships among the maintenance, enhancement, and replacement phases. Activities affecting the maintenance of computing applications require meaningful data and analysis, and for this purpose several concepts are introduced. They are:

1. Attributed Cause and Attributed Need,

2. Contamination Effects,

---

[2]Comments made here do not represent official views of the World Bank.

3. Cascading-Causal Chains and Linkages,

4. Indirect and Direct Tools.

The role of statistical theory and application is explored in order to indicate how statistics can help guide future research on needed software maintenance tools. Areas of needed research are outlined, together with some pitfalls to be avoided in pursuing the research challenges.

Introduction

The expenditure of resources on the maintenance of a computing application can be substantial. To what extent are such expenditures necessary? Can the expenditures be reduced by different ways of carrying out the steps leading to the design, implementation, and use of a computing application? Maintenance of a computing application is a little understood subject, and therefore its true role should receive special attention. It is not particularly difficult to define maintenance as is done below or to specify the activities associated with it. However, it is often surprisingly difficult to collect uncontaminated data to measure the effects of various policies or factors which influence the need to perform maintenance or to determine the amount of effort that is spent to perform maintenance. I believe that considerable research effort needs to be addressed to overcoming the obstacles mentioned in this paper if appropriate software metrics are to be developed to aid in understanding and managing maintenance activities. In particular, there is a need for software tools to aid both the maintenance activities and the collection of relevant data to support meaningful analysis. Employment of statistical theory can aid in describing what is taking place and can aid in predicting future events. Statistical theory can be an effective help in deciding how to collect, analyze, and present data underlying the software metrics. However, the appropriate use of statistical theory will require careful planning and the willingness to seek new statistical tools.

What is Maintenance?

Depending upon who is asking this question and who is answering, one can either fail to appreciate its complexity or be so absorbed with the complexity that useful communication does not take place. I have found it useful to answer the question by providing two definitions, *maintenance status* and *maintenance work* [6].

Maintenance status

For practical purposes here, let us consider the set of materials, including the program (or package, or system) and all related job controls, documentation, and test data, as a computing application.

Maintenance is being defined in terms of an application rather than a program since the needs of a user are usually greater than the boundaries of a single program. The application should be defined as being in maintenance status if it has been tested and distributed to the intended users on the assumption that it can provide the capabilities that were specified for the application.

Maintenance work

Maintenance work on a computing application in maintenance status is that effort spent on changing the actual programming (without enhancing the scope of the application), performing tests related to programming or programming changes, changing the documentation or test data, or providing assistance to those who have difficulty using the computing application. Maintenance work can also become necessary because of environmental changes such as the need to change controls because of equipment changes or operating system changes. In addition, maintenance work can relate to changing procedures to use the application, to training people in how to use the application following a change, or to ensuring that changes have been distributed to the user and correctly incorporated into the user's installation.

As we shall see below, other types of activities can masquerade as maintenance and many distortions arise from this source.

Why Consider a Life Cycle Approach?

The life cycle approach is being used because of the relationships among its maintenance, enhancement, and replacement phases.

A life cycle model may help one to understand better and measure the development and maintenance of a computing application. It should provide perspective for the many interdependent activities required to develop and use a computing application. There is a rich literature available on life cycle models, and the general conceptual framework helps to identify and relate the various stages throughout the life cycle of a computing application, illuminating the relationships among them — in particular, design, development, maintenance, enhancement, and replacement of the application.   Maintenance, enhancement, and replacement effort can be given consistent definitions within a life cycle framework, although in the real world these stages are often not easy to distinguish in terms of the available data.   Moreover, the physical life-cycle analogy is sometimes indistinct when applied to the intellectual effort represented by a computer program.   It is because it is difficult to translate the desirable characteristics of a life cycle model into the real world of collecting and analyzing data related to maintenance activities that many interesting and challenging research problems in software metrics arise, some of which are considered in later sections.   Only with the passage of time will it be possible to judge whether or not a life cycle model makes a significant contribution to understanding maintenance of computing applications.

Factors Influencing Maintenance

There are both technical and psychological factors that affect what is accomplished as maintenance activity and these factors influence the possible choice of data to establish useful metrics.   These factors are elucidated in the next few sections from several different viewpoints to illustrate how data are subject to contamination effects and activities in the   life   cycle   that   precede   or   follow   maintenance   activities. Contamination effects are considered in order to identify an obstacle to developing valid measures, i.e., software metrics.   It may happen that two different types of metrics are needed: those to aid in the explanation and description of the maintenance effort, and those to aid in predicting the future effort and cost of maintenance.

Attributed Cause and Attributed Need

Introduction

The title of this section identifies one type of information contamination in relation to maintenance that occurs due to psychological factors rather than technical considerations. These types of contamination must be identified and considered when collecting and analyzing data to avoid drawing invalid inferences from the data.   I know of no single and consistent process to eliminate the finger-pointing that arises between the user and developer of a computing application when a user asserts that the computing application is *working incorrectly.* Often one sees work on a computing application that is done as a maintenance task when in fact the resources are really being expended for an enhancement. The misclassification of effort as maintenance can arise because the person incompletely or incorrectly specified his need in the first place, or because the developer of the computing capability has misunderstood or failed to provide the *needed* capability, or because needs have changed. What an uninvolved observer can detect, usually after the fact, is a defective communication between the *user* and *developer* of a capability about an attributed need or the attributed cause of dissatisfaction.

Sleeping dogs and *open patients*

It is often the case that renewed user attention, or new users, will awaken the need (*sleeping dogs*) for doing something about an application that has escaped attention or has not been considered important enough to warrant formal maintenance in the past. Similarly, programmers frequently notice, during maintenance (i.e., while the patient is open), things that need correction or enhancement and proceed to make the necessary changes. Far from being harmful, these behavior patterns may bring about significant improvements; however, they tend to distort our data on maintenance work.

Are some *bugs* acceptable?

Most organizations will permit a needed maintenance change to a program, but many organizations require justification to establish why an enhancement is necessary. This adds to the information contamination. In an ideal situation, there would be no blame or no penalty to the user or developer so that one could easily separate maintenance and enhancement activities. Clear and complete design specifications may produce better accuracy. I believe that part of the problem arises because of the mistaken belief that a computing capability can and should be designed, implemented, and used in a single step. For the foreseeable future I believe a partial solution to this problem would be to have computing applications evolve through a series of design-implementation-use iterations. However, this iterative process requires careful data identification to separate maintenance, enhancement, and replacement activities.

The research questions that arise here relate to setting up reproducible human factor experiments to understand either how to avoid the *attributed need, attributed cause* syndrome and its resulting data contamination or how to adjust the data to offset the effect of human factors. One should question how much priority should be given to such research effort, because of the uncertain payoff. However, to make significant progress in software metrics for maintenance work, this problem must be overcome.

Contamination Effects

Introduction

Since contamination of data may result when users and developers of a computing application treat an enhancement requirement as a maintenance requirement, this problem might be reduced or avoided by having the maintenance done by someone other than developers, though this creates an inevitable transfer cost. However, there are also other forms of misclassification. Various stages in the life cycle affect tasks defined as maintenance and therefore contribute to the contamination of data identifying work done as maintenance. There are other types of contamination that also need to be understood and identified before research on software metrics can aid designers and maintainers of computing applications. Some are discussed below.

Cumulative Effects of Changes

The life cycle model seems most appropriate for a mechanical device subject to wear. For a computing application, the analogue of wear is the process of *deterioration* that occurs to a computing application as a result of maintenance or enhancements, or accommodation to shifting user needs. The deterioration or quasi-deterioration can be in the programs, controls, test data, or documentation. The end result is that the controls, a program or piece of documentation no longer has an evident integrity of design, or perhaps that the coherence of its design is no longer present. It could be argued that *pure* maintenance activities should not affect the useful life of a computing application if they were not contaminated by a concealed element of enhancement. Unfortunately, several myths have developed around typical attempts to maintain programs. There is a prevalent belief that computing applications become unmaintainable because of the cumulative effects of maintenance activities. Many applications are therefore replaced because *the old programs can no longer be maintained.* With the contamination of data related to maintenance, enhancement, and replacement, we find little valid data available. Maintenance must be studied in relation to the place it properly occupies in the life cycle. What is needed is research to measure and elucidate what is meant by program *deterioration*. The purpose of this research should be to provide guidance on how to perform maintenance rigorously without disturbing the integrity of the program. The research itself can become contaminated, if it fails to take into account the maintenance of test data and documentation consistent with the program.

A life cycle model with sufficient detail might also help to distinguish between *deterioration* and *obsolescence* with respect to maintenance. Even if programs, test data, documentation, and controls, have not deteriorated, their future maintenance cost could be significantly reduced if they were replaced by newer techniques — for example, higher level languages, table or parameter driven programs, data base systems, test data systems, a documentation system, or newer job control systems. In order to justify the cost of making replacements, one needs to forecast future maintenance demands, and this requires valid data and models.

The life cycle model can facilitate making reliable predictions of the cost of various stages of a computing application. Such cost estimates are useful in deciding to replace rather than maintain an application — i.e., if the cumulative actual cost of maintenance is near or beyond that amount adopted as the criterion for eliminating or replacing the application.

Faulty use of controls or documentation distortions

When measuring the effort spent on maintenance activities, the data must be identified with sufficient precision to distinguish effort spent in attempting to detect alleged bugs that are thought to exist because the user failed to understand the controls or the documentation. The resolution of such misunderstanding can require significant amounts of time. Such effort should be a signal to review the controls and documentation to determine if they are faulty or themselves need maintenance. Time spent on such evaluations and time spent on modifying controls, including preparation of clearer error messages or documentation, should itself be considered a necessary maintenance activity of a different kind. Software metrics should allow separate identification of time spent on detecting such limitations, correcting them, and making program changes if they are really required.

Distribution effects

When a computing application is distributed to multiple users, usually at multiple locations and possibly using different operating systems, distortions can easily occur in the data related to maintenance. There are many opportunities for contamination. For example, some users may fail to have releases of the controls, programs, documentation, or test data. More subtle problems occur when a sequence of several maintenance items has been distributed and not all have been incorporated, or some have been incorporated incorrectly. These problems can be attributed to defective administrative procedures of distribution; however, there may also be a technical failing: If the computing application had contained sufficient diagnostic capabilities, the omissions or errors might have been detected, perhaps should have been. Therefore, one research problem ought to be how to specify effective diagnostic capabilities. The challenge of software metrics in this situation would be to measure the cost-effectiveness and necessary trade-offs in development of needed diagnostic capabilities.

With the expected wide use of microprocessors; maintenance activity and data collection on maintenance activity will also be complicated by the use of distributed equipment, where some parts of the programs will be distributed among physically separated pieces of equipment.

Diagnostic limitations of test cases and data

How can one measure the cost of incorporating diagnostic capabilities in an application, including both the design and maintenance of such capabilities, and the overhead burden of executing the application when the diagnostic capabilities are included? Without better awareness of the cost of the problems cited in earlier sections, one will have difficulty in estimating the benefits derived from the presence of adequate diagnostic capabilities. An activity related to building and using these diagnostic capabilities is the effort required to modify them as the maintenance of a system requires changes or incorporation of additional diagnostic capabilities. An additional contamination effect may be introduced because changes to the diagnostic capabilities may not be true maintenance activities but in fact enhancement or replacement activities.

Malfunctions due to Equipment or Operating System

Often the consequences attributed to a maintenance activity can subsequently be traced to a problem with the equipment or the software of the operating system. Adequate diagnostic tools, such as those mentioned above, can aid in identifying and separating the causes of the problem. It is very tempting for those involved with maintenance activities to classify a problem as due to the hardware or the operating system. However, the result may be to mask a deficiency in the application or to contaminate the data by reporting that time spent to fix a deficiency was spent to ascertain that the cause of the problem was the hardware or operating system. One could argue that if the computing application is well designed there should be few, if any, instances when the cause of a reproducible problem due to hardware or the operating system cannot be quickly detected. The questions of the confounding of such problems with problems with the application, and how to distinguish these problems are an important challenge for those developing software metrics.

Unintended or Unexpected Uses of the Application

Often one can observe the spending of considerable effort on maintenance activity, only to discover afterwards that an attempt was made to use the application in an unforeseen way, by using the controls in an unforeseen manner or providing data which created unforeseen calculations. The situation raises additional questions of how to ensure adequate data identification. It is a demanding research problem to specify what kinds of software metrics will be useful here. Even with valid data, one still confronts the often-mentioned confusion over whether or not to make changes ostensibly as a maintenance activity to cope with the user's problem.

Errors Introduced by Maintenance

If a sequence of maintenance tasks has been performed and it is later discovered that one or more of them are in error, should further corrective maintenance effort be attributed to the design and implementation of the application or to faulty maintenance efforts? Data contamination from this source creates a serious difficulty to those who want to understand the software life cycle interactions among design, implementation, maintenance, enhancement, and replacement phases. The need for software metrics is undisputed, but it is not clear how best to proceed. Some of the difficulties relate to the cascade effects addressed below.

Cascading-Causal Chains and Linkages

The life cycle model is a formal way of acknowledging the interdependence of the various stages of work on a computing application from the inception of the planning. However, the model by itself does not have sufficient granularity to provide adequate event identification so that an action taken in an early stage can be traced to show its impact on subsequent stages. The interdependence of events at different stages needs more attention than at present, and a much richer data structure will be needed in order to identify events and the associated data. Physical phenomena are sometimes identified and analyzed as a set of cascading events with linkages or causal chains. In such a formulation, under some reasonable assumptions, one can sometimes describe a process as a sequence of transition events, simplifying both the data collection and storage and the data analysis. This type of formulation may be useful to understanding how design and implementation alternatives influence maintenance. Otherwise one must consider analytical approaches, which are far more complex, or lack sufficient detail to provide insight. A useful research question is whether or not such formulations are adequate. Until such research on software metrics is undertaken, we will hear many claims about the virtues of one or another particular approach, with little if any data to support or reject the proposed approach, be it top-down, bottom-up, structured, or something else.

Until we support research on metrics we will find it difficult to justify any particular design or implementation approach. For example, I believe that a computing application which is based on a modular design is easier to design, test, document, and maintain than one that does not use a modular design. However, there is little actual evidence bearing on this question, one way or the other. Furthermore, without diligent study we will not know why a program module included in a modular design fails to maintain its modularity during modification as part of a maintenance or enhancement effort. Without further development of software metrics, one can expect to see a continued flow of misleading or inconclusive results on this question, because of contamination effects that could have been taken into account through a cascade or causal-chain approach.

Indirect and Direct Tools to Aid Maintenance

Two classes of tools are needed to aid our understanding of the maintenance process and to aid in establishing software metrics. The tools are needed to support the collection of data of the comprehensive types suggested in earlier sections. Without such tools it is unrealistic to expect that the burden of data collection, retention, and analysis will take place at a level and on a scale that is needed.

Indirect tools to aid maintenance should come out of efforts to establish software metrics. These tools are indirect since they involve actions taken at other stages of the life cycle. Such tools should generate information to influence policy and planning decisions — for example, a decision to design and implement computing applications based upon using modularity of design, to require that applications include data collection capabilities to diagnose performance and to aid maintenance, or to develop an application as a sequence of iterative steps.

Direct tools are those that immediately affect how maintenance is done. These tools relate to the collection, retention, and analysis of valid data about the maintenance process, whether it be administration, control, programming, testing, documentation, training, or user assistance [1]. One of the most promising tools is the integration of the development and maintenance of programs with the development and maintenance of documentation. An example is the Programmer's Workbench, developed for use on UNIX [2,3,4,5]. With such tools it should be possible and cost-effective to retain an institutional history of all changes and to support a rich enough coding structure to analyze cascading or causal chains as described above. However, to make these tools effective, one must use them from the inception of the design of a computing application. One must adopt them out of appreciation for the interdependence of the various stages of the life cycle. Such tools must be included as an integral part of organizing how one performs maintenance activities. Otherwise, I fear that the identifying and collection of data on what takes place as maintenance activity will be viewed as an avoidable overhead cost or as an unnecessary burden on those doing maintenance, and the information will not receive adequate attention.

Human Factors

In earlier sections I have already mentioned how data related to maintenance can be contaminated as a result of failing to address human factors. The need to address the influence of human factors on developing effective software metrics is clear. What is not clear is how to proceed. Human factors often affect what we are trying to measure. To understand the implications of this for software metrics, we will have to establish well-designed and reproducible experiments. Such experiments present a challenge that is shared with all of the social sciences that depend upon statistical theory and techniques in order to make general inferences from a set of experiments. Much of the current literature on measuring the influence or the quality of effort devoted to software development or maintenance raises more questions than useful answers. One area where measurement seems to be effective is the evaluation of programming aptitude [7,8]. In this case, for example, using measured aptitude as a control variable, one could introduce a series of interesting questions concerning how programmer aptitude affects maintenance activities.

Role of Statistics

The possible role of statistics in software maintenance is suggested by statistics' concern with the theory and application of methodology for efficient and effective data collection and analysis. One uses the theory of statistics to aid in the description or explanation of events or to aid in prediction or forecasting of events. Statistical theory helps because analyses can be done in the presence of incomplete information and in the presence of uncertainty. In spite of many successful applications, it does not follow that statistical theory and techniques will be easy to use here, or that existing techniques will be appropriate. New theory or new tools may be needed. However, based on past experience, one might expect to be able to employ the modern theory of the design of experiments to aid in experimentation to find good software metrics or in understanding the influence of human factors. Another part of the theory of statistics is related to modeling. I believe that modeling, based upon statistical techniques, will help us to: a) cope with and understand the complexity of software metrics; b) develop methods by which we can predict the influence of factors affecting software; c) aid those making decisions affecting investments in software; and d) provide tools for selecting among methods for developing software.

If one accepts the usefulness of the life cycle approach to model building for software metrics, then I believe that the role of statistical techniques is vital to exploring model building as an iterative process. In particular, statistical techniques can aid in each of the iterative steps of conjecture, model building, data collection and analysis, model verification or modifications based upon model experiments, and model acceptance and use. However, neither statistical theory nor the life cycle model should be looked upon and accepted uncritically. Both should be carefully considered to determine whether they apply and help to gain effective understanding and progress.

Research Problems

Consistent with the objectives of the meeting for which this paper has been prepared, several research questions have been posed, following an explanation of why specific software metrics are needed and how this generates a need for research. Let me review some of these questions:

- The complex interactions among the various stages in the life cycle, in particular, maintenance, enhancements, and replacement. The need for better data and analysis to understand what takes place.
- Attributed Cause and Attributed Need — determine whether to have a one-step or iterative approach to developing computing applications.
- Contamination Effects — cumulative effects of changes, distortions due to faulty controls or documentation, what is meant by deterioration, distribution effects, diagnostic data limitations, separating the influence of hardware and software malfunctions, effects of unforeseen uses, and error corrections introducing new errors.
- Cascading-Causal Chains and Linkages — how to collect, retain, and analyze data when the events that occur as maintenance depend upon events for an earlier stage of the life cycle.
- Tools — the need for research to design tools.
- Human Factors — an almost unlimited horizon of interesting research questions.

In summary, I have suggested that use of a life-cycle model should be considered to determine if it can aid in the development of needed software metrics. However, many research questions persist. For example, how can one be sure that with a life cycle view of development, software metrics can indicate when to replace, extend, or correct existing software? Can software metrics aid in deciding how to replace, extend, or correct software? Merely defining the universe of discourse may be difficult — for example, how does one distinguish between an extension, correction, or replacement of software? We need to agree whether or not this distinction is important to the development of software metrics, though I believe it is.

If we can agree on the importance of these distinctions, we should next agree on the need for research to identify:

1. What factors contribute to achieving good software development? Use? Maintenance?
2. What factors contribute to accurate cost estimates of development? Use? Maintenance?
3. What factors contribute to establishing valid specifications to be met by a particular software product?

A Closing Remark

I hope that this paper has helped the reader to face twin questions: Why are software metrics needed? How can one proceed to establish needed metrics? I was pleased to be asked by the meeting organizers to concentrate on this neglected topic and to suggest research questions. Without adequate attention to maintenance, we will continue to see unnecessary and wasteful effort spent on maintenance, as well as premature replacement of *old* applications with *new-replacement* applications without building upon what already exists. I believe software metrics is a rich and challenging field for research and for the development of practical and useful tools.

Acknowledgement

I wish to thank George W. Barclay, Daniel Hoyle, and Leonard Steinberg for their helpful comments on an earlier draft of this paper.

References

[1]   J. R. Allen.
        Some testing and maintenance considerations in package
            design and implementation.
        In David Hogben and Denis W. Fife, editors, *Computer Science
            and Statistics: Tenth Annual Symposium on The Interface*,
            pages 211-214. U.S. Department of Commerce/National
            Bureau of Standards, Washington DC, 1977.

[2]   M. H. Bianchi and J. L. Wood.
       A user's viewpoint of a programmer's workbench.
       Proceedings of the Second International Conference on
           Software Engineering, pages 193-199. Institute of Electrical
           and Electronic Engineers, San Francisco, 1976.

[3]   T. A. Dolotta and J. R. Mashey.
       An introduction to the programmer's workbench.
       Proceedings of the Second International Conference on
           Software Engineering, pages 164-168. Institute of Electrical
           and Electronic Engineers, San Francisco, 1976.

[4]   S. I. Feldman.
       Make — a program for maintaining computer programs.
       Computer Science Technical Report Number 57. Bell
           Laboratories, Murray Hill, New Jersey, 1977.

[5]   E. L. Ivie.
       The programmer's workbench — a machine for software
           development.
       Communications of the ACM 20:746-753, 1977.

[6]   M. E. Muller.
       Maintenance and distribution of statistical software: Satisfying
           diverse needs.
       In David Hogben and Denis W. Fife, editors, *Computer Science*
           and Statistics: Tenth Annual Symposium on The Interface,
           pages 205-210. U.S. Department of Commerce/National
           Bureau of Standards, Washington DC, 1977.

[7]   J. M. Wolfe.
       Perspectives on testing for programming aptitude.
       Proceedings Annual Association for Computing Machinery
           Conference, pages 268-277. 1971.

[8]   J. M. Wolfe.
       A validation study — long-range predictive capabilities of the
           Aptitude Assessment Battery programming test.
       Programming Specialists, Inc., Brooklyn, New York, 13 pages,
           1972.

Chapter 15:
When is "Good" Enough? Evaluating and Selecting Software Metrics

Mary Shaw

Computer Science Department
Carnegie Mellon University
Pittsburgh, PA 15213

Abstract

In assessing the use of metrics for software, it is important to consider the quality of the metrics themselves. This has two components. First, we can determine some of the statistical properties of the metric itself. Second, we can assess the way a metric will be used and select one that provides appropriate information without excess expense. This note discusses some issues about the validation and efficiency of measurement techniques.

Introduction

This note addresses two questions related to the judicious use of software metrics. The first is how proposed metrics should be described and evaluated. The second is how to select metrics that are cost-effective, in the sense that they strike a reasonable balance between the amount and precision of the information delivered and the cost of collecting and processing raw data.

The first question is of concern to people who develop metrics. It pertains to the criteria that should be used for evaluating metrics and the guidance that should be provided to prospective users. It covers not only ways to state properties of individual metrics, but also ways to validate the models that underlie the metrics and ways to decide when it is appropriate to introduce new metrics.

The second question is of concern to people who use metrics. It pertains to criteria for deciding when imprecise measures offer good enough results — that is, to ways to determine the cost-effectiveness of a metric. Many people succumb to the temptation to demand as much detail as technologically possible, neglecting the costs which arise from its acquisition, comprehension, and use. We have many examples of detailed models and complex metrics; we should also look for some metrics that are both less expensive and less precise.

In a broader sense, I am discussing the problem of developing literacy and taste in the construction and use of metrics. At issue is a piece of culture — the attitude that we as scientists and engineers take toward all the work we do, the expectations that we as readers have of technical material, and the standards that we as editors enforce for material under consideration for publication.

Evaluating Proposed Metrics

The most desirable metric is a direct measurement of the property of interest. Unfortunately, such measures are rarely available; they may be unavailable at the time they are needed, they may be expensive to obtain, or there may be no known way to take a direct measurement. As a result, we frequently resort to indirect measurements. When we do, we become dependent on an analytic or empirical model of the system or process being measured.

It would be nice to have a common set of program dimensions — a *basis* — that is commonly accepted by all investigators as the object of measurement. Unfortunately, we are far from agreement on what might constitute such a basis for the measurement of software, so we tend to develop models that are idiosyncratic in their choices of source data. In another paper in this report, I argue that a serious attempt should be made to encourage the development of a common, consistent paradigm.

Whenever a metric is indirect — based on a model — two issues are involved in its evaluation. The first is validation of the underlying model; the second is determination of the properties of the statistics provided by the measurement technique. In the case of a direct measurement, only the latter is of concern.

Part of the validation of a proposed metric should include a comparison of its results with the results given by existing metrics. In addition to agreeing with other ways of measuring the same thing, a new metric should clearly provide an improvement over previous techniques along at least one dimension (e.g., some property of the measure or of the cost of its use).

We must exercise discretion in the standards we set, however. Some measures are based on static analysis of program text; these will be deterministic. Other measures are based on data gathered by monitoring the execution of a program; although in a strict sense these may be deterministic, it is often not practical to treat them that way. Still other measures are based on human performance, which is much more variable and far from deterministic. Different standards must be applied in all these cases; if, for example, correlation coefficients are used to evaluate metrics, higher correlations should be expected of deterministic than of nondeterministic metrics.

Properties of a Metric

We need to establish criteria for the evaluation of proposed software metrics. Unfortunately, the field of computer science offers little precedent or guidance. In the absence of exemplars in our own field, we may turn to other fields for ideas. When we do this, however, we must be cautious about drawing analogies uncritically. Techniques that work perfectly well in another field may, for some reason, be inapplicable to situations in computer science that are superficially similar. Nevertheless, we may turn to other fields for inspiration if we take care to avoid uncritical or inappropriate use of the ideas. This section surveys several properties of metrics that are recognized in other areas of measurement and may be pertinent for software.

When a metric can be cast as a traditional problem of statistical inference involving estimation or hypothesis testing, standard statistical techniques (e.g., [5] Chapters 9-11) can be applied. These are sufficiently familiar that there is no need to review them here.

Some less familiar concepts from psychometrics (e.g., [6,8]) are also worth considering. These may apply directly, particularly in productivity studies, or they may merely be suggestive of areas where we need to establish criteria of our own. I will describe criteria for *reliability* and *validity*.

A reliability measure for a metric indicates how much confidence we can have in the value of the metric for a particular individual being measured — a program, person, system, team, or whatever. It can be thought of as a consistency measure — an estimate of the degree to which repeated measurement of an individual would produce the same result. The reliability of a metric may be reduced by variability of several kinds:

- *Observer variability* refers to the possibility that the person taking the measurement may not always record the same events in the same way. It is unlikely to be an issue for an objective or analytic metric, but if subjective judgements are required of the observer, they may lower reliability. If the observer is a machine, this may be referred to as *instrument variability*.

- *Subject variability* refers to systematic or random changes in the individual being measured. For example, day-to-day variations in an individual's typing speed and improvement of his skill through time can both introduce variability.

- *Environmental variability* refers to uncontrolled factors that may affect measurement. It is common, for example, for the system load in a time-sharing system to affect the reliability of timings.

A number of methods are available for estimating the reliability of objective tests. The situation appears to be less well under control when the possibility for much variability exists.

A validity measure for a metric indicates how well it measures what it is supposed to measure. Several kinds of validity are recognized:

- *Content validity* or *face validity* is demonstrated by arguing that the questions asked or the data collected is pertinent to whatever is being measured. In other words, content validity can be established by getting an expert to say that the test measures what it claims to.

- *Predictive validity* is demonstrated by showing a correlation between the result of the metric and some criterion based on the future performance of the individual.

- *Construct validity* is an issue when a property is measured indirectly. Such a measurement depends on knowing a relation between the measured variables and the property of interest. Construct validity is demonstrated by showing that this relation does in fact hold.

In one sense, a validity measure should be straightforward, for validity is simply the correlation between the metric and some criterion. In practice, however, the criterion values may be expensive to obtain or not immediately available.

It is important to note that reliability and validity are independent concepts: a test can be quite reliable without being at all valid and conversely. In other words, the results of two tests may differ because of measurement error or because different things are being measured. The two effects should not be confused.

In addition to using general criteria as a matter of course, it is appropriate to set up specialized criteria for particular classes of metrics, For example, Roberts [11] studies techniques for evaluating computer-implemented text editors. She begins by setting up standards against which to measure the techniques. In the abstract she says,

> This thesis explores the possibility of performing an objective and thorough, but quick, evaluation of text editors from the viewpoints of their various users. The criterion of *objectivity* implies that the evaluation scheme not be biased in favor of any particular editor's user's model, its way of regarding text and operations on the text. As much as possible, data should be gathered by observing people who are equally familiar with each system, and when tests are analytic, the criteria for scoring must be unambiguous. *Thoroughness* implies that many aspects of editor use be considered. *Quickness* means that the tests are usable by editor designers, managers of word processing centers, or other non-psychologists who need this kind of information but have limited time and equipment resources.

In the thesis, she develops ways to answer several different categories of questions. She develops empirical methods and matching analytic (predictive) models, then shows how well the (cheaper) analytic methods do as substitutes for the (more expensive) empirical ones.

Models that Underlie Metrics

We have learned over the years that programs are easier to deal with when we abstract from details of the code to the important properties of the computation. The same principle applies to the problem of managing the complexity of the *measurement* of a program. When we introduce a model of a system, we are identifying certain properties as being of interest and suppressing the rest — which is precisely the same approach we use for program development. Kleinrock [9] has provided fundamental queueing-theoretic models for performance evaluation. Spirn [13] has used modeling extensively for evaluating paging systems. Svobodova [14] presents a more general description of modeling techniques, but does so in a heavily hardware-oriented setting.

In an *empirical model*, equations are fit to observed data in an attempt to capture the information contained in the data. Such models can be validated by determining the correlation between the equations and observed data (fresh data or the data on which the equations were based). A variety of empirical models can be found in [2].

An *analytic model*, on the other hand, proceeds from an assumption that the process being modelled is well understood — at least to the extent that a mathematical description of the mechanism can be written down. Parameters of such models may be tuned to correspond to actual systems, but the underlying description may be selected as much for its mathematical tractability as for its exact correspondence to observed data. Queueing-theoretic models for operating systems [9] exemplify this approach.

Whether a model is simple or complex, empirical or analytic, it is necessary to determine how accurately it matches reality. The techniques for validating models seem to be as varied as the models. It appears that efforts to find tractable, perspicuous models that can be re-used extensively in a variety of situations have considerable payoff potential.

The importance of validating a model critically can be demonstrated by an example. Feller [4] relates a cautionary tale:

> The *logistic distribution* function
>
> $$F(t) \; = \; 1/(1 + e^{-\alpha t - \beta}), \qquad \alpha > 0 \qquad\qquad (*)$$
>
> may serve as a warning. An unbelievably huge literature tried to establish a transcendental "law of logistic growth"; measured in appropriate units, practically all growth processes were supposed to be represented by a function of the form (*) with *t* representing time. Lengthy tables, complete with chi-square tests, supported this thesis for human populations, for bacterial colonies, development of railroads, etc. Both height *and* weight of plants and animals were found to follow the logistic law even though it is theoretically clear that these two variables cannot be subject to the same distribution. Laboratory experiments on bacteria showed that not even systematic disturbances can produce other results. Population theory relied on logistic extrapolations (even though they were demonstrably unreliable). The only trouble with the theory is that not only the logistic distribution but also the normal, the Cauchy, and other distributions can be fitted to the *same material with the same or better goodness of fit* [3]. In this competition the logistic distribution plays no distinguished role whatever; most contradictory theoretical models can be supported by the same observational material.
>
> Theories of this nature are short-lived because they open no new ways, and new confirmations of the same old thing soon grow boring. But the naive reasoning as such has not been superseded by common sense, and so it may be useful to have

an explicit demonstration of how misleading a mere goodness of fit can be.

Standard Validation Tasks

In order to help establish the expectation that new metrics will be evaluated against existing competitors, it would be useful to have a set of standard problems, tasks, or programs against which new metrics can (should) be validated. This role is played by sorting programs for algorithmic complexity, by the "reader-writer" problem for process synchronization, by stacks for data type specifications, by the M/M/1 queue in performance evaluation, and by the fruit fly *Drosophila melanogaster* for genetics. *bug* Such a problem or program can become a standard in its own right, simply because so much knowledge grows up around it.

Selecting Appropriate Metrics for a Task

As software measurement is currently practiced, we can observe two unfortunate patterns. The first is a tendency to use statistics uncritically; the second is a tendency to obtain as much detail or precision as possible, without regard for the cost. We must recognize that there are legitimate grounds for departing from the singleminded pursuit of exact measurements and detailed models.

The modern computer has an unparalleled capacity for producing data. The problem in applying software metrics is to find appropriate measures and make sense out of the data, not simply to obtain the data. It is important to bear in mind that collecting and analyzing statistics itself has cost, and that many parts of a system may require analysis. When much of a system is not analyzed, or only crudely analyzed, there may be little merit in going to great lengths to obtain exact measurements of individual parts.

Imprecise measures are often good enough, and they should be cheap to compute. They are particularly likely to be adequate in large systems where parts of the system other than the one being measured are even less well analyzed or understood.

A user cannot make reasonable decisions about the selection of a metric without data on both the cost and the precision of the metric. Thus the description of a metric should indicate how much of what kind of data is required and how expensive it is likely to be to collect the data and compute the measurement. In addition, the description of the metric should specify the precision, reliability, and validity of the results.

This point can be supported by citing a few specific examples:

Several investigators have explicitly recognized the importance of tailoring the detail of analysis to the goals of the analysis. For example, Svobodova [14] considers the question of carrying an appropriate level of detail through an analysis. Early in Chapter 3 (System Models), she says,

> Any system to be analyzed properly must be defined and understood to a sufficient level of detail. The level of detail in a model is an important factor. With too few details available, system performance cannot be properly assessed; too many details may conceal essential functions and relations. Adjustability of the level of detail in a system model to the needs of a project is an important consideration when selecting a representation medium.

In a similar vein, Smith and Browne [12] describe a current problem:

> Current computer performance evaluation techniques are too time consuming to obtain necessary answers to questions on the impact of new software, easily, accurately, and on short notice when data on the expected execution characteristics is unavailable... The need is for a quick, easy means of predicting the performance of software.

Card et al. [1] needed a model for predicting the time it would take for expert users to execute interactive tasks on an interactive system. They developed a model, the Keystroke Model, based solely on counting keystrokes and other low-level operations. Validation showed a root-mean-square prediction error of 21% for individual tasks. In addition, the model can be simplified in ways that directly trade ease-of-use for accuracy.

Wulf and Feiler [16] have developed a method for cheaply determining a figure of merit that estimates the improvement made by an optimizing compiler for various ⟨compiler, machine⟩ combinations. The figure of merit represents the code size of the optimized code, scaled to an arbitrary standard. It relies on an assumption about hierarchy and independence among optimization techniques, and it is limited to algebraic languages and conventional register-oriented machines. Within those limitations, the figure-of-merit for a new ⟨compiler, machine⟩ combination can be obtained by compiling and analyzing a small set of test programs; the time required is estimated to be a day or two. Initial validation studies across several languages and machines indicate that the figures of merit can be about 90% accurate (10% confidence level).

The *Fog Index* is a measure of the syntactic complexity of English text. Proposed by Gunning [7], it relies on counts of sentence lengths and the density of polysyllabic words to obtain an estimate of the number of years of education a reader would need in order to read a piece of text. The index can clearly be defeated, for it gives no consideration to the conceptual difficulty of the material, only to the sentence structure. Nevertheless, it proves a useful indicator to identify problem areas in written material. It is of interest here because it delivers a great deal of information in proportion to the (very small) amount of effort required to compute it.

A graphic demonstration of the tradeoff between precision and analysis cost is provided by the complexity analysis of Euclid's Algorithm for finding the greatest common divisor of two numbers, m and n (say $n > m$). Knuth [10] (sec 4.5.3, pp. 316-333) devotes seventeen pages to an empirical argument that in the worst case the number of divisions required is approximately $1.9405 \, log_{10} \, n$. However, the observation that each divisor is at least two, so the larger of the numbers under consideration must be halved at each step leads immediately to a bound of $2 \, log_2 \, n$, or $6.0206 \, log_{10} \, n$. If it is sufficient for your purposes to have a bound that is only within a factor of about 3, the analysis to support the bound is much simpler and intuitively plausible.

Summary

In this note I have sketched some issues concerning the evaluation and selection of software metrics. A number of questions remain open for investigation:

- Can we identify a reasonably small collection of techniques that satisfy a large fraction of software measurement needs? It would be unfortunate if we needed to devise new approaches for most new problems.
- We don't currently know which properties of a metric matter or how high we can reasonably expect correlations, reliabilities, or other indicators to be. We have lots of experience with particular models, but no good generalizations. How can we encourage the process of generalization?

- How can we best draw on traditional statistics? In particular, how do we (a) transfer knowledge from statistical fields; (b) educate computer scientists in statistical responsibilities; (c) determine whether techniques can be taken directly from statistical fields or whether they must be modified for computer science?

- Do traditional techniques deal with all of our problems, or do we need new techniques to cope with (a) the ease with which we generate large masses of data; (b) the fact that we are still developing our models; (c) the apparent malleability of our medium and the ease with which we can blend models with running systems?

- Recent developments in programming methodology have emphasized the use of abstraction and hierarchical organization to control detail. How can these program organizations be exploited by the metrician?

- Performance evaluation techniques now address hardware problems quite successfully. Are there significant differences between hardware and software problems, or do we just have more experience with measuring hardware?

- Tukey [15] makes the point that conventional statistical techniques are useful for testing hypotheses we have already formulated. Is software metrics now in such a state that we need assistance in formulating the hypotheses more than we need help with testing them? If so, we should be cautious about expecting conventional statistics to be applicable to all our problems.

It is important to note that understanding is much more important than tools. Although measurements may help us come to understand them, in the long run comprehension of the underlying processes is critical to useful metrics.

References

[1]   Stuart K. Card, Thomas P. Moran, Allen Newell.
        *The Keystroke-Level Model for User Performance Time with
            Interactive Systems.*
        Tech. Rept. SSL-79-1, Xerox PARC, March, 1979.

[2]   Data and Analysis Center for Software.
        Quantitative Software Models.
        U.S. Air Force, March, 1979.

[3]   William Feller.
        On the logistic law of growth and its empirical verifications in
            biology.
        Acta Biotheoretica 5 (1940), 51-66.

[4]   William Feller.
        An Introduction to Probability Theory and Its Applications.
        John Wiley and Sons, 1966.

[5]   John E. Freund.
        Mathematical Statistics.
        Prentice-Hall, 1971.

[6]   Edwin E. Ghiselli.
        Theory of Psychological Measurement.
        McGraw-Hill, 1964.

[7]   Robert Gunning.
        How to Take the Fog Out of Writing.
        Dartnell Press, 1964.

[8]   Paul Horst.
        Psychological Measurement and Prediction.
        Wadsworth, 1966.

[9]   L. Kleinrock.
        Queuing Systems: Theory.
        John Wiley & Sons, 1975.

[10]   D. E. Knuth.
        *The Art of Computer Programming: Semi-Numerical
            Algorithms.*
        Addison-Wesley, Reading, 1969.

[11]   Teresa Lynn Roberts.
        Evaluation of Computer Text Editors.
        Ph.D. Thesis, Stanford University, 1980.

[12]   Connie Smith and J. C. Browne.
        Performance Specifications and Analysis of Software Designs.
        In *Proceedings of the Conference on Simulation, Measurement,
            and Modeling of Computer Systems*, August 1979, 173-182.

[13]   J. R. Spirn.
        Program Behavior: Models and Measurements.
        Elsevier North-Holland, Ltd., New York, 1977.

[14]   Liba Svobodova.
*Computer Performance Measurement and Evaluation Methods:
Analysis and Applications.*
Elsevier Scientific Publishing Company, 1976.

[15]   John W. Tukey.
Exploratory Data Analysis.
Addison-Wesley, 1977.

[16]   W. Wulf, P. Feiler, J. Zinnikas, R. Brender.
*A Quantitative Technique For Comparing the Quality of
Language Implementations.*
In preparation.

Annotated Bibliography on Software Metrics

Compiled by Mary Shaw

Computer Science Department
Carnegie-Mellon University
Pittsburgh, PA 15213

This bibliography includes the significant references from the papers in the panel report together with other papers that have been identified as relevant to some aspect of software metrics. It is interesting to note that almost all of the papers were published within the past ten years.

Contributions of panel members and other interested members of the program measurement community were augmented with authors' abstracts and reviews from *Computing Reviews*. The source of each review is indicated in the annotation. No attempt has been made to make the bibliography complete -- the boundaries of the field are too fuzzy and the number of projects is too large. Nevertheless, the annotations provided here should serve as a useful resource.

The panel would like to express its appreciation to Brian Wichmann and Chris Harman of the National Physical Laboratory for allowing us to incorporate material from a draft survey of studies on the usage of high-level languages and to Richard Snodgrass of Carnegie-Mellon University for providing his extensive annotations on software monitoring. The material from *Computing Reviews* is reprinted by permission of the copyright owner, the Association for Computing Machinery; the auhor of each review is named in the original review.

The format of the bibliography is patterned on a software engineering bibliography developed at the University of Toronto in the mid-1970's [Barnard77]. The first section lists the papers on each of several topics, and the second section provides complete citations and annotations.

The bibliography is available in Scribe format on the ARPANet. Contact Shaw@CMU-10A for details.

Authors of Annotations

Attribution	Author and affiliation
Abstract	Abstract of the cited paper
CR12345	Computing Reviews (with review number; reprinted by permission of the Association for Computing Machinery)
FGS	Frederick G. Sayward, Computer Science Department, Yale University, New Haven, CT 06520
IF	Ivor Francis, Department of Economic and Social Statistics, Cornell University, Ithaca, NY 14853
JCB	J. C. Browne, Computer Science Department, University of Texas, Austin, TX 78712
JES	Jean Sammet, IBM Federal Systems Division, Bethesda, MD 20034
LAB	L. A. Belady, IBM Corporation, T. J. Watson Research Center, Yorktown Heights, NY 10598
MEM	Mervin E. Muller, Director of Computing Activities, World Bank, 1818 H Street N. W., Washington DC 20433
MS	Mary Shaw, Computer Science Department, Carnegie-Mellon University, Pittsburgh, PA 15213
RTS	Richard T. Snodgrass, Computer Science Department, Carnegie-Mellon University, Pittsburgh, PA 15213
VRB	V. R. Basili, Computer Science Department, University of Maryland, College Park, MD 20740
W&H	Brian A. Wichmann and Chris Harman, National Physical Laboratory, Teddington, TW11 0LW, England

Topic Lists

This section provides classified pointers into the main body of the annotated bibliography.

General

Basili78b, Beilner77, Belady79a, Boehm78, Chen76, Gepner78, Gilb77c, Mohanty79, QSM79, Shneiderman80, Spirn77, Svobodova76

Surveys and Bibliographies

Agajanian75, Atwood79, Barnard77, Basili78b, Belady79a, Bryant79, Calingaert67, Conti79, DACS79, Ferrari78a, Ferrari78b, Fitzsimmons78, Francis75a, Francis79a, Gannon75c, Gilb77a, Goodenough79, Jackson78, Mohanty79, Musa79, QSM79, Shneiderman80, Smith67

Application-Specific Measures

Compilers: Akka67, Arnborg74, Bloom74, Freiburghouse74, Grosse-Lindemann76, Hammond77, Hartmann77, Lurie73, Moulton67, Odemalm75, Palme68, Partridge75, Shaw74, Wirth71, Yuval77a, Yuval77b

Interactive Systems: Boies74, Card78, Card79, Card80, England73a, England73b, Ivie77, Jones80, Lantz69, Mamrack79a, Mamrack79b, Ostreicher67, Sackman68

Virtual Memory and Paging Systems: Arora78, Batson77, Denning70, Gupta78, Hawthorn79, Janson76, Lampson76, Lenfant75, Masuda79, Sprin77

Protection: Andrews74, Bishop77, Ellis78, Fabry74, Gehringer79, Jones73, Lampson69, Lampson76, Linden76, Neumann75, Redell74, Wilkes79

Reliability: Belady79c, DeMillo81a, Gilb77a, Gilb77b, Linden76, Littlewood75, Musa75, Naur78, Schafer79, Thayer76

Testing Techniques: Bicevskis79, BrinchHansen73, BrinchHansen78, Budd78, Goodenough79, Holthouse79, Howden78a, Howden78b, Howden79, Howden80, Myers78b, Ottenstein79, Schneidewind79, Scowen72, Sheppard79a, Sheppard79b, Sime77a

Statistical and Numerical Software: Boisvert79, Brown79,

Crowder79, Duff79, Enright79, Francis77, Francis81, Lyness79a,
Lyness79b

Case Studies

Baker77, Basili75, Basili78a, Basili79c, Bianchi76, Boisvert79,
BrinchHansen73, Browne70, Card78, Chambers73, Clark76,
Clark78, Clark79, Dunsmore79, Francis75b, Francis79b,
Francis81, Freberger79, Gannon75a, Gannon75b, Gannon75c,
Gannon77, Gehring77, Griswold75, Gupta78, Hansen78,
Herndon78, Jackson78, Longley67, Myers78b, Rye77, Sammet71,
Shneiderman80, Thisted77, Velleman77, Weiss79, Willman77,
Woodfield79

Cost Estimation

Armstrong78, Basili77a, Basili77b, Basili78b, Basili78c, Basili81a,
Belady76, DACS79, Doty77, Herd77, Herndon78, Jeffery??,
Jones78, Parr80, Putnam78, Walston77, Wolverton74

Data Collection Techniques

Allen77, Armstrong78, Baker77, Basili75, Basili77a, Basili77b,
Basili78c, Basili79c, Basili81b, Bergeron75, Cheung74, Cohen74,
Curtis81a, Ferrari78a, Fries77, Ripley75, Saltzer70,
Shneiderman80, Slavinski75, Walston77, Willman77

Direct Measurement of Programs

Belady79a, Bloom74, Meeson79, Shneiderman80

Static: Alexander72, Alexander75, Archer75, Baker79, Basili75,
Belady79b, Brailsford77, Chanon73, Chapin79, Chevance78,
Clark77, Conradi77, Curtis79b, Dunsmore80, Elshoff76a,
Elshoff76b, Elshoff77a, Elshoff77b, Elshoff78, Fitzsimmons78,
Forman71, Foxley78, Gannon75a, Gannon75b, Gannon75c,
Gannon77, Good73, Gordon78, Gordon79a, Halstead76,
Halstead77, Hehner74, Hoaglin73, Huahg79, Jeffery??,
Kamnitzer75, Kolence72, Knuth71, Laemmel78, Love77, Lurie73,
McCabe76, Morrison77, Moulton67, Pratt78, Ryder79, Saal77,
Salvadori75, Salvadori??, Shaw74, Shimasaki79, Slavinski75,
Smith67, Tanenbaum??, vanderKnijff78, Wichmann70,
Woodward79, Wortman72, Zelkowitz76, Zweben79

Dynamic: Akka67, Alexander75, Archer75, Ashby73, Barak78,
Batson77, Belgard78, Bergeron75, Bingham76, Brailsford77,
BrinchHansen73, BrinchHansen78, Calingaert67, Cambell68,

Cerf71, Cheng69, Chevance78, Cohen74, Cohen77, Connors70, Crowley79, Dearnley78, Elshoff76a, Elshoff76b, Fitch77, Foxley78, Freiburghouse74, Griss77, Griswold75, Grochow69, Hammond77, Hanson78, Ingalls71, Knuth71, Knuth73, Lenfant75, Lloyd74, Lyon75, Masuda79, Matwin76, Millbrant74, Model78, Morrison77, Newcomer73, Niedereichholz79, Partridge75, Perrott77, Peuto77, Robinson77, Saltzer70, Satterthwaite72, Shimasaki79, Sites78, Storey77, Thompson79, Waite73, Wichmann70, Wong74, Wortman72, Wortman76, Yuval75a, Yuval75b, Yuval77a, Yuval77b, Zelkowitz76

Error Studies

Allen77, Amory75, Basili77a, Basili77b, Basili79a, Basili79b, Basili79c, Belady76, Boies74, Curtis79a, Curtis79b, Dunsmore78, Dunsmore79, Dunsmore80, Fries77, Gannon75a, Gannon75b, Gannon75c, Gannon77, Motley77, Musa75, Odemalm75, Pfasterer78, Schafer79, Schneidewind79, Scowen72, Shneiderman77a, Shneiderman77b, Shneiderman80, Thayer76, Weiss79, Youngs74

Evaluation of Metrics

Basili78a, Basili78c, Basili79a, Beaton76, Belady81, Bloom74, Boehm78, Boisvert79, Budd78, Curtis80, Curtis81a, deFreitas78, Elshoff76a, Elshoff76b, Gehring77, Gordon79b, Halstead77, Howden78a, Howden78b, Howden79, Jackson78, Jain79, Lyness79a, Mamrak79a, Mamrack79b, QSM79, Rubey75, Sammet71, Shaw81, Sevcik74, Shneiderman80, Tuggle78, Turner79, Velleman75

Human Factors

Atwood79, Basili79b, Basili79c, Brooks78, Brooks80, Bryce75, Card78, Card79, Card80, Dunsmore80, Gannon75a, Gannon75b, Gannon75c, Gannon77, Gordon79a, Gould74, Gould75, Green77, Hansen78, Litecky76, Love77, Model78, Sammet71, Sayward81, Sheppard79a, Sheppard79b, Shneiderman77a, Shneiderman77b, Shneiderman80, Sime73, Sime77b, Weinberg74, Weissman73, Weissman74, Wolfe71, Wolfe72, Woodfield79, Youngs74

Language Selection, Evaluation, and Design

Barron72, Browne70, Brunt76, Dunsmore78, Gannon75a, Gannon75b, Gannon75c, Gannon77, Good73, Green77, Hoare76, Lauesen73, Litecky76, Parsons75, Pratt78, Rayner75, Sammet71,

Sammet81, Shaw74, Shaw80, Sime73, Sime77b, Weissman73, Weissman74

Maintenance and Enhancement

Belady76, Belady79c, Curtis79a, Curtis79b, Feldman77, Gilb77b, Herndon78, Ivie77, McKissick79, Muller77, Muller81

Measures of Productivity

Chrysler78, Comer79, Crossman79, Curtis79a, Curtis79b, Curtis81a, Dunsmore78, Fitzsimmons78, Freberger79, Herndon78, Jeffery??, Jones78, Myers78a, Sackman68, Sammet70, Sheppard79b, Shneiderman77a, Shneiderman77b, Walston77, Weinberg74, Woodfield79

Models

Basili81a, Beilner77, Belady79c, Browne81, Buzen76, DACS79, Drummond73, Francis80, Gilb77c, Halstead77, Peterson77, QSM79

Modeling Concerns: Armstrong78, Basili77a, Basili77b, Basili79a, Basili81b, Brown79, Browne81, Card78, Card79, Card80, Courtois77, Gehring77, Hellerman72, Lyness79a, Mamrack77, Mills76, Musa75, Naur78, Sevcik74, Shaw81, Smith79b, Smith79c, Smith80b, Spirn77, Svobodova76, Tuggle78

Structural: Bard79, Belady79b, Boehm78, Booth79a, Booth79b, Browne75, Chandy75, Chanon73, Courtois77, Denning78, Dowdy79, Ellis78, Franta75, Graham78, Gupta78, Hilborn80, Howden78a, Howden80, Jones78, Kienzle79, Kleinrock75, Lynch81, Lyness79b, McCabe76, Musa75, Parr80, Putnam78, Robinson79b, Schneidewind79, Sevcik74, Shaw74, Shaw79, Sheppard79a, Trivedi79, Turner79, Waters79

Empirical: Basili78a, Basili78c, Belady76, Cheng69, Cheung74, Chrysler78, Curtis81b, DeMillo81b, Dunsmore78, Dunsmore79, Elshoff76a, Elshoff76b, Fitsos79, Fitsoş80, Freberger79, Goel78, Howden78a, Jeffery??, Jones78, Laemmel78, Motley77, Myers78a, Schafer79, Schneider78, Smith79a, Smith80a, vanderKnijff78 Walston77, Weiss79, Weissman73, Weissman74, Wolverton74, Woodfield79

Performance Evaluation

Agajanian75, Bard76, Bard79, Beilner77, Booth79a, Booth79b, Bryant79, Buzen78, Calingaert67, Cambell68, Chandy75, Conti79, Crowley75, Denning78, Dowdy79, Drummond73, Ferrari78a, Ferrari78b, Feustel73, Graham78, Hawthorn79, Hellerman75, Jain79, Kienzle79, Kleinrock75, Lucas71, Lynch81, MacDougall75, Mamrack77, Mamrack79b, Noe73, Nutt75, Peterson77, Peuto77, Robinson79a, Smith79b, Smith79c, Smith80b, Storey77, Trivedi79, Turner79

Software Life Cycle

Basili78b, Basili81a, Belady79c, Belady81, Bianchi76, Curtis81b, Dolotta76, Dunsmore80, Feldman77, Gehring77, Gilb77b, Hoare76, Jeffery??, Lehman80, McKissick79, Mills76, Muller81, Myers78a, Parr80, Perlis81, Putnam78, Rubey75, Rye77, Sanguinetti79, Weiss79, Wolverton74

Software Monitoring

deFreitas78, Jones80, MacEwen74, Morrison77, Ousterhout80, Partridge75, Peuto77, Robinson77, Sevcik72, Sites78, Warren79, Wichmann70, Yuval75a, Yuval75b, Yuval77a, Yuval77b, Zelkowitz76

Timing: Bergeron75, Matwin76, Newcomer73, Shimasaki79, Wichmann72

Sampling: Brailsford77, Jasik71, Knuth71, Thompson79, Waite73, Wong74

Event Monitoring: Ashby73, BrinchHansen73, BrinchHansen78, Cohen74, Cohen77, Deutsch71, Griswold75, Hajioannan76, Hanson78, Model78, Perrott77, Ripley78,

Special Hardware: Almes80, Bonner69, Cockrum71, Estrin67, Gumpertz78, Nemeth71

Software Systems: Barak78, Cambell68, Cantrell68, Cheng69, Dearnley78, Grochow69, McGehearty80, Millbrant74, Saltzer70

Network Monitoring: Abrams77, Gertner80, Morgan75, Nutt79, Tobagi76

Transfer of Techniques from Other Disciplines

Armstrong78, DeMillo81a, DeMillo81b, McCabe76, Musa75, Sayward81, Shneiderman80, Wolfe71, Wolfe72

Annotated bibliography

[Abrams 77]   M.D. Abrams and S. Treu.
A Methodology for Interactive Computer Service
Measurement.
Communications of the ACM 20(12):936-944, December,
1977.
An extensive list of applicable measures of the service provided to an interactive terminal user is described. This list contains time-based measures (such as system delay, user delay, user transmit), lengths (system response in characters, session length in number of transactions), multiplicities (command use, system and user error counts), rates (characters per second, errors per hour), and ratios (relative response, reliability). After a discussion of the Network Measurement Machine (NMM) used to collect data, a multi-level model consisting of four measurement levels of abstraction (data channel, transaction, subsession, and session attributes) and three measurement conditions (control of context, comparison of system(s), and collection of sessions) is detailed. An example experiment using this model ends the paper. Although the list of measures is extensive, each measure needs further research to determine its range of applicability, its use in psychological models of the interactive user, etc. [RTS]

[Agajanian 75]A.H. Agajanian.
A Bibliography on System Performance Evaluation.
Computer 8(11):63-74, November, 1975.
This bibliography of 440 references covers the period January 1970 to March 1975. It is divided into eight major sections: conferences, bibliographies, books, review articles, applies performance evaluation techniques, performance evaluation: case studies, system comparison results, and reliability, availability, and serviceability (RAS). This bibliography is of limited usefulness concerning monitoring. [RTS]

[Akka 67]   David S. Akka.
A Quantative Comparison of the Efficiencies of Compilers.
Master's thesis, Department of Computer Science,
University of Manchester, England, 1967.
Introduction: This thesis concerns an investigation of the efficiencies of several compilers in three languages (Algol60, FORTRAN 4 and Atlas Autocode). In order to attach meaningful weights to the features in the benchmark program, dynamic counts of various types of features had to be obtained.

Analysis: The dynamic analysis was carried out on Atlas Autocode programs on an Atlas computer. The AB compiler was modified so that the object programs produced dynamic counts when they were run.

Programs analyzed: A total of 200 of the programs analyzed produced useful results. The programs varied from less than 1000 autocode statements to more than 100,000 autocode statements. All programs were picked at random from the input trays of the University computing service. Each test program produced a set of 27 counts.

Results: Results (for the dyamic analysis are given for:

1. The dynamic counts.

2. The dynamic counts as percentages of the number of statements obeyed.

3. The number of programs not using each particular feature.

The timings from the benchmark programs are also given, and also the program which modifies the compiler. [W&H]

[Alexander 72]

W. G. Alexander.
How a Programming Language is Used.
Technical Report CSRG-10, University of Toronto, 1972.

Introduction: An empirical study of programs written in XPL was carried out with the aim of determining properties of both the language and the object machine, the System/360.

Static analysis: The XPL compiler (XCOM) was modified to extract the static information, tabulate it and print it.

Dynamic analysis: The XPL interpreter was used to collect the runtime statistics and tabulate them. As this is a very slow process, a jump tracing program was also included, which executed System/360 instructions between branches in the flow of control at machine speed.

Programs analyzed: 19 programs were analyzed from various sources:

1. An undergraduate course in compiler writing.
2. A similar graduate course in compiler writing.
3. Graduate students who developed compilers in XPL for their own use.
4. The SPL compiler XCOM and a non-compiler.

Results: Static results are presented for:

Frequencies of statement types	XPL operators
Nesting of DO groups	Relations
Statements in DO groups in XCOM	Distribution of numeric constants
Nesting of procedures	References to variables
Data definitions	Build-in function calls
Where variables are declared	Length of identifiers

Dynamic and static results are presented for:

S/360 opcode usage	Triples of opcodes
Top 10 instructions	Opcodes in XCOM
Fetch and store by wordsize	Pairs in XCOM
Distribution of accumulators	Triples in XCOM
Distribution of condition code masks	Range of S/360 branches in
Conditional decoding	XPL programs

[W&H]

[Alexander 75]

W. G. Alexander and D. B. Wortman.
Static and Dynamic Characteristics of XPL Programs.
Computer 8(11):41-46, November, 1975.

Introduction: This paper summarises the results of a detailed study that was made of the static and dynamic characteristics of programs written in XPL. The implementation studied was for the IBM System/360.

Types of analysis:

    Static analysis: Static information was gathered by modifying the XPL compiler by including counters.

    Dynamic analysis: The technique used for this was "jump-tracing". Only the branches of the test programs were interpreted, and only these produced dynamic results. A second program was used to analyse the file of information produced.

Programs tested:

Static analysis - 19 programs tested
Dynamic analysis - 10 programs tested

Results: Results are tabulated for:

Distribution of statements by type
Distribution of operators in
   expressions
Distribution of numeric constants
Static instruction usage

Dynamic instruction usage
Instruction distribution (static and
   dynamic)
Distribution of branch distances

[W&H]

[Allen 77]   J. R. Allen.
Some Testing and Maintenance Considerations in Package Design and Implementation.
In *Computer Science and Statistics: Tenth Annual Symposium on the Interface*, pages 211-214. U.S. Department of Commerce/National Bureau of Standards, Washington, D.C., 1977.

Approaches taken to minimize errors prior to distribution of a major statistical package are presented. Design concepts are mentioned which can help avoid errors during implementation and maintenance. The inclusion of statistics-gathering tools within a package is discussed as a way to control errors and improve performance. [MEM]

[Almes 80]   G.T. Almes.
Garbage Collection in an Object-Oriented System.
PhD thesis, Carnegie-Mellon University, Computer Science Department, June, 1980.
Available as CMU-CS-80-128.

This thesis investigates the design, implementation, and testing of a garbage collector for Hydra, and provides a set of measurements of the usage of data objects in Hydra. Several pages are devoted to a description of the measurement tools available on Hydra, including the kernel tracer, the terminal emulator, the snapshot taker, and several ad hoc tools designed to measure particular attributes of Hydra kernel processes. [RTS]

[Amory 75]   W. Amory and J. A. Clapp.
                Engineering of Quality Software Systems (A Software
                Error Classification Methodology).
                Technical Report RADC-TR-74-325, Rome Air Develoment
                Center Technical Report, January, 1975.
This report presents preliminary results of a study in the area of error classification. A
general method of error classification is described which is designed to serve as a
guideline for experiment-specific application. A survey of error classification and analysis
work, both in the general literature and at MITRE, as well as a study of error experiment
design considerations, are reflected in the discussion and conclusions. [Abstract]

[Andrews 74] G.R. Andrews.
                COPS--A Protection Mechanism for Computer Systems.
                PhD thesis, University of Washington, July, 1974.
                Available as 74-07-12.
This dissertation describes a mechanism sufficient to conveniently solve a variety of
problems in the areas of isolation, controlled sharing, restricted access, mutually
suspicious computations, and confinement. In addition, a model of computer protection is
developed in order to abstract this mechanism and others, define types of protection
problems, and define a set of criteria by which to evaluate the utility and functional
completeness of any protection mechanism. COPS is a paper design; hence no discussion
is included on aspects such as user interfaces or control languages for such a system.
[RTS]

[Archer 75]   J. M. Archer.
                Dynamic and Static Analysis of COBOL Programs.
                Memo 46400-75-01, Burroughs Corporation, Paoli, USA,
                1975.
Introduction: This is a report on the dynamic and static analysis of COBOL programs. The
analysis was done to determine if a static analysis gave a true picture of the constructs
used in COBOL programs.

The analysis: The Burroughs COBOL compiler was modified so that a static and dynamic
analysis of user programs could be obtained. The static analysis is done by a procedure in
the compiler and the dynamic analysis is accomplished through the use of a dependant
process which is initiated at run-time.

The test programs: 32 programs were analyzed. 26 of these were benchmark programs
from the burroughs CSG/T library and the other 6 were from a bank's library.

Results: Results are given for:
        Dynamic and static analysis of various data references
        Dynamic analysis of MOVE statements
        Static Data Division summary
[W&H]

[Armstrong 78]
J. Scott Armstrong.
Long-range forecasting: from crystal ball to computer.
John Wiley & Sons, Inc., New York, 1978.

This book embarks on an ambitious task: to set forth everything that is known about forecasting methods in all aspects of business, government, and science. The methods are "applicable to all areas of the social, behavioral, and management sciences." It includes a "comprehensive synthesis of research in economics, sociology, psychology, transporation, education, and management -- with occational references to work in medicine, meteorology, and technology." It seeks to organize its material so as to be suitable for use not only as a reference book for experienced practitioners, but also as an introduction to the field for beginners.

It is divided into five parts, with an extensive bibliography, numerous appendices, a glossary of terms, and indices for subject-matter and persons. Part I distinguishes between forecasting and planning, discusses the role of forecasting in organizations, outlines a strategy for implementing the forecasting function in an organization, and suggests the role that theory and conceptualization should play in forecasting. Part II presents an overview of various types of forecasting methods: judgmental, extrapolation, econometric, segmentation, and "bootstrapping" (simulation) approaches. Part III discusses forecasting model application and use, and includes chapters on the evaluation of forecasting models. Part IV reviews issues related to forecasting costs and benefits and the question of forecasting accuracy. Part V assesses trends in the use of forecasting methods, and reviews current issues in the development of such methods. [Excerpted from CR36317]

[Arnborg 74]   Stefan Arnborg.
Simula Program Semantics and Code Generation
Effectiveness.
FOA P Report C 8408-M3(E5), Research Institute of
National Defense, Stockholm, Sweden, 1974.

Introduction: This report shows the use of a trace system on a Simula-67 compiler to obtain statistics on the semantic properties of user programs. The figures are presented and used to informally evaluate the effectiveness of code generation in DECsystem-10 Simula.

Analysis: A tracing system was included as part of the Simula compiler and this produces listings of the compiler code with frequency counts inserted for all instructions.

Program analyzed: 51 programs were selected according to the following criteria:

1. The program was written to solve a problem stated by comments in the source.
2. It was not written mainly to check the programming system itself.
3. It is not less than 150 lines.
4. Not more than 15 Algol programs were included.

Results: Statistics are presented for:

Frequency of constructs	Procedure and function calls
Literals	Indexed and remote variables
Identifiers	GOTO statements

[W&H]

[Arora 78]   Radha Krishan Arora and R. K. Subramanian.
                Exploiting the optimal paging algorithms.
                Inf. Process. Lett. 7(5):233-236, August, 1978.
From the title of this paper, I expected a discussion of a way to improve existing paging
techniques by applying new insights about optimal paging algorithms. What I found
instead was a presentation of methods for computing: 1) the number of page faults and the
average memory demand for a variable space page replacement algorithm which minimizes
the total cost of replacement and retention of pages; and 2) the minimum number of page
faults for a fixed space demand prepaging algorithm. Although these paging algorithms
are unrealizable (because they require knowledge of future references), they are often
useful as benchmarks for comparisons with realizable replacement algorithms.   The
methods for computing these values appear to be quite efficient, requiring only one pass
over the reference trace and one memory cell per program page. The paper explains the
methods clearly, and I would recommend it to any researcher desiring to compute these
performance measures. [CR34149]

[Ashby 73]   Gorden Ashby, Loren Salmonson, and Robert Heilman.
                Design of an Interactive Debugger for Fortran: MANTIS.
                Software--Practice and Experience 3:65-74, 1973.
A debugger for Fortran is described. Actions can be associated with individual statements.
The execution flow can also be traced. Objectives, implementation experience and system
features are discussed and are related to the general problem of designing debuggers for
language subsystems. [RTS]

[Atwood 79]   Michael E. Atwood, H. Rudy Ramsey, Jean N. Hooper and
                Daniel A. Kullas.
                Annotated Bibliography on Human Factors in Software
                   Development.
                AIR Technical Report P-79-1, June, 1979.
As part of a larger Army Research Institute effort to survey, synthesize, and evaluate the
state of the art in the area of human factors as applied to software development, a fairly
extensive literature survey was conducted. This resulting bibliography contains citatins of
478 articles or reports pertaining to the behavioral aspects of software design,
programming, coding, debugging, testing, evaluation, and maintenance. Most citations are
accompanied by descriptive abstracts, and all are indexed by author, publication source,
institutional affiliation, and subject.   To help the user unfamiliar wih the area, the
bibliography contains brief, basic reference lists in the areas of software engineering, the
psychology of software development, the Structured Programming Series, and the DoD
software program. Coverage is exhaustive through 1977 with a few references in 1978.
[Abstract]

[Baker 77]   W. F. Baker.
                *Software Data Collection and Analysis: A Real-Time
                   System Project History.*
                Technical Report RADC-TR-77-192, Rome Air
                   Development Center, June, 1977.
This report discusses the procedures used for, and the results obtained from, an analysis of
software error problem reports. The problem reports studied were generated during the

development of a large, real-time, highly sophisticated multi-processor data processing system. A brief profile of the development of this system is presented along with discussions of the procedures used in the analysis of the problem reports and the objectives to be met. The results of the analysis are discussed, and statistics reflecting the results are presented. Finally, some of the problems encountered during the course of the study are presented, as well as some pertinent observations. [Abstract]

[Baker 79]   Albert L. Baker and Stuart H. Zweben.
               The Use of Software Science in Evaluating Modularity
                 Concepts.
               IEEE Transactions on Software Engineering SE-5(2):110-
                 120, March, 1979.
An investigation is made into the extent to which relationships from software science are useful in analyzing programming methodology principles that are concerned with modularity. Using previously published data from over 500 programs, it is shown that the software science effort measure provides quantitative answers to questions concerning the conditions under which modularization is beneficial. Among the issues discussed are the reduction of similar code sequences by temporary variable and subprogram definition, and the use of global variables. Using data flow analysis, environmental consideration which affect the applicability of alternative modularity techniques are also discussed.

The results obtained using software science are compared with certain generally accepted methodologies involving modularity, and show strong agreement. Finally, the results suggest some areas of potential improvement in the technique used to obtain the software science measurements. [Abstract]

[Barak 78]   Amnon B. Barak and Moshe Aharoni.
               A Study of Machine Level Software Profiles.
               Software--Practice and Experience 8:131-136, 1978.
The instruction mix of a CDC CYBER/74 computer in a university environment was monitored, and frequencies of execution for the most commonly used instructions was determined. The percentages over various time intervals is constant, so a machine-level software profile (MLSP) can be computed. [RTS]

[Bard 76]   Yonathan Bard.
               An Experimental Approach to System Tuning.
               In Peter P. S. Chen and Mark Franklin, editor, *Proceedings
                 of the International Symposium on Computer
                 Performance Modeling, Measurement and
                 Evaluation*, pages 296-305. Harvard University, March,
                 1976.
It is desired to find the values of certain system parameters which maximize some performance criterion. Using standard experimental design techniques, one runs an initial set of experiments which explore the system's response surface. Subsequently, the data are smoothed, and a hill climbing technique is used to locate the maximum. This technique was employed successfully to tune the paramenters in an experimental version of the VM/370 scheduler.[Abstract]

The techniques of measurement described here have the great advantage of neither pretending to specious accuracy nor consuming the resources they are supposed to measure during the experimental period. This would seem a method with wide applicability in tuning systems, and one capable of useful refinement with experience. [CR34690]

[Bard 79]   Yonathan Bard.
Performance Analysis of Interactive Systems.
In *Quantitative Software Models*, pages 108-124. Data and Analysis Center for Software, 1979.
Many topics are covered by the science (art??) of system performance analysis. Among these are measurement of existing systems, tuning, performance evaluation, design of control algorithms, system modeling, workload characterization, and performance prediction. After giving a brief summary of these topics, the paper will concentrate on the last three. It will describe how existing workloads can be measured and analyzed routinely so as to produce the inputs required by analytic system models. These models employ queueing network formulations which allow the workload to consist of several user classes with different characteristics. Such models have been validated successfully against real systems, but some problems, particularly relating to paging in virtual memory systems, have so far not received definitive solutions. [CR34534]

[Barnard 77]   David Barnard (ed.).
An Annotated Bibliography on Computer Program Engineering.
Technical Report, University of Toronto, Computer Systems Research Group, May, 1977.
Collects extensive annotations on individual articles in the field of software engineering and includes subject classification and extensive topic cross-referencing. Many of the referenced articles are relevant to software metrics. [MS]

[Barron 72]   D.W. Barron and I.R. Jackson.
The Evolution of Job Control Languages.
Software--Practice and Experience 2:143-162, 1972.
This paper traces the historical development of command languages, and compares OS/360 and the George 3 CL. Modern CL's are shown to be akin to programming languages. Many of the problems of OS/360 JCL are illustrated. [RTS]

[Basili 75]   V. R. Basili and A. J. Turner.
Iterative Enhancement: A Practical Technique for Software Development.
IEEE Transactions on Software Engineering SE-1(4), December, 1975.
This paper recommends the "iterative enhancement" technique as a practical means of using a top-down, stepwise refinement approach to software development. This technique begins with a simple initial implementation of a properly chosen (skeletal) subproject which is followed by the gradual enhancement of successive implementations in order to build the full implementation. The development and quantitative analysis of a production compiler for the language SIMPL-T is used to demonstrate that the application of iterative enhancement to software development is practical and efficient, encourages the generation of an easily modifiable product, and facilitates reliability. [VRB]

[Basili 77a]   Victor R. Basili, Marvin V. Zelkowitz, Frank E. McGarry,
               Robert W. Reiter, Walter F. Truszkowski and David
               L. Weiss.
               The Software Engineering Laboratory.
               Technical Report TR-535, University of Maryland,
               Computer Science Center, College Park, Maryland,
               May, 1977.

The development of techniques to produce cost-effective reliable software first requires the collection of quantitative and qualitative data on the development process. Towards this end, the Software Engineering Laboratory has been organized in conjunction with NASA Goddard Space Flight Center. The purpose of the Software Engineering Laboratory is to monitor existing software methodologies and develop and measure the effectiveness of alternate methodologies.

Initially, three aspects of the software development life cycle are to be investigated. These are: (1) management aspects in estimating team organization, resource requirements, schedules and reliability factors in the finished software product, (2) error characteristics and their causes, and (3) program structure and its relation to well-developed software. [VRB]

[Basili 77b]   Victor R. Basili and Marvin V. Zelkowitz.
               The Software Engineering Laboratory: Objectives.
               In *Proceedings Fifth Annual Computer Personnel
               Research Conference*, pages 256-269. ACM, August,
               1977.

This paper describes the work being done at the Software Engineering Laboratory of NASA Goddard Space Flight Center in cooperation with the University of Maryland. The goals of the laboratory are "to analyze the software development process and software produced in order to understand the development process, the software product itself, the effect of various *improvements* on the process with respect to the methodology, and to develop quantitative measures that correlate well with intuitive notions of good software."

The paper includes 1) an overview of the research objectives and experiments being performed at the laboratory, 2) the current list of factors under study that may affect the software development process or product, 3) data collection and data management activities, and 4) the current status and future plans for the laboratory. Currently, about a dozen projects are being studies. No results are available as yet. [CR35656]

[Basili 78a]   Victor R. Basili and Robert W. Reiter, Jr.
               Investigating Software Development Approaches.
               Technical Report TR-688, University of Maryland,
               Department of Computer Science, August, 1978.

This paper reports on research comparing various approaches, or methodologies, for software development. The study focuses on the quantitative analysis of the application of certain methodologies in an experimental environment, in order to further understand their effects and better demonstrate their advantages in a controlled environment. A series of statistical experiments were conducted comparing programming teams that used a disciplined methodology (consisting of top-down design, process design language usage, structured programming, code reading, and chief programmer team organization) with programming teams and individual programmers that employed ad hoc approaches. Specific details of the experimental setting, the investigative approach (used to plan, execute, and analyze the experiments), and some of the results of the experiments are discussed. [VRB]

Reports on a controlled software experiment in which it was found that three man teams, in building a simple compiler, which were required to use modern programming methods required less effort than uncontrolled teams or individuals. [FGS]

[Basili 78b]   Victor R. Basili, Edward H. Ely and Donovan Young.
                Executive Summary of the Second Software Life Cycle
                    Management Workshop.
                Proceedings of Second Software Life Cycle Management
                    Workshop.
                Workshop held in Atlanta, Georgia in August, 1978.
This is the proceedings of a workshop sponsored by the U. S. Army Computer Systems Command, U. S. Army Institute for Research in Management Information and Computer Science. It contains a large volume of papers which deal with models, metrics, and studies in the software life cycle management process. Topics of interest include (1) description and understanding of various components of the life cycle, (2) ways to delineate and analyze relationships among component activities, (3) milestones and other tools to help direct, coordinate, understand and control research and development in software life cycle management, and (4) development of management tools using the results of life cycle management research to help plan and manage software development projects. [VRB]

[Basili 78c]   Victor R. Basili and Marvin V. Zelkowitz.
                Analyzing Medium-Scale Software Development.
                In *Proceedings Third International Conference on
                    Software Engineering*, pages 116-123. ACM, May,
                    1978.
The most fascinating aspect of this paper is the distance between the stated goals of the program and programming quality analysis and the state of the art as described.

The authors start well by putting forth an important problem: How do you assess new programming methodologies when there are no firm measures of programming effectiveness or program quality? There is a need for a better understanding of the attributes of good programs in order to understand the attributes of good programming technology. (In order to address this problem, the Software Engineering Laboratory has been established as a co-operative effort between NASA Goddard and the University of Maryland.)

The authors describe a procedure for collecting data about personnel skills and organization, assessments of problem magnitude, programming methodologies, tools, and resources. For a set of projects, with different degrees of monitoring, various expense curves are defined. An attempt is made to fit data to the Rayleigh curve which is investigated as an equation for predicting development cycle costs for medium scale projects.

The problem is well stated, the references are reasonable, and the paper holds great promise -- particularly for me, since Glen Myers is a close colleague and it would be nice if someone offered conclusive evidence that software technology of the kind he fosters is truly effective.

Unfortunately, perhaps through no fault of the authors, the paper soon lapses almost completely into issues of project management and cost estimation. Very little is reported about changes in cost patterns or quality due to different programming methodologies. Nothing is said about refined measures of software quality. Possibly this is because this is an early paper in a long-term effort. Still, given the initial statement of the problem, the paper is a disappointment.

The reviewer has the impression that the authors are surprised by some mismatches between predictions and actualities. But they are honest and intelligent and attempt to explain the phenomena.

Most disturbing is the fact that organizational practices which separate the development cycle from the maintenance cycle lead to some serious distortions in lifetime programming costs.

It is highly likely that this research will produce more results later, but, at the moment, it seems to be in a very initial state, and the paper seems to suggest how far we have to go rather than how far we have come. [CR35228]

The collection and analysis of data from programming projects is necessary for the appropriate evaluation of software engineering methodologies. Towards this end, the Software Engineering Laboratory was organized between the University of Maryland and NASA Goddard Space Flight Center. This paper describes the structure of the Laboratory and provides some data on project evaluation from some of the early projects that have been monitored. The analysis relates to resource forecasting using a model of the project life cycle based upon the Rayleigh equation and to error rates applying ideas developed by Belady and Lehman. [VRB]

[Basili 79a] Victor R. Basili and Robert W. Reiter, Jr.
Evaluating Automatable Measures of Software
Development.
IEEE Workshop on Quantitative Software Models,
October, 1979.

There is a need for distinguishing a set of useful automatable measures of the software development process and product. Measures are considered *useful* if they are sensitive to externally observable differences in development environments and their relative values correspond to some intuition regarding these characteristic differences. Such measures could provide an objective quantitative foundation for constructing quality assurance standards and for calibrating mathematical models of software reliability and resource estimation. This paper presents a set of automatable measures that were implemented, evaluated in a controlled experiment, and found to satisfy these usefulness criteria. The measures include computer job steps, program changes, program size, and cyclomatic complexity. [VRB]

[Basili 79b] Victor R. Basili and Marvin V. Zelkowitz.
Measuring Software Development Characteristics in the
Local Environment.
Computers and Structures 10, 1979.

This paper discusses the characterization and analysis facilities being performed by the Software Engineering Laboratory which can be done with minimal efort on many projects.

Some examples are given of the kinds of analyses that can be done to aid in managing, understanding and characterizing the development of software in a production environment. [VRB]

[Basili 79c]   Victor R. Basili and Robert W. Reiter, Jr.
                An Investigation of Human Factors in Software
                Development.
                Computer Magazine, December, 1979.
This paper gives a human factors interpretation of an experiment on software development. The experiment involves the development of software under three different environments which include disciplined teams, ad hoc teams, and ad hoc individuals. Low level programming aspects are used to predict high level software properties, such as reliability, cost effectiveness, and complexity. [VRB]

[Basili 81a]   Victor R. Basili.
                Resource Models.
                In Frederick G. Sayward, Mary Shaw and Alan J. Perlis,
                    editor, *Software Metrics: An Analysis and Evaluation*.
                MIT Press, Cambridge, Massachusetts, 1981.
In "Resource Models" Basili categorizes two approaches to predicting the resources (such as computer time, personnel, and dollars) needed for large scale software projects: formulating models based on historical data and relationships, and, deriving equations from assumptions such as how people solve problems.

He recommends that experiments be conducted aimed at substantiating the formulae which have been derived. He also feels that research aimed at gaining insights on the software lifecycle from the derived formulae should be supported. [FGS]

[Basili 81b]   Victor R. Basili.
                Data Collection, Analysis, and Validation.
                In Frederick G. Sayward, Mary Shaw and Alan J. Perlis,
                    editor, *Software Metrics: An Analysis and Evaluation*.
                MIT Press, Cambridge, Massachusetts, 1981.
In "Data Collection, Analysis, and Validation," Basili gives a variety of means for collecting data on software projects and suggests approaches to dealing with the validity of the data-forms and automated data-collecting programs. Validity considerations include incorrectly filled-out forms and redundant data.

He recommends that more effort be put into defining terms, reporting error bounds on collected data, and establishing and refining a very large data base on the software life cycle. It would be helpful to find ways of integrating metrics into the process of classifying the data base. [FGS]

[Batson 77]   A. P. Batson and R. E. Brundage.
               Segment Sizes and Lifetimes in Algol 60 Programs.
               Communications of the ACM 20(1):36-44, 1977.
Introduction: The research described in this paper is an empirical study of the nature of the memory demands made by a collection of Algol60 programs. The distributions are presented for several virtual memory components of the Algol programs.

Analysis: The B5500 Algol compiler and operating system were modified to collect the statistics.

Programs analyzed: 34 B5500 Algol programs made up the sample. They were production programs for scientific/engineering applications, and ranged considerably in size from 162 words to 89976 words.

Results: Johnson's Contour Model is used for describing the concepts of scope and computing environment. Results are plotted for:

Program segment sizes
Contour data segment sizes
Contour lifetimes and normalized average contour lifetimes
Array segment sizes
Array segment lifetimes
Total memory request associated with each contour

[W&H]

[Beaton 76]   A.E. Beaton, D.B. Rubin and J.L. Barone.
The Acceptability of Regression Solutions: Another Look
at Computational Accuracy.
Journal of the American Statistical Association
71(353):1958-1968, 1976.

This paper discusses the measurement of accuracy of computed solutions to multiple regression problem. It proposes that a *perturbation index* be computed by these programs to measure the sensitivity of the solution to rounding errors. [IF]

[Beilner 77]   H. Beilner and E. Gelenbe.
Measuring, modeling and evaluating computer systems.
Elsevier/North Holland, Inc., New York, 1977.

This book consists of the 26 papers presented at the Third International Symposium on Modeling and Performance Evaluation of Computer Systems organized in Bonn, W. Germany (October 1977) by GMD and cosponsored by IFIP Working Group 7.3, IRIA-LABORIA, and the Commission of the European Communities.

Five contributions aim at the evaluation of more or less total computer system configurations; four papers deal with models of program behavior and of memory management policies; seven others propose exact or approximate solutions for probabilistic models of queues and/or of networks of queues. There are two studies of optimal resource assignment under deadlock and cost constraints, respectively. Two papers discuss the use of timed Petri nets for performance evaluation. The remaining presentations deal with simulation models (2), measurement tools (1), statistical sequential methods (1), and reliability assessment of fault-tolerant computing systems (1).

Most papers are contributions to research; this book is therefore not tor the manager in search of a ready-made method for the evaluation of his computer installation. [Excerpted from CR34328]

[Belady 76]   L. A. Belady and M. M. Lehman.
A Model of Large Program Development.
IBM Systems Journal(3), 1976.

Discussed are observations made on the development of OS/360 and its subsequent enhancements and releases. Some modeling approaches to organizing these observations are also presented. [VRB]

[Belady 79a]   L. A. Belady.
               Survey of software complexity measures.
               Proceedings of the IEEE Workshop on Quantitative
                   Software Models.
               Workshop held in Kiamesha Lake, New York, in October,
                   1979.
The survey is presented in a two-dimensional classification of about seventy papers on complexity.   Both programming related and more general papers are considered. Following the approach taken by a paper, the survey distinguishes four classes: informal, based on counting, probabilistic, and experimental. Some examples are offered. [LAB]

[Belady 79b]   L. A. Belady and C. J. Evangelisti.
               System Partitioning and its Measure.
               Technical Report RC 7560 (# 32643), IBM T. J. Watson
                   Research Center, March, 1979.
Program modules and data structures are interconnected by calls and references in software systems. Partitioning these entities into clusters reduces complexity. For very large systems manual clustering is impractical. A method to perform automatic clustering is described and a metric to quantify the complexity of the resulting partition is developed. [Abstract]

[Belady 79c]   L. A. Belady and M. M. Lehman.
               The Characteristics of Large Systems.
               In *Research Directions in Software Technology*, pages
                   106-138. MIT Press, Cambridge, Massachusetts, 1979.
In this paper Belady and Lehman summarize their research of the last decade into the dynamics of large software systems. They view a large software system as being very much like an organism which changes throughout its lifetime in reaction to its environment. These changes continue long after traditional system implementation is complete. Following the normal practice in general systems theory, they formulate their observations as a set of laws. The most important of these laws are:

1. Law of Continuing Change: A system that is used undergoes continuing change until it is judged more cost effective to freeze and recreate it;
2. Law of Increasing Unstructuredness: The entropy of a system increases with time, unless specific work is executed to maintain or reduce it;
3. Law of Dynamic Evolution: Measures of global system attributes may appear stochastic locally in time and space, but statistically they are cyclically self-regulating, with identifiable invariances and recognizable long-range trends.

Belady and Lehman present many tables and graphs drawn from IBM software development experience to illustrate and explain their contention that large software systems are like other large systems in most ways. They urge software developers to apply general system theory to the development and maintenance processes.

This is an outstanding paper. Important arguments are clearly and persuasively presented. The approach is largely nontechnical. Everyone involved with large software systems, either as a developer or a user, should read and absorb this paper. [CR35552]

[Belady 81]   L. A. Belady.
Complexity of Large Systems.
In Frederick G. Sayward, Mary Shaw and Alan J. Perlis,
editor, *Software Metrics: An Analysis and Evaluation*.
MIT Press, Cambridge, Massachusetts, 1981.

In "Complexity of Large Systems" Belady finds that there are many speculative ideas around on the complexity of small programs but that few of them have been adequately tested. There is much duplicated uncoordinated effort. The two most important concepts for the complexity of large systems are evolutionary complexity and the time required to do a programming task. Little is known about evolutionary complexity.

Belady sees the need for a DOD coordinated effort to establish a large data base for validating a small standard set of complexity metrics. Also this data base could be studied in a search for patterns and trends in the evolution of large systems. This would lead to models of software evolution from which would emanate testable hypotheses. Another potentially fruitful study would be an exploration on the use of locality of information in large systems. [FGS]

[Belgard 78]   Richard Belgard and Victor B. Schneider.
A Comparison of the Code Space and Execution Time
Required for FORTRAN Assignment Statements on Six
Computer Architectures.
In *MICRO 11: Proceedings Eleventh Annual
Microprogramming Workshop*, pages 56-64. ACM,
IEEE, November, 1978.

This paper attempts a *topological* comparison of six different architectures for a class of instructions, namely, FORTRAN assignment statements. The qualifier *topological* is used here because the authors attempt a technology-and size-independent comparison. Since the memory access and addition time are taken to be the same for all architectures, the differences show up because of the organization and storage of parsing tree and access mechanisms employed to fetch instructions and data. The authors generate tables to indicate lower bounds on compiled code lengths and worst case execution times to make their point.

In the opinion of this reviewer, the chief merit of the paper is that the authors attempt a topological comparison, and the main drawback is that the result has no practical value since the instruction set chosen is too restrictive, and no consideration is given to the software environment which can exploit architectural features of a machine. [CR35449]

[Bergeron 75] R. Daniel Bergeron and Henri Bulterman.
A Technique for Evaluation of User Systems on an IBM
S/370.
Software--Practice and Experience 5:83-92, 1975.

The design and implementation of the System for System Development (SSD) Evaluation System is described. This system modifies load modules of the user's system in order to cause run-time invocation of the system at routine entry. Raw data on secondary storage is produced, and a post processor is used to interpret the data. The information produced by the post processor includes cummulative and differential times, execution counts, and a history of the calling sequences. [RTS]

[Bianchi 76]   M. H. Bianchi and J. L. Wood.
A User's Viewpoint of a Programmer's Workbench.
In *Proceedings of the Second International Conference on Software Engineering*, pages 193-199. IEEE, San Francisco, 1976.
This paper presents the benefits obtainable to a user of the facilities provided by Programmer's Workbench. [MEM]

[Bicevskis 79] Janis Bicevskis, Juris Borzovs, Uldis Straujums, Andris Zarins, and Edward F. Miller, Jr.
SMOTL -- A system to Construct Samples for Data Processing Program Debugging.
IEEE Transactions on Software Engineering SE-5(1):60-66, January, 1979.
The possiblity of automatic construction of a complete set of program tests is considered. A test set system is said to be complete if every feasible program branch (segment) is executed by it. The complete test set construction algorithm for commercially oriented data processing programs is outlined, and the results of its functioning on real programs are analyzed. [Abstract]

[Bingham 76] H. W. Bingham and K. T. Carvin.
Dynamic Usage of APL Primitive Functions.
In *APL-76, ACM-STAPL Conference*, ACM, September, 1976.
Introduction: Dynamic measurements of APL primitive functions and operators applied to shaped data objects (arrays) were routinely collected by the Burroughs APL/700 system. Actual usage of these primitives by all APL users was counted. Data collected from two sites is contrasted.

Analysis: Counters in the APL/700 processor are used to collect the dynamic information. Observations were collected for entire days, usually about a week apart. Some static information collected earlier is also included in the results.

The programs:

	Site A	Site B
primitives	30 million	7 million
sample days	19	3
principal applications	design assistance, text editing	mathematical modelling, graphics

Results: Results are presented for:
Dynamic and static percent usage of primitive functions
Dynamic and static percent usage of dyadic mixed functions
Dynamic and static percent usage of monadic mixed functions
Dynamic and static percent usage of operators
Dynamic and static percent indexing usage

Dynamic and static ranked usage of functions

[W&H]

[Bishop 77]   Peter B. Bishop.
                *Computer systems with a very large address space and
                    garbage collection.*
                PhD thesis, Massachusetts Institute of Technology, May,
                    1977.
                Available as MIT LCS TR-178.

A new computer system is proposed that provides hardware support for objects and object references that can be used in all applications of objects. The new system provides small object references that can be copied freely, makes very small objects efficient, and retrieves the storage for inaccessible objects automatically. This system is compared with some widely used existing system, and while its speed seems to be competitive, it is much easier to use.

Object references provide protection in the new system as do capabilities in capability systems. The object reference in the new system contains an address from a linear, paged virtual address space rather than a unique ID. Use of small objects is made feasible by efficiently grouping objects into areas. Objects in the same area may be placed on the same page. The system automatically and efficiently maintains lists of inter-area links that allow single areas to be garbage collected independently of the rest of the system. The garbage collector can determine whether objects have been inappropriately placed in an area and can move these objects to more appropriate area automatically. [Abstract]

[Bloom 74]   Burton H. Bloom, Mac H. Clark, Clare G. Feldman, Robert
                K. Coe.
                Criteria for Evaluating the Performance of Compilers.
                Technical Report RADC-TR-74-259, Rome Air
                    Development Center, October, 1974.

The main purpose of this study was to develop criteria by which it will be possible to qualitatively measure and evaluate the performance of compilers, possibly operating on different computers, and possibly having different features. To satisfy this purpose, three technical questions were studied:

1. How can two compilers with the same features and operating in the same environment be compared?
2. If two compilers with the same features operate in different environements, how can their measured differences in performance be attributed to the environmental differences vs. the compiler differences?
3. How should a compiler buyer deal with the problem of evaluating compilers with different special features?

These three questions were studied from a point of view that the answers should help provide a basis for conducting dollar cost/benefit analysis of compilers. [Abstract]

Introduction: The main purpose of this report is to develop criteria by which it will be possible to quantitively measure and evaluate the performance of compilers. In order to do this a static and dynamic analysis of Jovial programs compiled by the J3B and AEB compilers was made.

Analysis:

Static analysis   The compilers were modified to collect the static data.

Dynamic analysis   To obtain the dynamic data, weighting factors were applied to the static information.

Test programs: Two J3B programs were selected from a collection of such programs used for acceptance testing of the J3B compiler. The programs were modified so that two corresponding AED programs could be prepared.

Results: Static and dynamic results are presented for:

      Summary of usage of statement types, operators and labels
      Summary of usage of assignment statement forms
      Summary of usage of statement types used with conditionals and loops
      Summary of usage of FOR statement sub-types
      Summary of usage of integer forms in FOR statements
      Summary of usage of arithmetic form
      Summary of usage of boolean forms
      Histogram of occurrences of procedure and function calls
      Histogram of occurrences of assignment statements
      Histogram of occurrences of boolean expressions
      Histogram of occurrences of FOR loops
      Histogram of occurrences of executable statements in FOR loops
      % usage of statement types
      % usage of statement types following THEN
      % usage of statement types following ELSE
      % usage of statement types following DO
      % usage of arithmetic operators
      % usage of arithmetic forms
      % usage of boolean operators
      % usage of boolean forms
      % usage of arithmetic assignments
      % usage of boolean expressions
      % usage of function calls
      % usage of executable statements in FOR loops

[W&H]

[Boehm 78]   B. W. Boehm, J. R. Brown, H. Kaspar, M. Lipow, G. J. McLeod, M. J. Merritt.
Characteristics of Software Quality.
North-Holland Publishing Company, 1978.

The objectives of this study were to identify a set of characteristics of quality software and, for each characteristic, to define a metric such that:

1. Given an arbitrary program, the metric provides a quantitative measure of the degree to which the program has the associated characteristic.
2. Overall software quality can be defined as some function of the values of the metrics.

[Abstract]

[Boies 74]   S. J. Boies and J. D. Gould.
Syntactic Errors in Computer Programming.
Human Factors 16(3):253-257, 1974.
Introduction: This paper is mainly concerned with how programmers correct syntactic errors, but also contains statistics on how often this type of error occur on the IBM TSS/360 time-sharing system.

Programs: All programs were analyzed in two five day periods. Data for the two test periods are shown separately.

113/166 programs were submitted to the FORTRAN language processor
139/125 programs were submitted to the PL/I language processor
66/77 programs were submitted to the Assembler language processor

Results: As there are not many results, they are given below for both five day periods.

FORTRAN

16%/13% contained one or more errors
78%/83% contained no errors
6%/5% were terminated before any errors were detected

PL/I

17%/18% contained one or more errors
73%/75% contained no errors
10%/7% were terminated before any errors were detected

Assembler

12%/9% contained one or more errors
62%/81% contained no errors
26%/10% were terminated before any errors were detected

[W&H]

[Boisvert 79]   Ronald F. Boisvert, John R. Rice and Elias N. Houstis.
A System for Performance Evaluation of Partial Differential Equations Software.
IEEE Transactions on Software Engineering SE-5(4):418-425, July, 1979.
This paper describes a system to systematically compare the performance of various methods (software modules) for the numerical solution of partial differential equations. We discuss the general nature and large size of this performance evaluation problem and the data one obtains. The system meets certain design objectives that ensure a valid experiment: 1) precise definition of a particular measurement; 2) uniformity in definition of variables entering the experiment; and 3) reproducibility of results. The ease of use of the system makes it possible to make the large sets of measurements necessary to obtain confidence in the results and its portability allows others to check or extend the measurements. The system has four parts: 1) semiautomatic generation of problems for experimental input; 2) the *ellpack* system for actually solving the equation; 3) a data management system to organize and access the experimental data; and 4) data analysis programs to extract graphical and statistical summaries from the data. [Abstract]

[Bonner 69]   A.J. Bonner.
               Using system monitor output to improve performance.
               IBM System Journal(4):290-298, 1969.
First a simple hardware monitor is described which consists of multiple inputs, a patchboard for combining signals, and a set of sixteen registers which can count events or record durations. The use of this monitor in detecting bottlenecks and increasing performance is then discussed. [RTS]

[Booth 79a]   Taylor L. Booth.
               Performance Optimization of Software Systems
                  Processing Information Sequences Modeled by
                  Probabilistic Languages.
               IEEE Transactions on Software Engineering SE-5(1):31-
                  44, January, 1979.
The performance of a hardware/software system is a function of both the deterministic properties of the computation being performed and the probabilistic properties of the information sequence being processed. This paper develops the idea of a computational cost which can be used to measure system performance and shows how this cost can be related to the structure of the system and the information processed by the system. Different ways in which this cost can be used to study system performance are presented. [Abstract]

[Booth 79b]   Taylor L. Booth.
               Use of Computation Structure Models to Measure
                  Computation Performance.
               In *Proceedings Conference on Simulation, Measurement,
                  and Modeling of Computer Systems*, pages 183-188.
                  ACM, August, 1979.
This paper is a straightforward application of flowbalance equations and external constraints to a flowchart to obtain an independent set of flow counts in terms of which execution time costs can be evaluated. The procedure is illustrated by means of a program to look up two tables to find a given key.

The main achievement of the paper seems to be a significant reduction in the number of counters required to obtain the program profile via the application of the flowbalance equations and systems constraints. A section outlines the procedures for estimating the probability density function (in this case, the probability of finding a key in either one table or the other), based on the measurements.

This is mostly textbook material; nevertheless, it is a quite useful technique and worth serious consideration by those desiring information in the areas of software modeling and measurement. [CR35703]

[Brailsford 77] D.F. Brailsford, E. Foxley, K.L. Mander and D.J. Morgan.
               Run-Time Profiling of Algol 68-R programs using
                  DIDYMUS and SCAMP.
               SIGPlan Notices 12(6):27-35, June, 1977.
               Proceedings of the Strathclyde Algol 68 Conference.
Two programs are discussed. The first, DIDYMUS, is run together with the program to be

monitored, and builds a histogram of the program counter at regular intervals. A postprocessor which has access to the link table then prints the approximate time spent in each routine. The second program, SCAMP, is a preprocessor which inserts code to maintain counts of syntactic constructs. Since only a moderate amount of syntactic analysis is done, there are several restrictions on the allowable constructs. [RTS]

[BrinchHansen 73]
>   Per Brinch Hansen.
>   Testing a Multiprogramming System.
>   *Software--Practice and Experience* 3:145-150, 1973.

A central problem in program design is to structure a large program such that it can be tested systematically by the simplest possible techniques. This paper describes the method used to test the RC 4000 multiprogramming system. During testing, the system records all transitions of processes and messages between various queues. The test mechanism consists of fifty machine instructions centralized in two procedures. By using this mechanism in a series of carefully selected test cases, the system was made virtually free error free within a few weeks. The test procedure is illustrated by examples. [Abstract]

[BrinchHansen 78]
>   Per Brinch Hansen.
>   Reproducible Testing of Monitors.
>   *Software--Practice and Experience* 8:721-729, 1978.

This paper describes a systematic method for testing monitor modules which control process interactions in concurrent programs. A monitor is tested by executing a concurrent program in which the processes are synchronized by a clock to make the sequence of interactions reproducible. The method separates the construction and implementation of test cases and makes the analysis of a concurrent experiment similar to the analysis of a sequential program. The implementation of a test program is almost mechanical. The method, which is illustrated by an example, has been successfully used to test a multicomputer network program written in Concurrent Pascal. [Abstract]

[Brooks 78]   R. Brooks.
>   Using a Behavioral Theory of Program Comprehension in Software Engineering.
>   In *Proceedings 3rd International Conference Software Engineering*, pages 196-201. IEEE, 1978.

In a controlled software experiment the author found that dictionaries of program variables are superior to macro flowcharts as an aid to understand program control and data structures. [FGS]

[Brooks 80]   R. Brooks.
>   Studying Programmer Behavior Experimentally: The Problems of Proper Methodology.
>   *Communications of the ACM* 23(4):207-213, April, 1980.

Reviews the subject, material, and measure selections which have been used in software experiments. Concludes that the subject and material selections used thus far have been poor and recommends that past experiments be replicated with more realistic subjects and materials before the conclusions of these experiments can be widely accepted. Concludes that, although measure selection has not been as bad as subject and material selection, new measures of the effort required for program construction and program understanding based on cognitive models of program-programmer interaction are needed. [FGS]

[Brown 79]   W. Stanley Brown.
              Some Fundamentals of Performance Evaluation for
              Numerical Software.
              In *Performance Evaluation of Numerical Software*, pages
              17-30. Elsevier North-Holland, Inc., New York, 1979.
One aspect of the evaluation of numerical software concerns the performance for all valid inputs on a given computer. To be declared correct, a numerical algorithm must be proven to give results accurate to within the machine range.   To assist in the evaluation of numerical programs, the author has constructed a model of a floating point arithmetic system.   This model is described by means of some basic machine constants and in addition some derived constants depending on the basic parameters.   A technique is described for computing these parameters.   The model system is used in proving correctness of an algorithm for computing the mean of a vector. [CR35979]

[Browne 70]   P. H. Browne et al.
               *Data Processing Technologies, Volume I - High-Level
               Language Evaluation.*
               Army Contract No. DAH60-69-C-0037, Teledyne Brown
               Engineering, Huntsville, Alabama, May, 1970.
This paper discusses the evaluation criteria used for selecting languages for use in Ballistic Missile Defense Agency.   While most of the paper is devoted to a discussion of the relevance of the technical characteristics of the languages under consideration, the report is important for software metrics because it describes a weighted scoring technique and applies this to a practical situation. [JES]

[Browne 75]   J. C. Browne, K. M. Chandy, R. M. Brown, T. W. Keller,
               D. F. Towsley and C. W. Dissly.
               Hierarchical Techniques for the Development of Realistic
               Models of Complex Computer Systems.
               In *Proceedings of the IEEE 63*, pages 966-977. IEEE, 1975.
This paper is a case study on the application of hierarchically structured modeling to the performance analysis of a complex computer system.   This work preceded the formal development of hierarchical structures of queueing networks and thus gives intuitive and readable arguments for this technique. [JCB]

[Browne 81]   J. C. Browne and Mary Shaw.
               Toward a Scientific Basis for Software Evaluation.
               In Frederick G. Sayward, Mary Shaw and Alan J. Perlis,
                   editor, *Software Metrics: An Analysis and Evaluation*.
               MIT Press, Cambridge, Massachusetts, 1981.
In "Toward a Scientific Basis for Software Evaluation" Browne and Shaw explain how a great deal of energy is regularly invested in making measurements on software and its development process.   The techniques of description, measurement, and evaluation are, however, mostly ad hoc. Most of the analysis and data collection techniques haven't been

generalized beyond the local system for which they were developed. There is a general lack of a scientific foundation in this area on which to derive invariant principles from observations and experiments.

They recommend that future experimental work be based on the traditional principles of science where the first considerations are principles which are invariant across all software and hierarchies of abstract models. Although there now are several popular predictive models, they see more long term benefits coming from structural models of software. It is the development of this area for which they recommend support, with concentration first being on learning from structural models for specific systems. [FGS]

[Brunt 76]   R.F. Brunt and D.E. Tuffs.
A User-Oriented Approach to Control Languages.
Software--Practive and Experience 6:96-108, 1976.
This paper describes SCL, the command language of System B, the operating system of ICL's 2900 series computers. SCL is a block-structured, procedure oriented approach, with some control constructs (IF and GOTO) and macros. The parameters to procedure calls are rather extensive (8 data types). The data types available to the user include integer, boolean, string, vector, and array. VAR parameters are also allowed in procedure calls. [RTS]

[Bryant 79]   R. F. Bryant and J. B. Dennis.
Concurrent Programming,
Research Directions in Software Technology. MIT Press,
Cambridge, Massachusetts, 1979.
This paper is a readable survey of techniques for the management of concurrent and parallel programming. It is a research summary up-to-date as of about 1977. [JCB]

[Bryce 75]   G.R. Bryce and H.G. Hilton.
Local Installation of Packages.
In *Proceedings of the Statistical Computing
Section*, pages 13-15. American Statistical
Association, 1975.
The authors conduct an experiment to measure the difficulty of installing several competing statistical software systems. [IF]

[Budd 78]   Timothy A. Budd, Richard J. Lipton, Frederick G. Sayward,
and Richard A. DeMillo.
The Design of a Prototype Mutation System for
Programming Testing.
In *Proc. 1978 National Computer Conference*, pages 623-
628. AFIPS, November, 1978.
One of the most neglected areas of software development has been the area of software testing. There have, however, been many articles written on the inadequacy of the testing performed on software prior to release.

The authors are correct when they state that the "major question which must always be addressed is: If a program is correct for a finite number of test cases, can we assume it is correct in general."

We are presented with a "design of a prototype mutation system for program testing." This analysis is based upon the assumption that "competent programmers will produce programs which, if they are not correct, are 'almost' correct. That is, if a program is not correct it is a 'mutant'--it differs from a correct program by simple errors." Mutation analysis is designed to detect these errors. The prototype system is approximately 80 percent effective using 25 mutant operators. These operators range from simple to complex.

If the prodecures discussed are effective on subroutines, the question arises as to whether they can be as effective on larger, more complete programs. In any case, it is gratifying to see that more attention is being paid to testing software prior to release rather than waiting to correct errors detected by the user. [CR34263]

[Buzen 76]   J. P. Buzen.
Fundamental Laws of Computer Systems Performance.
In *Proceedings of the International Symposium on Computer Performance Modeling Measurements and Evaluation*, pages 200-210. March, 1976.
This is the original paper defining operational analysis of computer system performance. It develops the conceptual foundation for establishing macro-level relationships between work measures such as throughput and resource usage. [JCB]

[Buzen 78]   J. P. Buzen and P. J. Denning.
The Operational Analysis of Queueing Network Models.
Computing Surveys 10:225-262, 1978.
This paper elaborates on and gives a number of examples of the application of the operational analysis technique to performance evaluation. [JCB]

[Calingaert 67]
Peter Calingaert.
System Performance Evaluation: Survey and Appraisal.
Communications of the ACM 10(1):12-18, January, 1967.
The state of the art of system performance evaluation is reviewed and evaluation goals and problems are examined. Throughput, turnaround, and availability are defined as fundamental measures of performance; overhead and CPU speed are placed in perspective. The appropriateness of instruction mixes, kernels, simulators and other tools is discussed, as well as pitfalls which may be encountered when using them. [Abstract]

[Cambell 68]   D.J. Cambell and U.J. Heffner.
Measurement and analysis of large operating systems during system development.
In *Proceeding AFIPS Fall Joint Computer Conference*, pages 903-914. AFIPS Press, 1968.
After a summary of hardware and software measurement techniques, four specific methods for internal system measurement are given. These are (a) system design that allows for adequate measurement (ensuring that important information is available somewhere in the system); (b) built-in system auditing techniques (checkpointing and other techniques to increase reliability and detect inconsistencies); (c) event tracing (of some fifty different events for the operating system illustrated); and (d) performance analysis with exterior tools

(mainly event analysis and sampling tools). The paper is impressive in that it gives many examples of tools that were used in the implementation of a large operating system. The last two sections are particularly useful. [RTS]

[Cantrell 68]   H.N. Cantrell and A.C. Ellison.
Multiprogramming System Performance Measurement and Analysis.
In *Proceedings of the AFIPS Spring Joint Computer Conference*, pages 213-221. AFIPS Press, 1968.
This paper concerns the performance evaluation of an earlier version of the operating system described in [Cambell 68]. A scientific approach was taken to detect and correct performance bugs, namely determining where the problem might lie, and continually refining this probable location. Statistical sampling methods are intoduced in this paper. And finally, an operating system sampler program is described, and the uses such a program can be put to are outlined. [RTS]

[Card 78]   Stuart K. Card.
Studies in the Psychology of Computer Text Editing Systems.
Technical Report SSL-78-1, Xerox PARC, August, 1978.
Six studies of user interaction with on-line computer text editing systems are reported. Editing times for benchmark tasks on several editing systems were collected to gauge the range of performance across systems. Using the measured times, it was possible to predict when an editing system would outperform a typewriter. To model the user's behavior in greater detail, an information processing model of editing performance is proposed describing the user's "goals", "operators", "methods", and "selection rules". An important issue in such a model is how the model's accuracy depends on the grain of analysis. To find out, the model was recast at nine different levels of grain size and the accuracy of the different versions compared. From observations of users on several different systems, it was discovered that on each task, the users go through a similar sequence of task assimilation, target location, target modification, and verification. This concept of a "unit task cycle" was used to predict rough performance times for a proposed system prior to system specification. With respect to the target location part of a task, four devices for pointing to a target were compared and modeled. Using Fitts' Law, it is argued that the time for the best of these devices, the mouse, approaches the theoretical minimum. Finally, a Monte Carlo simulation model using gamma-distributed, with which sequences of user actions, time per task, and the distribution of time can be predicted.

The picture of user behavior that emerges from these studies is related to, but distinct from, behavior in classical problem-solving studies. The main difference is that the methods are almost certain of success. For any subproblem the user simply recalls the solution from his experience rather than working it out. Hence there is no search. Such behavior is expected to be found in many cognitive tasks in industrial work and daily life which people perform repetitively, tasks the report calls 'routine cognitive skills.' [Abstract]

[Card 79a]   Stuart K. Card, Thomas P. Moran, Allen Newell.
The Keystroke-Level Model for User Performance Time with Interactive Systems.
Communications of the ACM 23(7), July, 1979.
It is not common practice today for system designers to deal systematically with the issues

of user-computer performance. One reason is the lack of appropriate analysis tools. An easy-to-use model -- the Keystroke Model -- is proposed for predicting the time it will take expert users to execute given tasks on a system. The Model is based on counting keystrokes and other low-level operations, including the user's mental preparations and the system's responses. Methods for executing tasks are coded in terms of these operations, and standard times for the operations are then summed up to give predictions. Heuristic rules are given for predicting where mental preparations occur in the methods. Keystroke Model predictions were tested against data from 28 users, on 10 systems, and over 14 task types. The root-mean-square prediction error was 21% for individual tasks -- and much better for collections of tasks. An example illustrates how the Keystroke Model can be used to give parametric predictions and how sensitivity analysis can be used to redeem conclusions in the face of uncertain assumptions. Finally, the Keystroke Model is compared to several simpler versions, which trade ease-of-use for accuracy. [Abstract]

[Card 79b]   Stuart K. Card.
A Method for Calculating Performance Times for Users of
    Interactive Computing Systems.
    In *Proceedings of the 1979 International Conference on
        Cybernetics and Society*, pages ??. Cybernetics,
        October, 1979.
In order to design systems which are easy and pleasant to use, designers must trade off several different factors. Yet, at present, there is little scientific basis for how to do this. This paper presents a way in which one of the factors, time to perform a task, can be calculated at design time from a simple model. The technique gives estimates accurate to about 20% of actual times required by users (measured under laboratory conditions) in a variety of different tasks and systems. Several examples of the use of the model for interface design and analysis are discussed. [Abstract]

[Cerf 71]   V.G. Cerf and G. Estrin.
Measurement of Recursive Programs.
    In *Information Processing 71*, IFIP, 1971.
A simple model of recursive programs is presented. From the model, analytic measures of program efficiency are developed. The use of event counters for providing the parameters for the model is then discussed. [RTS]

[Chambers 73]
    J.M. Chambers.
Linear Regression Computations: Some Numerical
    Statistical Aspects.
    Bulletin of the Institute of Statistical Instruction 45(4),
        1973.
The author compares the accuracy of several algorithms for linear computations. [IF]

[Chandy 75]   K. M. Chandy, U. Herzog and L. Woo.
Parametric Analysis of Queuing Networks.
    IBM Journal of Research and Development 19:36-42,
        1975.
This paper develops the mathematical basis for collapsing a network of queues into a

single equivalent queue. The Chandy, Herzog, Woo (CHW) collapsing Theorem is the formal basis for much of the hierarchically structured modeling work in the performance evaluation area.

The formal basis for hierarchically structuring queueing network models is developed in this rather cryptic paper. The essential content is a procedure for defining a single queue which is equivalent in throughput to a network of queues. The class of networks for which this procedure is possible is basically satisfying local balance. [JCB]

[Chanon 73]   Robert N. Chanon.
On a Measure of Program Structure.
Technical Report, Department of Computer Science, Carnegie-Mellon University, 1973.

Program structure has been discussed as being an important influence on the ease with which programs can be constructed, verified, understood, and changed. Yet the notion of program structure has remained a vague and imprecisely defined concept. This thesis proposes a definition and a measure for program structure and evaluates the usefulness of the measure as a tool for determining and controlling structure in a program . . .

The measure uses the information theoretic concept of excess entropy -- entropy loading -- to determine the extent to which assumptions are shared. Entropy loading calculations also provide a way of comparing different decompositions of a program. Unfortunately, finding the best decompositions of all but small programs seems intractable. Consequently, several heuristics are stated that attempt to establish bounds on the growth of entropy loadings for elaborations of decompositions suggested at early stages in a development . . .

Without mechanical aids, however, applications of these techniques to practical problems would be tedious and difficult. This and other difficulties motivate further research about this important but elusive property of programs: their structure. [Abstract]

[Chapin 79]   Ned Chapin.
A Measure of Software Complexity.
In *Proceedings AFIPS 1979 National Computer Conference*, pages 995-1002. AFIPS, June, 1979.

This paper presents a proposed measure of how complex a program or system of programs will be when it is implemented. This Q measure is based upon design or documentation documents in which the proposed system has been split into modules. Each module performs a specific function. The input and output data for that function form the basis of the complexity measure. These data are divided into four categories depending on their use in the function, namely those for: 1) processing, 2) value-changing, 3) flow of control, and 4) passing to subsidiary or ancestor functions. The number of data items in each category is computed, these totals are weighted according to the type of usage and added to form a module complexity measure. The module complexity measures are averaged to produce an overall complexity measure. The major weakness of the presentation is that no reasons are given for the actual weightings used, although the author says several times that he has provided reasons. His arguments are purely qualitative, however.

The results of an example containing twelve modules are presented along with figures for the same modules using other previously proposed complexity measures. the analysis of differences among the complexity measures is disappointingly superficial. A good case is made, however, for contending that one complexity measure is about as valid as another.

This is a dangerous paper for a reader to take without a grain of salt. Numerous statements are made as if they were widely accepted facts, when they are not. No evidence is presented to support such statements as "It rarely mistakes the final complexity of the software as coded if the input-output tables were conscientiously prepared," or "The proposed Q measure reflects what will take the form of actual code complexity in implementation." [CR35088]

[Chen 76]   Peter P.S. Chen and Mark Franklin.
              Proceedings of the International Symposium on Computer
                  Performance Modeling, Measurement, and Evaluation.
The International Symposium on Computer Performance Modeling, Measurement, and Evaluation was held on March 29-31, 1976, at Harvard University, Cambridge, Massachusetts. This Symposium was jointly sponsored by the SIGMETRICS group of ACM and IFIP Working Group 7.3 (Computer System Modeling).

The main purpose of the Symposium was to bring together researchers and practitioners to discuss problems in computer system performance evaluation.

The papers ranged from model building and validation to measurement techniques. Several areas of current interest such as database systems, computer networks, and computer systems control were also covered. [CR34397]

[Cheng 69]   P.S. Cheng.
               Trace-driven system modeling.
               IBM System Journal(4):280-289, 1969.
The method described in the paper is to run the job stream sequentially using the OS under which a trace program can be executed. System activities that pertain to the execution of a given job are collected in a trace log. Then the data in the trace log is reduced to the level of detail the system is to be simulated at. The events present in the reduced trace log are used to drive the event-based simulation. [RTS]

[Cheung 74]   R. C. Cheung, K. H. Kim, C. V. Ramamoorthy, and S. S.
               Reddi.
               Automated Generation of Self-Metric Software.
               *Proc. of the Seventh Hawaii International Conference on
                   System Sciences*:149-151, 1974.
Self-metric software are programs that record their behavior statistics automatically during their execution. They are generated from existing software by inserting software measurement instruments into the program at appropriate locations after an automatic analysis by the system. In this paper, an algorithm to locate and insert the optimal (minimal cost) set of activity counters for generating the program activity profile is given. The use of the model for measuring execution time, branching characteristics, code activities, path activities, and other program statistics are discussed. The applications of these statistics in program testing, optimization, and program restructuring for virtual memory are presented. [Abstract]

[Chevance 78]R. J. Chevance and T. Heidet.
             Static Profile and Dynamic Behavior of COBOL Programs.
             SIGPLAN Notices 13(4):44-57, 1978.
Introduction: A sample of more than 50 COBOL programs from various application areas

were analyzed both statically and dynamically. The IRIS COBOL compiler was modified to make the necessary measurements.

Types of analysis: Dynamic and static analysis refers to the PROCEDURE DIVISION. Variables are only counted if they are accessed at least once in the PROCEDURE DIVISION. SORT/MERGE and REPORT operations were not found since they are performed as separate job steps. 45% of COBOL statements were IF statements.

Results: Seven tables are given as follows:

> Usage of constants.
> Distribution of references.
> Condition type in conditional expression.
> Operator frequencies.
> Operand types (static).
> COBOL statement distribution.
> Mean number of operands by type (static).
> Type of MOVE statement (static).

Note: All the tables not marked "static" are both static and dynamic. [W&H]

[Chrysler 78]   Earl Chrysler.
            Some Basic Determinants of Computer Programming
               Productivity.
            Communications of the ACM 21(6):472-483, June, 1978.

The purpose of this research was to examine the relationship between processing characteristics of programs and experience characteristics of programmers and program development time. The ultimate objective was to develop a technique for predicting the amount of time necessary to create a computer program. The fifteen program characteristics hypothesized as being associated with an increase in programming time required are objectively measureable from preprogramming specifications. The five programmer characteristics are experience-related and are also measurable before a programming task is begun. Nine program characteristics emerged as major influences on program development time, each associated with increased program time. All five programmer characteristics were found to be related to reduced program development time. A multiple regression equation which contained one programmer characteristic and four program characteristics gave evidence of good predictive power for forecasting program development time. [CR34959]

Investigates the effect of program characteristics and programming environment factors on development time. The experiment consisted of recording relevant data for 36 production COBOL programs. The general conclusion was that the occurance counts of the following program characteristics were the most significant predictor of development time: output fields, input files, control breaks and totals, input edits, output records, input fields, and input records. Also, programmer's age and years of formal education were the most significant predictors of development time. [FGS]

[Clark 76]   D. W. Clark.
            List Structure: Measurements, Algorithms and Encodings.
            PhD thesis, Computer Science Department, Carnegie-
               Mellon University, Pittsburgh, Pennsylvania 15213,
               USA, August, 1976.

This thesis includes material reported in "An Empirical Study of the List Structure in LISP" by Clark and Green, as well as some additional work on dynamic measurements of various kinds. All the LISP terminology used is explained.

Analysis: The static analysis is the same as in "An Empirical Study of the List Structure in LISP." To collect the dynamic statistics, a PDP-10 simulator was used, which wrote to a disk file, the address of every list cell accessed.

Programs: The programs tested are the same as in "An Empirical Study of the List Structure in LISP".

Results: Results are presented for:

    Percentage occurrence of data types in Car
    Percentage occurrence of data types in Cdr
    Cdr list pointers in PIVOT
    Histograms of list pointer distances in PIVOT
    Static percentage of list pointers pointing on the page
    Frequency distribution of atom pointers
    Frequency distribution of number pointers
    Static and dynamic percentages of data types in Car
    Static and dynamic percentages of data types in Cdr
    Histograms of static and dynamic list pointer distances in SPARSER
    Static and dynamic percentages of list pointers pointing on the page
    Atom pointers (static) and references (dynamic) in NOAH and SPARSER
    Scatter diagram of static and dynamic ranks of NOAH atoms
    Cumulative distributions of atoms in NOAH
    Cumulative distributions of atoms in SPARSER
    Execution frequency of LISP primitives
    Replacement of data types by replaced in SPARSER
    Cumulative distributions of inter-reference distances in CONGEN, NOAH and SPARSER
    Cumulative distributions of stack distances in CONGEN, NOAH and SPARSER
    References to list pages in CONGON, NOAH and SPARSER

The thesis also contains details of linearization algorithms, their effects and compact encodings of list structure. [W&H]

This thesis is about list structures: how they are used in practice, how they can be moved and copied efficiently, and how they can be represented by space-saving encodings. The approach taken to these subjects is mainly empirical. Measurement results are based on five large programs written in Interlisp. [Abstract]

[Clark 77]   D. W. Clark and C. C. Green.
        An Empirical Study of the List Structure in LISP.
        Communications of the ACM 20(2):78-86, 1977.

Introduction: Static measurements of the list structure of five large LISP programs are reported and analyzed in this paper. The measurements reveal substantial regularity, or predictability, among pointers to atoms and especially among pointers to lists.

Analysis: A measurement program was used in this study which found all lists which were either the top-level binding of an atom or the property list of an atom. The program found 87% and 94% of all the list structures of two programs respectively.

Programs: 5 large Lisp programs were measured, written in Interlisp-10 and running on a DECsystem-10. Details of the programs are given in the paper. Number of list cells in each are:

program	NOAH	= 49593
	PIVOT	= 42958
	SPARSER	= 48156
	STRGEN	= 65366
	WIRE	= 51120

Results: Results are presented for:

Percentage occurrence of data types in Car
Percentage occurrence of data types in Cdr
Histograms of list pointer distances in PIVOT
Percentage of Car list pointers pointing a given distance
Percentage of Cdr list pointers pointing a given distance
Frequency distributions of atom pointers (graph)
Percentage of list pointers pointing on the page
Percentage of list pointers pointing to a following cell
Percentage of all list pointers pointing on the page
Entropy before linearization
Entropy after linearization
Contributions to Car entropy by data type
Contributions to Cdr entropy by data types

[W&H]

[Clark 78]   Douglas W. Clark and Cordell C. Green.
              A Note on Shared List Structure in LISP.
              Inf. Process. Lett. 7(6):312-314, October, 1978.
LISP permits *shared cells*, that is cells which are pointed to more than once. This paper shows that fewer than 2 1/2 percent of all cells were shared for five particular applications. With so few shared cells, various clever garbage collection strategies are practical, as discussed and referenced in the paper. [CR34260]

[Clark 79]   Douglas W. Clark.
              Measurements of Dynamic List Structure Use in LISP.
              IEEE Transactions on Software Engineering SE-5(1):51-
              59, January, 1979.
This paper is an empirical study of how three large LISP programs use their list structure during execution. Most list-cell references are due to the functions *car* and *cdr*, which are executed about equally often and greatly outnumber other primitive functions. Executions of *cdr* yield the atom *nil* about 10 to 20 percent of the time, and nearby list cells most of the rest of the time. Executions of *car* yield atoms, small integers, and list cells in varying proportions in the three programs. Atom references by *car* tend to concentrate on a small number of atoms. The function *rplacd* increases static pointer locality, but *rplaca* is used idiosyncratically. Repeated reference to list cells is likely: over half of all references were to one of the ten most recently referenced cells. *Linearization* is the rearrangement of lists so that consecutive cdr's are adjacent in memory whenever possible. This property deteriorates slowly after a list structure is linearized. If all of a program's lists are linearized,

page faults are reduced slightly, but because of the high cost of a fault this small reduction has a large effect. [Abstract]

[Cockrum 71] J.S. Cockrum and E.D. Crockett.
Interpreting the results of a hardware systems monitor.
In *Proceedings of the AFIPS Spring Joint Computer Conference*, pages 23-38. AFIPS Press, 1971.

The interesting portion of this paper is a set of ten listings describing the operation of a monitoring system for System/360 machines. The first part of the paper descrines the types of events a hardware monitor can handle (single sensor events, multiple sensor and comparator events, and combination events). The second part describes how one can use this data to instigate corrective actions of system reconfiguration, data set reorganization, job scheduling, and operator procedures. [RTS]

[Cohen 74]   J. Cohen and C. Zuckerman.
Two Languages for Estimating Program Efficiency.
Communications of the ACM 17(6):301-308, June, 1974.

Two languages enabling their users to estimate the efficiency of computer programs are presented. The program whose efficiency one wishes to estimate is written in the first language, a go-to-less programming language which includes most of the features of Algol 60. The second language consists of interactive commands enabling its users to provide additional information about the program written in the first language and to output results estimating its efficiency. Processors for the two languages are also described. The first processor is a syntax-directed translator which compiles a program into a symbolic formula representing the execution time for that program. The second processor is a set of procedures for algebraic manipulation which can be called by the user to operate on the formula produced by the first processor. Examples of the usage of the two languages are included. The limitations of the present system, its relation to Knuth's work on the analysis of algorithms, and some of the directions for futher research are also discused. [Abstract]

[Cohen 77]   J. Cohen and N. Carpenter.
A Language for Inquiring about the Run-time Behaviour of Programs.
Software--Practice and Experience 7:445-460, 1977.

This paper describes a language for studying the behaviour of programs, based upon the data collected while these programs are executed by a computer. Besides being a useful tool in debugging, the language is also valuable in the experimental evaluation of the complexity of algorithms, in studying the interdependence of conditionals in a program, and in determining the feasibility of transporting programs from one machine to another. The program one wishes to analyze is written in an Algol 60-like language; when the program is executed it automatically stores, in a data base, the information needed to answer general questions about computational events which occurred during execution. This information consists (basically) of the list of labels passed while the program is being executed, and the current values of the variables. Since the list of labels is describable by regular expressions, these expressions can also be used to identify specific subparts of the list and therefore allow access to the values of the variables. This constitutes the basis for the design of the inquiry language. The user's questions are automatically answered by a processor which inspects the previously generated data base. The paper also presents examples of the use of the language and describes the implementation of its processor.

[Abstract]

[Comer 79]   Douglas Comer and Maurice H. Halstead.
             A Simple Experiment in Top-Down Design.
             IEEE Transactions on Software Engineering SE-5(2):105-
             109, March, 1979.

In this paper we: 1) discuss the need for quantitatively reproducible experiments in the study of top-down design; 2) propose the design and writing of tutorial papers as a suitably general and inexpensive vehicle; 3) suggest the software science parameters as appropriate metrics; 4) report two experiments validating the use of these metrics on outlines and prose; and 5) demonstrate that the experiments tended toward the same optimal modularity.

The last point appears to offer a quantitative approach to the estimation of the total length or volume (and the mental effort required to produce it) from an early stage of the top-down design process. If results of these experiments are validated elsewhere, then they will provide basic guidelines for the design process. [Abstract]

[Connors 70] W. D. Connors, V. S. Mercer and T. A. Sorlini.
              S/360 Instruction Usage Distribution.
              Technical Report TR-00.2025, IBM, May, 1970.

Introduction: This report gives results for the dynamic usage of machine instructions for different types of job stream on the System/360 computers.

Analysis: The method used for obtaining the profiles is the trace/timer technique, using a sample trace rather than a full trace. The method is described in the report.

Programs: Four job streams were analyzed:

1. Scientific stream - 20 short Fortran G jobs and a Fortran H background job.
2. Mixed stream - 12 Fortran, 2 PL/I, 2 COBOL, 1 RPG and 2 Sort jobs.
3. Commercial stream - 17 jobs using COBOL, COBOL with Sort option and COBOL with assembler subroutines.
4. LASER set of "sample job segments" (no details).

Results: Results are given for:

    Instruction distribution summary
    Instructions least used
    Instructions not used in sample traces
    Frequency usage: summary of streams
    Frequency usage: scientific stream
    Frequency usage: mixed stream
    Frequency usage: commercial stream
    Frequency usage: LASER sample
    Mnemonic code sequence: summary of streams
    Mnemonic code sequence: scientific stream
    Mnemonic code sequence: mixed stream
    Mnemonic code sequence: commercial stream
    Mnemonic code sequence: LASER sample

[W&H]

[Conradi 77]   R. Conradi.
              The Use of Compile-Time Constructs, Particularly Macros,
              in MARY.
              Technical Report, Division of Computer Science,
              University of Trondheim, Norway, 1977.

Introduction: This paper is a short survey of common compile-time facilities in modern programming languages. Static usage frequencies for 7 types of MARY macros is given, and compared with static frequencies of "typed" constructs such as procedure calls etc.

Analysis: The static usage of global macros in two MARY systems programs was counted and classified. Also static counts on the usage of all procedures, global-modes and global-data, of FI-brackets and ESAC-brackets, and on the occurrences of dot accesses (selections) were recorded.

The programs Two large systems programs were analyzed.
    1. The MARY-MARY compiler: 43K source lines,
    2. The MARY RUNSYS operating system: 21K source lines, 45K 16-bit instructions.

Results: Results are presented for:
       Static usage of certain program symbols in MARY RUNSYS
       Static usage of certain program symbols in MARY-MARY compiler
       Static usage of certain program symbols and of assignments
       Accumulated static usage of macros and coercion in IODRIVER (part of MARY RUNSYS)

The results are commented upon at the end. [W&H]

[Conti 79]   Dennis M. Conti.
              Findings of the Standard Benchmark Library Study Group.
              Technical Report 500-38, National Bureau of Standards,
              January, 1979.

This report presents the findings of a Government-industry study group investigating the technical feasibility of standard benchmark programs. As part of its investigation, the study group reviewed earlier efforts to develop and use standard benchmark programs. Several issues dealing with the implementation, maintenance, cost/benefit, and acceptability of standard benchmarks emerged as a result of this review. The problems encountered by the study group, notably the lack of an accepted definition of representativeness, prevented it from arriving at a definitive statement on feasibility. However, several areas were identified as topics requiring further investigation and are presented in this report. [Abstract]

[Courtois 77] P. J. Courtois.
              Decomposability: Queueing and Computer System
              Applications.
              Academic Press, New York, 1977.

Large computing systems, like many complex systems, can be regarded as nearly completely decomposable systems -- systems in which the density of interactions between elements is low and the interconnection matrices are sparse. The book presents techniques for analysis of software and hardware systems that can be modeled as nearly-decomposable systems. [MS]

The theory of queueing networks, developed by Gordon, Jackson, and Newell in the late

1950s and early 1960s, lay almost unnoticed by computer analysts until, in 1971, Buzen discovered fast algorithms for calculating queue-length distributions in these networks. Since then interest in analytic models of computer performance has grown explosively. The theory has grown too: the models handle a variety of queueing disciplines, load dependent servers, multiple job classes, and service distributions of phase type. Computational algorithms have been developed for each of the extensions.

But the technology of queueing networks has reached its limits. The computational procedures do not handle priorities, blocking, or synchronized servers -- all of which occur in real computer systems. Moreover, the algorithms become unwieldy for systems of reasonable size, and they often exhibit numerical instabilities. The exact solution methods, which use brute force, are being dropped in favor of approximations, which use cunning.

P. J. Courtois has written a highly original monograph about the most powerful approximation method of which we know: decomposability. The method overcomes the difficulties of exact solutions to queueing problems.

The analysis of systems which are (nearly) decomposable has been attributed to Simon and Ando who, in 1961, reported on state-aggregation in linear models of economic systems. The key observation is that the matrices which describe complex systems tend to be mostly empty. Courtois's insight is that computer systems are hierarchies of components, within which interactions are strong and fast compared to interactions between components at the same level. In developing the method of decomposability for analyzing computer systems, Courtois has also developed computational methods for any (nearly) decomposable system. [Excerpted from CR34612]

This book describes the mathematical requirement for decomposing queueing network representations of computer systems into component parts. This is a necessary prerequisite for hierarchical structuring in cases where the CHW theorem does not apply. This is a significant but rather difficult book. [JCB]

[Crossman 79]
Trevor D. Crossman.
Taking the Measure of Programmer Productivity.
Datamation:144-147, May, 1979.

[Crowder 79]   Harlan Crowder, Ron S. Dembo and John H. Mulvey.
On Reporting Computational Experiments with
Mathematical Software.
ACM Trans. Math. Software 5(2):193-203, June, 1979.
Given two items of mathematical software, both purported to be capable of solving a certain class of problems of interest, which one should be chosen? This question often faces the developer of program libraries, the consultant in scientific programming, and the individual applications programmer. The question persists whether the software items are highly polished and finished products, such as two subroutines for solving dense linear systems of low to moderate order using Gaussian elimination with partial pivoting, or are more modest works of the programmer's art. (An example of the latter is a subroutine presented in a research paper for the purpose of illustrating a proposed new algorithm.) Published papers that compare software items by evaluating their actual performance on some set of real or constructed test examples can be a definite aid in making the choice alluded to above.

The authors consider the methodological and pedagogical requirements for successful software evaluation papers of this type. They note that many of the papers published are of inferior quality when measured against their standards, an assertion that is supported in an earlier work of Jackson and Mulvey. The suggestions in the present paper are based on traditional principles of scientific experimentation, most importantly the need for reproducibility and for sufficiently complete and accurate documentation, so that later workers can confidently build upon the published work. Perhaps it is surprising that such basic tenets need to be stressed, but this reviewer has also observed weakness in published work in this area.

The paper is short and to the point. It contains a useful checklist of "important points to consider when evaluating or reporting a computational experiment." It is well worth reading by anyone working in mathematical software. [CR35227]

[Crowley 75]   C. P. Crowley and J. D. Noe.
               Interactive Graphics Simulation Using Modified Petri Nets.
               In *Proceedings on Simulation of Computer*
                    Systems, pages 177-185. August, 1975.
This paper extends the macro-E-net representation of Nutt and Noe and gives an application to the analysis of multi-drive disk sub-systems. [JCB]

[Crowley 79]   Charles Crowley and Gary Klimowicz.
               A Note on Procedure Timing.
               SIGPlan Notices 14(11):19-22, November, 1979.
The feasibility of procedure timing is discussed in relation to commonly used computers and operating systems. Some simple design criteria are described which facilitate such timing in an OS. Finally some observations are made on how clocks might be available at the hardware level to futher facilitate procedure timing. [RTS]

[Curtis 79a]   B. Curtis, S. Sheppard and P. Millian.
               Third Time Charm: Stronger Prediction of Programmer
                    Performance by Software Complexity Metrics.
               In *Proceedings of the 4th International Conference*
                    Software Engineering, pages 356-360. IEEE, 1979.
In a replication of the experiment done in *IEEE Transactions on Software Engineering SE-5* with larger multimodular programs and a wider variety of subjects, the authors found that Halstead's effort metric was better than lines of code by a factor of two for predicting debugging effort. [FGS]

[Curtis 79b]   Bill Curtis, Sylvia B. Sheppard, Phil Milliman, M. A. Borst
               and Tom Love.
               Measuring the Psychological Complexity of Software
                    Maintenance Tasks with the Halstead and McCabe
                    Metrics.
               IEEE Transactions on Software Engineering SE-5(2):96-
                    104, March, 1979.
Three software complexity measures (Halstead's E, McCabe's $v(G)$), and the length as measured by number of statements) were compared to programmer

performance on two software maintenance tasks. In an experiment on understanding, length and $v(G)$ correlated with the percent of statements correctly recalled. In an experiment on modification, most significant correlations were obtained with metrics computed on modified rather than unmodified code. All three metrics correlated with both the accuracy of the modification and the time to completion. Relationships in both experiments occured primarily in unstructured rather than structured code, and in code with no comments. The metrics were also most predictive of performance for less experienced programmers. Thus, these metrics appear to assess psychological complexity primarily where programming practices do not privide assistance in understanding the code. [*Authors' Abstract*]

The authors deliver what they promise. They neither overestimate nor underestimate the importance and strength of their results. This paper therefore represents another brick in the small but growing structure of knowledge of the psychological dimensions of programming. [CR35700]

Compares Halstead's effort metrics, McCabe's cyclomatic number metric, and the number of executable statements to programmer performance on two maintenance tasks. The experiment consisted of two parts: understanding the code and accurately implementing changes to it. Structured programming techniques and program documentation were varied in the FORTRAN programs used. The authors found that there was little to choose in the three metrics with respect to time and accuracy of maintenance. The metrics had most significance with unstructured, uncommented code and with inexperienced programmers. [FGS]

[Curtis 80]   B. Curtis.
Measurement and experimentation in software engineering.
Proceedings of the IEEE, September, 1980.
This paper has two major parts. The first is a summary of metrics based on product properties useful to predict productivity and schedule. The second is a review of experimental evaluation of metrics proposed to capture programming attributes, mostly complexity. Close to one hundred papers are referenced. [LAB]

[Curtis 81a]   Bill Curtis.
The Measurement of Software Quality and Complexity.
In Frederick G. Sayward, Mary Shaw and Alan J. Perlis, editor, *Software Metrics: An Analysis and Evaluation*.
MIT Press, Cambridge, Massachusetts, 1981.
In "The Measurement of Software Quality and Complexity" Curtis explains that while there are many software metrics for measuring the product (programs) there are few metrics for measuring the process (programming). There have been several software experiments conducted on relating these two concepts in order that the product metrics can be used to predict the process time. Several interesting relationships have resulted, but it is far too early to accept them as laws.

Curtis recommends support for efforts to refine metrics, weeding out the redundant ones, and for efforts to validate metrics on larger data bases. Another important area of research is the development and validation of predictive equations. [FGS]

[Curtis 81b]   Bill Curtis.
                Experimental Evaluation of Software Characteristics.
                In Frederick G. Sayward, Mary Shaw and Alan J. Perlis,
                    editor, *Software Metrics: An Analysis and Evaluation*.
                MIT Press, Cambridge, Massachusetts, 1981.
In "Experimental Evaluation of Software Characteristics" Curtis finds that most
experimental studies on software metrics do not demonstrate cause-effects relationships
between software characteristics and programmer performance.   There are many
uncontrolled factors which could have influenced the observed data. The biggest problem
lies in replicating the environmental conditions under which real-world software is built.

Curtis recommends establishing long term multiple institute research programs which
combine to replicate software experiments to see if the results are repeatable.   He also
recommends that experimental work be initiated on two forgotten areas -- programming
language differences and the early lifecycle stages such as requirements and specification.
[FGS]

[DACS 79]   Data and Analysis Center for Software.
                Quantitative Software Models.
                Technical Report, U. S. Air Force, March, 1979.
This report has been prepared by the Data and Analysis Center for Software for the U. S. Air
Force. The volume contains brief description of models and tabular classification of major
contributions in the following three areas:

> Life Cycle Cost/Productivity
> Reliability/Error Analysis
> Complexity

A fifty-two item bibliography is also attached. [LAB]

The purpose of this document is to disseminate information on the models and methods
that encompass software life-cycle costs and productivity, software reliability and error
analysis, and software complexity, and the data parameters associated with these
models/methods. [Preface]

For each of 44 models, the report provides a summary of the purpose and characteristics of
the model and a list of the model's parameters, outputs, etc. [MS]

[Dearnley 78]   P. Dearnley.
                Monitoring database system performance.
                The Computer Journal 21(1):15-19, 1978.
Monitoring is categorized into the areas of physical (sampling) and logical (modifying the
source text).   Logical monitoring is futher broken down into the areas of cummulative
(includes lower level routines) and differential. The DBMS was instrumented to record real
and processor time on both a cumulative and a differential basis, in addition to frequency
and number of transfers. [RTS]

[deFreitas 78] S. L. de Freitas and P. J. Lavelle.
                A Method for the Time Analysis of Programs.
                IBM Systems Journal 17(1), 1978.
Discussed is a technique for investigating the efficiency of compiled programs. Based on

research that uses FORTRAN as a test subject, the method is more widely applicable. Time analyses show programmers points at which efficiencies may be increased. Also discussed are uses of the technique for comparing the efficiencies of compilers and languages, and for making performance/cost analyses. Presented are validation data for the method under several sets of conditions. [Abstract]

[DeMillo 81a] Richard A. DeMillo and Frederick G. Sayward.
Statistical Measures of Software Reliability.
In Frederick G. Sayward, Mary Shaw and Alan J. Perlis,
editor, *Software Metrics: An Analysis and Evaluation*.
MIT Press, Cambridge, Massachusetts, 1981.

In "Statistical Measures of Software Reliability" DeMillo and Sayward list two current scales of software reliability. First is the Boolean scale of formal verification, formal testing, and special programming disciplines. These don't really address a degree of reliability. The other is the continuous scale gotten mainly by applying hardware reliability theory to software. These attempts have led to unnatural and often contradictory assumptions. Among other difficulties is the problem that software is not a fixed object and hence the stochastic requirements of hardware reliability theory cannot be satisfied.

They recommend that, rather than striving for ways to assign a probability of correct operation to software, attempts to assign a probability to the processes used to validate software be supported. These validation processes are fixed over time and thus distributions for them can be studied empirically. Then a Baysian based "level of confidence" in the correct operation of software validated by the process can be derived. [FGS]

[DeMillo 81b] Richard A. DeMillo and Richard J. Lipton.
Software Project Forecasting.
In Frederick G. Sayward, Mary Shaw and Alan J. Perlis,
editor, *Software Metrics: An Analysis and Evaluation*.
MIT Press, Cambridge, Massachusetts, 1981.

In "Software Project Forecasting" DeMillo and Lipton claim that the present searches for simple formulae for predicting the cost of large scale software efforts are very likely to fail. They explain how measurement theory rejects most of the formulae that have been suggested. On a positive side, they feel that the other popular method of predicting cost from historical data is more likely to produce useful results.

They recommend that predicting from historical data receive continued support and that more effort and thought go into establishing a better data base for these studies. They also recommend that an analogy from weather forecasting suggests a refinement which should be explored. That is, the development of micro theories of software costing (which don't necessarily scale up) and the development of large scale computational techniques (such as clustering) which integrate the micro theories to make a cost prediction for large systems. [FGS]

[Denning 70] Denning, Peter J.
Virtual memory.
ACM Computing Surveys 2(3):153-89, September, 1970.

The need for automatic storage allocation arises from desires for program modularity, machine independence, and resource sharing. Virtual memory is an ellegant way of achieving these objectives. In a virtual memory, the addresses a program may use to identify information are distinguished from the addresses a memory system uses to identify physical storage sites, and program-generated addresses are translated automatically to the corresponding machine addresses. Two principal methods for implementing virtual memory, segmentation and paging, are compared and contrasted. Many contemporary implementations have experienced one or more of these problems: poor utilization of storage, thrashing, and high costs associated with loading information into memory. These and subsidiary problems are studied from a theoretic view, and are shown to be controllable by a proper combination of hardware and memory management policies. [Abstract]

[Denning 78] Peter J. Denning.
The Operational Analysis of Queueing Network Models.
Computing Surveys 10(3):225-262, September, 1978.
Both Markovian queueing network theory and operational queueing network theory lead to the same mathematical equations. However, the derivations resulting from operational analysis are dependent upon one or more of the following operational principles: 1) All quantities are defined to be precisely measurable; 2) All assumptions are directly testable; 3) The system must be flow balanced; and 4) The system must be homogeneous.

These operational assumptions can be tested prior to applying the equations from this theory. Direct verification of the assumptions will allow analysts to more confidently apply queueing network analysis in their system evaluation endeavors. Hence, the difference between the Markovian and operational approaches is important.

The paper presents the results of operational queueing network theory and succinctly motivates its derivation. The concepts which are discussed include job flow balance, state transition balance, one-step behavior, homogeneity, and decomposition. Analysts not familiar with these concepts and their application should definitely study this tutorial. It is well written and highly recommended. [CR34957]

[Deutsch 71] P. Deutsch and C.A. Grant.
A Flexible Measurement Tool for Software Systems.
In *Information Processing 71*, pages 320-326. IFIP, 1971.
This paper describes a time-sharing system measurement tool called the Informer, which provides an environment in which user programs may serve as measurement routines. Measurement routines are inserted dynamically to be called when control reaches arbitrary locations within the measured program. An important quality of this measurement is that no error in its use can cause a system failure. Also, system degradation due to measurement error can be automatically controlled. [Abstract]

[Dolotta 76] T. A. Dolotta and J. R. Masher.
An Introduction to the Programmer's Workbench.
In *Proceedings of the Second International Conference on Software Engineering*, pages 164-168. IEEE, San Francisco, 1976.
A summary description is presented of the Programmer's Workbench as an aid to developers of computer programs. [MEM]

[Doty 77]   D. L. Doty, P. J. Nelson, and K. R. Stewart.
Software Cost Estimation Study; vol II: Guidelines for
Improved Software Cost Estimating.
Technical Report RADC-TR-77-220, Rome Air
Development Center, August, 1977.

This report contains guidelines for developing estimates of computer software cost. Consideration is first given to the initial program estimate which is often made with a paucity of supportive data. Adjustments are presented for modifying the estimate given the availability of additional data. Procedures are presented for assessing the affordability of the resulting estimates. Emphasis is placed on developing a conservative but reasonable best estimate for purposes of program budgeting. Separate consideration is given to steps that should be taken to bring the program in at or below budget. Frequently recurring problems are summarized in their time-phased order of occurence. [Abstract]

[Dowdy 79]   Lawrence W. Dowdy, Ashok K. Agrawala, Karen
D. Gordon and Satish K. Tripathi.
Computer Performance Prediction via Analytical Modeling
-- an Experiment.
In *Proceedings Conference on Simulation, Measurement,*
and Modeling of Computer Systems, pages 13-18.
ACM, August, 1979.

The experiment described here compares the predicted versus actual performance of a computer system when a second processor is added. Six different benchmarks are run first on a single-processor system, and the results are used to calibrate a queueing network model. This model is modified to predict the performance for a dual-processor system. These predictions are compared to actual results obtained by running the benchmarks on the reconfigured system.

The results show that the model does not predict throughput within 10 percent. The authors attribute this result to an assumption that certain parameters -- especially the degree of multiprogramming -- will remain fixed when the model is altered. They offer several good reasons why the degree of multiprogramming should not be expected to remain constant.

The authors are disturbed that their predictions are not better, given that they are using a *validated* model. In the reviewer's opinion, it is ill advised to treat validation so decisively. The prevailing view of validation is not as a binary decision variable, but rather as a measure of confidence that the model's performance is representative of the real system, and only over a specified range of applications. An experiment like this helps to establish that range. The contribution here is to test the suitability of the model as a predictive tool when a second processor is added. The paper succeeds in describing the experiment and its implications. [CR35679]

This paper describes an experiment the authors conducted using a simple central server queueing network model of a Univac 1100/41 computer system running under EXEC 8. They validated their model by comparing the system's behavior running a benchmark workload with that predicted by the model. They then reconfigured the system to include a second processor (CPU) and ran the same benchmark workload through the modified system.

The central server model was then updated to include the extra CPU; the values now predicted by the model were not as *close* to the actual system behavior as before. This discrepancy is not attributed to the model. Instead, the problem arises from not being able to accurately predict those parameters that were assumed to remain constant under the hardware change. Denning and Buzen's well written survey article on queueing network models has further details on this parameter prediction problem. [CR36007]

[Drummond 73]
   M. E. Drummond.
   Evaluation and Measurement Techniques for Digital Computers.
   Prentice-Hall, Englewood Cliffs, 1973.
This is an early and readable IBM-oriented book on basics of performance, measurement and modeling. [JCB]

[Duff 79]   I. S. Duff and J. K. Reid.
   Performance Evaluation of Codes for Sparse Matrix Problems.
   In *Performance Evaluation of Numerical Software*, pages 121-136. Elsevier North-Holland Inc., New York, 1979.
The authors make the statement that "There is a strict limit to the extent that analytical methods can be used to assess the effectiveness of techniques employed in sparse matrix codes. Any full evaluation therefore demands the running of a realistic set of test problems." In this paper the authors describe the collections of test matrices they have assembled at the Atomic Energy Research Establishment at Harwell. They provide details of how the test matrices have been used in their own algorithm development and in assessing computer software generated elsewhere. They concentrate on solving systems of linear algebraic equations because "it is a basic step used widely in the eigenvalue problem and in the solution of nonlinear problems." Direct methods are used. Writing a computer program to call the software for a given problem produces a qualitative answer to the question "Is the software easy to use?" Whether or not the software can be used to solve all of the test problems gives a tentative answer to the question "is the software reliable and robust?" In addition to these qualitative answers, quantitative assessments are given for each problem in relation to the computing time and storage required and the accuracy achieved. A qualitative assessment is given for the diagnostic and monitoring information returned. [CR35558]

[Dunsmore 78]
   H. E. Dunsmore and J. D. Gannon.
   Programming Factors--Language Features that Help Explain Programming Complexity.
   Proc. ACM 1978 Annual Conf. 2:554-560, 1978.
Programming complexity (the amount of difficulty in constructing a program) may depend upon certain programming factors (choices of programming language features). Using program changes as a programming complexity measure, previous research has identified five potential programming factors. This paper suggests that subjects tend to use the same levels of these factors in two different programming languages, supporting the conjecture that these factors are elements of individual programming style. It also describes five potential programming factors, and although each of these has intuitive appeal, only average procedure length was related to programming complexity. [CR34375]

[Dunsmore 79]
H. Dunsmore and J. Gannon.
Data Referencing: An Empirical Investigation.
Computer 12(12):50-59, December, 1979.
In a controlled experiment the authors found that average variables referenced per statement and average live variables per statement had a simplifying effect on program development and program maintenance. [FGS]

[Dunsmore 80]
H. E. Dunsmore and J. D. Gannon.
Analysis of the Effects of Programming Factors on Programming Effort.
The Journal of Systems and Software 1, 1980.
Programming effort appears to be related to choices of programming language features which we call programming factors. A series of experiments was conducted investigating program construction, comprehension, and modification. Ease of construction seemed related to average nesting depth, percentage of global variables used for data communication, average variables referenced, and average live variables per statement. Data communication and live variables were shown to be related to ease of modification as well. [VRB]

Investigates the effect program nesting, percentage of global variables, ratio of parameters to global variables, average variables referenced, and average live variables have on the effort required for program construction, comprehension, and modification. From a controlled expreiment the authors concluded that effort is related to all five parameters, and modification is easier when the ratio of formal parameters to global variable is high and when the average live variables per statement is low. [FGS]

[Ellis 78]   Clarence A. Ellis.
Analysis of Some Abstract Measures of Protection in Computer Systems.
International Journal of Computing and Information Science 7(3):219-251, September, 1978.
In this paper, Ellis has done a very good, very thorough, rigorous analysis of an uninteresting academic problem. It is embarrassing that such good work should be wasted on such an unrealistic approach to protection. The problem posed is based on protection by keys, similar to the method used in the IBM 360/370 computer storage protection system. The accesses of a set of subjects to a set of objects is to be controlled. A key is associated with each subject and each object. Access is allowed only if the key of the subject is properly related to the key of the object. A proper relation exists if the number of one-bits, resulting from a Boolean function of the keys of the subject and the object, exceeds a system threshold. By varying the function (equivalence, AND, ...) and the threshold, one can achieve various protection schemes.

This is not an unrealistic basis for a protection scheme (IBM actually built one version of it), but Ellis then assumes 1) that objects are associated one-to-one with subjects, and that a subject can only access its object; 2) keys are statically assigned; and 3) there are more subject/object pairs than there are distinct keys. In this situation, protection is not possible, so Ellis investigates how to minimize the amount of protection failure which can occur (worst case, average, ...), totally disregarding the fact that no one would ever build a system which is guaranteed to allow protection violations.

Given also that systems exist with the basic structure proposed, but with dynamic key assignments, we can only assume that since real systems are too difficult to analyze, a totally unreal system ws analyzed instead. [CR33988]

[Elshoff 76a]   James Elshoff.
              An Analysis of Some Commercial PL/I Programs.
              Transactions on Software Engineering SE-5(2):113-120,
              June, 1976.
The source code for 120 production PL/I programs from several General Motor's commercial computing installations has been collected. The programs have been scanned both manually and automatically. Some data from the scanning process are presented and interpreted.

The programs are considered with respect to five attributes: 1) the size of the programs, 2) the readability of the programs, 3) the complexity of the programs, 4) the discipline followed by the programmers, and 5) the use of the programming language. Each area is reviewed with pertinent data presented whenever it is available.

This report should be of interest to anyone involved with programming. The report helps explicitly identify some areas of programming in which a better job could be done. Although the programs analyzed are written in PL/I, those persons from installations using other languages, particularly COBOL, have indicated that the information presented is typical. [VRB]

[Elshoff 76b]   James L. Elshoff.
              A Numerical Profile of Commercial PL/I Programs.
              Software -- Practice & Experience 6(4):505-525, 1976.
Introduction: The paper concentrates on the data collected from the analysis of 120 commercial PL/I programs in 1974. It represents how PL/I was used in a commercial programming environment up to that year.

Types of analysis: The only analysis used is a **static** analysis. A scanning program was used to extract raw data from the set of sample programs. The data collected was manipulated by semi-automatic means to obtain the results presented in this paper.

Statistics: 120 programs were examined from a typical commercial programming environment. All programs were scheduled production programs.

    Number of records in study = 145,994
    Number of PL/I statements in study = 102,397

Results: Results are presented showing:

Distribution of program by size	Declared file constant usage
Distribution of statement types	Distribution of identifiers by reference
Program usage of statement types	type
Multiple data item assignments	Distribution of identifiers by length
DO statement type data	Label usage in control of flow
IF statements and ELSE clauses	Miscellaneous label data
Distribution of operators in	Distribution of statements spanned
expressions	between uses of an identifier
Distribution of expressions by number	Comparison of statements spanned

of operators
Program usage of expressions
Numeric constants
Program usage of lists of expressions
Distribution of expression lists by
    lengths
String constants
Identifier declaration information
Distribution of identifiers by
    data type
Program usage of data types
Some attribute data
Statements per block at each level

with program size
Distribution of blocks by level
Program usage of block levels
Distribution of statements by level
Distribution of blocks by size
Distribution of bottom level blocks
Statistics on block types
Pairwise combinations of blocks
The average program
The influence of program size
Consistency of program attributes
Miscellaneous reference information

[W&H]

[Elshoff 77a]   J. L. Elshoff.
        A Study of the Structural Composition of PL/I Programs.
        Technical Report GMR2444, General Motors Corporation,
        June, 1977.

This report investigates the relationship proposed by Halstead between the number of distinct operators and operands (n1, n2) and the total number of uses of operators and operands (N1, N2). this is the "length equation", which is:

    Program length $\equiv$ N1 + N2 = n1 * log2(n1) + n2 * log2(n2)

This report studies the operator frequency distributions. [W&H]

[Elshoff 77b]   J. L. Elshoff.
        The Influence of Structured Programming on PL/I
        Program Profiles.
        IEEE Transactions on Software Engineering SE-3(5), 1977.

Introduction: Two sets of PL/I programs were studied. One set represents programming practice before the introduction of structured programming techniques and the other set after their introduction.

Analysis: All the non-structured programs have been studied in a previous paper (see "A Numerical Profile of Commercial PL/I Programs" by James Elshoff) where the method of analysis is described.

Programs: 120 programs written without structured programming techniques were collected and 34 written with structured programming techniques were collected from two installations.

Results: Results are given for:

A comparison of the two samples
Distribution of statement types
DO statement data
ELSE clause usage
GOTO statement usage
Label usage in control of flow

Procedure statements and procedures
Distribution of blocks by level
Distribution of statements by level
Average block size at each level
Program usage of block levels
Distribution of blocks by size

Abstract view of program structures
[W&H]

[Elshoff 78]   J. L. Elshoff.
                An Investigation into the Effects of the Counting Method
                used in Software Science Measurements.
                SIGPLAN Notices 13(2):30-45, 1978.
This reports investigates the relationship proposed by Halstead between the number of
distinct operators and operands (n1, n2) and the total number of uses of operators and
operands (N1, N2). This is the "length equation", which is:

   Program length $\equiv$ N1 + N2 = n1 * log2(n1) + n2 * log2(n2)

This report investigates various counting methods for determining the four numbers (note
that a procedure is regarded as an operator). [W&H]

[England 73a] D.M. England.
              Operating System of System 250.
              Note 1S5.
This paper describes the OS of the Plessey System 250 in terms of a series of abstractions,
starting from the store allocator/manager, working up through the process
allocator/manager, and ending with the command interpreter and the user code. The
command interpreter consists primarily of a symbol table, which refers to capabilities and
data values. The capabilities can refer to either resources provided by the abstract
machine provided by the OS, or command programs, which are comprsied of existing
commands. [RTS]

[England 73b] D.M. England.
              Architectual Features of System 250.
              Plessey Telecommunications Research internal
              document.
This paper gives an overview of the hardware and software components of the Plessey 250,
a reliable, real-time telephone control system. The hardware consists of multiple CPU's
addressing multiple memory modules and busses. In addition to conventional data
registers, each CPU contains eight capability registers. Instructions exist for loading and
deleting capabilities in these registers, as well as providing a protected procedure call
mechanism. The operating system is described in terms of resource management, the
user/resource interface, and the user terminal system. The logical resources available to
the user are (a) store block, (b) process, (c) flag (i.e., semaphore), (d) stream, (e) textfile, (f)
directory, (g) job, and (h) command program. Except for store blocks, all the resources are
represented by 'enter' capabilities, which allow type specific operations to be performed on
the resource. Store blocks can be manipulated directly by the user, and a command
progiam may be either a code block which can be executed directly or a string of
commands which must be interpreted. There exist several standard command libraries that
extend the facilities provided by the command language. It appears possible for the user to
define new resources to be managed by the command language, but the mechanisms for
doing so are not discussed in this paper. [RTS]

[Enright 79]   W. H. Enright.
Using a Testing Package for the Automatic Assessment of
Numerical Methods for ODEs.
In *Performance Evaluation of Numerical Software*, pages
199-214. Elsevier North-Holland, Inc., New York, 1979.
The well-known testing packages, originating from the University of Toronto, for comparing
numerical methods for ordinary differential equations, both stiff and non-stiff, achieve an
equitable basis for comparison by insisting that all of the methods to be compared should
attempt to accomplish exactly the same task. Since different methods may be designed to
accomplish similar but different tasks, they sometimes have to be modified before being
tested on the Toronto packages, and the extent to which these modifications may upset the
conclusions one might draw from the results of the test is an open question . . .

In this paper an alternative philosophyu of testing is propounded, and a new package for
implementing it is described. Methods are not modified, but are assessed on how well they
accomplish their stated tasks. Comparison between different methods is then achieved by
normalizing the cost statistics to take account of the fact that different methods may have
different aims. [Excerpted from CR35982]

[Estrin 67]   G. Estrin, D. Hopkins, B. Coggan and S.D. Crocker.
SNUPER Computer -- a computer in instrumentation
automata.
In *Proceedings of the AFIPS Spring Joint Computer
Conference*, pages 645-656. AFIPS Press, 1967.
The first part of this paper characterizes information processing systems, discusses classes
of measurements, and describes artifact introduced by measurement. The second part
describes the characteristics of the SNUPER computer which was not implemented at the
time this paper was presented. [RTS]

[Fabry 74]   Robert S. Fabry.
Capability-based addressing.
Communications of the ACM 17(7):403-12, July, 1974.
Various addressing schemes making use of segment tables are examined. The
inadequacies of these schemes when dealing with shared addresses are explained. These
inadequacies are traced to the lack of an efficient absolute address for objects in these
systems. The direct use of a capability as an address is shown to overcome these
difficulties because it provides the needed absolute address. Implementation of capability-
based addressing is discussed. It is predicted that the use of tags to identify capabilities
will dominate. A hardware address translation scheme which never requires the
modification of the representation of capabilities is suggested. The scheme uses a main
memory hash table for obtaining a segment's location in main memory given its unique
code. The hash table is avoided for recently accessed segments by means of a set of
associative registers. A computer using capability-based addressing may be substantially
superior to present systems on the basis of protection, simplicity of programming
conventions, and efficient implementation. [Abstract]

[Feldman 77] S. I. Feldman.
Make - A Program for Maintaining Computer Programs.
Computer Science Technical Report 57, Bell Laboratories,
Murray Hill, New Jersey, 1977.

A description is given of *MAKE* -- a program for maintaining computer programs. The basic features of *MAKE* are described. [MEM]

[Ferrari 78a] Domenico Ferrari.
Performance of Computer Installations: Evaluation and
Management.
In Domenico Ferrari, editor, *Proceedings of the
International Conference on the Performance of
Computer Installations*, Elsevier/North-Holland, Inc.,
New York, June, 1978.

All computer installations are confronted with a variety of performance problems. When a new installation is to be set up, or an existing one is to be upgraded, such performance issues as the analysis of performance requirements for the system to be procured, the design of benchmarks or synthetic jobs to model the installation's projected workload, and the sizing of the system present themselves naturally to the parties involved. When the system is installed, it must be tuned to the actual workload, otherwise its performance would generally be lower than the one its capacity could produce. Since a system's performance is very sensitive to workload variations, and since the workload in most installations changes in time with many different patterns and frequencies, periodic retuning is often necessary or desirable. The procurement of systems software and applications software, that of external computing services, and various issues regarding machine room organization are some of the additional problems that are to be faced by scientific, administrative and commercial installations in their daily operation. To be successfully solved, these problems require that system performance be evaluated and managed. Evaluation methodoligies, techniques and tools provide the knowledge on which performance managers are to base their decisions.

What is the state of the art in the areas of performance evaluation and performance management in 1978? Has significant progress been made toward the solution of such classical problems as workload characterization, benchmark design, capacity planning? Is the field of performance evaluation ready to accept the challenges coming from new, rapidly emerging hardware and software techniques (distributed systems, database systems, multilevel automatically managed storage hierarchies, and so on)? The International Conference on the Performance of Computer Installations (ICPCI 78), of which this volume contains the proceedings, was organized to provide an answer to these questions. [CR34345]

[Ferrari 78b] D. Ferrari.
Computer System Performance Evaluation.
Prentice-Hall, Englewood Cliffs, 1978.

Ferrari gives an advanced and comprehensive view of the state-of-the-art in computer performance evaluation and analysis as of the time of publication of his book. The approach is both thorough and readable. [JCB]

[Feustel 73]   Feustel, Edward A.
                On the advantages of tagged architecture.
                IEEE Transactions on Computers C-22(7):644-656, July,
                1973.
The uses of tagged architecture in all software areas is shown. The ability to implement object-based systems using tagged architecture is briefly discussed.   Many of the advantages of object-based systems are also inherent in tagged architectures. [RTS]

[Fitch 77]   John Fitch.
                Profiling a Large Program.
                Software--Practice and Experience 7:511-518, 1977.
A profiling technique (provided by the BCPL compiler) was used on a large algebra system, CAMAL, in order to determine where time was being used. Savings of up to 70 per cent as a result of small changes were reported. [RTS]

[Fitsos 79]   George P. Fitsos.
                *Software Science Counting Rules and Tuning
                Methodology*.
                Technical Report TR 03.075, IBM General Products
                Division, Santa Teresa Laboratory, September, 1979.
Programming Development at IBM's Santa Teresa Laboratory has been investigating "The Elements of Software Science" as defined by Dr. Maurice H. Halstead.   A set of IMS and VSAM modules have been counted and were used to tune and specifically define the counting rules for assembler and PL/S. The method used for tuning the rules is presented, as are the rules themselves. Also discussed are some observations made during the tuning process.   While the specific experiments were limited to assembler and PL/5 languages, the methodology for tuning of rules would seem applicable to any language. [Abstract]

[Fitsos 80]   George P. Fitsos.
                Vocabulary Effects in Software Science.
                Technical Report TR-3926, IBM General Products
                Division, Santa Teresa Laboratory, January, 1980.
Programming Development at IBM's Santa Teresa Laboratory has been investigating the elements of software science as defined by Dr. Maurice H. Halstead of Purdue University. In conducting our experiments certain phenomena were observed, two of which are the subject of this report.   The first relates to the number of unique operators.   The number appears to be constant for a given higher level language.   The second relates to program length.   While the specific experiments were limited to assembler and PL/S languages, the observations would seem applicable to other programming languages. [Abstract]

[Fitzsimmons 78]
                Ann Fitzsimmons and Tom Love.
                A Review and Evaluation of Software Science.
                Computing Reviews 10(1):3-18, March, 1978.
During recent years, there have been many attempts to define and measure the "complexity" of a computer program. Maurice Halstead has developed a theory that gives objective measures of software complexity. Various studies and experiments have shown that the theory's predictions of the number of bugs in programs and of the time requried to

implement a program are amazingly accurate. It is a promising theory worthy of much more probing scientific investigation.

This paper reviews the theory, called "software science", and the evidence supporting it. A brief description of a related theory, called *software physics*, is included. [Abstract]

[Forman 71]   P. D. Forman.
            A Static Analysis of FORTRAN IV.
            Master's thesis, Department of Computer Science,
                University of Toronto, Canada, 1971.

Introduction: This thesis contains the results from a static analysis of the usage of FORTRAN constructs, particularly assignment statements.

Analysis: All Fortran statements were analyzed, but to varying degrees of complexity. Every statement was analyzed according to statement distribution, while only often used statements were analyzed further. No details of the analysis are given.

Programs: One set of programs were benchmark programs obtained from University research groups and the other set were obtained by randomly probing into the Computer Center program library. 49 programs were obtained, 36508 cards, 26282 statements.

Results: Statistics are given for:

Distribution of statement types	Arithmetic expressions
Mixed mode conversions	Logical expressions and their
Logical and arithmetic IF statements	structure
COMMON statements	Type statements
EXTERNAL statements	EQUIVALENT statements
Statement function definitions	Define file statements
DO and implied DO loops	DATA statements
GOTO statements	CALL statements
Function subroutines	PAUSE, RETURN and STOP
Subroutine and entry statements	statements
READ statements	WRITE statements
Direct access READ statements	Direct access WRITE statements
Unit reference number	Input and output lists
Hollerith fields	FORMAT statements
NAMELIST statements	Program structure
Production counts	

[W&H]

[Foxley 78]   E. Foxley and D.J. Morgan.
            Monitoring the Run-Time Activity of Algol 68-R Programs.
            Software--Practice and Experience 8:29-34, 1978.

A program profiling system for the Algol 68-R language is described. The system is a preprocessor using the language syntax analyzer. The profile consists of counts associated with each statement (some constructs were not monitored due to the lack of sophistication of the parser). [RTS]

[Francis 75a] I. Francis, R.M. Heiberger and P.F. Velleman.
Criteria and Considerations for the Evaluation of
Statistical Program Packages.
American Statistician 29(1):52-56, 1975.
This report to the American Statistical Association, incorporating the contributions of over one hundred people, presents the characteristics that have to be considered when evaluating statistical software. [IF]

[Francis 75b] I. Francis and R. Valliant.
The Novice with a Statistical Package: Performance
Without Competence.
In *Proceedings of the Computer Science and Statistics
Eighth Annual Symposium on the Interface*, pages
110-114. Computer Science and Statistics, 1975.
An experiment was conducted to compare the ease of use of the command language by novices of SPSS and SAS. [IF]

[Francis 77] Ivor Francis, editor.
A Comparative Review of Statistical Software.
In *Proceedings of the 41st Session of the ISI*, International
Association for Statistical Computing, 1977.
In this volume of the Proceedings of the 41st Session of the ISI, Professor Ivor Francis has assembled and presented a comprehensive collection of evaluations of 46 major statistical computing packages, describing their capabilities and use. Details for many of the program packages appeared as exhibits during the session and formed the basis for the material presented in this volume. This presentation was one of the innovations of the inaugural meeting of the International Association for Statistical Computing (IASC), held as part of the 41st Session of the ISI.

There is considerable need for evaluation of statistical software, and this large volume responds significantly to that need. A unique aspect of the presentation is the introduction of a self-evaluation approach, designed by Professor Francis in collaboration with his colleagues. Each developer prepared, in a standard format, an evaluation of the capabilities that are provided in the package. In addition, Professor Francis has summarized the evaluations. The evaluated software includes large, general-purpose statistical programs, special-purpose packages, packages for data management, editing, tabulation, survey analysis and subroutine libraries.

Software features evaluated include: capabilities for processing and displaying data; portability and availability; the ease of learning and using; reliability and cost. Also shown are concise, detailed package abstracts covering specific capabilities, illustrations of user languages, typical samples of output, and developer comments on recent and future development. The volume contains an extensive bibliography for statistical software. [Excerpted from CR36252]

[Francis 79a] I. Francis (ed.).
A Comparative Review of Statistical Software I: The
International Association for Statistical Computing
Exhibition of Statistical Software.
IASC, Voorburg, Netherlands, 1979.
Forty-six statistical programs and packages are reviewed.   Numerical ratings by the
developers on over fifty features are presented permitting comparisons across all systems.
Descriptive papers by developers include samples of input and output. A bibliography of
reviews and evaluations of statistical software is included. [IF]

[Francis 79b] I. Francis and J. Sedransk.
A Comparison of Software for Processing and Analyzing
Surveys.
Bulletin of the International Statistical Institute, 48.
This presents the results of three experiments: (1) to evalulate programs for computing
variances from complex sample surveys, (2) to evaluate programs for processing census
data, and (3) to evaluate programs to tabulate data from surveys. [IF]

[Francis 80]   I. Francis.
A Taxonomy of Statistical Software.
In COMPSTAT 1980: Proceedings in Computational
Statistics, 1980.
A system for describing and classifying statistical software is proposed and used to present
detailed ratings by users and developers of six widely-used statistical packages. [IF]

[Francis 81]   Ivor Francis.
A Scientific Approach to Statistical Software.
In Frederick G. Sayward, Mary Shaw and Alan J. Perlis,
editor, Software Metrics: An Analysis and Evaluation.
MIT Press, Cambridge, Massachusetts, 1981.
In "A Scientific Approach to Statistical Software" Francis summarizes what has been done
in evaluating statistical packages. Two questions of concern are software accuracy and
convenience for users. Some quantitative measures have been defined for both questions
and experiments have been conducted using these metrics. The experiments have relied
on developing standard test problems.

Francis recommends research to develop metrics for the evaluation of software. He also
recommends that a set of standard experiments be developed. [FGS]

[Franta 75]   W. R. Franta.
Process/Event Driven Simulation.
American-Elsevier, 1975.
This book gives a summary perspective on the fundamentals of simulation modeling. [JCB]

[Freburger 79]Karl Freburger and Victor R. Basili.
The Software Engineering Laboratory: Relationship Equations.
Technical Report TR-764, University of Maryland, Computer Science Center, College Park, Maryland, May, 1979.

Despite the fact that software costs are becoming a greater portion of the cost of using a computer system, very little research has been done to determine which factors impact the software development process. Presented are results of research into methods of estimating programming project variables such as effort, project duration, staff size and productivity. The results obtained are compared to the results of a previous study by Walston and Felix. [VRB]

[Freiburghouse 74]
R. A. Freiburghouse.
Register Allocation Via Usage Counts.
Communications of the ACM 17(11):638-642, 1974.

This short paper introduces the notion of usage counts, and describes how usage counts can provide a basis for register allocation. Two algorithms for loading registers are described (least-recently used and least-recently loaded).

In order to compare the two algorithms, results are given for:

1. Loads generated by each criteria
2. Relative performance of criteria

[W&H]

[Fries 77]   M. J. Fries.
Software Error Data Acquistion.
Technical Report RADC-TR-77-130, Rome Air Development Center, April, 1977.

Software error data was collected from a large DOD system development project. The errors were analyzed and put into a predefined set of categories. As part of the effort, the times to find and fix the errors were calculated, and the phase of the development project in which the errors arose was determined. Study results were also compared to results of a similar type of study performed by a second contractor who performed analysis of data from another DOD software project. [Abstract]

[Gannon 75a] J. D. Gannon and J. J. Horning.
Language Design for Programming Reliability.
IEEE Transactions on Software Engineering 1(2), June, 1975.

The language in which programs are written can have a substantial effect on their reliability. This paper discusses the design of programming languages to enhance reliability. It presents several general design principles, and then applies them to particular languages constructs. Since we can not logically prove the validity of such design principles, empirical evidence is needed to support or discredit them. Gannon has performed a major experiment to measure the effect of nine specific language-design decisions in one context. Analysis of the frequency and persistence of errors shows that several decisions had a significant impact on reliability. [Abstract]

[Gannon 75b] J. D. Gannon.
Language Design to Enhance Programming Reliability.
Technical Report CSRG-47, Computer Science
Department, University of Toronto, Canada, 1975.

Introduction: This thesis uses two related languages to compare the effects of certain language choices on program reliability. A chapter of the thesis is devoted to an examination of similar work in this area up to 1975.

Analysis: The analysis consists of recording the results of 40 subjects coding problems in the two languages. The 40 subjects were divided into two groups (25, 15), one for each language. The subjects had very varied but matched experience. Comparisons of the recorded errors etc, were made by elaborate statistical techniques. Four classifications were used in the analysis to indicate the property of the error.

Programs: Two sample tasks were taken for the comparison. The first was a simulation of a card game, the second a very simple output spooler. The solution consists of between 123 and 306 statements.

Results: About a dozen language decisions were analyzed by each of the four classification methods. Twenty results were statistically significant. The most important one was that having a semicolon as a statement terminator was better than having a semicolon as a statement separator.

A summary of this work appears in "The Impact of Language Design on the Production of Reliable Software" by Gannon and Horning, *ACM Conference on Software Reliability,* 1975. [W&H]

[Gannon 75c] John D. Gannon and James J. Horning.
The Impact of Language Design on the Production of
Reliable Software.
*Proceedings of International Conference on Reliable Software:*10-22, 1975.

Gannon has performed a major experiment to measure the effect of nine specific language design decisions in one context. Analysis of the frequency and persistence of errors shows that several decisions had a significant impact on reliability. [Abstract]

[Gannon 77] J. D. Gannon.
An Experimental Evaluation of Data Type Conventions.
Communications of the ACM 20(8), August, 1977.

This paper discusses an experiment that compares the programming reliability of subjects using a statically typed language and a "typeless" language. Two languages were designed by the author and attempts were made to make the two languages identical in all features not affected by the issue of data types. This particular experiment showed that in that particular environment, the features of a statically typed language increased programming reliability more than the features of a "typeless" language. [JES]

Investigates the effect of programming in statically typed (ST) versus typeless (NT) languages with respect to the number of errors made and the number or runs made in arriving at the final program. From a controlled experiment the author was able to conclude was that ST has positive effect over NT with respect to making fewer errors and taking fewer runs in arriving at the final program. [FGS]

[Gehring 77] Philip F. Gehring, Jr. and Udo W. Pooch.
A Quantitative Analysis of the Accuracy of Estimating in Software Development.
In *Proc. 16th Annual Technical Symposium on Systems Software: Operational Reliability and Performance Assurance*, pages 61-70. National Bureau of Standards, Gaithersburg Md., 1977.

The authors hypothesize that there are specific activities within a software development project whose estimate accuracy consistently reflects the estimate accuracy of the project as a whole. That is, if the resource consumption of these key activities is predicted accurately, then the resource consumption of the whole project will also be predicted accurately. Similarly, if a bad estimating job is done on the key activities, the estimate for the whole project will also be bad.

The authors tested this hypothesis by applying a statistical technique known as SEQUIN (for sequential item analysis) to data on some 39 software projects collected by the PARMIS project control system of the US Air Force Data System Design Center in Montgomery, Alabama. SEQUIN has previously been used to identify key questions in the Scholastic Achievement Test (SAT), such that scores on the key quesions are strongly correlated to overall score. Such information is of use to educators in reducing the length of the SAT (not to mention its value to the students who take it).

The authors found that there are indeed specific key activities in the sense described above. The three activities leading the list are : 1) defining input data, 2) system design review, and 3) flowcharting of system processes.

The benefits of this knowledge are not made clear. The implication is that if effort were concentrated on producing an accurate estimate of, say, the resources to do input data definition, then overall project estimate accuracy could be significantly improved. But there is nothing in the remainder of the paper to suggest how the accuracy of key activities are in fact"key". It is a bit like knowing what links will cause a chain to fail, but being unable to do anything about those links.

The authors conclude that "estimation of software development continues to be as bad as, or worse than, it has ever been." They recommend a number of remedial measures, chief of which is replacing the classical phase structure of software development (feasibility, requirements, system design, etc.) by the Research-Development-Production model, in which each of the three phases is estimated on the basis of the preceding phase. "The RDP model will heighten management's awareness of the complexity of what has to be done to eliminate the historically impossible requirement to accurately estimate the cost and time for the entire software development project. [CR34785]"

[Gehringer 79]
Edward F. Gehringer.
Functionality and performance in capability-based operating systems.
PhD thesis, Purdue University, May, 1979.

Early capability-based operating systems provided a rather coarse control over protection domains, but recent designs have been tending toward the support of finer-grained protection. This has resulted in complex process structures and run-time inefficiencies. A detailed simulation model is employed to compare the performance of several capability designs. The model reveals that by far the most important factor affecting performance is the number of segments which must be independently swapped; the effects of capability-segment size and call/return efficiency are minro by comparison.

To solve this problem, a virtual memory design is presented which allows for the support of arbitrarily small objects without a significant run-time penalty. The basis for the design is a generalization of tagged memory, which associates a hardware-interpreted type field with extended-type objects as well as hardware-defined data types; and the concept of variable length capabilities, which allows most capabilities to be very short -- 16 to 32 bits in length. The virtual memory design is extended to provide efficient and flexible means for domain switching and subprocess creation. This organization provides elegant solutions to several problems which previous capability designs have handled only in an ad hoc fashion. [Abstract]

[Gepner 78]   Herbert L. Gepner.
        User Ratings of Software Packages.
        Datamation 24(13):163-227, December, 1978.
Users of proprietary software packages rated 260 packages subjectively in the categories Overall Satifaction, Throughput and Efficiency, Ease of Installation, Ease of Use, Documentation, Vendor Technical Support, and Training. Average opinion, price, and brief notes on advantages and disadvantages are given for each. This article is abstracted from a Datapro 70 report. [MS]

[Gertner 80]   I. Gertner.
        Performance Evaluation of Communicating Processes.
        PhD thesis, Computer Science Department, University of
            Rochester, May, 1980.
        Available as TR76.
This dissertation is concerned with performance analysis of distributed systems using finite state automata, with the arcs signifying messages sent between processes. Various time durations are associated with messages, and the performance evaluator is able to compute task execution times and overheads, for example, from these times. [RTS]

[Gilb 77a]   T. Gilb.
        Software Metrics Technology: Some Unconventional
            Approaches to Reliable Software.
        In *Software Reliability*, pages 101-115. Infotech
            International Ltd., 1977.
A brief survey of techniques classified under the umbrella of "software metrics," i.e., they all relate to measurability of software reliability and closely related concepts, is presented. The subjects are classified into four categories, although most techniques could be said to belong to more than one:

1. Quantification of reliability
2. Automation of the reliability/maintainability task.   This includes, for example, assertion language tools, automatic program structuring, and automatic test case construction.
3. Management technology for reliable software. This includes, for example, design

and code inspection, and the multi-element component comparison and analysis method.

4. Redundancy based reliability technology. This includes, for example, dual programming; advocated as the cheapest way to achieve reliability

The paper might be useful for project managers, although it is extremely superficial and fairly ad hoc. The author also seems to have a somewhat strange understanding of the notion "structured programming". [CR33990]

[Gilb 77b]   T. Gilb.
Distinct Software: A Redundancy Technology for Reliable Software.
In *Software reliability*, pages 117-133. Infotech International Ltd., Maidenhed, Berkshire, UK, 1977.

Distinctness is used to mean that there is some degree of redundancy in the software.

Some advantages of creating software distinctness for the software development process are described. 100% distinctness, i.e., there is for each program at least one other program which functionally performs identically, is argued to have great advantages during operational testing for automatic correction of bugs, maintenance, and adds far less to the total costs of the software than generally believed. Some advantages of data redundancy are also mentioned.

Finally, a number of mostly very favorable experiences with the application of distinct software are described.

The paper makes a reasonably good case for software distinctness as a means of achieving high reliability. The examples and experiences described are interesting and illustrative. [CR33968]

[Gilb 77c]   Tom Gilb.
Software Metrics.
Winthrop, 1977.

An extensive survey of settings in which software metrics could be used and numerous proposals on metrics for various properties of programs. [MS]

[Goel 78]   Amrit L. Goel and K. Okumoto.
Bayesian Software Prediction Models.
Technical Report RADC-TR-78-155, Rome Air Development Center, July, 1978.
Five volumes.

These reports explore the use of a stochastic model for software failure phenomena for the case when the errors are not corrected with certainty. [MS]

[Good 73]   J. Good and B. A. M. Moon.
FORTRAN - As Provided by Some Major Machine Manufacturers.
Software -- Practice & Experience 3(1):9-14, 1973.

Introduction: This paper is concerned with a FORTRAN benchmark analysis of 10 computer systems, to assess the quality of them. The results contain some static information on the test programs.

Analysis: No details of the analysis are given.

Test programs: The original batch of test programs consisted of 34 Fortran programs. From these, nine main programs and subroutines were extracted, to obtain the results.

Systems tested are:

B5500   B6500
CDC 3300   CDC 6400
360/44(44PS)   360/series(OS level G)
1900 series (GEORGE 3 XFAT)   1100 series
DECsystem-10

Results: Results are given for:

1. Core utilization

   Average core per routine for instructions
   Average number of instructions per routine
   Bits per variable
   Bits per instruction
   Average core occupied by programs
   Size of supervisor and I/O areas
   Total core used

2. An indication of the effects of word lengths on floating point precision.

[W&H]

[Goodenough 79]
John B. Goodenough.
A Survey of Program Testing Issues.
In *Research Direction in Software Technology*, pages 316-342. MIT Press, Cambridge, Massachusetts, 1979.

There is some confusion in the literature about the utility of software testing. Goodenough's comprehensive and careful remarks on program testing should dispel this confusion. Software product managers know that testing is absolutely necessary. With the author's organization of the testing problem, this necessity is made understandable and academically respectable.

For anyone unfamiliar with Goodenough's ideas on testing, this paper is a good introduction. For practitioners, it also provides useful guidelines on the proper choice of specific testing methods. With the exception of some minor changes, this is the same paper that was published by Infotech in *Software Reliability*. [CR35851]

[Gordon 78]   J. D. Gordon, C. K. Capstick and A. Salvadori.
An Empirical Study of COBOL Programmers.
INFOR 15(2):229-241, 1978.

Introduction: This report compares the statistics obtained from student and professional programmers using COBOL.

Types of analysis: Static analysis is given of the final programs produced. Diagnostic counts for the entire development process is given. Finally, the number of runs to complete the task, the size of the final program, etc. is given.

Statistics: 37 trainee programmers were used who produced 27 successful programs. Three professional programmers were used on coding the same two tasks given to the students.

Results:

Use of COBOL verbs - trainees
Use of COBOL verbs - professionals
Diagnostic distribution - General - Each of the four COBOL divisions.
Variability of parameters monitored.

Note: One of the main differences between the groups was that the professionals used the GOTO much less. [W&H]

[Gordon 79a] Ronald D. Gordon.
            Measuring Improvements in Program Clarity.
            IEEE Transactions on Software Engineering SE-5(2):79-
            90, March, 1979.

This paper is one of a *software science* series. If you liked its predecessors, you'll probably like this one as well. This reviewer is in substantial agreement with Paul B. Moranda in his paper titled, "Software quality technology: (sad) status of; (unapproached) limits to; (manifold) alternatives to."

The author sought, and claims to have found, an objective measure of program clarity. Like other software science measures, his is computed by simple counts on operators and operands. The author then applies his measure to a number of programs that have been previously published as examples of improvement in clarity. He shows that his measure is in substantial agreement with subjective opinion in the overwhelming number of cases. He resorts to subjective discussion of program clarity to *explain* the remaining cases. In spite of the weight of the evidence, this reviewer is unconvinced that the results really indicate that the measure is a measure of what I mean by clarity. Since the program pairs involved consist of two very similar algorithms, many measures that indicate simplifications might coincide with subjective measures of clarity.

I suspect that a deeper cause of my disagreement with the author is that we have a different definition of what it means to understand a program. I propose two alternative definitions:

1. I have understood a program if I can follow it (that is, see what it will do) in various cases that I consider.
2. I have understood a program if I have found a convincing way of showing that it is correct.

I use the second of these two definitions because I find that feeling reasonably certain that a program works and knowing why it works are intrinsic to understanding that program. The author's discussions of the examples, and his choice of a measure, indicate that he uses the first. [CR35699]

[Gordon 79b] Ronald D. Gordon.
            A Qualitative Justification for a Measure of Program
            Clarity.
            IEEE Transactions on Software Engineering SE-5(2):121-
            127, March, 1979.

A form of mental effort measure from software science is proposed as an appropriate indicator of program clarity. The measure chosen is the ratio of program volume to an estimate of implementation level. This measure is subjected to an analysis of its behavior under a variety of program transformations which seek to remove six identifiable forms of impurities. These impurities have been used in various ways by several authors to develop principles of programming, or *DOs* and *DON'Ts*. It is shown that these principles of programming are in fact supported by the proposed clarity measure in nearly all cases, in the sense that the value of the measure (which "attempts to assess the amount of mental effort required to understand a program by a person fluent in the programming language") is less for the *purified* version than for the *unpurified* one.

It is gratifying to see software science measures being treated in a more solid analytical manner, and encouraging that the results of this analysis are good. Software science needs more of this kind of general analytic investigation in order to receive wider acceptance. The study shows that software science techniques support principles of programming on which there is general agreement, and also points out that they might be useful in clarifying and shedding new light upon issues on which there is controversy.

It is interesting that the estimated implementation level, rather than its definition from software science, was used in the study. Since the two versions occasionally exhibit different behavior, this suggests that different results might have been reached had the definition been used. For example, it would appear that using the definition of *level* as the ratio of potential volume to program volume would satisfactorily explain the removal of superfluous assignment statements which define synonymous operands, which the author shows is not satisfactorily explained by the use of the estimation of level. However, it also appears that the use of this definition of level would not satisfactorily explain the removal of a variable which represents different types of values in different parts of a program (ambiguous operands). This bears investigation and explanation, if true. [CR35806]

[Gould 74]   J. Gould and P. Drongowski.
An Exploratory Study of Computer Program Debugging.
Human Factors 16(3):258-277, 1974.

In comparing two types of errors, syntactically correct but semantically incorrect assignment statements versus array bound found that the former took five times as long to detect as the latter. Also the author found that debugging aids such as telling the subjects the type of errors or the line in which an error occurred had little effect on the subjects' debugging performance. Found a difference of 4 to 1 in debugging ability for experienced subjects having equivalent backgrounds. [FGS]

[Gould 75]   J. D. Gould.
Some Psychological Evidence on How People Debug
Computer Programs.
International Journal of Man-Machine Studies 7:151-182, 1975.

Introduction: This study examines the way programmers debug programs, how long they take and the facilities they use to do it (for example, an interactive computing system).

Analysis: Ten experienced FORTRAN programmers were used as subjects in this experiment. Four statistical analysis programs from the IBM Scientific Subroutine Package were modified. 3 classes of non-syntactic bug were inserted into each program - an assignment bug, an iteration bug, and an array bug - to produce 12 listings. All the programs were compiled using the TSS/360 compiler. Each subject was told to debug each of the 12 listings. The time it took time to debug each one, the number of times the interactive computing system was used, and the number of bugs not found were all measured, and finally the programmer was interviewed to find out what debugging techniques he used.

Results: Results are given showing:

The 12 program bugs used in the experiment
Frequency distribution of 120 debug times, including those in which the subject did not find the bug
Performance measures for each subject
Debug times, number of bugs not found and number of errors
Median debug times for each of the three classes of bugs
Debug times, number of bugs not found and number of errors for each program
Debug times, number of bugs not found and number of errors for each class of error
Summary of each listing
Output from TAB-1 array listing
Output from TAB-1 iteration listing

(TAB-1 is one of the test programs)

[W&H]

During a replication of the experiment described in Gould 74, the author found examples of debugging tasks and program modifications which require little to no understanding of the programs under consideration. Also, the author found that the subjects were reluctant to use the available interactive debugging facilities. [FGS]

[Graham 78] G. S. Graham.
  Guest Editors Overview: Queueing Network Models of
    Computer Systems Performance.
  Computing Surveys 10:219-224, 1978.

This paper is the Editor's summary for the September, 1978 issue of Computing Surveys which is a special issue on network models of computer systems. This issue of Computing Surveys is a good source for a state-of-the-art analysis of solution techniques and applications of queueing network models. [JCB]

[Green 77] T. Green.
  Conditional Program Statements and Their
    Comprehensibility to Professional Programmers.
  Journal of Occupational Psychology 50:93-109, 1977.

The author found that professional programmers were better able to answer difficult questions about programs written in a language which used an IF THEN ELSE having redundant predicate information rather than the standard IF THEN ELSE. [FGS]

[Griss 77] M. L. Griss and M. R. Swanson.
  MBALM/1700: A Microprogrammed LISP Machine for the
    Burroughs B1726.
  In *Proceedings, Tenth Annual Workshop on
    Microprogramming*, IEEE, 1977.

Introduction: BALM is an Algol-like extension of LISP. The paper describes an implementation of BALM on the B1726 which is coded partly in itself and partly interpreted via microcode. The code which in interpreted (MBALM) consists of about 100 opcodes of one to four bytes in length. These opcodes correspond to the LISP primitives.

Analysis: Extensive static and dynamic analysis has been made, a summary of which appears in the paper.

Programs: A simple program is used to illustrate system overheads. The source of the main analysis is not given but 90,000 opcode uses are utilized.

Results: Tables given in the paper list:

> Sizes of system on 1108, PDP-10 and B1700 (with and without microcode)
> Translate and execute time for a simple program (on above systems)
> Static counts of 13 most commonly occurring primitives
> Static counts of 22 most commonly occurring pairs of primitives
> Dynamic counts of 13 most frequently used primitives
> Dynamic counts during compilation of 9 support functions

[W&H]

[Griswold 75] Ralph Griswold.
A Portable Diagnostic Facility for SNOBOL4.
Software--Practice and Experience 5:93-104, 1975.

In programming systems based on abstract machine modeling concepts, the underlying structure of the abstract machine can be made available to the software implemented on it. The result is an unusual facility for diagnosis and exploration of software structure. Such a facility has been added to the macro implementation of SNOBOL4. This paper describes the nature of the facility, illustrates its use, and presents some results of using it for language implementation and development. [Abstract]

[Grochow 69] J.M. Grochow.
Real-time graphic display of time-sharing system operating characteristics.
In *Proceedings of the AFIPS Fall Joint Computer Conference*, pages 374-386. AFIPS Press, 1969.

The Graphic Display Monitoring (GDM) System is an experimental facility for Multics which runs on a PDP-8 connected to a display processor, a disk, and a 2400 baud line to Multics. The GDM can request the value of any memory location within Multics; up to 20 such samples may be requested a second. Some use of the graphics display facilities is provided though stored display templates. Unfortunately, the slow sampling rate is a severe limitation of the system. [RTS]

[Grosse-Lindemann 76]
C. O. Grosse-Lindemann and H. H. Nagel.
Postlude to a Pascal Compiler Bootstrap on a DECSystem-10.
Software -- Practice & Experience 6(1):29-42, 1976.

Introduction: This paper is concerned with the problem of bootstrapping a Pascal compiler onto a DECsystem-10, and getting accepted by the general public. It also contains some statistics on the compiler.

Analysis: The static and dynamic distribution of instructions have been determined, but no details of the analysis are given except that the compiler had some minor modifications made to it.

Test program: The results given relate to the compilation of the compiler.

Results: Results are given for core requirements in tabular form. No other results are tabulated, but runtime support and dynamic and static distribution of instructions are discussed, though not in much detail. [W&H]

[Gumpertz 78] R. Gumpertz.
Hydra Kernel Tracer.
Unpublished Internal Memo.

The Hydra Kernel Tracer consists of microcode for recording kernel entries, exits, I/O interrupts, context swaps, and internal events, along with various postprocessors for converting the data so generated into usable forms. The time the event occurred, as well as a small anount of event-specific information, is recorded for each event. The microcode assist makes it practical to trace events with a granularity of less than 1 ms with little perturbation. There are at least seven postprocessor formats; two of the more important are process time lines and processor time lines. [RTS]

[Gupta 78]   Ram K. Gupta and Mark A. Franklin.
Working Set and Page Fault Frequency Paging
Algorithms: a Performance Comparison.
IEEE Transactions on Computers 27(8):706-712, August,
1978.

The authors analyze the performance of the two paging algroithms mentioned in the title. Both analytic and empirical results are presented. The former are based on a program behavior model which assumes an inter-page-fault interval distribution which depends only on the size of the program's resident set. The empirical results are based on traces of two real programs. Performance comparison is based on the value of the space-time product, with time defined as the sum of virtual and page transfer times. Unfortunately, the value of the latter quantity is not given. The authors conclude that the PFF algorithm is more sensitive to the value of its control parameter than is the WS algorithm, and they therefore express preference for the latter. Their diagrams, however, show PFF to be clerly superior on one of the real program and, with proper tuning, capable of beating WS on two of the three analytic cases; thus the superiority of WS is far from proven, at least by the results of this paper. [CR34395]

[Hajioannan 76]
M. Hajioannan.
Debugging of Parallel Programs.
In *Proceedings of the Ninth Hawaii International
Conference on System Sciences*, pages 20-22.
January, 1976.

This paper proposes a method for producing well-structured parallel programs. A set of constructs is listed, and it is claimed that several useful properties result. Debugging aspects of these restricted programs are minimally considered. This paper is not recommended, since it merely lists results without motivation or proof. [RTS]

[Halstead 76] M. H. Halstead, R. D. Gordon and J. L. Elshoff.
On Software Physics and GM's PL/I Programs.
Technical Report GMR 2175, General Motors Corporation,
June, 1976.

This report investigates the relationship proposed by Halstead between the number of distinct operators and operands (n1, n2) and the total number of uses of operators and operands (N1, N2). This is the "length equation", which is:

Program length $\equiv$ N1 + N2 = n1 * log2(n1 + n2 * log2(n2)

This report gives an introduction with results for PL/I, Algol 58, FORTRAN and machine language. [W&H]

[Halstead 77] Maurice H. Halstead.
Operating and Programming Systems: Elements of Software Science.
Elsevier, New York, 1977.

This book contains the first systematic summarization of a branch of experimental and theoretical science dealing with the human preparation of computer programs and other types of written material. Application of the classical methods of the natural sciences demonstrates that even such relatively intangible objects as written abstracts and computer programs are governed by natural laws, both in their preparation and in their ultimate form. [VRB]

[Hammond 77]

J. Hammond.
Basic - An Evaluation of Processing Methods and a Study of some Programs.
Software -- Practice & Experience 7:697-711, 1977.

Introduction: The main aim of this paper is to assess various processing methods for BASIC, that is, compiling, interpreting and throw-away compiling. The performance of each method is assessed by six benchmark programs whose characteristics are listed.

Analysis: The main analysis in the paper consists of measurements of the compiling/running characteristics of the three methods on a 4130 computer (at the University of Kent).

Programs: Six programs are considered. In some cases, three variants of one program is used, the program being a Computer Aided Instruction application.

Results: Apart from the analysis of the performance of the compiling systems, the details given about the programs is as follows:

Counts, both static and dynamic of

Statement types	Array variables
Constants	Operations
Simple variables	Function calls (standard and defined)

[W&H]

[Hansen 78]   Wilfred J. Hansen, Richard Doring, and Lawrence
R. Whitlock.
Why an Examination was Slower Online than On Paper.
Int. J. Man-Mach. Stud. 10(5):507-520, September, 1978.
The authors looked at the use of a program which carries out interactive examinations on
the PLATO system. They found that the length of time students took to complete
interactive examinations were sometimes as much as twice the length of time taken to
complete similar examinations given conventionally on paper. The authors sought to
explain their finding by analyzing the two examination situations, including the collection of
a limited amount of videotape evidence of students being examined. On the basis of this
analysis, the authors propose suggestions, e.g., for faster display speeds which "may
eventually" make PLATO a faster examination medium than paper. [CR34479]

[Hanson 78]   David Hanson.
Event Associations in SNOBOL4 for Program Debugging.
Software--Practice and Experience 8:115-129, 1978.
An event association facility for the SNOBOL4 programming language is described. This
facility permits the execution of a programmer-defined function to be associated with the
occurrence of a specified event. The set of valid events includes variable referencing,
statement execution, program interruption, function call and return, and execution-time
errors. The use and implementation of this facility is described. [RTS]

[Hartmann 77] A. C. Hartmann.
A Concurrent Pascal Compiler for Minicomputers.
In *Lecture Notes in Computer Science 50*, pages 59-?.
Springer-Verlag, 1977.
Introduction: This paper describes a seven-pass compiler for Concurrent Pascal. It
contains some static information on types of compiler failures during testing and also some
performance data such as space requirements for each pass.

Analysis: Compiler failures occurring during testing were detected by runtime checks in the
virtual machine. Three types of checking were performed - variant checking, pointer
checking and range checking.

Programs: No details of the test programs are given, but a total of 64 failures were detected.

Results: Results are given for percentage of variant, pointer and range errors. Results are
also presented showing the space requirements of the seven-pass Concurrent Pascal
compiler, and a six-pass Sequential Pascal compiler. Detailed data is given for each pass
of the Concurrent compiler. [W&H]

[Hawthorn 79] Paula Hawthorn and Michael Stonebraker.
Performance Analysis of a Relational Database
Management System.
In *Proceedings ACM-SIGMOD 1979 International
Conference on Management Data*, pages 1-12. ACM,
May, 1979.
The performance characteristics of INGRES, a relational database management system
which runs on the DEC PDP 11 with the UNIX operating system, are analyzed and
discussed in this clearly written paper. The authors are conservative about suggesting

extensions of their results to other DBMS, but their methodology is clearly of wider applicability.

Two types of queries are considered: data-intensive and overhead-intensive. More system overhead is required to process an overhead-intensive query than the data processing time to actually fetch and manipulate the data. In contrast, a data-intensive query requires much more processing time than overhead time. The latter case arises when the query itself is inherently data intensive and when the database is not well structured to respond to the query.

The authors ran three benchmarks for each type of query. I/O reference patterns and CPU usage patterns are shown for each benchmark. These patterns differ greatly for the two types of query. In general, overhead-intensive queries are CPU-bound and exhibit high locality of reference to INGRES system files. Data-intensive queries show a significant degree of sequentiality of data reference.

The authors conclude that caching read-ahead data blocks can significantly improve DBMS performance on data-intensive queries, provided that the system has space available, and that the data is organized on disk to take advantage of sequential reads. Overhead-intensive queries, and interactions with a terminal-oriented DBMS user interface in general, may be processed much more effeciently through the use of intelligent terminals to handle the interface. The type of analysis carried out to reach these conclusions could have significant impact on decision making regarding the most effective use of new technology to improve DBMS performance. [CR35255]

[Hehner 74]   E. C. R. Hehner.
Matching Program and Data Representations to a Computing Environment.
Technical Report CSRG-44, Computer Science Department, University of Toronto, Canada, 1974.

Introduction: This thesis is a study of the use of highly variable length encoding for both program and data in order to achieve better use of memory.

Analysis: The starting point was the XPL compiler for the 360. The output code was altered to generate code for the new machine. Measurements were done on the resulting compiler to determine what further changes seemed desirable.

Program: The only program considered is the XPL compiler itself.

Results: Relatively few figures are given which can be related directly to the use of XPL. However, this report seems to be one of the few to consider more complex addressing schemes to handle variable length data, for instance, integers and strings of variable length. The main table is the static frequency of the target operation codes in the final machine design. [W&H]

[Hellerman 72]
          L. Hellerman.
          A Measure of Computational Work.
          IEEE Transactions of Computers 21:439-446, 1972.

Hellerman attempts to lay a foundation for a formal theory of information processing work. The paper gives a good insight into the problems of developing such a theory. [JCB]

[Hellerman 75]
　　　H. Hellerman and T. F. Conroy.
　　　Computer System Performance.
　　　McGraw-Hill, New York, 1975.
This text gives a basic approach to computer system performance evaluation and analysis. It offers introductions to queueing theory among its other coverage. [JCB]

[Herd 77]　　James H. Herd, John N. Postak, William E. Russell, and Kenneth R. Stewart.
　　　Software Cost Estimation Study; vol I: Study Results.
　　　Technical Report RADC-TR-77-220, Rome Air Development Center, June, 1977.
The study identified factors that have an adverse effect on software cost estimates, determined their impact on software cost estimates, discussed methods for controlling the effect of these factors, and developed an overall methodology for estimating the costs of software development. In addition to a generalized model for estimating software development costs, separate models have been generated for estimating the development cost of command and control, scientific, utility, and business software. [Abstract]

[Herndon 78]　Mary Anne Herndon and Ann P. Keenan.
　　　Analysis of Error Remediation Expenditures During Validation.
　　　In *Proceedings Third International Conference on Software Engineering*, pages 101-206. IEEE, May, 1978.
The costs of remediation of errors in a formal in-house validation procedure for a real time communication system are described in this paper. Cost is expressed in an equation which reflects the expenditures for reportng, analysis, remediation, retesting, and managerial overhead. This case study concludes that for this project an underinvestment in the validation phase caused by underallocation of time and resources for this and previous chronological phases led to large expenditures for correction and retesting procedures.

The paper is definitely worth reading for those involved in the management of programming projects, despite some juxtaposition of definitions with the references to these definitions. [CR35807]

[Hilborn 80]　Gene Hilborn.
　　　Measures for Distributed Processing Network Survivability.
　　　In *Proceedings of AFIPS 1980 National Computer Conference*, pages 157-164. AFIPS, 1980.
This paper views a network as a graph, and develops an axiomatic measure, defined on (0, 1), of network survivability in the face of node and edge failure. The survivability measure defined reflects the number of, size of (in number of nodes), and connectivity of subgroups formed when the network graph becomes disconnected. In a sense, the survivability measure reflects the degree to which the disconnected subgraphs are able to communicate and continue functioning (survive) when failure occurs.

The paper is nicely organized, and except for a few rather horrible sentences is well written.

The survivability measure developed has interesting, desirable, axiomatic properties; e.g., the survivability measure is best improved by adding a node to the largest size subgraph.

Following statement of the axioms which the survivability measures, σ, must obey, and after discussing the properties σ will have if it obeys the axioms, the measure

$$\sigma(X) = \Sigma_i^\ell \, [x_i^2/n^2]^{1/2}$$

is settled upon, with n the number of nodes in the network, and X, a vector,

$$X = (x_1, x_2, \ldots, x_\ell)$$

with x_i the number of nodes in the ith of ℓ subgraphs formed after failure of a specified set of nodes and/or links.

The model is capable, therefore, of comparing the effect of (node/edge) failures for a collection of topologies. An example of a sixteen node network organized into seven topologies is used to compare survivability measures. Obviously, as survivability improves, the number of edges increases. It is not surprising, therefore, to learn that the star, (bi-directional) loop, and bus (called a string tree in the paper) topologies score low as survivors. What is puzzling is that the opening paragraph and title bill the results as applicable to distributed processing networks, including distributed architecture computers, etc. Clearly they are not, at least as most distributed systems are being organized.

In short, the model is fine as far as it goes; i.e., as with any model, we must be aware of its limitations, assumptions, and applicability. [CR36411]

[Hoaglin 73] D. C. Hoaglin.
An Analysis of the Loop Optimization Scores in Knuth's "Empirical Study of FORTRAN Programs".
Software -- Practice & Experience 3(2), 1973.

Introduction: The optimization scores for Knuth's random sample of inner loops are analyzed to provide a unified comparison of the five optimization levels. The techniques used are those of exploratory data analysis.

Type of analysis: The logarithms of the scores are calculated and the technique of "median polish" used to analyse the results. This involves iteratively removing the median of each row and column. The method is described step by step in the paper.

Results: Results are given for:

    Optimization scores for inner loops
    Logarithms of optimization scores
    Result of first step of median polish
    Result of second step of median polish
    Result of third step of median polish
    Result of fourth step of median polish
    Optimization level effects as percentages
    Example grouped by pattern of interaction
    Optimization level effects by group

[W&H]

[Hoare 76]   C. A. R. Hoare.
The High Cost of Programming Languages.
In *Software Systems Engineering*, pages 413-429. Online
Conferences Ltd., Uxbridge, UK, 1976.
This paper investigates the high cost of computer programming, including direct, indirect and consequential costs. It identifies eight major headings: organization, design, program construction, error, change, running costs, software procurement, and finally, delay. It then lists sixteen ways in which a programming language and its implementation can contribute to these costs, namely, by unfamiliarity, application-orientation, instability, independent compilation, debugging and optimizing compilers, machine dependence, obscurity of specification, freedom of expression, unreadability, inefficient translation, inefficient object code, unreliability, insecurity, lack of structure, illogicality, and complexity. The paper concludes with some advice of immediate and long-term benefit to programmers and their managers. [CR34245]

[Holthouse 79]
Mark A. Holthouse and Mark J. Hatch.
Experience with Automated Testing Analysis.
Computer 12(8):33-36, August, 1979.
In this paper, the authors discuss automated techniques associated with adequate flow path coverage by functional testing. They emphasize the fact that "schemes for automatic generation of test data, to cause untested paths, may be counterproductive unless the tester is still intimately involved in the process."

Their coverage goal is 90 percent of the outcomes of program flow decisional branches. The paper gives results showing that executing additional runs to improve coverage does indeed lead to the detection of additional errors. However, they state that a "major source of the branch testing technique's power comes from the close inspection of the software it forces."

The authors' manual efforts lead to their identification of certain problems in their test strategy. The problems characterized as most important are unreachability, large system problems, bypassed loops, and omissions. [Excerpted from CR35397]

[Howden 78a] William E. Howden.
Theoretical and Empirical Studies of Program Testing.
Proc. 3rd International Conference Software Engineering
20(4), April, 1978.
This paper starts off by distinguishing between the theoretical and empirical approaches to the study of program testing. Various theoretical (nonmathematical, graph-theoretical, and algebraic) and empirical approaches (path, branch, structured, special values, and symbolic testing, interface consistency, anomaly analysis, and specifications requirements) are described.

Next, the results of a research project are reported. A total of 28 errors were introduced into six working programs. Various test techniques were then used in attempts to identify these errors. Path testing was the most effective single technique. It found 18 of the errors. All techniques combined found 26 of the errors.

Two of the six programs were written in Algol. The others were written in COBOL, PL/I, FORTRAN, and PL360. Very little information is presented on the nature or size of these programs or on the nature of the errors introduced.

The author concludes that further empirical studies of testing are needed. This reviewer agrees. Considering the magnitude of the resources devoted to program testing, any guidance in the selection of the most effective test techniques for a given program (considering its nature, size, and source language) would be extremely valuable. [Excerpted from CR34958]

[Howden 78b] William E. Howden.
> *Functional Program Testing.*
> Technical Report DM-146-IR, University of Victoria, August, 1978.

An approach to functional testing is described in which the design of a program is viewed as an integrated collection of functions. The selection of test data depends on the functions used in the design and on the value spaces over which the funcitons are defined. The basic ideas in the method were developed during the study of a collection of scientific programs containing errors. The method was the most reliable testing technique for discovering the errors. It was found to be significantly more reliable than structured testing. The two techniques are compared and their relative advantages and limitations are discussed. [Abstract]

[Howden 79] William E. Howden.
> *An Analysis of Software Validation Techniques for Scientific Programs.*
> Technical Report DM-171-IR, University of Victoria, March, 1979.

Different empirical methods for assessing the effectiveness of software validation methods are discussed. *Error analysis* involves the examination of a collection of programs whose errors are known in advance. Each error is analyzed and the validation techniques are identified whose use would result in the discovery of the error. The results of an error analysis study of a package of FORTRAN scientific subroutines are described. The errors that were present in version five of the package and then later corrected in version six were analyzed. The results of the study indicate that the use of an integrated collection of static and dynamic analysis methods would have resulted in the discovery of the errors in edition five before its release. The paper is organized so that it describes the features of an integrated approach to validation as well as the effectiveness of individual methods. [Abstract]

[Howden 80] William E. Howden.
> Functional Program Testing.
> *IEEE Transactions on Software Engineering* SE-6(2):162-169, March, 1980.

This paper describes a project which took a set of known errors in a release of a program library and investigated how various testing methods could have found these errors before release. Both functional testing and structural testing are considered, with emphasis on the former. A refinement of functional testing is presented; in this, the program is not regarded as a black box but is analyzed and split into sub-functions. The conclusion of the paper is that functional and structural testing should be regarded as partners rather than as rivals, since each can find different kinds of error. Functional testing, however, finds more, particularly if the refined method is used.

The paper is quite interesting and readable, in spite of a tendency to labor the obvious. [CR36382]

[Huang 79]   J. C. Huang.
Detection of Data Flow Anomaly Through Program Instrumentation.
IEEE Transactions on Software Engineering SE-5(3):226-236, May, 1979.

A data flow anomaly in a program is an indication that a programming error might have been committed. This paper describes a method for detecting such an anomaly by means of program instrumention. The method is conceptually simple, easy to use, easy to implement on a computer, and can be applied in conjunction with a conventional program test to achieve increased error-detection capability. [Abstract]

[Ingalls 71]   Daniel Ingalls.
Fete: A Fortran Execution Time Estimator.
Technical Report, Stanford University, February, 1971.

This report describes a preprocessor which takes a Fortran program and inserts code to accumulate counts for each statement. A postprocessor is also described which takes the modified program and correlates the text with the final counter values. Although counts rather than times are stored, the postprocessor tries to estimate the cost of each statement as a function of the operators which compose the statement. [RTS]

[Ivie 77]   E. L. Ivie.
The Programmer's Workbench -- A Machine for Software Development.
Communications of the Association for Computing Machinery 20(10), 1977.

A discussion of the concepts underlying the Programmer's Workbench (PWB) is presented to explain how PWB can aid program development and maintenance. Information is given on a specific implementation of PWB using UNIX. [MEM]

[Jackson 78]   Richard H.F. Jackson and John M. Mulvey.
A Critical Review of Comparisons of Mathematical Programming Algorithms and Software.
J. Res. N.B.S. 83(6):563-585, Nov.-Dec., 1978.

This paper surveys fifty articles spanning the period 1953-77 which report the computational testing of mathematical programming algorithms. The authors' intention is to document the methods employed in conducting these experiments, including the selection of problems, algorithm description, experiment design, and the form of reported results.

The survey is arranged according to the following topics: elements of the experiment (algorithms, software, problem class); experiment design (test problems, computer environments, experiment controls); empirical results (performance measures, statistical methods, mathematical checks, reporting of empirical evidence, interpretation of results); and suggestions for future work.

The papers included for critical review cover the major areas of mathematical programming: LP, IP, unconstrained optimization, shortest paths, NLP, networks (mincost flow), geometric problems, system of nonlinear equations, quadratic programs, and knapsack problems . . .

The authors of the paper suggest that fundamental research in the area of computer-algorithm performance is long overdue. Some initial attempts to rectify the situation in this area have been made. One of the authors of the reviewed paper has co-authored a report addressing the issue under discussion. [Excerpted from CR34894]

[Jain 79]   Aridaman K. Jain.
               A Guideline to Statistical Approaches in Computer
               Performance Evaluation Studies.
               Performance Evaluation Review 8(1/2):63-77,
               Spring/Summer, 1979.
This paper suggests that better experimental design and statistical analysis could alter the conclusions of some computer performance evaluation studies. It does not provide a *guideline* for applying statistical approaches in computer performance studies. It does, however, discuss various topics in the design of experiments and in statistical data analysis, and give references which include bibliographies and conference proceedings on computer performance evaluation. [CR35701]

[Janson 76]   P.A. Janson.
               *Using type extension to organize virtual memory
               mechanisms.*
               PhD thesis, Massachusetts Institute of Technology,
               September, 1976.
               Available as MIT LCS TR-167.
Much effort is currently being devoted to producing computer systems that are easy to understand, to verify and to develop. The general methodology for designing such a system consists of decomposing it into a structured set of modules so that the modules can be understood, verified and developed individually, and so that the understanding/verification of the system can be derived from the understanding/verification of its modules. While many of the mechanisms in a computer system have been decomposed successfully into a structured set of modules, no technique has been proposed to organize the vitual memory mechanism of a system in such a way.

The present thesis proposes to use type extension for that purpose. The virtual memory mechanism consists of a set of type manager modules implementing abstract information containers. The structure of the mechanism reflects the structure of the containers that are implemented. While using type extension to organize a virtual memory system is conceptually simple, it is hard to achieve in practice. All existing or proposed uses [of] type extension assume the existence of information containers that are uniformly accessible, can always be grown, and are protected. Using type extension inside a virtual memory mechanism raises implementation problems since such containers are not implemented. Their implementation is precisely the objective of the virtual memory mechanism. In addition to explaining how type extension can be supported inside a virtual memory mechanism, the thesis demonstrates its use in a case study involving a commercial, general-purpose, time-sharing system. It concludes by providing some insights into the organization of virtual memory mechanisms for time-sharing systems. [Abstract]

[Jasik 71]   S. Jasik.
Monitoring Program Execution on CDC 6000 series
Machines.
In R. Rustin, editor, *Proceedings of the Conference on
Design and Optimization of Compilers*, pages 129-136.
Prentice-Hall, 1971.

This paper describes a sampling routine which runs on a peripheral processor (PPU), monitoring the program in the central processor (CPU). A histogram is accumulated by sampling the program counter of the CPU approximately 35,000 times a second. Using the PPU eliminates any causes of interference. A postprocessor relects the information back to the source text of the program. [RTS]

[Jeffery ??]   D. R. Jeffery and M. J. Lawrence.
*An Inter-Organizational Comparison of Programming
Productivity.*
Technical Report, University of New South Wales,
Department of Information Systems, ??.

The factors which influence program size and program development time have been investigated across three dissimilar organizations. Data on a total of 93 COBOL programs has been collected and analyzed. Eighteen variables covering the characteristics of the program, programmer and programming environment were recorded. Program size and program development time were found to have a strong program characteristic and organization dependency. Programmer characteristics did not appear to play a role in influencing program size or program development time. The best determinant of program development time was found to be procedure division lines of code, which gave a simple regression R^2 in excess of .79 for the two organizations using well formulated programming standards. Productivity measures based on lines of code per hour are shown to be misleading in inter-organizational comparisons. [VRB]

[Jones 73]   Jones, A. K.
Protection in programmed systems.
PhD thesis, Carnegie-Mellon University, June, 1973.

This dissertation investigates the control of access to objects within programmed systems. The vehicle for this study is a model of protection that isolates a small set of mechanisms needed to provide access control, leaving the policy for invoking theses mechanisms to vary naturally with applications. Emphasis is placed on access control required for parameters that accompany a process crossing between execution environments; and a new concept called amplification is defined.

The model is shown to provide structure and terminology sufficient for describing and comparing diverse protection systems, for expressing and proving boundary conditions that characterize the manipulation of objects within environments independent of the code executed, and for partially ordering protection services according to the services they provide. In addition, the dissertation introduces the concept of a centralized protection facility capable of providing access control for user defined objects and accesses. [Abstract]

[Jones 78]   T. C. Jones.
Measuring Programming Quality and Productivity.
IBM Systems Journal 17(1), 1978.

Discussed is the unit-of-measure situation in programming. An analysis of common units of measure for assessing program quality and programmer productivity reveals that some standard measures are intrinsically paradoxical. Lines of code per programmer-month and cost per defect are in this category. Presented here are attempts to go beyond such paradoxical units as there. Also discussed is the usefulness of separating quality measurements into measures of defect removal efficiency and defect prevention, and the usefulness of separating productivity measurements into work units and cost units. [Abstract]

[Jones 80]   A.K. Jones and E.F. Gehringer, eds.
The Cm* Multiprocessor Project: A Research Review.
Technical Report CMU-CS-80-131, Carnegie-Mellon
University, Computer Science Department, July, 1980.

This snapshot of the Cm* project contains details on two object-based operating systems, StarOS and Medusa, as well as several chapters on monitoring. The performance monitoring aspects are concerned with how fast addressing, communication, and synchronization primitives execute in the various operating systems, and how memory contention affect total running time of a program. This report is certainly recommended for those interested in Cm* or one of its operating systems. [RTS]

[Kamnitzer 75]
S. H. Kamnitzer.
Bootstrapping XPL from IBM/360 to Univac 1100.
*SIGPLAN Notices:*14-20, May, 1975.

Introduction: This paper is concerned with the implementation of the SPL Compiler Generator System on the Univac 1100 series computers. The paper consists of a brief description of the SPL system, the techniques used to produce the XPL/1100 system from XPL/360, details of the structure of the compiler and finally some statistics giving information on instruction usage.

Results: Results are given for:

Usage of registers by XPL/1100 as compared to XPL/360
An XPL/1100 program in memory giving relative size of each routine
% of instruction types as compared with XPL/350 and Pascal/6600
Number of most frequently used instructions

[W&H]

[Kienzle 79]   M. G. Kienzle and K. C. Sevcik.
A Systematical Approach to the Performance Modeling of
Computer Systems.
In *Performance of Computer Systems*, pages 3-28.
Elsevier North-Holland, Inc., New York, 1979.

This paper presents a design methodology for generating computer system performance models. The modeling process is subdivided into three stages. In the first, a measurement model is derived from system data collected by monitors within the system. This measurement model is then transformed into a logical system model, which represents such features as program behavior, interference pattern, multiprogramming mix, workload, and resource attributes. The system model is described from both queueing and birth-death process viewpoints. The final state of the model is the mathematical, computational model, which is derived from the system model. This stage is used to generate the desired performance measurements for the computer system.

Overall, the use of the multi-stage model provides excellent insight into the anatomy of the performance modeling process. The transition from measured system parameters to a queueing network model becomes considerably more straightforward, and thus has the potential to be applied systematically to any computer system. The case study presented in the paper, done on an IBM S/370-165 II system, illustrates this point well. [CR35680]

[Kleinrock 75] L. Kleinrock.
Queuing Systems: Volume 1: Theory; Volume 2: Applications.
John Wiley & Sons, 1975.

Kleinrock's Volumes 1 and 2 are the standard references for queueing network model mathematics and applications as they existed in 1974. Volume 1 is a readable survey of single queue and network of queue mathematics. Volume 2 surveys applications in communication, computer systems, etc. Both volumes are readable by the non-specialist although acquaintance with the early chapters of Volume 1 is essential for reading of Volume 2 or the later chapters of Volume 1. [JCB]

[Knuth 71] Donald E. Knuth.
An Empirical Study of FORTRAN Programs.
Software -- Practice & Experience 1(2):105-133, 1971.

Introduction: A sample of programs written in FORTRAN IV by a wide variety of people for a wide variety of applications, was chosen at random in an attempt to see what programmers "really do". Statistical results are presented, together with some of their apparent implications.

Types of analysis: Three types of analysis are used:

1. Static analysis - the occurrence of easily recognizable syntactic constructions were counted.
2. Dynamic analysis - the frequency with which each construction actually occurs during one run was counted. Two test programs were used, FORDAP and PROGTIME which shows how much time was spent in system subroutines.
3. The inner loops of several programs were considered. They were translated into machine language by hand using 5 different optimizing techniques in an attempt to weigh the utility of various local and global optimizing techniques.

Programs analyzed:

33 programs from Stanford University students
9 programs from CSD subroutine library
3 programs from "Scientific Subroutine" library and various others

For static analysis - 440 programs analyzed at Lockheed
For dynamic analysis - 25 programs analyzed
17 inner loops studied

Results: Results given are:

Static analysis   Distribution of statement types
                       Length and depth of DO loops
                       Complexity of assignments
                       Occurrence of operators

Dynamic analysis   Profile of a short program
                       Distribution of executable statements
                       Histogram corresponding to PROGTIME run

Inner loops   The instructions used after compilation are weighted, and the results
                       discussed from each loop.

[W&H]

Static and dynamic statistics on a sample of programs were gathered. The principle conclusion is the importance of a program profile, which is a table of frequency counts which record how often each statement is performed in a typical run. It appears that the nth most important statement of a program from the point of execution time accounts for about $(a - 1)a^{-n}$ of the running time, for some a and for small n (very approximately). Generally less than 4 per cent of a program accounts for more than half of its running time. [RTS]

[Knuth 73]   Donald Knuth and Francis Stevenson.
                Optimal Measurement Points for Program Frequency
                    Counts.
                BIT 13:313-322, 1973.

A procedure recently devised by A. Nahapetian reduces an arbitrary flowchart to the minimal one, on which program frequencies can be measured. The algorithm is optimal, in that the minimum number of measurements is determined. An example implementation in Simula is given. [RTS]

[Kolence 72]   K. Kolence.
                Software Physics and Computer Performance
                    Measurements.
                In *Proceedings of the ACM National Conference 25*, pages
                    1024-1040. Association for Computing Machinery,
                    1972.

This is another of the basic papers in the attempt to establish a fundamental information theory basis for information processing work and computer performance analysis. [JCB]

[Laemmel 78]   A. Laemmel and M. Shooman.
                Software Modeling Studies.
                Technical Report RADC-TR-78-4, Rome Air Development
                    Center, April, 1978.

This report discusses the application of concepts of statistical language theory (Zipf's Laws) to the derivation of formulas for measuring program and language complexity. Experimental data from several different programs and programming languages, such as PL/I, assembly and FORTRAN, is presented which is used to verify the necessary underlying assumption and to verify formulas for program length by comparison with actural statistics. Finally, the derived formulas are compared with those of Software Physics derived by Halstead. [Abstract]

[Lampson 69] B.W. Lampson.
Dynamic Protection Structures.
In *Proceedings of the AFIPS Fall Joint Computer Conference*, pages 27-38. AFIPS Press, 1969.
This paper describes the positive and negative aspects of the use of capabilities in the BCC 500. The concepts of domain, capability and access key are investigated, and the ramifications these ideas have on addressing and transfers of control (including traps and interrupts) are examined. The command language for the system is dealt with only peripherally. [RTS]

[Lampson 76] B.W. Lampson and H.E. Sturgis.
Reflections on Operating System Design.
Communications of the ACM 19(5):251-265, May, 1976.
The main features of the CAL system, developed for the Control Data 6400, are presented, and its good and bad points are discussed. The positive aspects included the use of capabilities, the idea of protected layering, and the conversion of input-output devices into processes with a minimum of interpretation. The negative aspects included the attempt to provide the illusion of a mapped address space on unsuitable hardware, and the way in which the disk was incorporated into the memory hierarchy. The user interface is not dealt with in this paper. [RTS]

[Lantz 79]   K. Lantz and R.F. Rashid.
VTMS: A Virtual Terminal Management System for RIG.
In *Proceedings of the Seventh Symposium on Operating System Principles*, pages 86-97. ACM, December, 1979.
Rochester's Intelligent Gateway provides its users with the facilities for communicating simultaneously with a large number of processes spread out among various computer systems. We have adopted the philosophy that the user should be able to manage any number of concurrent tasks or jobs, viewing their output on his display device as he desires. To achieve this goal the Virtual Terminal Management System (VTMS) converts a single physical terminal into multiple virtual terminals, each of which may be written to or queried for user input. VTMS extends the features of the physical terminal by providing extensive editing facilities, the capacity to maintain all output in disk-based data structures, and sophisticated mechanisms for the management of screen space. Virtual terminals are device-independent; the specific characteristics of the physical terminal are known only to the lowest-level I/O handlers for that device. VTMS is currently running on a network of six minicomputers supporting various text and raster-graphics displays. [Abstract]

[Lauesen 73] S. Lauesen.
Program Control of Operating Systems.
BIT 13:323-337, 1973.
Traditional JCLs are eliminated if existing programming languages are extended slightly. The process described in this paper is to extend the existing language by (1) make a set of new basic data types and introduce them into all languages; (2) define declarations for them; (3) introduce the necessary basic operations working on them; (4) introduce a suitable set of standard functions covering the frequently used composite functions now expressed by means of control cards.

A set of operating system functions which make this scheme easy to implement is specified: (1) processes, communicating through shared queues; (2) parent/child processes; (3) processes for device I/O; and (4) an internal control language. [RTS]

[Lehman 80]   M. M. Lehman.
               Programs, programming and the software life cycle.
               Proceedings of the IEEE, September, 1980.
This paper clarifies the difference between the evolution dynamics of program development and the dynamics of program execution. Also, a classification of large programs is offered, following the difficulty and severity of continuous enhancement and maintenance. Extensive bibliography attached. [LAB]

[Lenfant 75]   J. Lenfant and P. Burgevin.
               Empirical Data on Program Behaviour.
               In *International Computing Symposium*, pages 163-169.
               North-Holland, 1975.
Introduction: The main aim of this paper is to analyse the store accesses of programs in order to describe the general paging behaviour of programs.

Analysis: A simulation was made of more than 20 programs in order to obtain the complete data accessing string. This string was then analyzed further to obtain the properties of various paging algorithms with different page sizes.

Programs: A very varied sample of programs was taken, but the only ones not written by students were in Fortran.

Results: A good number of tables are included as well as additional comments on the more interesting data. Results come from a CII 10070 computer. (excluding the supervisor which was not monitored). Between 6% and 93% of cpu time was spent on I/O.

Tables include:
    Machine instruction type: Frequency for 6 programs.
    Machine addressing mode: Frequency for 10 programs.
    Branch instructions and branches taken: 10 programs.
    Frequency of Branch and Link: 8 programs.
    Percentage of instruction access: 10 programs.
    Page fault rates and related data: 11 tables.
[W&H]

[Linden 76]   Linden, Theodore A.
               Operating system structures to support security and
                  reliable software.
               ACM Computing Surveys 8(4):409-45, December, 1976.
Security has become an important and challenging goal in the design of computer systems. This survey focusses on two system structuring concepts that support security: small protection domains and extended-type objects. These two concepts are especially promising because they also support reliable software by encouraging and enforcing highly modular software structures -- in both systems software and in applications programs. Small protection domains allow each subunit or module of a program to be executed in a restricted environment that can prevent unanticipated or undesirable actions by that

module. Extended-type objects provide a vehicle for data abstraction but allowing objects of new types to be manipulated in terms of operations that are natural for these objects. This provides a way to extend system protection features so that protection can be enforced in terms of applications-oriented operations on objects. This survey also explains one approach toward implementing these concepts thoroughly and efficiently -- an approach based on the concept of capabilities incorporated into the addressing structure of the computer. Capability-based addressing is seen as a practical way to support future requirements for security and reliable software without sacrificing requirements for performance, flexibility, and sharing. [Abstract]

[Litecky 76]   C. R. Litecky and G. B. Davis.
A Study of Errors, Error-Proneness and Error Diagnosis in COBOL.
Communications of the ACM 19(1):33-37, 1976.

Introduction: This paper provides data on COBOL error frequencies, for correction of errors in student oriented compilers, improvement of teaching, and changes in programming language.

Analysis: Firstly a pilot study was set up to establish an error classification scheme for COBOL. This scheme was then applied to a second group of programs. The classification scheme was developed by observation and tallying of errors.   132 errors were distinguishable.

Programs: The pilot study consisted of approximately 1000 runs of 50 student programs. For the actual study, 1777 errors from 1400 runs of 73 programs were gathered. All programs were written by students beginning a COBOL course.

Results: Results are presented for:
Classification structure and frequency of COBOL errors.
Top twenty percent of errors.
[W&H]

[Littlewood 75]
B. Littlewood.
A Reliability Model for Markov Structured Software.
Proceedings of International Conference on Reliable Software:204-207, 1975.

A system is considered in which switching takes place between sub-systems according to a continuous parameter Markov chain. Failures may occur in Poisson processes in the sub-systems, and in the transitions between sub-systems.   All failure processes are independent. The overall failure process is described exactly and asymptotically for highly reliable sub-systems. An application to process-control computer software is suggested. [Abstract]

[Lloyd 74]   E. Lloyd.
FORTRAN - A Structural Analysis.
Memo 46400-74-38, Burroughs Corporation, Paoli, USA, 1974.

Introduction: This is a report on the structure of FORTRAN programs. An analysis is made of the constructs programmers use when writing FORTRAN programs. The report gives suggestions on what processors and compilers should be concerned with in regard to FORTRAN. There is also a special report on performance with regard to the B6700 and B7700.

Types of analysis: The compiler was modified to produce static information and to modify the resultant code to produce the dynamic information. A program was written to analyse the results to show how many times a particular construct appears in a given Fortran program.

Test programs: 15 benchmark programs were obtained, being representative of Fortran programs currently being run on Burroughs' machines. They totalled 15000 cards and ranged from 32 to 4868 statements. They were all computation oriented.

Results: Results are given for:

DO-loops	Static distributions of statements
GOTO statements	Dynamic distributions of statements
IF statements	Static: dynamic comparison of statements
Variable accesses	Arithmetic operations
Function usage	Static: dynamic comparison of variable accesses

[W&H]

[Longley 67]   J. Longley.
                An Appraisal of Least Squares Program.
                Journal of the American Statistical Association 62:819-
                841, 1967.
The ability of several statistics systems to compute a solution to a poorly-conditioned problem is examined. [IF]

[Love 77]   Tom Love.
             An Experimental Investigation of the Effect of Program
             Structure on Program Understanding.
             *Proc. ACM Conference on Language Design for Reliable
             Software*:105-113, March, 1977.
A within-subjects experimental design was used to test the effect of two variables on program understanding. The independent variables were complexity of control flow and paragraphing of the source code. Understanding was measured by having the subjects memorize the code for a fixed time and reconstruct the code verbatim. Also, some subjects were asked to describe the function of the program after completing their reconstruction. The two groups of subjects for the experiment were students from an introductory programming class and from a graduate class in programming languages.

The major findings were that paragraphing of the source had no effect for either group of subjects but that programs with simplified control flow were easier for the computer science students to understand as measured by their ability to reconstruct the programs. The dependent varible, rated accuracy of their description of the programs functions, did not differ as a function of either independent variable.

The paper is concluded with a description of the utility of this experimental approach relative to improving the reliability of software and a discussion of the importance of these findings. [CR34498]

[Lucas 71]   H.C. Lucas.
Performance Evaluation and Monitoring.
ACM Computing Surveys 3(3):79-91, September, 1971.

Three major purposes for evaluating the hardware and software performance of computer systems -- selection evaluation, performance projection, and performance monitoring -- are described. Eight techniques that have been used or suggested for evaluating performance are discussed. Each of these techniques is rated on its suitability for the three purposes of evaluation. Recommendations are made on the most appropriate technique for each evaluation purpose. These suggestions include the development of a comprehensive set of synthetic programs on an industry-wide basis for selection evaluation purposes. Simulation is recommended as the most suitable technique for performance projection. Finally, a number of hardware and software monitors are available for performance monitoring. [Abstract]

[Lurie 73]   D. Lurie and C. Vandoni.
Statistics for FORTRAN Identifiers and Scatter Storage Techniques.
Software -- Practice & Experience 3(2):171-177, 1973.

Introduction: Statistical data is presented on the distribution of FORTRAN identifiers as a function of length and initial character. The performance of two hash coding algorithms is tested with random probing and linear probing on a pool of FORTRAN identifiers.

Type of analysis: A **static** analysis was carried out by scanning each line from left to right to pick out all fields which 1) begin with an alphabetic character and 2) are followed by a non-alphanumeric character. All standard FORTRAN words such as READ, FORMAT etc. and Hollerith constants were sifted out.

Number of programs: 214 programs were scanned from the CERN library. They consisted of 92463 cards and contained 205030 identifiers.

Results: Results are given for:

Fortran system words not included in statistical survey with frequency of occurrence.
Percentage distribution of Fortran keys as a function of length.
Percentage distribution of Fortran keys as a function of initial letter.
Frequency of occurrence of leading character as a function of length of key.

The rest of the paper concerns the comparison of two hash coding algorithms using the data obtained, for setting up symbol tables. [W&H]

[Lynch 81]   W. C. Lynch and J. C. Browne.
Performance Evaluation: A Software Metrics Success Story.
In Frederick G. Sayward, Mary Shaw and Alan J. Perlis, editor, *Software Metrics: An Analysis and Evaluation.*
MIT Press, Cambridge, Massachusetts, 1981.

In "Performance Evaluation: A Software Metrics Success Story," Browne and Lynch describe the generally accepted metrics for both external aspects (e.g., response time) and internal aspects (e.g., queue length) of software systems. A set of abstract models capture the salient aspects for performance and system tuning.

They recommend that support be given to a fundamental performance evaluation lack: software engineering procedures for developing software systems with desired values for given performance metrics. [FGS]

[Lyness 79a]   J. N. Lyness.
A Benchmark Experiment for Minimization Algorithms.
Math. Comput. 33(145):249-264, January, 1979.

Among the gound rules for the empirical evaluation of an algorithm one should list a) the need for a statistical approach which is not unduly influenced by an occasional lucky or unlucky break, b) the need for a parametric set of test problems so that the algorithm can be tested under all conditions, easy through impossible, c) the need for condensing a large volume of test results into a small number of figures which characterize the properties of the algroithm.

In test minimization programs the author's proposal for b) is a multiparameter family of "Helical Valley Objective Functions". He accommodates a) and c) by producing a probability distribution funciton for costs. This has the merit that occasional failures can be seen in proper perspective, without going to the extreme of either ignoring or treating them as fatal flaws. He demonstrates the test sequence on several standard programs. [CR34822]

[Lyness 79b]   J. N. Lyness.
Performance Profiles and Software Evaluation.
In *Performance Evaluation of Numerical Software*, pages 51-58. Elsevier North-Holland, Inc., New York, 1979.

The author distinguishes two types of problems in evaluating competitive software based on *performance profiles*:   class 1, in which the performance profile exhibits general microscopic errors -- such as when a function evaluation is being compared, e.g., sin(λ); and class 2, in which the performance profile exhibits general macroscopic errors -- as possibly when functional evaluations are compared, e.g., $\int f(\lambda,t)dt$. Traditionally, competitive software for class 1 problems are compared via some statistical analysis (mean values, error distributions, etc.) over a random set of λs. Class 2 problems generally do not enjoy such behavior, since varying λ may vary the behavior of $f(\lambda, t)$ over critical regions which may then affect the gross behavior of the method. The author suggests that much more information is needed, and that this information should be obtained in spite of the cost. The resulting data can be saved on tape for later processing "in different ways at leisure." The amount of work is enormous, but the rewards lead to "subsequent evaluation" that is "childishly straightforward." In designing the set of experiments, one should keep in mind some sort of standard so that software developed subsequently can be evaluated without redoing the entire data. The choice of what functions to use in the testing is also a matter for some thought. This approach could make critical evaluation of competitive software relatively easy at an appropriate cost. [CR35850]

[Lyon 75]   Gordon Lyon and Rona Stillman.
Simple Transforms for Instrumenting FORTRAN Decks.
Software--Practice and Experience 5:347-358, 1975.

A preprocessor is described which divides the source into code segments and adds calls to a monitoring routine which accumulates counts at the segment (statement) level. A division of monitoring is also given: clock interrupts via the operating system, counters inserted into a program, calls to a system clock, and event driven hardware probes. [RTS]

[MacDougall 75]
M. H. MacDougall.
Process and Event Control in ASPOL.
In *Proceedings Symposium on the Simulation of Computer Systems*, pages 35-51. IEEE, August, 1975.

This is a readable and straightforward paper describing the implementation of processes and events in the ASPOL simulation system. [JCB]

[MacEwen 74] G.H. MacEwen.
On Instrumentation Facilities in Programming Languages.
In *Information Processing 74*, pages 198-203. IFIP, 1974.

This paper examines the issues involved in designing instrumentation facilities for high level languages. A list of capabilities necessary for instrumentation facilities is given, and an example environment is illustrated in Simula. This paper makes no specific proposals, and hence is of little use. [RTS]

[Mamrak 77] Sandra A. Mamrak and Paul D. Amer.
A Feature Selection Tool for Workload Characterization.
In *Proceedings 1977 SIGMETRICS/CMG VIII Conference on Computer Performance*, pages 113-120. ACM, November 29-December 2, 1977.

A representative test workload is required for various computer system performance evaluation activities. Two critical issues in generating representative test workloads are 1) definition of the performance variables which are to be used to characterize the workload, and 2) development of an appropriate technique for test workload generation that provides a metric to quantitatively describe the *distance* between the real and test workloads. While some particularly useful approaches to the second problem have been developed, little attention has been paid to the selection of performance variables or job *features* upon which a characterization is based. Though the set of available variables is relatively large, in practice the maximum number of variables used for workload characterization is usually constrained. This paper describes a feature selection technique which can be used as a tool to aid the analyst in choosing a reduced variable subset while minimizing the probability of incorrect job classifications based on the new subset. An experimental application of the methodology is presented, along with an interpretation of the results in light of a sample system and user population. [*Authors' Abstract*]

The abstract above accurately describes the work.

The work justifies the intuitive assumption regarding the relative ordering of features in an IBM system: memory requested, number of files defined, number of lines printed, number of tape records read and written, number of disk records read and written, number of cards read, and CPU time used. [CR35978]

[Mamrak 79a] Sandra A. Mamrak and Paul D. Amer.
  *A Methodology for the Selection of Interactive Computer
    Services.*
  Technical Report 500-44, National Bureau of Standards
    Special Publication, January, 1979.

This publication addresses the comparison and selection of remote access interactive computer services. The comparison methodology presented relies principally on the statistical analysis of measurement data obtained from the interaction between a computer service and a user. One of the most important propertiesof the methodology is that it incorporate confidence statements about the probability of having made a correct selection. Experimental data are presented to illustrate an application of the methodology, and serve as a basis for a discussion of the cost and appropriateness of using the methodology in various procurement efforts. [Abstract]

[Mamrak 79b] S. A. Mamrak and P. D. Amer.
  Comparing Interative Computer Services-Theoretical,
    Technical, and Economic Feasibility.
  In *Proceedings AFIPS 1979 National Computer
    Conference*, pages 781-788. AFIPS, June, 1979.

The authors are concerned with the problem of computer comparison measurements. They divide the problem into the theoretical -- are the statistical techniques representative, the technical -- does the technology exist to apply the statistical techniques, and the economic -- is it economically feasible to perform the measurements. The ensuing discussion highlights the computer model, technical aspects of data collection and analysis, and the economic feasibility of the data collection and analysis.

The article is brief, but should provide the reader with a well organized approach to this classic problem, which many of us have faced in the past. I recommend this article as a good starting point in the process, along with the bibliography the authors have provided. [CR35119]

[Masuda 79] Takashi Masuda.
  Methods for the Measurement of Memory Utilization and
    the Improvement of Program Locality.
  IEEE Transaction on Software Engineering SE-5(6):618-
    631, November, 1979.

This paper will be of interest to those concerned with improving the performance of large programs running under paged virtual memory systems. The author presents the results of extensive analysis of the memory reference patterns of two large programs (a FORTRAN compiler and a virtual memory operating system) obtained through interpretive tracing of the addresses of executed instructions. By focusing on memory utilization in program sectors (a sector being defined as a unit of relocatable object code -- typically a subroutine), the author was able to formulate guidelines for constructing programs with a high locality of reference, and to suggest a procedure for improving the locality of existing programs . . .

Experimental results are presented for the FORTRAN compiler showing impressive reductions in working set size through the use of such methods.

The one question left unanswered concerns the practicality of using the procedure described above for tuning the performance of production software. The paper mentions *the tremendous amount of computing time and budget required* as limiting analysis of the trace data to approximately one-third of the instructions executed by the two programs studied. This left the reviewer wondering if such a procedure could be justifiably applied, from the standpoint of cost-effectiveness, to any but the largest and most intensively used programs. [Excerpted from CR36251]

[Matwin 76] S. Matwin and M. Missala.
A Simple, Machine Independent Tool for Obtaining Rough Measures of Pascal Programs.
SIGPlan Notices 11(8):42-45, August, 1976.
This paper describes a profiling system written in standard Pascal which consists of a preprocessor and a postprocessor. The preprocessor inserts statements into the source of the program to be monitored. As the program runs, it outputs an event record each time a routine starts or returns. A postprocessor uses this event file to determine execution counts and times for the routines in the program. [RTS]

[McCabe 76] Thomas J. McCabe.
A Complexity Measure.
IEEE Transactions on Software Engineering SE-5(4), December, 1976.
This paper describes a graph-theoretic complexity measure and illustrates how it can be used to manage and control program complexity. The paper first explains how the graph-theory concepts apply and gives an intuitive explanation of the graph concepts in programming terms. The control graphs of several actual Fortran programs are then presented to illustrate the correlation between intuitive complexity and the graph-theoretic complexity. Several properties of the graph-theoretic complexity are then proved which show, for example, that complexity is independent of physical size (adding or subtracting functional statements leaves complexity unchanged) and complexity depends only on the decision structure of a program.

The issue of using nonstructured control flow is also discussed. A characterization of nonstructured control graphs is given and a method of measuring the "structuredness" of a program is developed. The relationship between structure and reducibility is illustrated with several examples.

The last section of this paper deals with a testing methodology used in conjunction with the complexity measure; a testing strategy is defined that dictates that a program can either admit of a certain minimal testing level or the program can be structurally reduced. [Abstract]

[McGehearty 80]
P.F. McGehearty.
Performance Evaluation of a Multiprocessor under Interactive Workloads.
PhD thesis, Carnegie-Mellon University, Computer Science Department, August, 1980.
Available as CMU-CS-80-137.
This thesis describes the performance evaluation of C.mmp, running under Hydra. A detailed simulation model is developed and validated using synthetic workloads generated

by a terminal emulator. All validation was relative to response time, although some work was done on identifying processing power as it related to memory interference and basic Hydra software overheads. [RTS]

[McKissick 79]
John McKissick, Jr. and Robert A. Price.
Software Quality Assurance.
Proceedings 1979 Annual Reliability and Maintainability Symposium, 1979.

The continuing need for improved computer software demands improved software development techniques such as the Software Development Notebook. The organization, content, use and audit of Software Development Notebooks are documented in this paper. Experience and results from the application of this technique are also presented. [Abstract]

[Meeson 79]   Reginald Meeson and Arthur Pyster.
Overhead in FORTRAN Preprocessors.
Software Practice and Experience 9(12):987-1000, December, 1979.

FORTRAN code, generated by the IFTRAN and RATFOR preprocessors, is compared with hand-coded FORTRAN for relative execution time and size. The authors note: "This experiment was repeated on three computers, and five compilers with various optimization levels. The results indicate that a substantial overhead in storage space may be paid by using a preprocessor rather than direct coding in FORTRAN, and that in some cases execution time may be increased somewhat by using a FORTRAN preprocessor." The paper contains a number of tables presenting data to support these claims. However, this reviewer feels that the benchmarks producing the data were quite artificial: e.g., the given IF-THEN-ELSE test contained 4 FORMAT, 4 WRITE, 9 simple variable assignment, and 22 lines of control statements. Any use of FORTRAN preprocessors for real-life programs is likely to be less costly than the authors claim. [CR36218]

[Millbrant 74] W.W. Millbrant and J. Rodriguez-Rosell.
An interactive software engineering tool for memory management and user program evaluation.
In *Proceedings of the NCC*, pages 153-158. AFIPS Press, 1974.

This paper describes an interpreter which counts the references made to memory pages and periodically transfers its tables to a satellite display processor. This tool was developed to fill the need for user feedback systems by enabling the programmer to interactively monitor the memory referencing behavior of his modules in order to increase the locality of the program. [RTS]

[Mills 76]   Harlan D. Mills.
Software Development.
IEEE Transactions on Software Engineering SE-2(4), December, 1976.

Software development has emerged as a critical bottleneck in the human use of automatic data processing. Beginning with ad hoc heuristic methods of design and implementation of software systems, problems of software systems, problems of software maintenance and changes have become unexpectedly large. It is contended that improvement is possible only with more rigor in software design and development methodology. Rigorous software design should survive its implementation and be the basis for further evolution. Software development should be done incrementally, in stages with continuous user participation and replanning, and with design-to-cost programming within each stage. [VRB]

[Model 78]   M. Model.
Monitoring System Behavior in a Complex Computational Environment.
PhD thesis, Stanford University, January, 1978.
Available as Stan-CS-79-701.

This work is directed at the development of appropriate monitoring tools for complex systems, in particular, the representation systems of Artificial Intelligence research. The first half of this work provides the foundation of the design approach put forth and demonstrated in the second. Certain facts concerning limitations on human information processing abilities which formed the background for much of the research are introduced. Observation of program behavior ('monitoring') is shown to be the main function of most debugging tools and techniques.

The second half presents an approach to the design of monitoring facilities for complex systems. A new concept called 'meta-monitoring' replaces traditional dumps and traces with selective reporting of high-level information *about* computations. The importance of the visually-oriented analogical presentation of high-level information and the need to take into account differences between static and active processes are stressed. A generalized method for generating descriptions of system activity is developed. Some specific display-based monitoring tools and techniques which were implemented for this work are exibited. [Abstract]

[Mohanty 79] Siba N. Mohanty.
Models and Measurements for Quality Assessment of Software.
Computing Surveys 11(3), September, 1979.

Several software quality assessment methods which span the software life cycle are discussed. The quality of a system design can be estimated by measuring the system entropy function or the system work function. The quality improvement due to reconfiguration can be determined by calculating system entropy loading measures. Software science and Zipf's law are shown to be useful for estimating program length and implementation time. Deterministic and statistical methods are presented for predicting the number of errors. Testing theory is useful in planning the program test process; as discussed in this paper, it includes measurement of program structural characteristics to determine test effectiveness and test planning. Statistical models for estimating software reliability are also discussed. [VRB]

[Morgan 75] D.E. Morgan, W. Banks, D.P. Goodspeed and R. Kolanko.
A Computer Network Monitoring System.
IEEE Transactions on Software Engineering SE-1(3):299-311, September, 1975.

This paper discusses the motivation and derivation of the Computer Network Monitoring System (CNMS), then provides functional descriptions of most of the major hardware and software components, illustrates use of the CNMS, and lists experiments and applications. The CNMS consists of 1) a set of hybrid monitors, each of which is controlled by a locally or remotely located computer (these monitors consist of a PDP-11 controlling a patch panel connected to a number of specialized modules); 2) monitor control and data analysis software; 3) a network traffic generator; and 4) measurement software in each computer monitored. Each computer to be monitored is attached to a monitor, which is connected to the controlling computer by telephone lines, possibly different from those of the network. [RTS]

[Morrison 77] R. Morrison.
        A Method of Implementing Procedure Entry and Exit in
        Block Structured High Level Language.
        Software -- Practice & Experience 7(4):537-539, 1977.
This short communication is concerned with an alternative method of implementing block entry and exit in Algol programs. In order to do this, four programs were studied in order to look at the distribution of procedures, local and global variables.

A table of static and dynamic results is given for:

>   Number of procedure calls
>   Number of local variable accesses
>   Number of global variable accesses

[W&H]

[Motley 77]   R. W. Motley and W. D. Brooks.
        Statistical Prediction of Programming Errors.
        Technical Report RADC-TR-77-175, Rome Air
        Development Center, May, 1977.
This report presents and discusses the results obtained for statistical predictions of programming errors using multiple linear regression analysis. Programming errors were predicted from linear combinations of program characteristics and programmer variables. Each of the program characteristic variables were considered to be measures of the program's complexity and structure. Two distinct data samples comprising 783 programs with approximately 297,000 source instructions written for command and control software applications were analyzed. Background data on both samples is provided which includes discussions related to each sample's software development environment, testing conditions, predictor variables, definition of programming errors, and general data characteristics. Results are presented which give the prediction equations obtained and a discussion of the predictability of errors and error rate in each sample. Conclusions of the study and recommendations for further research are also provided. [Abstract]

[Moulton 67]   P. G. Moulton and M. E. Muller.
        DITRAN - A Compiler Emphasizing Diagnostics.
        Communications of the ACM 10(1):45-52, 1967.
Introduction: This paper contains a description of the DITRAN (DIagnostic FORTRAN) system on a CDC 1604. DITRAN is an implementation of FORTRAN IV with extensive error checking both at compilation time and runtime. The paper also contains some relevant statistics.

Analysis: No details of the analysis are given, but both static and dynamic results are presented.

Programs: 5158 programs were tested. They were written by 151 students on an introductory programming course and 83 students on an introductory numerical analysis course.

Results: Results are given for:

Static distribution of statements
Distribution of compilation errors
Distribution of execution errors

Average compilation time per program = 3 seconds
Average execution time per program = 3 seconds
Average core requirement per program = 793 words
Average number of statements per program = 38

Number of programs with compilation errors = 1859
Average number of compilation errors per program = 3.8
Number of programs with execution errors = 1699

[W&H]

[Muller 77]   M. E. Muller.
Maintenance and Distribution of Statistical Software:
   Satisfying Diverse Needs.
In *Proceedings of the Computer Science and Statistics:*
   Tenth Annual Symposium on the Interface, pages 205-
   210. U.S. Department of Commerce/National Bureau
   of Standards, Washington, D.C., 1977.
Reasons are given for a computer science statistical interface workshop on maintenance and distribution of statistical software. A formal definition of maintenance is presented. A list of technical issues affecting maintenance is given. [MEM]

[Muller 81]   Mervin E. Muller.
Software Maintenance Tools and Statistics.
In Frederick G. Sayward, Mary Shaw and Alan J. Perlis,
   editor, *Software Metrics: An Analysis and Evaluation.*
MIT Press, Cambridge, Massachusetts, 1981.
In "Software Maintenance Tools and Statistics" Muller finds little actual use of metrics in the maintenance lifecycle phase. Although considerable data is gathered, there is no conceptual model of maintenance, and hence no related set of software metrics has developed. The best things generally available are software tools such as the Programmer's Workbench, which are aimed at easing bookkeeping tasks.

In order to initiate steps to improve this situation, Muller proposes several research directions to achieve precise definitions of maintenance terms, a refinement of the maintenance data collection process, ways of detecting program deterioration, and ways of detecting errors introduced by maintenance activities. [FGS]

[Musa 75]   John D. Musa.
A Theory of Software Reliability and Its Application.
IEEE Transactions on Software Engineering SE-1(3),
September, 1975.

An approach to a theory of software reliability based on execution time is derived. This approach provides a model that is simple, intuitively appealing, and immediately useful. The theory permits the estimation, in advance of a project, of the amount of testing in terms of execution time required to achieve a specified reliability goal (stated as a mean time to failure (MTTF)). Execution time can then be related to calendar time, permitting a schedule to be developed. The reliability model that has been developed can be used in making system tradeoffs involving software or software and hardware components. The model has been applied to four medium-sized software development projects, all of which have completed their life cycles. [VRB]

[Musa 79]   J. D. Musa.
Software Reliability Measures Applied to Systems
Engineering.
In *Proceedings AFIPS 1979 National Computer
Conference*, pages 941-946. AFIPS, June, 1979.

The paper is somewhat a tutorial on execution-time theory wherein the previous work by this author and others is summarized. Formulas for finding software mean-time-to-failure and other parameters are given and explained.

The author states that execution time theory has been applied and validated on 16 diverse projects, has a good conceptual framework, and is a useful tool for systems engineering, project management and maintenance. In addition, it is parameter dependent and has side benefits in setting failure time objectives. [CR35554]

[Myers 78a]   Ware Myers.
A Statistical Approach to Scheduling Software
Development.
Computer 11(12):23-38, December, 1978.

This paper is mostly a summary of Putnam's work in resource estimation on large-scale software developments. In fact, a more appropriate title would have been "The Putnam/Norden Statistical Approach to Scheduling Software Development" since it is essentially about Putnam's extensions to Norden's original work at IBM in the early 1960s.

It is assumed that there is a natural cost curve governing software development. This curve is stated to be a Rayleigh curve, $y = 2Kat\ exp(-at**2)$, where y is the expenditure on a project per year, t is the elasped time in years, K is the total project cost (including maintenance), and a is a shape parameter of the curve. With data obtained from the US Army Computer Systems Command, Putnam has shown that real projects agree with this curve quite closely.

If td is defined to be the development time (or the time until the Rayleigh curve reaches a maximum), then the Rayleigh curve can be rewritten as a differential equation of the form $y = (K/td**2)t\ exp(-t**2/[2td**2])$. (Note: The paper contains a typographical error at this point.) The term $K/td**2$ is defined to be the difficulty of a project, and again empirical data seems to agree with this assumption.

Comparing these equations with the gradient of a function, the effects of modifying time (t)

or cost (y) on the difficulty can be measured, and a potential practical measure results. For example, if a project is required in 10 percent less time with the same staff, the increase in difficulty can be measured. Or if 10 percent less time is needed, how much larger a staff is needed to keep the same level of difficulty. The paper points out that there are limits to how much of a tradeoff can be made for time and people--the two are not totally interchangeable.

This paper is a well written summary of Putnam's work. Unfortunately, it suffers from the same deficiency as much of his other work--a lack of clear explanation of the underlying theory. To the uninitiated or skeptical the basic Rayleigh curve assumption looks quite ad hoc; it is, however, based upon a formal theory. The curve derives from hardware reliability theory, and is based upon the following assumptions:

1. A project has a fixed number of problems to solve.
2. Each problem requires so much time to be solved.
3. Solving a problem leads to fewer remaining unsolved problems (e.g., fixing a bug fdoes not introduce a new bug).
4. Increasing the number of people leads to an increased rate of problem solving.

The Rayleigh curve is a natural consequence of these assumptions. While the assumptions may not be totally accurate, they are a good beginning to an explicit mathematical theory of cost estimation. Unfortunately, it took this reviewer several months to track down any clearly written reference to this development. A good theoretical basis is needed to increase acceptance of the empirical data, and I hope that more will be written about the underlying theory. (The same comments apply to the other phases of the theory as well.)

While the formalism may not be totally correct, this paper is quite important. This is one of the few areas of research that is trying to get a firm grip on software costs and estimates. Software is just too expensive and unreliability is too dangerous for such current estimates as "about 10 lines of code a day" to be satisfactory in estimating the costs of multi-million dollar projects. [CR34649]

[Myers 78b]   Glenford J. Myers.
             A Controlled Experiment in Program Testing and Code
             Walk-Throughs/Inspections.
             Communications of the ACM 21(9):760-768, September,
             1978.

This very carefully detailed paper concerns the testing of a PL/I program patterned after the by now famous text reformatter program by P. Naur. Although the abstract states that seven methods were used to test the program, there were only three essentially different methods used; the test results of the application of these three were combined (ex post facto) in four additional ways. The three methods used are: 1) computer-based testing with specifications, but with the listing; 2) computer-based testing with both listing and specifications; 3) noncomputer-based testing by a team of three programmers using the walkthrough/inspection method on the listing. Groups were formed for each of the three methods and balanced as much as possible with respect to testing experience, knowledge of PL/I, and experience with walk-through procedures. [Excerpted from CR34125]

In a controlled software experiment the author compares the relative effect of three testing methodologies: specifications and executable program; specifications, executable program, and source listing; and, specifications and source listing (walkthrough). Experiment was of a group nature in which the subjects were to find as many errors as possible in a 69 statement PL/I program which contained 15 errors. Conclusions were that the three methods were about equally effective, surprisingly few errors (34%) were found, there were significant differences in the error types found by group, and the walkthrough was significantly more costly than the other two methods. [FGS]

[Naur 78]   P. Naur.
Software Reliability,
In R. K. D. Rees, *Software Reliability*. Infotech
International Ltd., Maidenhead, Berkshire, UK, 1978.

This excellent paper gives a very good clarification of the concept of software reliability. The author argues, with convincing examples, that reliability can only be understood as a relation between a certain system behavior and certain human expectations. In other words, we cannot judge the reliability of a system by observing its behavior. We have to compare this behavior with some expected standard of behavior. Reliability cannot be reduced to a single dimension, therefore any attempt to measure it along a one dimensional scale is misleading.

The author also briefly discusses reliability and correctness, reliability as related to systems controlled by software, stability of software systems, and reliable software design policies. [CR33969]

[Nemeth 71]   A.G. Nemeth and P.D. Rovner.
User Program Measurement in a Time-Shared
Environment.
Communications of the ACM 14(10):661-666, October,
1971.

A general discussion of the measurement of software systems is followed by a description of a hardware and software scheme for measuring user programs in a time-shared environment. The TX-2 computer at MIT Lincoln Laboratory was used for the implementation of such a system and the characteristics of this implementation are reported. Finally, it is shown how other time-sharing systems may provide similar measuring facilities. [Abstract]

[Neumann 75] Peter G. Neumann, L. Robinson, K.N. Levitt, R.S. Boyer, and A.R. Saxena.
A provably secure operating system.
Technical Report Project 2581 final report, Stanford
Research Institute, Menlo Park, California, June 13,
1975.

This paper describes the Provably Secure Operating System (PSOS). This system is a paper design of a hierarchical (over 12 levels) capability-based operating system, on which a formal proof of correctness was attempted. This paper contains concise sections on the basis of protection and the rationale for capabilities. The paper is well written and informative. [RTS]

[Newcomer 73]
J. Newcomer.
BLISS Timer Package--User's Manual.
PQCC Internal Memo.

This document is the user reference manual for the Bliss Timer Package, a collection of general-purpose measurement tools designed for the Bliss/10 (and recently Bliss/36) language. Included is a good description of sources of timing errors, including several non-obvious implications of monitoring programs running on a DecSystem-10. [RTS]

[Niedereichholz 79]
J. Niedereichholz.
Performance Tests with a CODASYL Database System.
Angew. Inf. 11:471-479, November, 1979.
The contents as well as the significance of the paper is easily guessed directly from the title: several time measures are offered and corresponding results for benchmarks run on UNIVAC 1108 with DMS 1100 for a small personal database are given. Several interesting and even unexpected recommendations deduced from the experiment conclude the paper. [CR36087]

[Noe 73]   J. D. Noe and G. J. Nutt.
Macro E-nets for Representation of Parallel Systems.
IEEE Transactions on Computers C-22:718-727, 1973.
E-nets are an extension of Petri nets to serve as a basis for the modeling of computer systems. This approach to modeling of parallel systems has not received the attention it deserves. [JCB]

[Nutt 75]   G.J. Nutt.
Tutorial: Computer System Monitors.
Computer 8(11):51-61, November, 1975.
This paper provides an introduction to the considerations involved in measuring computer system performance once the what and why have been determined. After introducing some basic terminology and listing the major reasons for monitoring a computer system, the factors in choosing a technique are discussed. These factors include tradeoffs such as tracing verses sampling, five monitoring methods to be chosen from, some potential pitfalls, and data presentation issues. Finally, pure software monitoring methods, pure hardware monitors, and hybrid monitors are discussed in detail. [RTS]

[Nutt 79]   G.J. Nutt.
A Survey of Remote Monitoring.
Technical Report NBS Special Publication 500-42,
National Bureau of Standards, January, 1979.
This report describes remote monitoring with regard to performance evaluation, diagnostic testing, performance assurance and system security testing. After a history of remote monitoring, seven catagories of current systems are developed: remotely controlled software monitors, internally distributed monitors, programmable monitors, hybrid monitors, computer network monitors, fault diagnosis monitors, and intelligent and extended consoles. Several example systems are discussed for each classification, along with their capabilities in each application area. An extensive bibliography is included. [RTS]

[Odemalm 75] H. Odemalm and J. Palme.

Error Messages in 360-Algol, 360/370 Simula and DEC-10 Algol.

FOA P Report C 8364-M3(E5), Research Institute of National Defense, Stockholm, Sweden, 1975.

Introduction: Several test programs, most of them containing errors, were run on three Algol compilers, the IBM 360 Algol F compiler, the IBM 360/370 Simula 67 compiler and the DECsystem-10 Algol compiler. For each program, marks are awarded to each compiler for the quality of the error messages obtained.

Analysis: The errors were divided into 7 classes, such as compile-time errors, run-time errors, precision errors etc. Altogether 38 programs were checked for errors.

Results: For each test program, the errors messages obtained are printed and points awarded depending on their quality. The final scores are:

IBM Algol F	61 points
360/370 Simula	69 points
DEC-10 Algol	59 points

[W&H]

[Oestreicher 67]

M.D. Oestreicher, M.J. Bailey, and J.I. Strauss.

George 3--A General Purpose Time-sharing and Operating System.

Communications of the ACM 10(11):685-693, November, 1967.

An operating system is described which will run on a variety of configurations of the I.C.T. 1900, and can handle a large number of users while at the same time running several background jobs. The most interesting aspect of this system is the command langauge, which includes macros, conditional statements, and software interrupts. [RTS]

[Ottenstein 79]

L. Ottenstein.

Quantitative Estimates of Debugging Requirements.

IEEE Transactions on Software Engineering SE-5:504-514, September, 1979.

The Author derives from the formulas of software science an estimate for the number of bugs present in delievered software. The estimate is the program volumn divided by 3000, where program volumn is based on the number of operators and operands present in the program. For three sets of data taken from the literature, the predicted initial bug content is compared to the reported figure. Applications to estimating the time needed for finding bugs are given. [FGS]

[Ousterhout 80]
    J. Ousterhout.
    Partitioning and Cooperation in a Distributed Multiprocessor System.
    PhD thesis, Carnegie-Mellon University, Computer Science Department, April, 1980.
    Available as CMU-CS-80-112.

This thesis describes Medusa, an object-oriented operating system for CM*. Although no command language for Medusa is described, the Medusa debugger, called Mace, is discussed briefly. This debugger is a combination of an extended multiple-process DDT and a simple performance monitor. [RTS]

[Palme 68]   J. Palme.
    A Comparison Between Simula and FORTRAN.
    BIT 8:203-209, 1968.

Introduction: The paper compares Simula and FORTRAN using the implementations on an 1107 by coding a military simulation model.

Analysis: The paper introduces the concept of *atoms*, that is, basic lexical units, in order to compare the textual lengths of the source programs. This overcomes the differing representation of equivalent statements.

Results: The main results are as follows:

Source program length in atoms	SIMULA 24% shorter
Memory requirement	FORTRAN 34% shorter
Compilation time	SIMULA 50% shorter
System overhead	FORTRAN 50% shorter
Execution time	FORTRAN 39% shorter

[W&H]

[Parr 80]   F. N. Parr.
    An Alternative to the Rayleigh Curve Model for Software Development Effort.
    IEEE Transactions on Software Engineering SE-6(3), May, 1980.

A new model of the software development process is presented and used to derive the form of the resource consumption curve of a project over its life cycle. The function obtained differs in detail from the Rayleigh curve previously used in fitting actual project data. The main advantage of the new model is that it relates the rate of progress which can be achieved in developing software to the structure of the system being developed. This leads to a more testable theory, and it also becomes possible to predict how the use of structured programming methods may alter patterns of life cycle resource consumption. [VRB]

[Parsons 75]   I.T. Parsons.
    A High Level Job Control Language.
    Software--Practice and Experience 5:69-82, 1975.

This paper presents a high-level command language design incorporating block structure, type-free variables, conditional statements, and list and string manipulation. Procedures are used to invoke operating system functions. The system inputs a job control program and outputs JCL statements for the ICL System 4, the ICL 1906A running George 3, or the CDC 7600 machine running Scope 2.0. [RTS]

[Partridge 75] D. Partridge.
A Dynamic Database Which Automatically Removes Unwanted Generalisation for the Efficient Analysis of Language Features that Exhibit a Disparate Frequency Distribution.
Computer Journal 18(1):43-48, 1975.

Introduction: A self organizing database was developed as part of a general language analysis system. The periodic, automatic reorganisation of the database was aimed at increasing the efficiency of analysis of a language in which the constituent features exhibit a Zipfian type rank frequency. Such a distribution means that only a small number of possible features account for a large proportion of the information.

Types of analysis: The mechanism described in the paper aims at reconciling two conflicting procedures - condensation by generalization of language features to minimize the total size of the database, and the particularisation of the few commonly occurring features to minimize the average analysis time. Results are presented for the application of this mechanism to the **static** analysis of a batch of Fortran programs.

Results: Results are given for:

1. The frequency distribution of Fortran statement types (5 data sets, total of 20121 samples)
2. Percentage frequency distribution of arithmetic expressions of differing length (5 data sets, total of 22151 samples)
3. Percentage frequency distribution of types of arithmetic operands (5 data sets, total of 31525 samples)
4. Percentage frequency distribution of alphabetic characters within Fortran statements (5 data sets, total of 107892 samples)
5. Percentage frequency distribution of arithmetic operators (5 data sets, total of 9475 samples)

[W&H]

[Perlis 81]   Alan J. Perlis.
Controlling Software Development Through the Life Cycle Model.
In Frederick G. Sayward, Mary Shaw and Alan J. Perlis, editor, *Software Metrics: An Analysis and Evaluation.*
MIT Press, Cambridge, Massachusetts, 1981.

In "Controlling Software Development Through The Life Cycle Model" Perlis states that almost no present systems are designed by taking a total view of the software lifecycle into account. Systems are designed to minimize design stage feedbacks, to local' ..e effects of maintenance, and to delay enhancements. No one ever think' ,oout making replacement easy. This view is what Perlis calls the "pre-structured approach." It assumes that there is but one pass through the lifecycle which, if all else is held constant, yields a perfectly designed and built system. Little attention is paid to building prototype systems -- they aren't necessary under this view.

Perlis recommends that a serious look be given to the sequence of executable prototype systems approach to software design as an alternative to the pre-structured approach. When coupled with the proper choice of language quite possibly this approach is more effective in dealing with the inevitable design changes, maintenance activities, and system enhancements. [FGS]

[Perrott 77]   R.H. Perrott and A.K. Raja.
Quasiparallel Tracing.
Software--Practice and Experience 7:483-492, 1977.
A description of different methods of program tracing in a quasiparallel environment, as well as a specific automatic tracing facility, is given. This facility traces process activation, entrance, exit, waiting, signaling, resuming, and restarting of monitor processes. Space and time overhead is examined. [RTS]

[Peterson 77] J. L. Peterson.
Petri Nets.
Computing Surveys 9:223-252, 1977.
This paper gives both the fundamentals of Petri nets and their applications in the context of computer science. The best source for computer scientists to learn about Petri nets. [JCB]

[Peuto 77]   B. L. Peuto and L. J. Shustek.
An Instruction Timing Model of CPU Performance.
In *Fourth Annual Symposium on Computer Architecture*, March, 1977.
Introduction: A model of high-performance computers was derived from instruction timing formulas. The model was used to predict the performance of the IBM 370/168 and the Amdahl 470 V/6. The model results are compared with actual benchmark results.

Types of analysis: The programs to be measured in user state and all the information required to compute the instruction execution time from the formulas was collected. Thus the final results reflect the **dynamic** performance of the machines.

Programs analyzed: 7 programs were tested:

FORTC	- compilation by IBM Fortran H compiler
FORTGO	- execution of program compiled by FORTC
PLIC	- compilation by IBM PL/I - F compiler
PLIGO	- execution of PL/I program
COLOLC	- compilation by IBM ANSI COBOL compiler
COBOLGO	- execution of COBOL program
LINSY2	- execution of Fortran subroutine - no I/O

Results: Results are presented in tabular form for:

SVC times and cache effects	Instructions which caused branching
Program characteristics	Branch distances for successful branches
Model and Benchmark times	Execution distances
Opcode frequency distributions	Opcode pair distributions
Opcode time distributions	Length distribution for STM
Instruction lengths	Length distribution for LM
Analysis of branch instructions	Length distribution for MVC

Register use for RX-instruction effective address calculation

All the results obtained are explained in detail. [W&H]

[Pflasterer 78] D. C. Pflasterer.
An Approach to Efficient, Fault Tolerant Programming.
SIGPLAN Notices 13(2):67, 1978.

Introduction: A report about a Computer Aided Instruction (CAI) system written in an Algol-like language (CAMIL) for CAI and CMI work. The report tabulates the errors detected in the system from over 200 errors.

Results: The errors found were as follows:

ERROR	FREQUENCY
Array subscript out of range	26
Length of substring negative	21
Division by zero on real divide	16
Invalid character in string to integer conversion	14
Division by zero on integer divide	9
Base of exponent invalid	8
Extended core storage read invalid	3
Close of unopened file	2
Invalid character in string to real conversion	.4

[W&H]

[Pratt 78]   T. W. Pratt.
Control Computations and the Design of Loop Control Structures.
IEEE Transactions on Software Engineering SE-4:81-89, 1978.

Introduction: A specialized paper analysing the 170 loop structures in the Pascal 2 compiler. The purpose of the analysis is to determine what forms of loop control are most appropriate for languages. [W&H]

[Putnam 78]   Lawrence H. Putnam.
A General Empirical Solution to the Macro Software Sizing and Estimating Problem.
IEEE Transactions on Software Engineering SE-4(4), July, 1978.

Application software development has been an area of organizational effort that has not been amenable to the normal managerial and cost controls. Instances of actual costs of several times the initial budgeted cost, and a time to initial operational capability sometimes twice as long as planned are more often the case than not.

A macromethodology to support management needs has now been developed that will produce accurate estimates of manpower, costs, and times to reach critical milestones of software projects. There are four parameters in the basic system and these are in terms managers are comfortable working with -- effort, development time, elapsed time, and a state-of-technology parameter.

The system provides managers sufficient information to assess the financial risk and investment value of a new software development project before it is undertaken and provides techniques to update estimates from the actual data stream once the project is underway. Using the technique developed in the paper, adequate analysis for decisions can be made in an hour or two using only a few quick reference tables and a scientific pocket calculator. [VRB]

[QSM 79]
Workshop on Quantitative Software Models for Reliability, Complexity, and Cost: An Assessment of the State of the Art.
Workshop held in Concord Hotel, Kiamesha Lake, New York, in October, 1979, IEEE Catalog No. TH0067-9.
This is the proceedings of a workshop on quantitative software models for reliability, complexity and cost, and contains a large number of papers related to both models and metrics of software development. Included are the evaluation of many models by various organizations. [VRB]

[Rayner 75]   D. Rayner.
Recent Developments in Machine Independent JCL.
Software--Practice and Experience 5:375-393, 1975.
This paper gives a general survey of recent developments in the field of job control languages. Three high-level job control languages (Unique, GCL, and Able) are presented in outline, and their merits and disadvantages are discussed. The approaches of the MU5 and of single language machines are discussed together with the question that they pose: 'Is a JCL really necessary?' In conclusion particular reference is made to the question of standardization and to continuing work in this field. [RTS]

[Redell 74]   David D. Redell.
Naming and protection in extendible operating systems.
PhD thesis, University of California, Berkeley, September, 1974.
Reprinted as Project MAC TR-140, Massachusetts Institute of Technology.
This thesis explores the design and implementation of a capability system providing both free distribution and orderly revocation of capabilities. A generalized capability sealing mechanism is shown to provide selective revocation of capabilities as well as a flexible type extension facility. [RTS]

[Ripley 75]   G. D. Ripley and R. E. Griswold.
Tools for the Measurement of Snobol 4 Programs.
SIGPLAN Notices 10(5):36-52, May, 1975.
Introduction: The work described in this paper is part of a project to design and develop effective tools for the measurement of high-level programming languages. The facilities described in this paper are being developed on a macro implementation of Snobol 4.

Analysis: Three methods are used to measure programs:

1. Measurement of entire program by specifying a switch to the Snobol interpreter.
2. Program controlled measurement by using the built-in MEASURE function.

3. Interactive code design and measurement using a program called SPIDER.

Results: Sample results are given for:

A performance profile	Controlled monitoring
Profile of simple reversal	Profile summary
Controlled monitoring of a pattern	Profile of reversal by replacement

[W&H]

[Ripley 78]   C. D. Ripley, R. E. Griswold, and D. R. Hanson.
               Performance of Storage Management in an
               Implementation of SNOBOL4.
               IEEE Transactions on Software Engineering SE-4(2),
               March, 1978.

Results of measuring the performance of the storage management subsystem in an implementation of SNOBOL4 are described. By instrumenting the storage management system, data concerning the size, lifetime, and use of storage blocks was collected. These data, like those obtained from conventional time measurement techniques, were used to locate program inefficiencies. In addition, these measurements uncovered some difficiencies in the storage management system, and provided the basis upon which to judge the heuristics used in the garbage collector. [Abstract]

[Robinson 76] S. K. Robinson and I. S. Torsun.
              An Empirical Analysis of FORTRAN Programs.
              Computer Journal 19(1):56-62, 1976.

Introduction: This paper describes the results obtained from a static analysis of FORTRAN programs written and run in a university environment.

Analysis: The **static** analysis was performed by a syntax analyzer designed to specifically analyse source program statements and produce a report containing the totals of each factor concerned.

Programs analyzed: Two distinct types of source program was analyzed. The first consisted of programs written by undergraduate students, and the second included such programs as library programs, research programs etc.

In all, 29971 Fortran statements were analyzed.

Results: Results are presented for:

Distribution of basic statement types
Percentage distribution of operators
Percentage distribution of logical operators
The breakdown of the "left part" of assignments with details of those within DO-loops
Detailed analysis of arithmetic expressions
Logical IF expression complexity
Details of statements following logical IF
DO-loop length
DO-loop nesting
Number of subroutine arguments
Statistics of identifiers

Field descriptors
[W&H]

[Robinson 77] S. K. Robinson and I. S. Torsun.
Dynamic Analysis of Program Performance (DAP) in a
FORTRAN Batch Environment.
Software -- Practice & Experience 7(3):307-315, 1977.
Introduction: This paper describes a DAP environment which effects changes to the execution of a program so that when the object code is run, the output of the program includes a list of the executable statements and their execution counts.

Analysis: The 1900 Fortran Batch System (FIBS) has a tracing option and when this is set, it sets a flag in the code generator which alters the object program so that a frequency profile is updated for each statement executed.

Programs: Sample results are given for two simple programs, written by first year students, which are also reproduced in the paper.

Results: Results are given for:
Output from original FORDAP system
FIBS profile output, detailed format
FIBS profile output, simplified format
[W&H]

[Robinson 79a]
John T. Robinson.
Some Analysis Techniques for Asynchronous
Multiprocessor Algorithms.
IEEE Transactions on Software Engineering SE-5(1):24-31, January, 1979.
Efficient algorithms for asynchronous multiprocessor systems must achieve a balance between low process communication and high adaptability to variations in speed. Algorithms that employ problem decomposition may be classified as static (in which decomposition takes place before execution) and dynamic (in which decomposition takes place during execution). Static and dynamic algorithms are particularly suited for low process communication and high adaptability, respectively. For static algorithms the following analysis techniques are presented: finding the probability distribution of execution time, deriving bounds on mean execution time using order statistics, finding asymptotic mean speedup, and using approximations. For dynamic algorithms the technique of modeling using a queueing system is presented. For each technique, and example application to parallel sorting is given. [Abstract]

[Robinson 79b]
K. A. Robinson.
An Entity/Event Data Modeling Method.
Computing Journal 22(3):270-281, August, 1979.
To date, system and data modeling techniques have concentrated almost exclusively on static views of the systems being modeled. What is modeled is a time slice of a given system's existence. The system dynamics are only modeled

implicitly and obscurely in the transaction consistency rules.

The explicit modeling of the system dynamics -- the system behavior -- has only been attempted hitherto in simulation languages... This paper shows how the technique can be applied in more realistic cases. [From the Abstract]

The author has accomplished what is set forth in the abstract. The paper is a gem in a relatively barren field, and I strongly recommend it to all students of the topic. My only reservation is that it will be difficult to assimilate for anyone but the initiate. I myself wished the author had been somewhat more generous in his explanations at some points. It requires re-reading to really glean the full value of what he is conveying. [CR35975]

[Rubey 75]   R. J. Rubey.
              Quantitative Aspects of Software Validation.
              Proceedings of International Conference on Reliable
                  Software:246-251, 1975.

This paper discusses the need for quantitative descriptions of software errors and methods for gathering such data. The software development cycle is reviewed and the frequency of the errors that are detected during software development and independent validation are compared. Data obtained from validation efforts are presented, indicating the number of errors in 10 categories and three severity levels; the inferences that can be drawn from this data are discussed. Data describing the effectiveness of validation tools and techniques as a function of time are presented and discussed. The software validation cost is contrasted with the software development cost. The applications of better quantitative software error data are summarized. [Abstract]

[Ryder 79]   Barbara G. Ryder.
              Constructing a Call Graph of a Program.
              IEEE Transactions on Software Engineering SE-5(3):216-
                  226, May, 1979.

The proliferation of large software systems written in high level programming languages insures the utility of analysis programs which examine interprocedural communications. Often these analysis programs need to reduce the dynamic relations between procedures to a static data representation. This paper presents one such representation, a directed, acyclic graph named the call graph of a program. We delineate the programs representable by an acyclic call graph and present an algorithm for constructing it using the property that its nodes may be linearly ordered. We prove the correctness of the algorithm and discuss the results obtained from an implementation of the algorithm in the PFORT Verifier. [Abstract]

[Rye 77]   P. Rye, F. Bamberger, W. Ostanek, N. Brodeur, and
              J. Goode.
              Software Systems Development: A CSDL Project History.
              Technical Report RADC-TR-77-213, Rome Air
                  Development Center, June, 1977.

This report provides a description of the data delivered to RADC for inclusion in a Software Data Repository. The data consists of a complete history of software modifications to the APOLLO on-board flight software for the period 1967 through 1971. Background material on the project that was the source of the data is provided, as well as tabular and graphic summaries of the data. Some recommendations for future work are made. [Abstract]

[Saal 77]   H. J. Saal and Z. Weiss.
              An Empirical Study of APL Programs.
              Computer Languages 2(3):47-59, 1977.
Introduction: The statistical results of a study of the APL language is presented in this
paper. The distributions of the appearance of APL primitive functions and the functions
derived from APL operators are presented.

Types of analysis: As no suitable data was available to actually executed APL programs in
order to observe their dynamic behaviour, only the static appearance of APL constructs
could be measured. An analysis program written in APLSV was used to analyse the
workspaces.

The test programs:

        Number of workspaces tested = 32
        Number of user functions = 697
        Number of lines of code = 8593

The programs tested were drawn from many different application areas. They include:

        IBM Installed User Programs
        PERT analysis and numerical integration
        STATPAK statistical analysis
        digital computer simulation and various others.

They were not chosen randomly, but were supposed to represent a high quality sample of
bug free code.

Result: Results are presented in tabular form except where otherwise stated:

        Distribution of lines of code per user defined function (graph)
        Distribution of nodes in parse tree per line (graph)
        Usage of major classes of APL operations
        Coordinate specification (2 graphs)
        GOTO statements
        Special branch operations
        Usage of inner products
        Constants as operands to APL primitives
        Monadic, dyadic and outer product primitive usage (6 graphs)
        The 80-20 rule (graph)

[W&H]

[Sackman 68] H. Sackman, W. Erikson and E. Grant.
                Exploratory Experimental Studies Comparing Online and
                Offline Programming Performance.
                Communications of the ACM 11(1):3-11, January, 1968.
In a controlled software experiment the authors found that on-line debugging took less time
than off-line debugging with no significant increase in CPU time. [FGS]

[Saltzer 70]   Jerome Saltzer and John Gintell.
                The Instrumentation of MULTICS.
                Communications of the ACM 13(8):495-500, August, 1970.
An array of measuring tools devised to aid in the implementation of a prototype computer

utility is discussed. These tools include 1) a hardware calendar clock (52 bit, 1 microsecond resolution) and an associated match register; 2) a memory reference counter; 3) an input/output channel which can be used by an attached processor to read memory; 4) a general metering package which records time spent executing selectable supervisor modules while the system is running; 5) a segment utilization metering facility which periodically probes for the current segment number; 6) a facility which records on a per-segment basis the number of missing pages and segments encountered during execution in that segment; 7) a tool which counts the number of times procedures are called; 8) a software package implemented on a PDP-8 which utilizes the special I/O channel [Growchow 69]; 9) the CLI, which prints out the time of day, the CPU time, and the number of times the process had to wait for a page to be brought in after every 'ready message'; 10) a ring buffer containing the segment, page number, and time of day of the last 256 missing pages of the process under measurement; 11) a package to monitor the effect of the system's multiprogramming effort of an individual program; 12) a script driver implemented on a PDP-8; and 13) an internal script driver. [RTS]

[Salvadori 75] A. Salvadori, J. Gordon and C. Capstick.
Static Profile of COBOL Programs.
SIGPLAN Notices 10(8):20-33, August, 1975.

Introduction: This paper describes a system for obtaining static profiles of COBOL programs in order to record both programmer behaviour and program development in COBOL in an industrial environment.   •

Analysis: The system records a static profile each time a program is compiled and run and also a "history" profile of all the runs of a particular, recording the number of run and the interval since the last one.

When the COBOL compiler is invoked, a routine is called which logs the statistics and optionally produces a report.

Results: Only sample results are given. They are:

> Listing of all the facilities used in the Identificaiton Division, Environment Division and Data Division.
> Usage per run of all verbs used in Procedure Division.
> Total number of source records, statements etc.
> History of errors by number.

[W&H]

[Salvadori ??] A. Salvadori, J. Gordon and C. Capstick.
Profiles of COBOL Programs.
Technical Report, Department of Computing and
Information Sciences, University of Guelph, Canada, ??.

Introduction: This report is an extension of "Static Profile of COBOL Programs" by Salvadori et al. and includes information on a dynamic analysis of COBOL programs.

Analysis: The static profiling system is the same as the one described in "Static Profile of COBOL Programs" by A. Salvadori et al. The dynamic system provides frequency counts of how often a particular segment of code is executed at run-time, where a segment of code is defined as a set of sequential instructions in the program which are executed consecutively.

Results: Sample results are given for:

Example program divided into segments
Listing of facilities used in Identification, Environment and Data Divisions
Static usage per run of all verbs and related constructs in Procedure Division
Other statistics such as number of source records etc.
Percentage figures for each verb
History of errors by run number
Output from dynamic analysis
Histogram of program development

[W&H]

[Sammet 70]   Jean E. Sammet.
Perspective on Methods of Improving Software
Development.
In Julius Tou, editor, *Software Engineering*. Academic
Press, 1970.

The concept of improving software development is important but ambiguous. The two major difficulties lie in attempting to measure the various aspects and the need to recognize the vast amount of tradeoffs required. By using a formula which permits (and requires) the manager to assign weights to the various facets, some quantitative information can be obtained on various tradeoffs. The productivity of an individual is important, but is only one facet of the entire development cycle. A number of specific technical and management techniques for improving software development have been described. [Summary]

[Sammet 71]   J. E. Sammet.
Problems in, and a Pragmatic Approach to Programming
Language Measurement.
In *Proceedings AFIPS Fall Joint Computer
Conference*, pages 243-251. AFIPS, 1971.

This appears to be the first published paper to discuss measurements in programming languages (as contrasted with measurements in or of programs). The paper describes the problem and its importance. Part of the paper discusses the need for consideration of non-technical (as well as technical) issues in selecting a programming language. A weighted scoring technique is described and illustrated with one example. A second part of the paper discusses the problem of defining the terms "dialect" and "language-L-like" and presents a method for measuring numerically the amount of deviation of one language from another. [JES]

[Sammet 81]   Jean E. Sammet.
High Level Language Metrics.
In A. Perlis, F. Sayward and M. Shaw, editor, *Software
Metrics: An Analysis and Evaluation*, chapter 8. MIT
Press, Cambridge, Massachusetts, 1981.

This paper points out the difference between program metrics and language metrics, and discusses only the latter. It mentions some possible high level language metrics, and indicates that some broad purposes for such metrics include: language selection/comparison, and language design. Several potential areas of future research are given, along with an indication of why valid experiments are difficult to perform in this area. [JES]

In "High Level Language Metrics" Sammet observes that language metrics and program metrics are quite different, although they are often confused or interchanged in casual discussion. High level languages are intellectual entities worthy of study and measure in their own right. The main purposes for which language metrics have been used are for language selection and/or comparison, and (separately) for language design. Some of the issues and measurements are subjective, whereas others can be objective.

Sammet contends that the more important areas of research are finding ways to measure the non-procedurality of languages, and deriving measures of programmer productivity through measures of language functionality. Other research topics include measuring the deviations from one language to another, the relationship of the language to various program measurements, and measuring the applicability of a language to a specific application area. [FGS]

[Sanguinetti 79]
> J. Sanguinetti.
> A Technique for Integrating Simulation and System Design.
> In *Proceedings of Conference on Simulation, Measurement and Modeling of Computer Systems*, pages 163-172. August, 1979.

Sanguinetti proposes a basis whereby simulation will become an integral part of the design process. [JCB]

[Satterthwaite 72]
> E. Satterthwaite.
> Debugging Tools for High Level Languages.
> *Software--Practice and Experience* 2:197-217, 1972.

The design of an integrated programming and debugging system using the language Algol W is described. The debugging tools are based entirely upon the source language but can be efficiently implemented. The most novel such tool is a selective trace, automatically controlled by execution frequency counts. System performance information is included. [Abstract]

[Sayward 81]   Frederick G. Sayward.
> Design of Software Experiments.
> In Frederick G. Sayward, Mary Shaw and Alan J. Perlis, editor, *Software Metrics: An Analysis and Evaluation.* MIT Press, Cambridge, Massachusetts, 1981.

In "Design of Software Experiments" Sayward summarized the principles used in conducting the many on going software experiments aimed at understanding and improving software development, testing, and maintenance. The designs of these experiments have nearly all followed the orthodox many subject random group design popularized by Sir Ronald Fisher. This area has led to the formulation of many interesting hypotheses. However, there are some basic problems with internal and external experiment validity which this area must overcome.

Sayward recommends continued support for the type of small scale many subject experiments which have been done since they will lead to interesting new hypotheses and they will produce a gradual refinement of design techniques for strengthening internal validity. He also suggests that a new approach, the single subject design, might be more natural for software experiments and recommends conducting intermediate scale single subject experiments as a potential way of strengthening external validity. [FGS]

[Schafer 79]   R. E. Schafer, J. E. Angus, J. F. Alter, and S. E. Emoto.
    Validation of Software Reliability Models.
    Technical Report RADC-TR-79-147, Rome Air
    Development Center, June, 1979.

This report presents the results of a study and investigation of software reliability models. In particular, the purpose was to investigate the statistical properties of selected software reliability models, including the statistical properties of the parameter estimates, and to investigate the goodness of fit of the models to actual software error data. The results indicate that the models fit poorly, generally due to in most part the vagaries of the data rather than shortcomings of the models. [Abstract]

[Schneider 78]
    Victor Schneider.
    Prediction of Software Effort and Project Duration -- Four
    New Formulas.
    SIGPLAN Notices 13(6):49-59, June, 1978.

This report uses the Rome Air Development Center (RADC) data on 400 software projects in order to develop estimating equations relating man-months of effort to lines of delivered source code. Beginning with Halstead's software science measure, the relationship is:

$$MM \text{ (man-months)} = 41.8 I^{1.83}$$

(where I is delivered source instructions), or for higher-level languages:

$$MM = 28 I^{1.83}$$

(or 162 instructions per man-month), and for assembly languages:

$$MM = 59.2 I^{1.83}$$

(or 107 instructions per man-month).

Several transformations are performed on these equations in order to validate their use of the RADC data. These transformations are then used to develop several additional cost estimating relationships.

This paper is reasonably short and straightforward. It would be useful for anyone involved in estimating project size or duration. [CR35116]

[Schneidewind 79]
    N. F. Schneidewind and Heinz-Michael Hoffman.
    An Experiment in Software Error Data Collection and
    Analysis.
    IEEE Transactions on Software Engineering SE-5(3):276-
    286, May, 1979.

This paper would be better entitled "A small study of a small set of small programs written by one programmer." The authors' stated purpose was "... to test our hypothesis that program structure has a significant effect on error making, detection, and correction as measured by various software error characteristics, such as the number of errors found and labor time required to detect and correct errors." To test this hypothesis, four programs were written by one programmer. The effort involved in completing them, from smallest to largest, was three, four, thirteen, and sixteen person-days. Each error discovered during the design, coding, debugging, and testing phases was logged and categorized. For each procedure in each program, five different complexity measures were calculated: minimum number of paths through the procedure, McCabe's cyclomatic number, reachability (number of ways of reaching each node in a directed graph representation of the procedure, summed over all nodes), average reachability per node, and number of source statements. The complexity measures were assumed to be related to program structure. As an example, low values of cyclomatic numbers were assumed to mean well-structured programs. The authors' hypothesis was first tested by calculating correlation coefficients between the values of the complexity measures for each procedure and various error properties of each procedure. The error properties used were number of errors, effort to find an error, and effort to correct an error. No significant relationship was found between any complexity measure and any error property. Error properties were then partitioned according to high and low values of cyclomatic number. A (subjectively measured) significant relationship was then found between procedures that had no errors and those that had errors and low and high values of cyclomatic number.

The paper leaves the reader with little insight into the causes of errors that were costly to find or correct and says nothing about the programming methodology used. It appears that there is no way to compare these results with others, or to generalize them. [Excerpted from CR35553]

The authors report on a software experiment to test the hypothesis that the rates of making programming errors, detecting programming errors, and correcting programming errors are all dependent on the structural complexity of the program under consideration. The experiment consisted of a single programmer writing and debugging four programs. The above rates were measured and correlated with five complexity measures: path count, cyclomatic number, aggregate statement reachability, average reachability, and number of executable statements. The experimental results support the hypothesis, at least for a stable personnel environment concentrating on small (<1000 lines) programs. [FGS]

[Scowen 72]   R. S. Scowen.
Debugging Computer Programs - A Survey with Special Emphasis on Algol.
Technical Report NAC 21, National Physical Laboratory, Teddington, England, June, 1972.

Introduction: This report considers the problems of debugging computer programs and some of the tools which can simplify the task. It also contains results obtained from a survey of the errors made by programmers at NPL.

Analysis: For the survey of runtime errors, the Whetstone Algol controller was modified so that it counted in a file the total number of programs which fail for each error.

For the survey of translation errors, the "red-box" Whetstone Algol translator was modified to record the failures.

Programs: For the analysis of runtime errors, 8902 programs which failed were examined. For the analysis of translation errors, 1383 programs which failed were examined.

Most programs cover a wide range of mathematic, scientific and engineering applications and were written by scientists at NPL.

Results: Results show:

Frequency of 25 runtime errors
Frequency of 12 translation errors

All the results are discussed in some detail. [W&H]

[Sevcik 72]   K.C. Sevcik, J.W. Atwood, M.S. Grushcow, J.J. Horning, and D. Tsichrizis.
Project SUE as a learning experience.
In *Proceedings of the AFIPS Fall Joint Computer Conference*, pages 331-338. 1972.

Project SUE was an effort to develop an efficient, extensible, reliable, understandable state of the art operating system for the IBM System/360. Processes are organized in a partially ordered hierarchy, with a form of message passing (facility calls) for communication and synchronization. A restricted capability mechanism is used for authorization and accounting purposes. The system was written in a custom implementation language. There is no mention of user interface issues. [RTS]

[Sevcik 74]   Kenneth C. Sevcik.
Computer System Modelling and Analysis: Assessing Some Common Assumptions.
Proc. Seventh Hawaii International Conference on System Sciences:37-39, 1974.

Certain assumptions have been made frequently in studying analytical models of computer systems. Before applying conclusions derived from such models, the validity of the assumptions must be judged. Any assumption of questionable validity must be further investigated to determine extent to which its variation caneffect the conclusions drawn from the model. Here, we investigate assumptions about various quantities of significance in several types of computer system models. Some suggestions for increasing the relevance of future modelling studies are given. [Abstract]

[Shaw 74]   Mary Shaw.
Reduction of Compilation Costs Through Language Contraction.
Communications of the ACM 17(5), 1974.

Introduction: This paper describes the use of simulation techniques to predict the savings in compilation cost achievable by removing unwanted features from a general purpose language.

Decomposition graph for contraction of Algol:

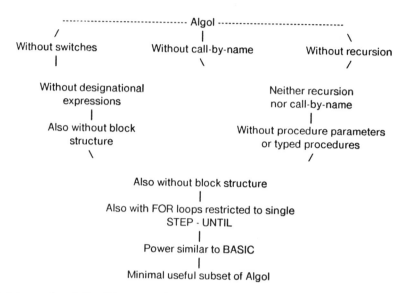

```
------------------------------ Algol ------------------------------
      /                          |                          \
Without switches          Without call-by-name        Without recursion
      |                          \                          /
 Without designational                    Neither recursion
    expressions                            nor call-by-name
         |                                       |
 Also without block                   Without procedure parameters
    structure                              or typed procedures
        \                                        /
```

Also without block structure
|
Also with FOR loops restricted to single
STEP - UNTIL
|
Power similar to BASIC
|
Minimal useful subset of Algol

Programs analyzed: For this paper, the results from tests on two algorithms are given. They are:

1. A "typical" program based on the results of several studied of the style of Algol and Fortran programmers.
2. The inner product procedure of the Algol report.

Results:

1. Compiler size estimates (table)
2. Billing cost vs. language size for typical program along call-by-name line
3. Billing cost vs. language size for inner product procedure along call-by-name/recursion/switch lines
4. Lexical size vs. language size for typical program
5. Lexical size vs. language size for inner product procedure
6. General form for compilation cost function

[W&H]

Simpler languages tend to have simpler compilers than more complex languages, but programs in simpler languages may have to be larger to accomplish the same tasks. This paper uses a combination of measurement and simulation techniques to establish the nature of the tradeoff between program size and language size. [MS]

[Shaw 79]   Mary Shaw.
             A Formal System for Specifying and Verifying Program Performance.
             Technical Report CMU-CS-79-129, Department of Computer Science, Carnegie-Mellon University, June, 1979.

This paper gives a formal technique for specifying the performance of program modules in a form analogous to that commonly used for specifying functional properties for formal verification. [JCB]

Formal techniques for specifying performance properties of programs (e.g., execution time) and for verifying the correctness of these specifications are developed. These techniques are extensions of well-known predicate transformer techniques for specifying purely functional properties of programs. [Abstract]

[Shaw 80]   Mary Shaw, Guy T. Almes, Joseph M. Newcomer, Brian K. Reid, and Wm. A. Wulf.
A Comparison of Programming Languages for Software Engineering.
Software -- Practice and Experience, 1980.

Four programming languages (FORTRAN, COBOL, Jovial and the proposed DOD standard) are compared in the light of modern ideas of good software engineering practice.The comparison begins by identifying a *core* for each language that captures the essential properties of the language and the intent of the language designers. These core languages then serve as a basis for the discussion of the language philosophies and the impact of the language on gross program organization and on the use of individual statements. [Abstract]

[Shaw 81]   Mary Shaw.
When is "Good" Enough? Evaluating and Selecting Software Metrics.
In Frederick G. Sayward, Mary Shaw and Alan J. Perlis, editor, *Software Metrics: An Analysis and Evaluation*.
MIT Press, Cambridge, Massachusetts, 1981.

In "When is 'Good' Enough? Evaluating and Selecting Software Metrics" Shaw examines the methods used by researchers to evaluate their proposed metrics and to compute the efficiency of metrics. Software metrics are either direct (e.g., cost) or indirect (e.g., time for cost). The majority of those found are indirect. The reason that there is a proliferation of software metrics is that there is little attempt to find a basis set of direct metrics accompanied by models relating them to indirect metrics. Also metrics are applied without regard to precision or cost.

She recommends research into finding a small set of basis metrics which span most needs. This would avoid the syndrome of inventing a new metrics for each study and would entail finding models which relate direct and indirect metrics. Also recommended is a more critical use of classical statistics in evaluating metrics. [FGS]

[Sheppard 79a]
S. Sheppard, M. Borst, M. Millman and T. Love.
Modern Coding Practices and Programmer Performance.
Computer 12(12):41-49, December, 1979.

In a software experiment authors found that one could use the number of languages known and the familiarity with FORTRAN concepts to predict comprehension, modification, and debugging performances for programmers having three or less years of FORTRAN experience, but not for programmers having more FORTRAN experience. [FGS]

[Sheppard 79b]
> Sylvia B. Sheppard, Phil Milliman and Bill Curtis.
> Factors Affecting Programmer Performance in a
> Debugging Task.
> *General Electric Software Management Research* TR-79-
> 388100-5, February, 1979.

This report is the third in a series investigating characteristics of software which are related to its psychological complexity. Three independent variables, length of program, complexity of control flow, and type of error, were evaluated for three different FORTRAN programs in a debugging task. Fifty-four experienced programmers were asked to locate a single bug in each of three programs. Documentation consisted of input files, correct output, and erroneous output. Performance was measured by the time to locate and successfully correct the bug.

Small but significant differences in time to locate the bug were related to differences among programs and presentation order. Although there was no main effect for type of bug, there was a large program by error interaction suggesting the existence of context effects. Among measures of software complexity, Halstead's E proved to be the best predictor of performance followed by McCabe's $v(G)$ and the number of lines of code.

Number of programming languages known and familiarity with certain programming concepts also predicted performance. As in the previous experiments, experiential factors were better predictors for those participants with three or fewer years experience programming in FORTRAN. [Abstract]

[Shimasaki 79]
> M. Shimasaki, S. Fukaya, K. Ikeda, and T. Kiyono.
> A Pascal Program Analysis System and Profile of Pascal
> Compilers.
> In *Proceedings of the 12th Hawaii International
> Conference on System Sciences*, pages 85-90. ACM,
> 1979.

Static and dynamic analyses of two Pascal compilers written in Pascal are described and compared with similar studies on Fortran and PL/I programs. The static analysis determined that 33% to 45% of the statements are procedure call statements, compared to 2% to 8% for Fortran or PL/I. [RTS]

[Shneiderman 77a]
> B. Shneiderman.
> Measuring Computer Program Quality and
> Comprehension.
> *International Journal of Man-Machine Studies* 9:465-478,
> 1977.

In a controlled software experiment the author found that even a few months difference in experience for intermediate level programmers can have a significant effect on performance. Advocates the use of memorization and recall as a basis of measuring program understanding based on the assumption that programmers read foreign code bottom up by organizing knowledge into ever larger units. [FGS]

[Shneiderman 77b]
B. Shneiderman, R. Mayer, D. McKay and P. Heller.
Experimental Investigation of the Utility of Detailed
Flowcharts in Programming.
Communications of the ACM 20(6):373-384, June, 1977.

The authors report on a controlled software experiment to investigate whether flowcharting provides significant benefit in coding, comprehension, debugging, and modification. All experiments were of a group nature having subject sizes around 100. The subjects were beginning or intermediate student programmers. Subjects either did or did not have flowcharts as part of their assignments. Materials consisted of short (less than 100 lines) FORTRAN programs. General conclusion was that flowcharts are redundant and have a potential negative affect. [FGS]

[Shneiderman 80]
B. Shneiderman.
Software Psychology: Human Factors in Computer and Information Systems.
Winthrop, Cambridge, Massachusetts, 1980.

This is a very new book which discusses a number of issues which are relevant to software metrics. A large number of experiments which have been conducted by many people over a period of time are described. A chapter discusses the software metrics which have been developed by various people. While the book contains several chapters which are not related to metrics, it nevertheless appears to be the most complete single source of material on the numerous approaches to software metrics and experiments. [JES]

[Sime 73]
M. Sime, T. Green and D. Guest.
Psychological Evaluation of Two Conditional
Constructions Used in Computer Languages.
International Journal of Man-Machine Studies 5(1):105-113, 1973.

In a controlled software experiment the authors found that the IF THEN ELSE type of conditional statement is superior to the IF THEN GOTO in terms of programming time and number of errors made. [FGS]

[Sime 77a]
M. Sime, A. Arblaster and D. Guest.
Reducing Programming Errors in Nested Conditionals by
Prescribing a Writing Procedure.
International Journal of Man-Machine Studies 9:119-126, 1977.

In a controlled software experiment the authors found that tools for helping format conditional statements reduced the initial program error content but didn't help in locating the error initially present. [FGS]

[Sime 77b]   M. Sime, T. Green and D. Guest.
               Scope Marking in Computer Conditionals -- A
               Psychological Evaluation.
               International Journal of Man-Machine Studies 9(1):107-
               118, 1977.
In a controlled software experiment on program comprehension, the authors found that for
nonprogrammers nesting is superior to jumps as a method of representing conditionals.
[FGS]

[Sites 78]   Richard Sites.
               Programming Tools: Statement Counts and Procedure
               Timings.
               SIGPlan Notices 13(12):98-101, December, 1978.
It is argued that execution time statement counts and procedure timings are needed in
even the first implementation of a high level language. Counts are useful in debugging,
algorithm analysis and reliability (for example, which statements have never been executed
in testing runs). It is important that the procedure times reflect real time, rather than CPU
time, since I/O overhead may present problems which can totally swamp any possible
improvements in the CPU-bound part of the code. An example of the usefulness of these
techniques is illustrated in the CRAY-I Pascal compiler. 'It would perhaps be instructive to
direct such programmers to take a routine low on the list of percentage of total time, and re-
write it to be ten times slower, but 20% smaller and 100% reliable!' [RTS]

[Slavinski 75] Richard T. Slavinski.
                Static FORTRAN Analyzer.
                Technical Report RADC-TR-75-275, Rome Air
                Development Center, November, 1975.
The National Bureau of Standards (NBS) Static FORTRAN Analyzer (SFA), which samples
FORTRAN programs and collects statistics on the utilization of predetermined FORTRAN
syntactic constructs, was adapted to operate under the FORTRAN-Y compiler of RADC's
HIS-635 GCOS operating system. The conversion process and subsequent analysis of 258
sample programs, consisting of approximately 22,000 lines of source code, are provided.
The statistical results of this effort may directly support the activities of FORTRAN language
study and standardization efforts which address language and compiler design,
optimization, and subsetting. [Abstract]

[Smith 67]   Lyle B. Smith.
               *A Survey of Most Frequent Syntax and Execution-Time
               Errors.*
               Technical Report, Stanford Computation Center, Stanford,
               California, 1967.
Introduction: This paper gives a survey and some discussion of the most common syntax
and execution-time errors encountered by students using Burroughs B5500 Extended
Algol.

Analysis: In order to avoid recording incorrect syntax errors, brought about by earlier
errors, only the first 6 errors encountered in a program were recorded. To collect data on
execution-time errors, all output from student runs was examined.

Programs: Six problems were set for 127 students, studying a variety of courses, and they were required to program them, their errors being recorded for each run. for the syntax error collection, over 5000 runs were analyzed, of which half contained syntax errors, and for the execution-time error collection, over 2000 runs were analyzed, of which 1500 produced errors.

Results: Results are given showing:

Most common syntax errors

Most common execution-time errors

[W&H]

[Smith 79a]   Charles P. Smith.
Practical Applications of Software Science.
Technical Report TR 03.067, IBM General Products
Division, Santa Teresa Laboratory, June, 1979.

Programming Development at IBM's Santa Teresa Laboratory has been investigating the elements of software science as defined by Maurice H. Halstead. A set of modules have been counted from a large IBM data base program product and the resulting analysis is presented in this report. Program length, vocabulary, volume, difficulty and language level are also discussed as is the possobility of defect prediction in existing code. This paper also discusses some of our problems and concerns. [Abstract]

[Smith 79b]   C. Smith and J. C. Browne.
Performance Specifications and Analysis of Software
Designs.
In *Proceedings of Conference on Simulation,
Measurement and Modeling of Computer
Systems*, pages 173-182. August, 1979.

This paper develops and applies techniques for developing performance specifications for large software systems and for predicting the performance of large software systems from these extended design specifications. [JCB]

[Smith 79c]   C. Smith and J. C. Browne.
Modeling Software Systems for Performance Predictions.
In *Proceedings of the CMG Group X*, December, 1979.

This paper develops and applies techniques for developing performance specifications for large software systems and for predicting the performance of large software systems from these extended design specifications. [JCB]

[Smith 80a]   Charles P. Smith.
*A Software Science Analysis of IBM Programming
Products.*
Technical Report TR-3925, IBM General Products
Division, Santa Teresa Laboratory, January, 1980.

Programming Development at IBM's Santa Teresa Laboratory has been investigating the elements of software science as defined by Maurice H. Halstead. This report summarizes the findings after several large products have been counted. Program *length, vocabulary, volume, difficulty,* and *language level* are discussed. [Abstract]

[Smith 80b]   C. Smith and J. C. Browne.
               Aspects of Software Design Analysis: Concurrency and
                  Blocking.
               In *Performance '80*, May, 1980.
This paper develops and applies techniques for developing performance specifications for
large software systems and for predicting the performance of large software systems from
these extended design specifications. [JCB]

[Spirn 77]   J. R. Spirn.
               Program Behavior: Models and Measurements.
               Elsevier North-Holland, Ltd., New York, 1977.
Spirn summarizes the work done on program behavior, paging, reference string behavior
and locality behavior up to the time of publication of this book. [JCB]

[Storey 77]   Tony Storey and Stephen Todd.
               Performance Analysis of Large Systems.
               Software--Practice and Experience 7:323-369, 1977.
A hybrid analytic and experimental approach to the analysis of large systems is described.
The approach is iterative under the assumption that a correct analysis will not be made the
first time. The process is 1) make an analysis of the system in terms of basic components;
2) create an estimation model; 3) calculate the cost of the components; 4) create a
quantitative estimation model; 5) verify the model experimentally; 6) if verification fails,
reiterate; 7) analyze the potential modifications to make an estimation model of the
modified system; and 8) evaluate the modifications. [RTS]

[Svobodova 76]
               Liba Svobodova.
               *Computer Performance Measurement and Evaluation
                  Methods: Analysis and Applications.*
               Elsevier Scientific Publishing Company, 1976.
Good general discussion of modeling techniques and problems, but in a heavily hardware-
oriented setting. [MS]

[Tanenbaum ??]
               A. S. Tanenbaum.
               *Implications of Structured Programming for Machine
                  Architecture.*
               Informatica Rapport IR-12, Computer Science Group, Vrije
                  Universiteit, Amsterdam, ??.
Introduction: Empirical measurements of a collection of procedures written in a GOTO-less
language (SAL) are presented. Based on the results, a machine architecture is proposed
which could reduce program size by a factor of 3.

Analysis: The compiler was modified to collect the static information on the test
procedures. No dynamic analysis was carried out.

Programs: 300 procedures written in SAL were tested. All programs were written by the
faculty and graduate students of the Computer Science Group at Vrije Universiteit. All
programmers made a deliberate effort to produce "clean" well structured procedures.

Results: Results are presented in tabular form for:

    Distribution of executable statements
    Distribution of assignment statement types
    Distribution of arithmetic expression length
    Distribution of condition expression length
    Distribution of operand types
    Distribution of arithmetic operators
    Distribution of relational operators
    Distribution of number of formal parameters
    Distribution of local scalar variables
    Distribution of local arrays
    Distribution of constants in expressions
    Distribution of number of statements in the *then part* of IF statements
    Mean number of various things per procedure
    Miscellaneous measurements
    Comparison of static controllable statement distributions (SAL, XPL, FORTRAN)

Finally the results are discussed and proposals made for a new machine architecture. [W&H]

[Thayer 76]   T. A. Thayer, et al.
    Software Reliability Study.
    Technical Report RADC-TR-76-238, Rome Air
    Development Center, August, 1976.

A study of software errors is presented Techniques for categorizing errors according to type, identifying their source, and detecting them are discussed. Various techniques used in analyzing empirical error data collected from four large software systems are discussed and results of analysis are presented. Use of results to indicate improvements in the error prevention and detection processes through use of tools and techniques is also discussed. [Abstract]

[Thisted 77]   R.A. Thisted.
    User Documentation and Control Language: Evaluation
    and Comparison of Statistical Computer Packages.
    In *Proceedings of the Statistical Computing
    Section*, American Statistical Association, 1977.

An experiment is conducted to compare the usefulness of several statistical systems for trained statisticians. [IF]

[Thompson 79]
    K. Thompson and D. M. Ritchie.
    UNIX Programmer's Manual.
    Technical Report, Bell Laboratories, January, 1979.

The UNIX operating system supports the collection of an execution histogram for every process that requests one. The data is stored in a buffer located within the process' address space, and is based on the value of the program counter during interrupts. A postprocessor exists for mapping the counts back to the original source text of the program. [RTS]

[Tobagi 76]   F.A. Tobagi, S.E. Lieberson, and L. Kleinrock.
On measurement facilities in packet radio systems.
In *Proceedings of the NCC*, pages 589-596. AFIPS Press, 1976.

The Packet Radio Network measurement facilities, consisting of the measurement tools and the techniques for data collection, were described. The measurement functions required for analysis were identified, as were the data items required to support these functions. Three types of measurement items were necessary: pickup packets (accumulating data in the information area of the packet as it travelled to its destination); individual unit-based cummulative statistics (counters and histograms) and end-device cummulative statistics. The cummulative statistics are either transmitted at regular intervals, or are requested by the controlling station(s). [RTS]

[Trivedi 79]   Kishor S. Trivedi and Robert A. Wagner.
A Decision Model for Closed Queuing Networks.
IEEE Transactions on Software Engineering SE-5(4):328-332, July, 1979.

This paper considers a computer configuration design problem. The computer system is modeled by a closed queuing network. The system throughput is the objective function to be maximized and the speed of the devices are the decision variables. A rich class of nonlinear cost functions is considered. It is shown that any local optimum of the optimization problem is also a global optimum. It is also shown that the cost constraint is active and that the method of Lagrange multipliers can be used to solve the problem efficiently. [Abstract]

[Tuggle 78]   Francis D. Tuggle.
Theory Content and Explanatory Power for Simulation Models.
Behav. Sci. 23(4):271-290, July, 1978.

A concise methodology for the efficient modeling of behavioral phenomena in living systems at the levels of organisms, groups, organizations, societies, and supranational systems is proposed. The methodology helps resolve questions such as: When a model is to be made more complex? What variables are useful ones to add? When should the model development process cease? The methodology is founded upon 1) the precise identification and delineation of the set of behavioral phenomena to be explained, and 2) the "size" of alternative explanatory models. From these data, measures of explanatory power (relative amount of the phenomena explained) and explanatory yield (the average amount of explained per unit of theory content) may be derived. Explanatory power is shown to be an increasing function of theory content, and explanatory yield is shown to be a decreasing function of theory content. The methodology is illustrated in detail in the context of six successive simulation models of the cognitive behaviors of a subject solving a job shop scheduling task. The success of the final model in providing a complete description of one large class of the subject's behavior corroborates the usefulness of the methodology. [Abstract]

The above abstract is presented with the published manuscript. Little more need be said; the abstract is quite complete. For individuals interested in modeling behavioral phenomena, or perhaps having an interest in general systems, the paper may be of interest. [CR34458]

[Turner 79] Rollins Turner.
An Investigation of Several Mathematical Models of Queueing Systems.
Performance Evaluation Review 8(1-2):36-43, Spring-Summer, 1979.

The author reports on an experiment which was undertaken to investigate alternative models for predicting system response time. The mathematical models considered were compared in their abilities to predict average response time in an interactive system. The bases for comparison were the response times calculated by using a simplified simulation model.

The understood goal of this project was to compare the practicality of various mathematical models for predicting system behaviors. The comparisons of the simulation results were interesting; more interesting might have been comparisons of actual measured response times. The author's analysis of the reasons for the failures of the models was on target. The results of sensitivity analysis of the workload files which were used to drive the simulation calculation emphasized the fact that blind application of a model without understanding the data which was used to determine the model's parameter can lead to unacceptable results.

Mathematical tools are valuable aids in performance evaluations. This paper does a good job of demonstrating the care which must be taken in their application. [CR35849]

[Van der Knijff 78]
D. J. J. Van der Knijff.
Software Physics and Program Analysis.
Australian Computer Journal 10(3):82-86, August, 1978.

Software physics is a term used to describe the analysis of programs to extract software engineering measures from particular general properties of the programs. It may be used to compare programs and languages, and to improve estimation procedures in the software industry. This paper introduces the reader to the terms used in software physics and its application to some problems. A selection of recent empirical analyses are presented to enable the reader to make comparisons with other methods. [CR33992]

[Velleman 75] P.F. Velleman and I. Francis.
Measuring Statistical Accuracy of Statistical Regression Problems.
In *Proceedings of the Computer Science and Statistics: Eighth Annual Symposium on the Interface*, pages 122-127. U.S. Department of Commerce/National Bureau of Standards, Washington, D.C., 1975.

The authors proposed that a program's accuracy in solving multiple regression problems be related to the numerical difficulty of the data. A measure of difficulty of regression problems is proposed, and several measures of accuracy of a solution. [IF]

[Velleman 77] P.F. Velleman, J.R. Seaman and I.E. Allen.
Evaluating Package Regression Routines.
In *Proceedings Statistical Computing Section*, pages 82-83. American Statistical Association, 1977.

The accuracy of several widely-used statistical packages in computing multiple regressions is evaluated on a series of problems of increasing difficulty. [IF]

[Waite 73]   W.M. Waite.
A Sampling Monitor for Applications Programs.
Software--Practice and Experience 3:75-79, 1973.
A set of monitoring conventions are specified for sampling. If the operating system does not allow interrupt handling by the user, it is necessary to put some of the routines in the monitor. A set of interface conventions for such a facility is described. [RTS]

[Walston 77]   C. E. Walston and C. P. Felix.
A Method of Programming Measurement and Estimation.
IBM Systems Journal 16(1), 1977.
Improvements in programming technology have paralled improvements in computing system architecture and materials. Along with increasing knowledge of the system and program development processes, there has been some notable research into programming project productivity estimation. Also presented are preliminary results of research into methods of measuring and estimating programming project productivity estimation. Also presented are preliminary results of research into methods of measuring and estimating programming project duration, staff size, and computer cost. [VRB]

[Warren 79]   S.K. Warren and D. Abbe.
Rosetta Smalltalk: A Conversational Extensible Microcomputer Language.
In *Proceedings of the Second Symposium on Small Systems*, pages 36-45. October, 1979.
Rosetta Smalltalk is a personal information handling environment for low-cost microcomputers based on Smalltalk-72. Windows are dealt with in detail, as are the predefined objects available in the system. The system's most interesting aspect is that it requires very little resources to run, occupying approximately 16K bytes and running about as fast as interpreted Basic. [RTS]

[Waters 79]   Richard C. Waters.
A Method for Analyzing Loop Programs.
IEEE Transactions on Software Engineering SE-5(3):237-247, May, 1979.
This paper presents a method for automatically analyzing loops, and discusses why it is a useful way to look at loops. The method is based on the idea that there are four basic ways in which the logical structure of a loop is built up. An experiment is presented which shows that this accounts for the structure of a large class of loops. The paper discusses how the method can be used to automatically analyze the structure of a loop, and how the resulting analysis can be used to guide a proof of correctness for the loop. An automatic system is described which performs this type of analysis. The paper discusses the relationship between the structure building methods presented and designed to assist a person who is writing a program. The intent is that the system will cooperate with a programmer throughout all phases of work on a program and be able to communicate with the programmer about it. [Abstract]

[Weinberg 74] G. Weinberg and E. Schulman.
Goals and Performance in Computer Programming.
Human Factors 16(1):70-77, 1974.

In a software experiment aimed at understanding the programmer-program process, the authors found that programmers construct quite different software to satisfy the same objectives of fast programming, efficient programs, minimal program size and program readability. [FGS]

[Weiss 79] David M. Weiss.
Evaluating Software Development by Error Analysis: The Data from the Architecture Research Facility.
The Journal of Systems and Software(1), 1979.

In software engineering, it is easy to propose techniques for improving software development but difficult to test the claims made for such techniques. This paper suggests an error analysis technique for use in gathering data concerning the effectiveness of different software development methodologies. The principal features of the error analysis technique described are the formulation of questions of interest and a data classification scheme before data collection begins, and interviews of system developers concomitant with the development process to verify the accuracy of the data. The data obtained by using this technique during the development of a medium-size software development project is presented. This project was known as the Architecture Research Facility (ARF) and took about 10 months and 192 man-weeks of effort to develop. The ARF designers used the information hiding principle to modularize the system, and interface specifications and high-level language coding specifications to express the design. Several error detection aids were designed into the system to help detect run-time errors. In addition, quality control rules were established that required review of specifications before coding, and review of code after compilation but prior to testing. A total of 143 errors was reported. Analysis of these errors showed that there were few problems caused by intermodule interfaces, that error corrections rarely required knowledge of more than one module, that most errors took less than a few hours to fix, and that the error detection aids detected more than half of the errors that were potentially detectable by them. [VRB]

[Weissman 73]
Lawrence M. Weissman.
Psychological Complexity of Computer Programs: An Initial Experiment.
Technical Report CSRG-26, University of Toronto, July, 1973.

In order to reduce the complexity of programs many ideas and techniques have been expounded. However, no quantitive evidence has been given that the quality of the programs has indeed been imporved. We believe that experimental studies should be performed to measure those factors which make programs complex. An initial experiment has been conducted to measure the effects of theree such factors, comments, paragraphing, and mnemonic variable names. This report summarizes the results of this experiment. [Abstract]

[Weissman 74]

Laurence M. Weissman.

A Methodology for Studying the Psychological Complexity of Computer Programs.

Technical Report CSRG-37, University of Toronto, August, 1974.

There are many reasons for empirically testing hypotheses about the effects of various factors on the psychological complexity of computer programs. (By "psychological complexity" we mean the intrinsic property of programs that affects their understandability and maintainability.) This thesis develops a methodology for such experimentation, and discusses the results of ten experiments involving the following factors: use of comments, control flow paragraphing, choice of variable names, and locality of data references. [Abstract]

[Wichmann 70]

Brian A. Wichmann.

Some Statistics from Algol Programs.

Technical Report CCU-11, National Physical Laboratory, Teddington, England, 1970.

Introduction: This report contains a substantial amount of statistical information on Algol60 programs run under the Whetstone interpretive system. From the results, weighting factors were calculated and an Algol mix formed for measuring machine times.

Dynamic analysis: The Whetstone interpreter was modified to count the number of times each type of operation was executed.

Static analysis: An "anti-compiler" was used to scan through the interpretive code and print out the static occurrence of each operation.

Finally an analysis was carried out to count the occurrences of certain "rare" symbols.

Programs analyzed:

Dynamic analysis - 949 programs analyzed in 7 batches
Static analysis - 40 programs analyzed

Most programs were written by scientists at NPL with little programming experience.

Results: Results are presented for:

Dynamic analysis

Operators	Procedures
Use of constants	Parameters
Labels and switches	Jumps
FOR loop code	Arithmetic variable store and fetch

Static analysis

Frequency of operators
Frequency of Algol Basic Symbols

Analysis of *rare* symbols

The occurrences of FOR, :, ↑ and / were counted and the results discussed.

[W&H]

[Wichmann 72]
Brian A. Wichmann.
The Performance of Some ALGOL Systems.
In *Information Processing 71*, pages 327-334. IFIP, 1972.
The problem of measuring the processing speed of an Algol system is considered in this paper. The work is based upon the time taken to execute 42 simple Algol statements on 18 machines. Two methods of analysis have been used. Firstly a technique which does not require weights for the individual statements, but gives a clear indication of the strength and weakness of each system. The second method uses a weighted 'mix' of the statements. This mix is derived from the monitoring of 155 million operations. [Abstract]

[Wilkes 79]   M.V. Wilkes and R.M. Needham.
The Cambridge CAP Computer and its Operating System.
Elsevier North Holland, New York, NY, 1979.
This book provides a well-written overview of the design of the CAP hardware and operating system. Emphasis is placed on the general design of the capability protection mechanism, the file system (which allows capabilities to be preserved on secondary storage), and the use of Algol68 as an implementation language. Specimen programs from the virtual memory manager and the file system comprise over a third of the book. The bibliography is minimal; it contains few references to other capability-based systems. There is also no discussion concerning the user interface. [RTS]

[Willman 77]   H. E. Willman, Jr., T. A. James, A. A. Beaureguard and P. Hilcoff.
Software Systems Reliability: A Raytheon Project History.
Technical Report RADC-TR-77-188, Rome Air
Development Center, June, 1977.
This report presents results of a project to collect software data from the records of development of a large Department of Defense ground-based system. A description of the subject systems software development process, characteristics, tools, and test methods are presented. Qualitative and quantitative data gathered from configuration management files are included as well as statistical summaries of this data. A detailed description of the data base files is included as well as portions of the actual data base. Recommendations are made for the use of the data as well for the future collection of such data.

The data consists of three files, viz:

a) Module Description file (109 entries)

b) Software Problem Report File (2165 entries)

c) Error Category File (193 entries)

Each problem report was assigned an error category from the fault taxonomy and the data was cross correlated and summarized. The most frequent problems were in the categories of:

a) User Requested Changes (35%)

b) Data Handling   (19%)

c) Logic   (18%)

[Abstract]

[Wirth 71]   N. Wirth.
The Design of a Pascal Compiler.
Software -- Practice & Experience 1(4):309-333, 1971.

Introduction: This paper is primarily concerned with the development of a Pascal compiler, which is described in some detail. The paper also gives some statistical information on the compiler.

Analysis: No details are given of the method of collecting the data.

Results: Results give information on:

Size of compiler

number of lines
number of characters
number of blanks, letters, digits etc.
number of identifiers and word delimiters

Object program size
Composition of machine code instructions
Usage of X-registers in CDC-6000
Usage of B-registers in CDC-6000

Four simple programs (which are reproduced) were written in Pascal, Algol 60 and Fortran and the total compilation and execution times measured. [W&H]

[Wolfe 71]   J. M. Wolfe.
Perspectives on Testing for Programming Aptitude.
In *Proceedings 1971 Annual Conference*, pages 268-277.
Association for Computing Machinery, Chicago, Illinois, 1971.

Limitations of programming aptitude tests are discussed. Factors which bias the usefulness of uncritical tests are reviewed, such as educational level, prior knowledge, and speed. The paper emphasizes the need to have a test which is relevant to the job to be performed, that is, a test that would measure what is required to perform the intended work. [MEM]

[Wolfe 72]   J. M. Wolfe.
A Validation Study -- Long Range Predictive Capabilities of the Aptitude Assessment Battery: Programming Test.
Programming Specialists, Inc., Brooklyn, New York, 1972.

The results of a validation study of an analysis of an *Aptitude Assessment Battery Programming* (AABP) test is presented. Aptitude test ratings and the evaluations of the programming supervisors are analyzed at an average interval of two and a half years after the testing. The study may be viewed as longitudinal rather than a time-slice. [MEM]

[Wolverton 74]
Ray W. Wolverton.
The Cost of Developing Large-Scale Software.
IEEE Transactions on Computers C-23(6), 1974.

The work of software cost forecasting falls into two parts. First we make what we call structural forecasts, and then we calculate the absolute dollar-volume forecasts. Structural forecasts describe the technology and function of a software project, but not its size. We allocate resources (costs) over the project's life cycle from the structural forecasts. Judgement, technical knowledge, and econometric research should combine in making the structural forecasts. A methodology based on a 25 x 7 structural forecast matrix that has been used by TRW with good results over the past few years is presented in this paper. With the structural forecast in hand, we go on to calculate the absolute dollar-volume forecasts. The general logic followed in "absolute" cost estimating can be based on either a mental process or an explicit algorithm. A cost estimating algorithm is presented and five tradition methods of software cost forecasting are described: top-down estimating, similarities and differences estimating, ratio estimating, standards estimating, and bottom-up estimating. All forecasting methods suffer from the need for a valid cost data base for many estimating situations. Software information elements that experience has shown to be useful in establishing such a data base are given in the body of the paper. Majoy pricing pitfalls are identified. Two case studies are presented that illustrate the software cost forecasting methodology and historical results. Topics for further work and study are suggested. [VRB]

[Wong 74]   K. Wong and J.C Strauss.
Use of a Software Monitor in the Validation of an Analytic Computer System Model.
Software--Practice and Experience 4:255-263, 1974.
A sampling monitor is described which examines OS/360 system tables and control blocks periodically for CPU activity, the priority mapping of certain tasks, I/O queuing activity and I/O activity of the devices on the selector channels. The monitor is a normal task which is loaded into a 20K partition with high priority. The data derived from the monitoring process was then used to validate an analytic model. [RTS]

[Woodfield 79]
Scott N. Woodfield.
An Experiment on Unit Increase in Problem Complexity.
IEEE Transactions on Software Engineering SE-5(2):76-79, March, 1979.
The effect of a variation in problem complexity and how the variation relates to programming complexity is predicted and measured. An experiment was conducted in which eighteen graduate students programmed two variations of the same small algorithm where the problem complexity varied by 25 percent. Eight measurable program characteristics are compared with predicted values obtained using only two known parameters. The agreement between observed and predicted values is very good. Both predicted and observed measurements indicate that the 25 percent increase in problem complexity results in a 100 percent increase in programming complexity. [Abstract]

The author reports on measuring the predicted values of software science versus the observed values for 18 programmers doing a common programming task. The task consisted of translating a small Algol program to FORTRAN and then extending the program. Predicted and observed values correspond to within .6 standard deviations. General conclusion is that a 25% increase in problem complexity, as defined by the number or input and output parameters, results in a 100% increase in the program complexity, as defined by counting operaters and operands. [FGS]

[Woodward 79]

Martin R. Woodward, Michael A. Hennell and David Hedley.

A Measure of Control Flow Complexity in Program Text.

IEEE Transactions on Software Engineering SE-5(1):45-50, January, 1979.

This paper discusses the need for measures of complexity and unstructuredness of programs. A simple language independent concept is put forward as a measure of control flow complexity in program text and is then developed for use as ameasure of unstructuredness. The proposed metric is compared with other metrics, the most notable of which is the cyclomatic complexity measure. Some experience with automatic tools for obtaining these metrics is reported. [Abstract]

[Wortman 72] D. B. Wortman.

A Study of Language Directed Computer Design.

Technical Report CSRG-20, Department of Computer Science, University of Toronto, Canada, 1972.

Introduction: A dialect of PL/I, called Student PL/I, is the language chosen for a detailed study in this thesis. The approach is to design an ideal machine for Student PL/I and to see how this compares with a conventional implementation. An initial implementation of the ideal machine was improved by collecting statistics on the use of the language by instrumenting the compiler.

Analysis: The parser was modified to obtain complete counts of every syntactic unit for static analysis. The generator was modified to count the occurrences of the basic machine instructions. The interpreter was modified to give dynamic usage counts.

Programs: 1494 programs were analyzed statically and 419 completed execution successfully. About 20 million "ideal" machine instructions were executed.

Results: The tabulated results include:

> Counts for each syntactic construct for 1494 programs.
> Static and dynamic count for 40 instructions of the ideal machine.
> Instruction pair frequencies.
> Distribution of order numbers as a function of the lexical level.
> Distribution of the compiled and executed address references as a function of the lexical level and current lexical level.
> Distribution of constant types.
> Distribution of FIXED constant values.
> Distribution of length field in program segment descriptors fetched to data stack during execution.
> Distribution of number of parameters per procedure call.
> Distribution (static and dynamic) of instructions in improved machine.
> Ratio of the following characteristics between old and new machine:

Program space	Data memory references
Data space	Instruction fetches
Instructions executed	Data fetches
Program memory references	

[W&H]

[Wortman 76] D. B Wortman.
A Study of High-Resolution Timing.
IEEE Transactions on Software Engineering SE-2(3):135-137, June, 1976.

This article describes an experimental comparison of timing information provided by a large multiprogramming system (OS/370 MVT) with timing information derived directly from a high resolution hardware clock. The hardware clock was found to be a superior source of timing information. [Abstract]

[Youngs 74] E. A. Youngs.
Human Errors in Programming.
International Journal on Man-Machine Studies 6:361-376, 1974.

Introduction: Thirty novices and twelve professional programmers volunteered as subjects for an experiment. They coded tasks from an elementary teaching course in roughly equal numbers in the languages Algol, BASIC, FORTRAN and PL/I.

Analysis: The rate and type of errors were analyzed, both for the advanced and novice programmers. On any one program, there was an exponential decay in the error rate. Algol and COBOL error rates were higher due to no default declarations. PL/I had problems due to the lack of reserved words which made error recovery hard for the compiler. Errors themselves were classified into *syntax, semantics, logical* and *clerical*.

Programs: A total of 69 programs were considered. Due to the specification, all were quite small.

Results: The main tables are:

Summary of errors by statement type.
Error frequencies tabulated by system diagnostic and programmer action (first run only).
Error frequencies tabulated by system diagnostic and run number.
Error frequencies tabulated by general cause and system diagnostic (first run only).
Proportion of errors in general cause for beginners and advanced programmers.
Proportion of errors in specific cause for beginners and advanced programmers.

[W&H]

In a software experiment aimed at understanding the programmer debugging process the author found that experienced programmers use different debugging strategies than those used by beginning programmers. [FGS]

[Yuval 75a] G. Yuval.
Gathering Run-Time Statistics Without Black Magic.
Software--Practice and Experience:105-108, 1975.

The Pascal/6000 compiler was modified to add a 'turnstile' program, a piece of code that will count how often it has been passed through, to the prologue of each routine. A postprocessor is used to construct a profile by searching through memory looking for turnstiles. The CDC 6000 smallest turnstile is 1 word (containing a subroutine call and a counter); the fastest is 105 bits long (a word is 60 bits long) and takes 1.2 to 1.5 microseconds. [RTS]

[Yuval 75b]   G. Yuval.
               A Snobol 4 Execution Profile.
               SIGPLAN Notices 10(12):40, December, 1975.
This short paper gives a trace function for gathering a dynamic profile of Snobol4
programs. The results obtained for a very small program are given. [W&H]

[Yuval 77a]   G. Yuval.
               Is Your Register Really Necessary?.
               Software -- Practice & Experience 7(2):295, 1977.
This is a short communication discussing register usage for Bliss-11 programs running on
a PDP-11. A table of results is given for code size versus number of registers in use for 6
Bliss-11 programs. [W&H]

[Yuval 77b]   G. Yuval.
               The Utility of the CDC 6000 Registers.
               Software -- Practice & Experience 7(4):535-536, 1977.
This is a follow-up of the above short communication and continues the discussion on
register usage. A table of results is given of code size versus number of X-registers in use
on a CDC 6000 for a series of 31 Pascal test routines. [W&H]

[Zelkowitz 76] M. V. Zelkowitz.
               Automatic Program Analysis and Evaluation.
               In *Proceedings Second International Conference on
               Software Engineering*, IEEE, 1976.
Introduction: This paper contains results of a static and dynamic analysis of 16000
programs written in PL/I and compiled using the Univac 1108 PLUM compiler.

Analysis: The analysis was divided into three phases

       Translation Phase, where the compiler collected static statistics
       Execution Phase, where program can be traced and variables altered
       Post-Execution Phase, where data which has been collected is printed.

Programs analyzed: A total of 16027 runs were tapped for data, average program size
being 100 statements, maximum size 884 statements.

Results: Results are given for:

       Data collected by PLUM
       Distribution of program size on sample of 4583 programs
       Statement profiles for 1294 programs
       Data for two classes which were processed
       Range in statement distribution across several files of programs
       Clustering based upon background and current instructions
       Plot of statement complexity vs. program size
       Frequency profiles for small and large programs
       Causes of program termination

[W&H]

[Zweben 79]   Stuart H. Zweben and Maurice H. Halstead.
              The Frequency Distribution of Operators in PL/1
                 Programs.
              IEEE Transactions on Software Engineering SE-5(2):91-
                 95, March, 1979.

During the past few years, several investigators have noted definite patterns in the distribution of operators in computer programs. Their proposed models have provided explanations for other observed software phenomena and have suggested possible relationships between programming languages and natural languages. However, these models contain notable deficiencies.

This study concentrates on a set of production programs written in PL/I. Using some basic relationships from software science, and a previously published algorithm generation technique, a model for computing operator frequencies is constructed which is based only on the number of distinct operators in the program and the total number of operator occurrences. The model provides a considerable statistical improvement over existing models for the PL/I programs studied. [Abstract]

Index